PROMOTING DEMOCRACY

Promoting Democracy

The Force of Political Settlements in Uncertain Times

Manal A. Jamal

NEW YORK UNIVERSITY PRESS

New York

NEW YORK UNIVERSITY PRESS
New York
www.nyupress.org
© 2019 by New York University
All rights reserved

Library of Congress Cataloging-in-Publication Data
Names: Jamal, Manal, author.
Title: Promoting democracy : the force of political settlements in uncertain times / Manal A. Jamal.
Description: New York : New York University Press, 2019. | Includes bibliographical references and index.
Identifiers: LCCN 2018048486| ISBN 9781479811380 (cl : alk. paper) | ISBN 9781479878451 (pb : alk. paper)
Subjects: LCSH: Pacific settlement of international disputes. | Diplomatic negotiations in international disputes. | Democracy—International cooperation. | Peaceful settlement
Classification: LCC JZ6010 .J36 2019 | DDC 327.1/72—dc23
LC record available at https://lccn.loc.gov/2018048486

For my late father, Ahmad Jamal, and to all nameless heroes everywhere who work selflessly to improve the world and the lives of those around them.

CONTENTS

LIST OF ABBREVIATIONS

ADEMUSA   Asociación Democrática de Mujeres / Democratic Association of Women

AMES   Asociación de Mujeres de El Salvador / Association of Women of El Salvador

AMS   Asociación para la Autodeterminación y el Desarrollo de Mujeres Salvadoreña / Association for the Self-Determination and Development of Salvadoran Women

ANM   Arab Nationalist Movement

ARENA   Alianza Republicana Nacionalista / Republican Nationalist Alliance

ASMUSA   Asociacón de Mujeres Salvadoreña /Association of Salvadoran Women

CEMUJER   Instituto de Estudios de Mujer "Norma Virginia Guirola de Herrera" / Institute of Women's Studies "Norma Viginia de Herrera"

CERP   Commander's Emergency Response Program

CG   Consultative Group

CIDA   Canadian International Development Agency

CID   Council for International Development

CPA   Coalition Provisional Authority

COMADRES   Comité de Madres y Familiares de Presos, Desaparecidos y Asesinados de El Salvador "Monseñor Romero" / Committee of Mothers and Relatives of the Disappeared, Assassinated and Political Prisoners

CONAMUS   Coordinadora Nacional de Mujeres Salvadoreñas / National Coordinating Committee for Salvadoran Women

CORAMS   Centro de Orientación Radial Para la Mujer Salvadoreña / Training Center for Salvadoran Women on Radio

CREA   Creative Associates International, Inc.

CRS   Creditor Reporting System

CSOS   civil society organizations

DAC   Development Assistance Committee

DFLP   Democratic Front for the Liberation of Palestine

DOP   Declaration of Principles

EC   European Commission

EIB   European Investment Bank

ERP   Ejercito Revolucionario del Pueblo / Revolutionary Army of People

EU   European Union

FAPU   Frente de Acción Popular Unificada / United Popular Action Front

Fatah   Harakat al-Tahrir al-Watani al-Filastini / Palestinian National Liberation Movement

FDR   Frente Democrático Revolutionario / Revolutionary Democratic Front

FIDA   Palestinian Democratic Union

FLACSO   Facultad Latinoamericana de Ciencias Sociales / Latin American Faculty for the Social Sciences

FMLN   Farabundo Martí para la Liberación Nacional / Farabundo Marty for National Liberation

FPL   Fuerzas Populares de Liberación / Popular Forces of Liberation

FPWAC   Federation of Palestinian Women's Action Committees

FPWAC-FIDA Federation of Palestinian Women's Action
Committees-Palestinian Democratic Union

FUSADES Fundación Salvadoreña para el Desarrollo Económico
y Social / Salvadoran Foundation for Economic and
Social Development

GFTU Palestinian General Federation of Trade Unions

GTZ German Agency for Technical Cooperation

GUPW General Union of Palestinian Women

HIVOS Humanistisch Instituut voor
Ontwikkelingssamenwerking / International
Humanist Institute for Cooperation with
Developing Countries

ICCO Interkerkelijke Organisatie voor
Ontwikkelingssamenwerking / Dutch Interchurch
Organization for Development Cooperation

ICG International Crisis Group

INCLE US Bureau of International Narcotics and Law
Enforcement Affairs

IMU Instituto de Investigación, Capacitación y Desarrollo
de la Mujer "Norma Guirola de Herrera" / Institute
of Research, Training, and Development of Women
"Norma Guirola de Herrera"

ISDEMU Instituto Salvadoreño para el Desarrollo de la Mujer /
Salvadoran Institute for Women's Development

JMCC Jerusalem Media and Communication Center

MAM Movimiento de Mujeres 'Mélida Anaya Montes' /
Melida Anaya Monte Women's Movement

MEA Municipios en Acción / Municipalities in Action

MIFTAH Palestinian Initiative for the Promotion of Global
Dialogue and Democracy

MNR Movimiento Nacional Revolucionario / National
Revolutionary Movement

MOPIC Ministry of Planning and International Cooperation

MPCS   Movimiento Popular Social Cristiano / Popular Social Christian Movement

MSM   Movimiento Salvadoreño de Mujeres / Salvadoran Movement of Women

NGO   nongovernmental organization

NOVIB   Oxfam-Netherlands

NRP   National Reconstruction Plan

OCHA   United Nations Office for the Coordination of Humanitarian Affairs

ODA   Official Development Assistance

OECD   Organization for Economic Cooperation and Development

ONUSAL   Observadores de las Naciones Unidas en El Salvador / United Nations Observer Mission in El Salvador

ORMUSA   Organización de Mujeres Salvadoreñas / Organization of Salvadoran Women

PA   Palestinian Authority

PANORAMA   Palestinian Center for the Dissemination of Democracy and Community Development

PARC   Palestinian Agricultural Relief Committees

PASSIA   Palestinian Academic Society for the Study of International Affairs

PCP   Palestinian Communist Party

PDC   Partido Demócrata Cristiano / Christian Democratic Party

PFLP   Popular Front for the Liberation of Palestine

PLC   Palestinian Legislative Council

PLO   Palestine Liberation Organization

PNC   Palestine National Council

PNF   Palestine National Front

PNGO   Palestinian Nongovernmental Organization Network

PNUD	Programa de la Naciones para el Desarrollo / United Nations Development Program
PPP	Palestinian People's Party
PRTC	Partido Revolucionario de los Trabajadores Centroamericanos / Revolutionary Party of Central American Workers
PRUD	Partido Revolucionario de Unificación Democrácia / Party of Revolutionary Democratic Unification
PCS	Partido Comunista de El Salvador / Communist Party of El Salvador
PTT	Programa de Transferencia de Tierras / Land Transfer Program
PVOS	Private Volunteer Organizations
PWWSD	Palestinian Working Women's Society for Development
RN	Resistencia Nacional/ National Resistance
SCF	Save the Children Federation
SHARE	Salvadoran Humanitarian Aid, Research, and Education Foundation
SWGS	Sector Working Groups
TAP	Tripartite Action Plan
TFPI	Task Force on Project Implementation
TIM	Temporary International Mechanism
TAC	Tunnel Affairs Commission
UCA	University of Central America
UDN	Unión Democrática Nacionalista / Nationalist Democratic Union
UNDP	United Nations Development Program
UNICEF	United Nations Children Fund
UNRWA	United Nations Relief Works Agency
UNSCO	United Nations Special Coordinators Office
UPA	United Palestine Appeal

UPWC	Union of Palestinian Women's Committees
UPWWC	Union of Palestinian Working Women's Committees
USAID	United States Agency for International Development
USSC	United States Security Coordinator
VAT	Value-Added Tax
WATC	Women's Affairs Technical Committees
WBGS	West Bank and Gaza Strip
WCLAC	Women's Center for Legal Aid and Counseling
WCSW	Union of Women's Committees for Social Work
WWC	Women's Work Committee

LIST OF FIGURES AND TABLES

PREFACE

In the late 1990s, I worked as a journalist and researcher in Jerusalem. As part of my daily routine, I would park my car—or, more accurately, my mother's car—on Highway 1, the 1950 armistice line separating East and West Jerusalem. Then I would walk to my morning job at the Alternative Information Center, a research institute, in West Jerusalem. At noon, I would return to the car and proceed to my full-time job in East Jerusalem at the Jerusalem Media Research Center, another research institute where I worked as a journalist and researcher on a project on donor assistance to the Palestinian territories.[1] One damp Tuesday morning, however, I returned to Highway 1 only to realize that the car was no longer there. Two bystanders informed me that two young Arab men had driven away with it.

I decided to go to the nearest police station, which happened to be in West Jerusalem, the predominantly Israeli side of the city. The officer on duty patiently listened, then informed me that I would likely never see the car again—32,000 cars are stolen in Israel per year. Dissatisfied with his response, I proceeded to the nearest Palestinian Authority (PA) police station in Abu Dis. There I filed a report for a stolen car. The officers on duty put out an alert to all personnel guarding Palestinian - Authority checkpoints near Jerusalem to look out for a gray Subaru with a yellow license plate—the plate color reserved for Palestinians with foreign passports, Palestinian residents of Jerusalem, Israelis, and foreigners. The alert noted that the car was owned by a Palestinian American with a US passport.

By late afternoon on Wednesday, I had heard from no one. I returned to Highway 1, hoping to find the car or evidence that would lead me to it, but it was still nowhere to be found. Across the street, a crowd of Palestinian laborers were waiting for transport to their jobs across the Green line.[2] I approached and asked if anyone knew any of the car thieves in the area and explained that my car had been stolen the previous day. I even offered a US$200 award to anyone who could help me find the car. Nonetheless, by evening, I had to return home without my mother's car.

Early the next morning, I received a call from one of the laborers I had spoken to the previous day; he informed me that he had found the car, and that I should proceed to meet him alone near a large sign by the entrance to a remote village. Wary of what awaited me, I asked the first person I met that morning, my friend Mohammed, to accompany me to the meeting. Shortly thereafter, we arrived at the meeting point and three vans approached. By coincidence, it turned out that Mohammed and the young men in the vans actually knew one another. They exchanged news about family members, and we eventually set off to retrieve the car. We arrived at a remote house on top of a hill with a number of cars parked outside. Inside the house, a group of men awaited. Since Mohammed knew some of the men, they did not ask for an award, and refused to take the US$200 I had initially offered. Instead, we drank tea with mint and exchanged information about common acquaintances.

The men informed me that I was very lucky because the owner of the "chop shop" to which my car had been sent was committed to a "nationalist policy" and would only buy stolen cars previously owned by Israelis. Since my case was one of mistaken identity, the partly stripped car would be returned to me. To ensure that there were no hard feelings, they suggested that I should meet with the owner of the chop shop and the young men who took the car, and that they would then apologize to me directly.

Mohammed knew an old woman in the village, so we agreed to meet the young men at her house. When we arrived, the house was dark because the electricity had been cut. I was perplexed, to say the least, and trying to absorb all that had happened. The car's theft and imminent return were no longer the focus of my attention. I was struck by the realization that there were villages in the West Bank that did not have continuous access to electricity. Here I was in a village that had not been touched by any post-Oslo development projects, let alone any promises of future development or reconstruction projects.[3] The West Bank central region of Jerusalem-Ramallah of the 1970s and 1980s had been more developed than this village now in the late 1990s. Many of the activists in this village were associated with a political organization that opposed the Oslo Accords, and I wondered if this was one of the reasons that explained this inequitable state.

The young men finally arrived. They entered the room and timidly offered their apologies, explaining that I had been mistaken for an Israeli Jew. Mohammed and I countered that mistaken identity did not make stealing any more legitimate. The owner of the chop shop laughed and rationalized that stealing cars was now one of their only means of continuing their nationalist resistance against the Israeli occupation. Prior to the Oslo Accords, they were all political activists, affiliated with one of the major leftist political factions. The owner of the chop shop had spent five years in jail between the ages of 13 and 20 for grassroots political organizing, and the other thieves shared similar backgrounds. He went on to explain that, after the 1993 Oslo Accords, they found themselves abandoned by the leadership of the political opposition, and increasingly marginal and irrelevant to the development promises of the new era. One of the few options available to former political activists with little education was to join the Palestinian police force. From the onset, it was becoming clear that the police force would serve as a security contractor of Israeli occupation and would require officers to act against fellow Palestinians. For activists affiliated with a political faction that opposed the Oslo Accords, this option was not very enticing. I left that afternoon with a deeper awareness of the dubious nature of the economic and political developments of the post-Oslo era. The events of that day would consume my thoughts for months to come.

The convening of the first elections of the PA in January 1996 was a euphoric moment for many who were concerned with the prospects for peace and stability in the region. Even those who were skeptical about the Oslo Accords and the durability of the interim agreements that paved the way for elections were cautiously supportive. But optimism slowly gave way to dismay as many began to realize that the lives of the majority of Palestinians would remain unaltered, totally untouched by the promises of the "conflict-to-peace" transition. The peace process, and the peacebuilding initiatives associated with it, remained a mere out of reach illusion for many Palestinians.[4]

In order to buttress support for the peace accords, the international community provided the PA, as well as Palestinian nongovernmental organizations (NGOs), with attractive aid packages, making the Palestinian territories one of the world's highest per capita recipients of Western donor assistance. Much of the assistance to the PA was earmarked for budget support and institutional development. A substantial portion of assistance was also allocated to democracy promotion efforts, which included funding to electoral commissions, labor rights, human rights, civic education, and women's NGOs. The initial focus of much of this support was the central regions of the Gaza Strip and the West Bank—regions that would become the seat of power of the PA, which is dominated by Harakat al-Tahrir al-Watani al-Filastini (Palestinian National Liberation Movement, or Fatah). The impact of this assistance was uneven, and only a fraction of Palestinian society had access to, or was even aware of, the developments taking place elsewhere. A related development was the demobilization of Palestinian grassroots organizations. Having come of political age during the first Intifada, I was intimately familiar with the extent to which mass-based political organizing flourished within and defined Palestinian society. This legacy of grassroots organizing, however, appeared a distant memory; most grassroots organizations, including the women's mass-based movements, had demobilized and become mere shadows of the institutions they once were. In 2006, Hamas won the legislative elections and slowly a worst-case scenario began to unfold as political polarization, with the help of Western donor assistance, virtually paralyzed Palestinian political life.

I began to notice a significant contrast between the Palestinian case and other cases of conflict-to-peace transition. As someone who previously worked with Salvadoran Humanitarian Aid, Research and Education Foundation fundraising to support election monitoring for their first postwar election, I noticed how in El Salvador, active mass-based organizations, including women's groups, had managed to maintain more similar levels of political activity in the postaccord period. Moreover, they seemed to have more equal access to resources and opportunities to adapt to the new political situation. In contrast to the Palestinian case, among the many mass-based organizations that became formal, professionalized NGOs in El Salvador there was a concerted effort to include and maintain relations with former grassroots constituencies. Hence, the nature of emergent civil society organizations (CSOs) in El Salvador differed markedly from those in the Palestinian territories in terms of their respective ability to incorporate and forge horizontal linkages with other sectors of society, especially the grassroots, and by extension portended more promising prospects for democratization. Two principal sets of questions emerged from these observations: Why did a case like the Palestinian territories (which received relatively higher amounts of Western donor assistance, including substantial allocations to democracy promotion)[5] lead to a more incoherent process, in which organizations had unequal access to resources, grassroots, and institutions to engage the state? Conversely, why did other cases such as El Salvador (which had actually received substantially less donor assistance, and democracy and civil society assistance in particular) seem to result in a more coherent democratic development process. Second, and more generally, what does this comparison tell us about democracy promotion efforts and the longer-term prospects for democratic development in different contexts, and why are democracy promotion efforts more successful in some contexts as opposed to others?

These questions have assumed even greater importance given the dramatic increase in Western donor assistance for democracy promotion in recent years. Since 1991, bilateral and multilateral Western donor assistance for democracy promotion, particularly civil society development, has also become a central pillar of US foreign policy. The Middle East Partnership Initiative,[6] the Broader Middle East and North Africa Partnership Initiatives,[7] and the Millennium Challenge Account are only a few such recent initiatives.[8] In the late 1980s, less than US$1 billion a year went to democracy assistance; by 2015, the estimated total was more than US$10 billion from all donors.[9] Many new democracies have also committed themselves to spreading democracy abroad.[10] In recent years, democracy promoters have even called for more heightened political intervention to shape desired "democratic" outcomes.[11]

These initial reflections would guide my PhD research and later the development of this book project. What follows draws from over a decade of research, close to 150 interviews,[12] and five research trips. My biggest challenge throughout this project has been to assess these political changes (to the extent possible) from the perspective of understudied groups and individuals who lived through this era. It was their stories and experiences that initially motivated this research project. Some of the activists were national leaders. Others were local community activists. Some continued their activism after the start of the peace accords, and others withdrew from political life. Among those who continued their political engagement, some continued through more formal structures such as in professionalized NGOs or government institutions, and others through informal structures and activities such as car theft. Regardless of the nature of their political participation (or lack thereof), I hope to shed light on how broader political developments and Western donor assistance informed these changes.

Along the way, I accumulated a debt of gratitude to countless individuals who helped me with my journey. I am perhaps most indebted to my numerous interviewees for their time and boundless generosity. In both the Palestinian territories and El Salvador, my interviewees often went out of their way to arrange interviews on my behalf, to provide me with supporting documents, and to invite me to all sorts of events and activities. I was deeply touched by the openness with which so many people received me, and humbled by the stories I heard and the life experiences they embodied. I extend special recognition to three women interviewees, who paved the way for others, and who are no longer with us: Rabiha Diab, Maha Nassar, Nihaya Mohammed.

Special thanks go to Juliet Johnson. Her feedback on an earlier draft of the manuscript and her support have been invaluable throughout this journey. I also thank Ellen Lust for her helpful comments on different chapters and her ongoing support. Numerous other colleagues also generously read and commented on parts of the manuscript, specific chapters, or presentations leading to this manuscript. These colleagues include: Lisa Andersón, Yesim Bayar, Eva Bellin, Sarah Bush, Chris Blake, Rosalind Boyd, Benoit Challand, Mona El-Ghobashy, Michael Hudson, Nadine Naber, Wendy Pearlman, Mouin Rabbani, Siham Rashid, Jillian Schwedler, Seteney Shami, John Scheperel, Richa Singh, Gopika Solanki, Berna Turam, and Devrim Yavuz. Nathan Brown and Yezid Sayigh also provided comments on an article published in *Comparative Political Studies* where I introduced the argument I develop in this book. I also thank the anonymous reviewers.

I had the opportunity to present parts of the manuscript and to receive feedback at numerous conferences and invited talks, including the American Political Science Association, the Middle East Studies Association, Georgetown University's Center for Contemporary Arab Studies, Harvard University's Kennedy School of Government, UC Berkeley's Center for Middle Eastern Studies, the Dubai School of Government, and the Politics of the Middle East Working Group Workshop at Princeton University.

The number of people who I owe a debt of gratitude to in El Salvador and Palestine are numerous and beyond what I can list here, but a few stand out: Ghassan al-Khatib; whose thoughtful political analysis has always been so valued; Raja Rantisi and Amal Hassan, for their support and willingness to always help; and Salim Tamari, has always been, and continues to be, so supportive of junior scholars. In El Salvador, Leslie Schuld, my former housemate, was beyond generous with her contacts and political expertise; Joceyln Viterna, helped me navigate my way when I first arrived in El Salvador; David Holiday for his expertise on everything El Salvador–related; and Raquel Hernandez, who helped me with translation and getting to and from interviews. Then, there was El Ché—the taxi driver—who helped me get around San Salvador. And thanks also to the many others who made my stays in El Salvador and Palestine such wonderful experiences.

I owe a debt of gratitude to colleagues who have always been generous with their support and mentorship. Special thanks go to Amal Amireh, Laurie Brand, Charles Butterworth, Frances Hasso, Mervat Hatem, Suad Joseph, Mehran Kamrava, Smadar Lavie, Ann Lesch, Zachary Lockman, Gwenn Okrulik, T. V. Paul, Glenn Robinson, and the late Dwight Simpson.

I also thank my friends, old and new (and whose names do not appear elsewhere in these acknowledgments), for their camaraderie and support, for remaining interested in this project, and for cheering me along the way: Hayfa Abdel Jabbar, Rabab Abdulhadi, Naser Abu Diab, Hussein Agrama, Muge Aknur, Canan Aslan, Mona Atia, Alia Ayyad, Dima Ayouob, Zahra Babar, Rita Bahour Lahoud, Anne Marie Bayloumi, Sabine Beddies, Leyla Binbrek, Iain Blaire, Nayiri Boghossian, Mesky Brahane, Matt Buehler, Renda Dabit, Rabab el Mahdi, Malia Everette, Awad Halabi, Rola Husseini, Zeynep Kadirbeyoglu, Arang Keshvarzian, Ismail Kushkush, Sherry Lapp, Khalid Madani, Amal Sood Muhyeddin, Saime Oscurmez, Nadia Rahman, Najat Rahman, Shira Robinson, Jennifer Zacharia Said, Wadie Said, Farnoosh Safavi, Charmaine Seitz, Erin Snider, and Atiyeh Vahidmanesh. And I extend special recognition to the late Samia Constandi, who unfortunately did not live long enough to see this book come to light.

Special thanks also go to my exceptional colleagues and friends at James Madison University, especially (also whose names do not appear elsewhere) Robert Alexander, Andreas Broschild, Keith Grant, David Jones, Bernie Kaussler, Jon Keller, Hakseon Lee, Lili Peaslee, Valerie Sulfaro, Nick Swartz, Amanda Tee, and Robyn Teske. Their support has been invaluable. And of course, thanks to my students for their endless curiosity about this book.

I had the tremendous privilege of receiving numerous fellowships and institutional affiliations that supported the research and writing of this book. These include UC Berkeley's Center for Middle Eastern Studies, the Dubai School of Government, and the Dubai Initiative and more recently the Middle East Initiative at Harvard University's Kennedy School of Government. Special thanks go to Emily Gottreich for her support during my time at UC Berkeley. A visiting scholar position at Georgetown University's Center for Contemporary Arab Studies provided me with an office and library access, and an opportunity to present parts of my work. FLACSO-El Salvador also provided me with office space and a computer, and the staff and researchers were exceptionally welcoming.

I am also grateful for the editorial assistance of Allison Brown and Lucy Malenke, and to my former student Grace Anderson who helped format and edit the final bibliography. At New York University Press, I thank everyone I worked with, especially Maryam Arain, Ilene Kalish, and Martin Coleman.

And my family, especially Eman, Khalid, Randa, my aunts Nathmia and Zahia, and the late Hajjeh Fatmeh, for their unconditional love, Eyad, Aissa, and the next generation.

1

The Primacy of Political Settlements
in Democracy Promotion

Grassroots organizations in the Palestinian territories reached their zenith during the first Intifada (which literally means "shaking off") between 1987 and 1993. This episode of coordinated mass upheaval and civil disobedience campaign throughout the West Bank and Gaza Strip was not instigated or organized by the Palestine Liberation Organization (PLO); rather, it was a popular mobilization initiated by a number of different organizations, committees, and institutions established in the occupied territories to resist Israel's military occupation and to empower communities. Within the first weeks of the Intifada, grassroots committees had organized an array of local popular committees (*lijan sha'biyya*) throughout the occupied territories that would sustain and strengthen the Intifada.[1] The popular committees were responsible for key tasks such as coordinating the daily activities of the Intifada, preparing for emergencies, cultivating self-sufficiency, and patrolling neighborhoods during the night.[2] The degree of popular participation in this Intifada was unprecedented compared to earlier uprisings. Mass involvement in nonviolent forms of resistance was a radical departure from the earlier period in which only armed struggle was recognized as a legitimate form of resistance. Moreover, the Intifada represented a fundamental shift in the site of power from the PLO to the people under occupation in the West Bank and Gaza Strip (WBGS). The Intifada had its own leadership structure, the United Leadership Command, in which all major political organizations of the PLO were represented.

Similar to other grassroots organizations, the Palestinian women's committees also reached their pinnacle of organizational success during this period. Countless women I interviewed who were directly involved in the daily activities of the Intifada highlighted the pivotal role of women during that period.[3] It was this particular feature of the Intifada—the widespread participation of women—that, perhaps more than anything else, dramatized the extent to which Palestinian society had been stirred. Women's widespread, grassroots-based, nonviolent civil disobedience was pivotal in supporting the uprising during this period.

The organizational efficacy of the first Intifada owed its success to decades of mass organizing by Palestinian political organizations.[4] By the early 1980s, all factions of the PLO had established their own volunteer grassroots structures throughout the WBGS. These organizations included labor unions, agriculture unions, health unions, student groups, women's groups, and various other professional unions and syndicates. These groups served to defend the interests of the various constituencies and enabled the participation and empowerment of local sectors of society. Each association, union, and grassroots organization was disparate and issue-oriented and reported to its respective parent political organization. These organizations were also volunteer based, and in line with the PLO's *sumoud* policy (policy of steadfastness), they stressed self-help, a continuation of national resistance, and more hands-on participatory development.[5]

In sync with the developments that were taking place in the broader national movement, women members of the various political organizations also established women's committees that would aid and facilitate mass mobilization. In 1978, women cadres from the Democratic Front for the Liberation of Palestine (DFLP) founded the first women's committee, the Women's Working Committee (WWC). The goal of the committee was to lend support to the national movement by involving women in resistance activities against the Israeli occupation and to empower and involve them in improving their daily living conditions. Though the founders were politically affiliated, the organization was not supposed to be partisan and was open to all women, regardless of their political affiliations. By 1981, the women's group began to splinter along factional lines, and each of the political organizations established its own women's committees.[6] Women leaders from other political factions worried that the leaders of the WWC would later recruit some of the members to the DFLP and hence embarked on establishing their own committees (see table 5.2, which indicates the year in which each of the political organizations established its respective women's committee).

During the 1980s, activities of the women's sector were an integral and essential component of Palestinian political and social life. Most towns and villages had an array of women's committees or groups that hosted weekly seminars, occasional courses, annual bazaars, and International Women's Day events. The women's committees were successful in assisting their members in their day-to-day lives, as well as in encouraging collective action among them. Projects addressed women's practical needs such as health, sustenance, and small-scale vocational training, childcare, and literacy.[7] Recruitment and the preservation of voluntary membership were contingent on genuine incorporation and inclusion. The potential to build on these local forms of sociopolitical organization were immense, especially in the emergence of a robust civil society. That potential, however, failed to materialize.

By the late 1990s, after the Madrid Peace Conference and the Oslo Accords, the extent of demobilization and weakening of these once thriving movements was evident to everyone. Membership in the labor unions, women's mass-based organizations, student groups, and professional syndicates had decreased dramatically. These once thriving movements no longer had the capability to organize and coordinate any mass action. Despite mounting dissatisfaction with the Oslo Accords and the newly established PA, civic protest was limited to individual disputes, with little in the way of collective organizing. In contrast, however, Fatah, the PLO's leadership party behind the Oslo Accords, still had the power to convene larger gatherings to lend support to the PA.

The absence of more organizing and protest was even more glaring considering the improvement in the security situation in the PA controlled areas. The redeployment of the Israeli military from the main town centers made reprisals against Palestinian protesters less likely. Moreover, the Palestinian territories were among the highest per capita recipients of Western donor funding in the world, with substantial allocations to democracy and civil society promotion.[8] This amount translated to $1,820 per capita (per Palestinian living in the WBGS) each year in the first decade after the peace accords. Theoretically, the level of mass organization, which had become an essential feature of Palestinian political life, facilitated by improvements in the security situation and a massive influx of Western democracy promotion assistance, should have laid the groundwork for a strong civil society. On the contrary, Palestinian civil society became increasingly elitist, characterized predominately by professionalized NGOs, often run by a single individual, with limited societal reach.

After the start of the Madrid Peace Process in 1991, numerous mass-based organizations became recipients of Western donor assistance and professionalized their operations. The organization of civil society became distinguished by its vertical linkages between the professionalized NGOs and the grassroots. In this new structure, the previously active grassroots constituencies, at best, were merely recipients of services from the professionalized NGOs and not active, engaged members. Moreover, civil society development did not lead to the establishment of regular, constructive patterns of interaction with state institutions. Local government remained restricted in representing constituent interests. Electoral political competition also remained limited, and perhaps more accurately, was stunted in its infancy. In the 1996 Palestinian legislative elections, the overwhelming majority of candidates were Fatah members, and in the 2006 legislative elections, Hamas's legislative victory led to a vicious backlash from Fatah and the international community, and the cessation of Western donor funding to the Hamas-led government. Despite massive discontent in the WBGS with the handling of the electoral outcome and Hamas's reaction, Palestinian civil society groups did little to voice their grievances.

NGO Professionalization: An Inadequate Explanation

Many analysts—academics, policy makers, and activists alike—attributed this demobilization within these once-thriving movements to NGO professionalization triggered by the influx of Western donor assistance in the post-Oslo period.[9] In agreement with an established and growing body of literature on the negative impacts of NGO professionalization, they argued that Palestinian social movements and the longer-term prospects for civil society and democratic development were undermined by this massive influx of Western donor funding. Western donors often required recipient institutions to institutionalize and professionalize their operations so that they are better able to keep detailed financial records and submit regular evaluation reports to their funders.[10] This process includes a host of organizational changes, such as increased specialization, hierarchies of pay, more formal channels of communication and decision-making, and often a greater need for better-educated, English-speaking employees. Among the most obvious outcomes of NGO professionalization are a loss of autonomy,[11] a focus on short-term goals as opposed to longer-term developmental goals, questionable sustainability, and greater accountability to donors rather than to the constituencies they are supposed to serve.[12]

This process of professionalization, which is not unique to the Palestinian territories, often results in the emergence of a new NGO elite.[13] The creation of this new elite class affects local forms of political organizing in three fundamental ways. First, it contributes to the atomization of civil society, since the people who move to the NGO sector are usually former leaders of grassroots movements. Second, privileging the leaders of these groups, or those "more qualified" to participate in these NGOs, exacerbates social schisms between those who do and do not have a Western education, proficiency in English, and familiarity with Western standards and modes of operation of NGO activity.[14] The NGOs serve as a lucrative alternative for the urban elite,[15] as Western-funded NGOs provide salaries that are often three to six times higher than the local standard. The discrepancy in salaries attracts the most talented and skilled workers to the Western-funded NGO sector, away from the public sector, civil service, local political parties, or local grassroots organizations. Third, professionalization and NGO reliance on Western funding entails depoliticization and an embrace of less politically controversial endeavors as a way for the organization to survive.[16] Professionalization-centered explanations, however, do not explain why the introduction of Western donor assistance and the outcomes of NGO professionalization vary in different contexts. Moreover, these explanations fail to take into account the primacy of political contexts. In particular, they neglect to consider how political contexts also determine variation in amounts and types of funding and inequitable access to resources and institutions, and how this variation shapes broader political developments. The continuation of Israel's military occupation and disillusionment also do not fully explain this trajectory. If these were sufficient explanations, the Palestinian population of the WBGS would not have succeeded in organizing previously, under even more repressive security conditions.

Very importantly, political developments in the Palestinian terri-tories contrasted sharply with other cases, such as El Salvador, which shared a number of important organizational and temporal similarities, but ultimately exhibited far more positive outcomes in terms of civil society and democratic development. In 1992, the Frente Farabundo Martí para la Liberación Nacional (FMLN) and the government of El Salvador signed the Chapultepec Accords in Mexico. Similar to the Palestinian case, Western donors provided extensive postsettlement assistance that facilitated the professionalization of certain mass-based organizations. NGO professionalization in El Salvador, however, did not result in the same extent of demobilization of previously active sectors. Rather, civil society development encouraged the incorpo-ration of grassroots constituencies and facilitated citizens' ability to engage the state. The development of civil society entailed the institu-tionalization of productive patterns of engagement with local govern-ment (see figure 1.1). Moreover, competition and a smooth turnover became defining features of El Salvador's presidential, legislative, and local elections. After two decades of Alianza Republicana Naciona-lista (Nationalist Republican Alliance, ARENA), presidential victories, the FMLN won both the 2009 and 2014 presidential elections. Indeed, the degree of political competition and the smooth turnover of power from ARENA, El Salvador's right-wing party, to the FMLN in presi-dential and legislative elections reflected the vigor of political life in the country.

Similar to the PLO, the political-military organizations of what be-came the FMLN embarked on mass-movement mobilization in the mid-1970s and established their own mass-based structures in the controlled zones[17] that included rural workers, teachers, students, women, and re-populated and war-displaced persons.[18] In the preaccord period, these associations shared similarities in terms of grassroots character, func-tions, and relationship to the political organizations. As in the Palestinian case, such organizations played central roles in resistance, consciousness-raising, provision of community services, and organization of coopera-tive economic enterprises.

Similar to the Palestinian case, during the late 1970s and early 1980s, the political-military organizations succeeded in recruiting women in large numbers, and in genuinely involving them in the struggle through mass-based organizations.[19] Each political-military organization established its own mass-based women's organizations (see table 5.3, which shows the year that each political-military organizations established its affiliated mass-based women's organization). The level of organization during this period, especially among the leftist opposition, laid the groundwork for what could become an effective civil society that could represent large segments of the population who would not otherwise be represented. In both contexts, the programs and projects of the women's sector addressed women's practical needs such as health, sustenance, childcare, literacy, and small-scale vocational training.

Following the election of Christian Democrat José Napoleón Duarte in 1984, political openings in El Salvador increased; because US engagement required the appearance of democracy, blatant repression was less tolerated. Consequently, many of the political-military organizations of the FMLN and the Christian base communities were able to operate more openly and established their own women's mass-based organizations between 1985 and 1988, many of them in San Salvador and not in the controlled zones[20] (see table 5.3).

After the signing of the Salvadoran peace accords in 1992, there also was an influx of donor assistance. Even after professionalizing their operations, however, these women's organizations, as with many other mass-based organizations, retained their mass character. In fact, donors often required these organizations to maintain regular engagement with their mass constituencies. The Palestinian case, however, and specifically the formerly active mass-based organizations, pointed to how unequal access to resources as well as institutions to engage the state became a defining feature of post-Oslo political life. This unequal access and the polarization that transpired were not simply an outcome of foreign donors requiring institutions to professionalize their operations. Even in the absence of the massive influx of Western donor assistance and requirements for institutional professionalization, Palestinian civil society and democratic developments would have remained constrained because, ultimately, the Oslo Accords were not meant to deliver and promote democracy. The massive influx of foreign aid that followed, including assistance to develop civil society and democracy, was intended to buttress the Oslo Accords and to promote those groups and constituencies that did not oppose the Oslo Accords.

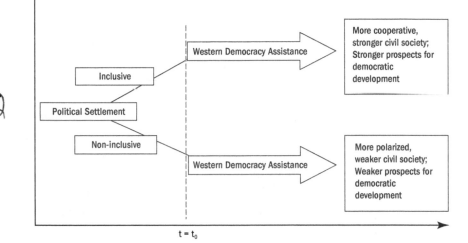

Figure 1.1. Political settlements, donor assistance, and civil society outcomes. This figure was slightly modified from the original that first appeared in Manal A. Jamal, "Democracy Promotion, Civil Society Building, and the Primacy of Politics," *Comparative Political Studies* 45, no. 1 (January 2012): 3–31. Reprinted by permission of SAGE.

The Centrality of Political Settlements

In this book, I depart from predominant explanations of civil society and democracy outcomes that solely focus on foreign donor assistance and related professionalization dynamics.[21] My analysis takes the argument a step back and concentrates on those factors that shape the emergent political context. I argue that political settlements, broadly understood as the formal and informal political agreements that define political relations in certain contexts, shape the impact of democracy promotion assistance. The "inclusivity" of political settlements (assessed by the extent of participation of major political groups and the degree of societal support) shapes the relative effectiveness of democracy promotion efforts and the impact of Western donor assistance on civil society and democratic development more generally. Democracy promotion efforts are bound to fail in contexts where the political settlement enjoys limited societal support and key political constituencies are excluded—despite the backing of dominant political groups and Western state-sponsored donors. In these contexts, Western donor assistance will minimize cooperation, exacerbate political polarization, and weaken civil society by promoting favored groups over others. This is especially true if the interests of dominant political groups and Western foreign donors coalesce to marginalize important political sectors. Conversely, in inclusive contexts, Western donor assistance will play a more positive role, helping civil society and democratic development.

Political settlements frame political relations and outcomes, determine key players, and shape societal conflict management systems.[22] In conflict-to-peace transitions, political settlements specifically refer to peace agreements. According to Stephan Haggard and Robert Kauffman, the settlement terms refer to both "formal constitutional rules and the informal understandings that govern political contestation in the new democratic system. . . . Terms include military prerogatives, rights of participation in political life, design of representation and decision making institutions."[23] In many ways, they are most similar to pacted transitions,[24] or what Guillermo O'Donnell and Philippe Schmitter define as

> an explicit, but not always publicly explicated or justified, agreement among a select set of actors which seeks to define (or better, to redefine) rules governing the exercise of power on the basis of mutual guarantees for the "vital interests" of those entering into it.[25]

Transition theorists generally concur that "pacted transitions" lead to the most stable and successful transitions to democracy.[26] These transitions ensure that the rules of democratic politics are acceptable to the largest proportion of the elite population.[27] Although stability may characterize these transitions, scholars agree that noninclusive arrangements may ultimately marginalize certain groups and sectors of the population, thus affecting the quality of the emergent democracies.[28] Similarly, during conflict-to-peace transitions, political settlements play a pivotal role in defining the most and least relevant actors. External actors also often play key roles in negotiating political settlements in these transitions, as sed to in ordinary democratic transitions, which tend to be more of an internal, domestic affair. Ultimately, noninclusive political settlements undermine the conflict-to-peace transition, as well as the quality of the emergent democracy.

During conflict to peace transitions, political liberalization and democratization processes may inherently exacerbate polarization and conflict,[29] especially where preexisting religious and ethnic schisms may exist.[30] Furthermore, the prospects for peace and democratization are bleak when there are unsatisfactory political pacts,[31] and especially when the settlements are noninclusive.[32] The more prescriptive peace-building[33] and conflict-resolution literatures concur that the broader inclusion of different actors and constituencies enhances the longer-term prospects for the cessation of violence, peace-building, and democratic development.[34] However, this fundamental understanding does not appear to figure prominently in the programming of Western donors who work in the promotion of democracy (what is often referred to as the Western democracy promotion establishment). This oversight has profound implications for the impact of their work. Although the extant literature has acknowledged how political bargaining influences the institutions that emerge[35]—and in turn, how institutional engineering influences electoral outcomes,[36] conflict resolution goals,[37] and the emergent state[38]—these works tell us little about the broader contexts that spawn political bargaining dynamics, the institutions that emerge, and the role of Western donors.

A growing body of literature has sought to assess the impact of Western democracy promotion assistance on democratic outcomes. A number of these works, often quantitative in approach, have examined the relationship between foreign aid, including democracy assistance, and democratic outcomes. Scholars, however, do not agree on the nature of this relationship. Some have found positive relationships[39] or negative relationships,[40] while others have found no direct relationship at all.[41] Although the quantitative research overwhelmingly establishes a positive relationship between foreign aid (including democracy assistance) and civil society and democratic outcomes, I do not fundamentally disagree with this approach. For the most part, however, as my analysis illustrates, in-depth case study examination illuminates the limitations of this approach since multiple dimensions and dynamics of these relationships simply cannot be captured by quantitative macro correlations. The amount of assistance per country is one factor, but the type and approaches of assistance are as important, if not more important. Fewer works have elaborated more explicit causal mechanisms. Pertaining to Western donor assistance and civil society development in particular, some scholars have focused on institutional professionalization, political and cultural constraints,[42] or on preexisting ethnic and religious cleavages that may inhibit civil society development.[43] Institutional professionalization, as I have explained, is not an adequate explanation to account for divergent outcomes. And although preexisting cleavages are important to consider, the political settlement remains pivotal to institutionalizing these divisions, or in harnessing ethnic, political, and social divisions. Moreover, in post-Communist regimes, although Western donors are inclined to support nonleftist groups that support liberal democracy, it is fair to say that the political settlements (even if informally) are noninclusive in these societies, but to a lesser degree than in conflict to peace transitions where a settlement is formally defined. Other scholars have focused on the importance of civil society's legacy in a given context, or its embrace of "universally embraced" norms.[44] Societies with a strong legacy of grassroots organization will persist in that tradition,[45] regardless of the type and quantity of Western donor assistance they receive. There are many cases, however, that may have had a strong legacy of civil society organizing that experience a decline regardless of the historical precedent or prevalent norms.

A number of works have focused on Western donors' lack of understanding of the contexts in which they operate and their reluctance to address the key challenges at hand while prioritizing their geostrategic interests.[46] Jason Brownley, for example, forcefully argued that the United States has often worked to ensure that democracy does not take root, as in the case of Egypt, prioritizing its own geostrategic interests over political reform.[47] Benoit Challand provided a cogent explanation of how donors can play a role in promoting and excluding certain NGOs.[48] These explanations, however, fail to fully account for how political contexts lead to divergent outcomes, and, more specifically, how noninclusive arrangements exacerbate these negative outcomes. Foreign donors are not operating in vacuums. Some may counter that the variation in democracy assistance may account for the difference in outcomes, but it is important to note that democracy programs do not vary extensively depending on the donor. The difference lies in the types of programs and projects that are prioritized in certain countries or contexts and the amounts of funding.[49]

This book addresses these omissions head on. It focuses on how political settlements shape the institutional engineering process and the unfolding relations between different civil society and political groups in these contexts, as well as how Western donor assistance mediates these processes. Western donors mediate these outcomes by encouraging certain patterns of engagement between different civil society and political groups, as well as with state institutions. Western donors also influence the degree of impact by the amount of funding they provide.

The inclusivity of the political settlement (in a given context), my key explanatory factor, shapes the impact of donor assistance on civil society and democratic development in three fundamental ways: who is included and who is not; degree of foreign donor involvement and program priority; and levels of institutionalization.

Inclusivity and Who Is Included and Who Is Not?

First, political settlements affect who receives funding and who does not and thus the strategies adopted by different actors. As a result, these settlements shape the degree of horizontal and vertical polarization between individuals, groups, and organizations that receive funding (and hence can professionalize) and those that do not receive funding. In turn, the settlements affect the degree of vertical hierarchy between those organizations that receive Western donor funding and those that do not. Funded organizations are required to professionalize their operations and often become service providers to the unfunded organizations. As I discuss in more detail in chapter 5, in the post-Oslo era, the mass-based women's organizations in the Palestinian territories that were affiliated with the Oslo opposition were often not able to access Western donor funding. In the new reconstituted women's sector, these mass-based organizations became the recipients of services and training from those organizations that were not as vocally opposed to the Oslo Accords. In this way, Western donors mediated relations between those who were included and those who were shunned by the settlement. These findings are not limited to the Palestinian territories and El Salvador, but extend to other cases. In noninclusive contexts such as Iraq, Western donors, and especially United Stated Agency for International Development (USAID), allocated all its assistance to anti-Ba'ath groups. In inclusive contexts, such as postapartheid South Africa, Western donor assistance was far less political and did not work to promote and exclude different political and civil society groups.

Inclusivity and Degree of Foreign Donor Involvement and Program Priority

Second, the political settlements determine the amounts of funding and types of programs donors are more likely to promote. Donors, especially state-sponsored donors, will likely be more involved and commit higher amounts of funding where settlements are more fragile and their geostrategic interests figure more prominently. Geostrategic considerations may influence which programs are implemented, and donors may not prioritize a stronger civil society or democratic development. Where donors become more involved and commit higher amounts of funding, their impact is greater. Higher amounts of funding also often require more stringent professionalization criteria. As I will explain in more detail in chapter 4, foreign donors prioritized aid to civil society development in the Palestinian territories in contrast to El Salvador, where they were more likely to prioritize economic development programs in the post-accord period. Along these same lines, the United States was more heavily involved supporting right-wing groups in El Salvador during the Cold War. By the late 1990s and early 2000s, it had appeared that liberal market-democracy had nearly triumphed in Latin America in contrast to the Middle East. All Latin American countries had adopted neo-liberal economic reform policies.[50]

Inclusivity and Institutionalization—Articulated versus Disarticulated Spaces

Third, in addition to determining suffrage and equal opportunity to formulate preferences and have preferences equally considered by the state,[51] the political settlement will impact political institutionalization at the local and national levels of government in a given context,[52] as well as electoral institutional design, and, in turn, shape citizen participation. These two levels of government are of particular relevance to this study because they facilitate relations between the state and civil society, and hence shape citizen participation. Through electoral laws and the frequency of elections, dominant groups influence the ability of opposition groups to participate in elections and prevail at certain levels of government. In turn, electoral outcomes influence how much and what type of access opposition groups (and affiliated NGOs) will have to council or assembly representatives in local government and the national legislative bodies.[53] As I will elaborate in chapter 3, because of the noninclusivity of the political settlement in the Palestinian territories, Fatah, the leadership party of the PA, has repeatedly postponed elections.

In noninclusive contexts, opposition groups and individuals will either not have access to these institutions (in this case, national legislative bodies or municipalities) or will remain a step removed from them compared to included groups. Western donors are less likely to fund programs and projects that will require cooperation or interaction with these institutions if "unfavored" groups may become represented in them, or the donors will simply avoid them altogether. Under these circumstances, CSOs are more constrained by the institutional setting since they are limited in terms of both their access to the state and their ability to make demands on it. Given the noninclusivity of these institutions and the lack of Western donor programs to encourage citizen participation between civil society and state institutions, what I refer to as "disarticulated spaces" pervade. In these spaces, institutions that should provide connecting channels between civil society and the state are lacking or discriminate against certain groups by not allowing them the same access.

Conversely, in politically inclusive contexts, if all major political groups are involved, ruling groups are more likely to design and endorse more inclusive political institutionalization at both levels. More representative national and local government bodies will also provide civil society with more institutional openings. Moreover, Western donor-promoted civil society development will not necessarily play a discriminating role favoring certain groups over others, and will likely promote programs that encourage more regular citizen engagement with the state, leading to more "articulated spaces," and hence to a more effective civil society.

In the post–Cold War era of liberal market-democracy consensus, the interests of key Western state-sponsored donors and dominant political groups often align to exclude certain political groups; this has had important implications for civil society and democratic development. In transition contexts, Western donors pay significant attention to civil society's promise to promote and entrench political settlements and promote what I refer to as a "post–Cold War liberal order." This political-economic order is committed to market-democracy and the advancement of civil and political rights, with lesser regard for economic rights and economic well-being. It is also more Western and liberal in its social orientation.[54] Given the priorities of Western geostrategic interests in the immediate post–Cold War period, these dynamics were most pronounced in the Middle East. It is important, however, not to reduce this state of affairs to the incompatibility between the West and Islam; rather, Western state-sponsored donors have worked to exclude parties that do not support Western-endorsed status quos. Hence, those excluded often not only oppose dominant political settlements but also are not well positioned to promote a "post–Cold War liberal order." This category includes Islamists, as well as leftists who refuse to embrace this status quo. What is remarkable about this state of play is that the West and many dominant political groups embrace the notion of democratic governance that is based on exclusion.

Civil Society

Before proceeding, it is important to clarify what exactly is meant by civil society and how it relates to this study.[55] Scholars generally agree that civil society is "a sphere of activity in which private citizens first constitute a public."[56] It speaks to the conditions of citizenship in a given polity, including both the virtues and dispositions of individual citizens.[57] Of specific concern to this study, however, are those organizations and social collectivities that facilitate political participation and influence and make demands on the state.[58] Civil society facilitates political participation by aggregating and representing citizen interests, countering state power, and furthering the struggle for citizenship rights. This study does not subscribe to the notion that all NGOs are part of civil society.[59] Rather, NGOs that seek to influence state policy or demand greater inclusion in national political structures are CSOs. Local NGOs that are part of civil society should be able to organize various constituencies, drawing on their needs and demands, and not simply implement the agendas of foreign donors or external actors. Civil society can contribute to the delivery of humanitarian relief, support the reintegration of former combatants, facilitate refugee return, improve the performance of political and economic institutions, and cultivate greater trust between different parties through civic engagement.[60] However, unless a service-provider NGO is simultaneously concerned with influencing and shaping broader political processes, including state policies, it should not be considered part of civil society. Social movements are involved in conflictual relations with clear opponents, are linked by dense networks, and have a collective identity, but they are not necessarily facilitating political participation and making demands on the state.

For civil society to accomplish these tasks, certain characteristics and contextual factors must obtain.[61] A more dense and plural civil society that is inclusive of broad social sectors will better contribute to the development of democracy; in such contexts, citizens from all walks of life, not only the elite or certain political groups, are afforded greater opportunities to participate in civic life.

Horizontal versus Vertical Networks

CSOs should also be rooted in society and be able to forge horizontal linkages with other CSOs and with grassroots constituencies.[62] Horizontal linkages are necessary for the strengthening of civil society and the longer term prospects for democratic development, because, as Robert Putnam explained, "a vertical network, no matter how dense and no matter how important to its participants, cannot sustain social trust and co-operation."[63] Furthermore, vertical networks are not likely to generate citizen participation or engagement because they reinforce existing hierarchy and polarization and decrease the likelihood of cooperation.[64] A cross-cutting, horizontally organized civil society will incorporate grassroots constituencies beyond simply providing services to them.

More effective incorporation will contribute to the better organization of interests and, in turn, to the growth of cooperative networks.

Access to Resources and Networks

Access to resources and networks is also critical, because, although a level of trust is necessary for citizens to engage in political participation, a conception of social capital that solely focuses on trust provides little insight into the "actual mechanisms by which social relations facilitate or block individual and collective access to resources."[65] Social capital (conceived as both the social trust and "norms of reciprocity" that facilitate cooperation, as well as access to resources and networks that facilitate civic engagement) will strengthen civil society.[66]

Political Institutionalization

Lastly, the extent of political institutionalization in a society, specifically at the national and local government levels, will also impact the performance of civil society.[67] These institutions provide the connecting channels between civil society and the state. Well-developed institutions of local government in particular will provide more political openings for local participation and thus facilitate the emergence of an effective civil society.[68] In contexts in which these political institutions are weak or absent, the performance of civil society will suffer.

The Imprecise Demarcation between Civil Society and Political Society

Although the autonomy of civil society is an important criterion, the relationship between civil society and political society[69] is not necessarily one of separation. A closer observation indicates that much of civil society during transitions—democratic transitions or conflict-to-peace transitions more generally—is often borne out of political society. According to most accepted Western liberal understandings, political society and civil society are two demarcated political realms, and political society represents those forces that seek to capture state power. However, one can more accurately describe the interactions between these two realms as forever shifting sites of contest, as individuals move from one site to another. Moreover, a less autonomous society that has greater capacity to reach broader constituencies is far more promising than a more autonomous civil society that is limited in its societal reach. An appreciation of this actual relationship puts into perspective how autonomous civil society actually is or can be.

The Study and Methodology

The book casts a broad lens on the question of why democracy promotion efforts are more successful in some cases as opposed to others. It begins with an examination of the divergent outcomes pertaining to democracy promotion in two cases of conflict-to-peace transitions, the Palestinian territories and El Salvador. It examines these developments at a more macro, general level in terms of democratic outcomes and then at the level of civil society by tracing transformations in one social movement sector—the women's sector—in each case. The book then generalizes these findings by expanding the temporal and geographic aperture of the study. First, it examines developments in the Palestinian territories surrounding Hamas's election victory in 2006. Then it expands this discussion to Iraq and South Africa to illustrate how the respective political settlements shaped the different outcomes and how Western donor assistance mediated these processes.

The more general discussion about the divergent democratic outcomes in the two cases brings the study to the present period. The more specific examination of developments in the women's sectors in each case, however, focuses on the immediate post-settlement period.[70] As opposed to a more recent examination, this time frame captures the immediate changes these societies underwent after the influx of post-settlement foreign donor assistance. This ten-year period allowed me to assess how the influx of postsettlement aid transformed the sector, as well as how it impacted the relations that transpired in the decade that followed. This time period also comprehensively captured the scope of transformation in each case in the postsettlement period; a more focused time period would not have encapsulated the breadth of organizational change and adjustment in each context. In this section of the study, I employed a structured, focused comparison that is historically sensitive but conducive to generalizing across cases. This method allowed for a more rigorous examination of the different outcomes by isolating certain variables. Political settlements are the key explanatory variable I examined. In keeping with the requirements for structured focused comparison, I collected data on the same variables across cases. I assessed the quality of civil society and prospects for democratic development by evaluating the extent to which different civil society groups forged horizontal linkages with one another, and their capacity to engage local and national levels of government. In both cases, I focused on the political centers, the Jerusalem-Ramallah access area in the Palestinian territories and San Salvador in El Salvador.

Research

This book draws from research conducted during five fieldwork trips: February 2002 to June 2002 in El Salvador, and June to October 2001, September to October 2006, July to August 2009, and August 2013 in Palestine. My research draws from over 150 formal semistructured and open-ended interviews. I conducted these interviews in the Palestinian Territories and El Salvador with grassroots activists, political leaders, directors and program officers in donor agencies, and directors of NGOs (for a more detailed discussion of interview case selection and sampling, refer to appendices I and II). My research also entailed participant observation, especially in terms of attending political events and protests and visiting professionalized organizations and the offices or headquarters of grassroots committees. It also relied heavily on the collection of primary and secondary materials, including newspaper articles, reports, government documents, and books in Arabic, English, and Spanish. I also examined in detail donor funding to El Salvador and the Palestinian territories, focusing more in depth on funding to civil society, democracy promotion, and women. This research project relied on several donor funding data sources, including primary reporting from donor agencies and NGOs, interviews with directors of donor agencies and NGOs, and country national-level reporting. To enhance data comparability and to corroborate and validate findings, the project also drew from data of the Organisation for Economic Cooperation and Development (OECD).

The Comparative Examination: Similarity and Divergence

The Palestinian and Salvadoran cases illustrate how the inclusivity of political settlements and the mediating role of Western donor assistance can lead to drastically divergent outcomes in cases that shared similar political and organizing trajectories during a certain phase of the respective conflicts. The comparison is across cases as well as between the presettlement and postsettlement periods in each case. Both cases experienced protracted conflicts in the latter part of the twentieth century. Furthermore, both contexts have also been shaped by extensive imperial encounters. The temporal parallels and similar trajectories of what became FMLN and PLO grassroots organizing justify this comparison. During the 1970s and 1980s, the political factions and organizations of the PLO and the FMLN both adopted policies of mass mobilization and established their own grassroots structures that included labor unions, agriculture unions, health unions, student groups, women's groups, and various other professional unions. In the early 1990s, the Palestinian territories and El Salvador began conflict-to-peace transitions, and Western donors provided extensive donor assistance.

Notwithstanding the historical and temporal similarities, key features distinguished the Palestinian and Salvadoran cases. In the Palestinian case, the conflict was between Israel and the Palestinian territories and their main representative, the PLO, and based on a history of colonial settlement, land appropriation, and military occupation; Palestinians were internally divided vis-à-vis an external enemy and occupier.[71] In El Salvador, the conflict was a civil war grounded in class conflict between the government of El Salvador and the FMLN—two domestic parties.[72] Conceivably, a civil war resolution is more likely to involve a larger number of domestic actors, necessitating higher levels of domestic support as opposed to "interstate" conflict. The Salvadoran conflict also centered on class conflict and economic grievance, whereas the Israeli-Palestinian conflict was more political and polarized along national lines.[73] Some would argue that the inequality-based differences in El Salvador were more amenable to amelioration than nationality-based differences. Moreover, the Israeli-Palestinian conflict was complicated by its colonial settlement nature, and that the Palestinian leadership was predominately based abroad. It is important to note, however, that much of the Salvadoran FMLN leadership was also based abroad in the period before the peace accords. Very importantly, however, regardless of the type of conflict, polarization will result when a political settlement fails to garner the support of major domestic political actors or important societal constituencies. Moreover, the Israeli-Palestinian conflict and the internal divisions among Palestinians are rooted in political differences and not identity-based differences. Just as the economic basis of the conflict was not fully addressed in the Salvadoran case, the political bases of the conflict were not fully addressed in the Palestinian case.

Others may contend that the Palestinian territories do not constitute a full-fledged state, and that this accounts for the divergent outcomes. The WBGS, however, are recognized as a state and treated as such by the international community and by the people who inhabit that territory.[74] Moreover, the PA is an institutionalized political organization that carries out the functions of a state, such as tax extraction, education, and health provision.[75] I am also examining the impact of the political settlement and Western donor assistance on social movement sectors. These social movement sectors were able to organize before the establishment of the PA.

The political settlements also differed in terms of the stages embodied, the scope of the agreements, and, most significantly, the levels of inclusivity and extent of societal support they enjoyed. In the Palestinian case, the initial Declaration of Principles (DOP) culminated in agreements involving renegotiation and the spelling out of implementation details. Fatah, the leadership party, negotiated these agreements on behalf of the PLO. Although the accords in this case were meant to serve as only interim agreements and were nonbinding, they did not meet minimal Palestinian nationalist aspirations. Critics pointed out that the Palestinians had not received any guarantees for a future independent, sovereign, viable state, nor any guarantees to halt Israeli settlement expansion in the occupied territories. Ultimately, the Oslo peace process and related initiatives would enjoy little support among Palestinians in the territories.[76] Most of the Palestinian political organizations, both leftist and Islamist, as well as prominent secular Palestinian intellectuals, did not support or endorse the peace accords. The renegotiation agreements did not expand beyond the bilateral, narrow participation of the PLO (represented by Fatah) and Israel that characterized the DOP interim agreements.[77] While negotiations in the Palestinian context moved toward interim arrangements that sought independent statehood, in El Salvador negotiations moved toward a final and comprehensive agreement addressing human rights, land redistribution, and ex-combatant reintegration. Also, a United Nations peace operation was actively involved.

By 1989, the Salvadoran government and the FMLN had reached a military stalemate with no clear victors.[78] As a result, both parties agreed to a negotiated settlement. The Salvadoran agreements built consensus on the different issues and culminated in a comprehensive final framework agreement that included agreements reached over the preceding two years. In contrast to the Oslo Accords, the Salvadoran peace accords enjoyed high levels of political inclusion and societal support. Although groups such as the Christian Democrats and the Social Democrats did not sit at the negotiating table, they were part of the Inter-Party Commission that endorsed the accords and were not marginalized by the terms of the agreement. Had these parties opposed the accords and been excluded as a result, similar polarization dynamics as in the Palestinian case would have transpired despite the variation in conflict type or extent of UN involvement. The conclusion of the Salvadoran civil war became known as the "negotiated revolution."[79]

Relatedly, some may argue that a key distinguishing feature that led to the divergent outcomes was the "settledness" or the extent to which the conflicts have been settled in these two cases. Democracy promotion will be a smoother process in more settled cases, and Anna Jarstad and Timothy Sisk's recommendation that it is better to settle a conflict and then promote democracy certainly applies here.[80] Regardless of the settledness of a conflict, however, democracy promotion in noninclusive contexts will exacerbate polarization and undermine the longer term prospects for democratization.

More restrictive security environments and limited governmental support conceivably could also account for different civil society outcomes. Most notably, the outbreak of the Al-Aqsa Intifada in 2000 and the continuation of Israel's encroachments against the Palestinian territories may have further challenged civil society institutions, resulting in different trajectories. These factors alone, however, do not explain variation within a case, or the underlying rationale for governments or other dominant groups to favor one group over another. The Palestinian case had experienced a restrictive security environment prior to the Oslo Accords, and this did not prevent political mass-based mobilization. Moreover, such factors do not explain why cases also experiencing societal insecurity related to crime and poverty may undergo more constructive civil society developments, as in El Salvador.

In chapter 7, I examine Iraq and South Africa. This examination departs from our standard two-by-two analysis that seeks to show the impact of my key explanatory factor in the absence of mediating factors. Such a treatment is not possible given that almost every country in the world is or has been a recipient of some form of democracy promotion assistance in the post–Cold War era. In both cases, however, associational life emerged from the political organizations of the pretransition period, yet we see divergent outcomes in the transition period. In Iraq, as a result of the noninclusive settlement, almost all institutions affiliated to the former ruling Ba'ath Party were marginalized in the transition, and Western democracy promotion efforts worked to exclude all former affiliated associations and promote nonaffiliates, further exacerbating the ensuing polarization. Alternatively, in South Africa, the political settlement ensured that all political organizations and their affiliated institutions would be included in the transition. Democracy promotion efforts worked to facilitate this inclusion, and thus we witness the emergence of a much more coherent civil society and democratic development process.

Assessing the Quality of Civil Society and Democratic Development

Although the breadth of citizenship in a society is a useful indicator for gauging the quality of civil society and democracy in a given polity,[81] a sole focus on rights does not tell us much about how broader changes affect the exercise of democracy. To this end, this study focuses on democratic outcomes, including changes in civil society. Pertaining to democratic outcomes, I assessed presidential, legislative, and local elections, focusing on the impact of timing, frequency, and the laws that govern these elections. I assessed changes in civil society by tracing how the mass-based organizations, and specifically women's mass-based organizations, were reconstituted after the start of the conflict to peace transitions, and how access to funding, including Western donor assistance, shaped these processes. I studied the impact of the political settlement by determining which organizations and individuals could access Western donor funding depending on their position vis-à-vis the peace accords. Then I examined the patterns of interaction that transpired between the different tendencies, paying particular attention to the degree to which the relationship is horizontal versus vertical, and the degree of cooperation and polarization. I assessed the extent of horizontal linkages and cooperation between the professionalized NGOs by examining the number of cooperative meetings, joint programs, and coordinating mechanisms in which they participated. I assessed the quality of horizontal linkages between the professionalized NGOs and mass-based groups by examining the extent of incorporation and interaction that went beyond simply service provision. Throughout, I compared these dynamics to the presettlement period, the period before the peace accords. My examination also focused on the accessibility of the state to different women's groups, and the ability of different tendencies of the women's movement to make representative demands on the state at both the local and national levels. To this end, I also examined the extent of meetings and interactions between activists of the women's sector and local and legislative government representatives.

I assessed these patterns by examining all the women's sector programs of the professionalized NGOs and grassroots organizations in the Ramallah and San Salvador areas. This examination included the careful screening of program documents and the websites of all the major women's organization, as well as interviews with the NGO directors, heads of gender desks, or program coordinators who could provide more detail about these programs. I also interviewed activists of the women's sector who had also been active in the preaccord period and could discuss changes between the pre- and postaccord periods. I corroborated my findings by examining program descriptions from donor agencies, and through interviews with activists who participated in these programs. (I elaborate on my interview selection in appendices I and II.)

In both cases, I focused on the women's organizations in the political centers of the Palestinian territories and El Salvador. To guarantee that my findings in the Ramallah-Jerusalem access area were representative of developments in the women's sector in other geographic locations in the Palestinian territories, I conducted additional semistructured interviews with women activists in the Gaza Strip and Hebron. In El Salvador, my interviews also addressed women's organizing in different regions of the country.

Foreign donor assistance is my key intervening variable.[82] Most of the funding received by CSOs in the cases I examined was from foreign sources, especially Western sources. To comprehensively capture the mediating role of foreign donor assistance on civil society and democratic development, this book examined democracy promotion related assistance and broader compositions of aid to more carefully determine who received aid and who did not, and for which programmatic priorities. To this end, I first examined general flows of donor assistance to the Palestinian territories and El Salvador in the immediate postsettlement period, including assistance to government and civil society, and then focused more specifically on donor assistance allocations to the women's sector, which extended well beyond democracy promotion assistance. This more comprehensive approach was necessary since ultimately both democracy assistance and development assistance shaped political outcomes. As Thomas Carothers explained, "The initial gulf between democracy support and development aid has indeed diminished."[83] Development assistance can very well impact civil society groups, or democratic outcomes more generally, and vice versa. Moreover, although institutionally, the bridges are partial, when examining the impact on a sector, there is no compelling rationale to assess these foreign donor assistance domains in isolation. Pertaining to the post-2006 Hamas electoral victory period, I focused predominately on the aid mechanisms put in place and the broader impact on associational life.

Why the Women's Sectors?

The women's sectors in both cases were successful in incorporating women in large numbers as well as addressing their needs. The women's sectors also produced a number of leaders who went on to become major actors in the national politics of both the Palestinian territories and El Salvador.[84] During the 1980s, the women's organizations in both contexts relied predominantly on solidarity funding, or funding funneled through the FMLN or the PLO in the respective cases. In the early 1990s, more readily available Western funding served as an impetus for many of these organizations to professionalize and institutionalize. After the initiation of the peace accords in both contexts, women's organizations attracted considerable amounts of foreign donor assistance. Women's socioeconomic status also did not vary extensively in these two societies, and therefore cannot account for the variation in outcomes in the two cases (see table 5.1).

It is important to note, however, that two key factors distinguished the women's organizations in the two contexts. In the Salvadoran case, women's participation in the opposition, and especially among the leadership, was not limited to the mass movements but often also extended to the guerrilla organizations. Additionally, each political organization, and by extension its women's groups, operated in its controlled territory through its vertical chain of command. In contrast, in the Palestinian territories, founders of the women's organizations for the most part did not have a military background, and the political organizations did not limit their organization to a designated territory of the WBGS but organized throughout the territory. These differences, however, cannot account for the variation in outcomes. In disagreement with the literature that focuses on the gendered outcomes in the women's sector,[85] I argue that the developments in this sector are not unique, but rather are representative of developments in other sectors of civil society. The parallel historical and organizational trajectories between the women's sector and other sectors, such as labor unions, student groups, and agricultural development committees, make these findings generalizable to other sectors of civil society. In "Beyond the Women's Sectors" section of chapter 7, I illustrate how these findings extend to other sectors such as labor.

Outline of the Remaining Chapters

Chapters 2 sets the stage for this study. It begins with a brief historical overview of the conflict in the two cases, and a more detailed discussion of the emergence of the political-military organizations and their affiliated mass-based organizations, including the women's sectors. The chapter draws from interviews with the leaders of the women's committees and organizations since many were members of the political organizations tasked with establishing the affiliated mass-based women's groups.

I develop my argument in chapters 3, 4 and 5. Chapter 3 illustrates how the degree of inclusivity of the political settlement affected civil society and electoral institutional design, as well as legislative and local government institutionalization in the two cases. Chapter 4 develops the second part of my argument about how the political settlement determined the amounts and types of foreign donor funding, and specifically Western donor funding, as well as the programs that donors prioritized given the context in which they were operating. It examines the history and changes in donor assistance in the two cases from the start of the conflict-to-peace transitions. Chapter 5 examines the impact of the political settlement and the mediating role of Western donor assistance at the level of civil society. It assesses these changes by examining transformations in the women's sector in the postsettlement period in each case. It draws heavily from primary interviews with the women who established these organizations, and the women who shaped and lived through these changes. Their reflections about these processes and the broader political changes these societies underwent anchor this chapter. Chapter 6 broadens the temporal aperture of the study. It examines the impact of the evolving political settlement and the mediating role of Western donor assistance in the Palestinian territories, and the Gaza Strip in particular, in the aftermath of Hamas's 2006 electoral victory. Unlike chapter 5, this chapter does not trace changes in a sector of civil society, but it looks at the more general transformations in the political landscape and in associational life. Chapter 7 returns to the question I started with: Why are democracy promotion efforts more successful in some cases as opposed to others? I also briefly discuss two other cases of conflict-to-peace transitions, namely Iraq and South Africa, to evaluate the defining impact of political settlements and the mediating role of Western donor assistance to illustrate how the findings in this book are by no means limited to the initial two cases.

What historical trajectories in the two cases led to the establishment of the political organizations and their affiliated mass-based organizations? This is the central question that chapter 2 tackles.

2

The Political-Military Organizations and the Emergence of Mass-Based Grassroots Organizations

Men make their own history, but they do not make it just as they please; they do not make it under circumstances chosen by themselves, but rather under circumstances found, given, and transmitted.
—Karl Marx, "The Eighteenth Brumaire of Louis Bonaparte"[1]

A rich history of civic organizing in El Salvador and the Palestinian territories underpinned the mass mobilization of the 1970s and 1980s. These mobilization efforts and much of the associational life that grew out of them were responses to conflicts with long historical roots: the British Mandate and Zionist colonial settlement in Palestine and, later, Israel's military occupation in the WBGS, and massive and enduring socioeconomic inequality, characterized by extreme concentration of land ownership in the hands of a very small minority (fourteen families to be exact)[2] in El Salvador. This conflict in El Salvador ultimately culminated in a civil war between the FMLN and the right-wing government. In both cases, the establishment of political-military organizations began in the latter part of the 1960s. The Arab-Israeli War in 1967 resulted in Palestinians seeking less Arab tutelage and more Palestinian autonomy and led to the establishment of various guerrilla/political-military organizations. In El Salvador, proponents of armed struggle in the Partido Comunista de El Salvador (Communist Party of El Salvador, PCS) broke away in 1969 and established the Fuerzas Populares de Liberación (Popular Forces of Liberation, FPL), which similarly set in motion the founding of various guerrilla/political-military organizations.

The Political-Military Organizations: Precursors to Mass Mobilization

The Palestinian Nationalist Movement Asserts Its Autonomy

By the early 1960s, and certainly following the 1967 war, the struggle for historic Palestine assumed an increasingly Palestinian character involving diasporic Palestinians themselves. This was a marked departure from the post-1948 defeat period in which the struggle for Palestinian independence assumed an Arab character that increased the involvement of neighboring nation-states.[3] Ironically, it was Palestinian students, studying and living in neighboring Arab countries, who questioned the commitments of other Arab leaders and cast into doubt the ability of these states to liberate historic Palestine.

In the late 1950s, these students founded a number of political organizations throughout the Arab world. Among these students were Khalil Wazir, Salah Khalaf, and Yasir Arafat, who took over the PLO in 1969. Two different streams dominated the Palestinian nationalist movement, the Harakat al-Qawmiyyin al-'Arab (Arab Nationalist Movement, ANM) which was more leftist in its political orientation, and Fatah, which is more nationalist in its orientation. Many of the Palestinian guerrilla and political organizations that emerged in the 1960s and thereafter owe their roots to one of these political strands.[4] Eventually, Fatah emerged as the largest and strongest of the Palestinian political factions, and is the current-day leadership party of the PA and the PLO.

The defeat of Egypt, Jordan, and Syria during the 1967 Six-Day War severely undermined the legitimacy of these states in the eyes of the Arab public, further eroding any notions that they would ultimately play an important role in the liberation of Palestine. In the aftermath, a number of Palestinian guerrilla organizations emerged.[5] The ANM's Palestinian branch, along with three other small guerrilla organizations, founded the Popular Front for the Liberation of Palestine (PFLP) in 1967. In 1968, the Palestine Front for the Liberation of Palestine–General Command broke away from the PFLP. Then in 1969, another group splintered from the PFLP, and called itself the Popular Democratic Front for the Liberation of Palestine (now called the DFLP).[6] These groups were predominately leftist in their orientation and would come to be among Fatah's major opposition. Fatah, the PFLP, and DFLP would come to represent the largest Palestinian political factions in the PLO, and play an important role in mass mobilization in the occupied territories, amassing substantial followings.

Communist Party activities in the Palestinian territories date back to the early 1920s, though the party became increasingly active in the late 1960s and early 1970s.[7] The West Bank Communists were firmly committed to mass mobilization and nonviolent protest.[8] In 1969, they reactivated the General Federation of Labor Unions, and later played a leadership role in the founding of the voluntary work programs among university and high school students.[9] In 1982, the West Bank Communists founded the PCP, despite the protests of the Jordanian Communist Party.[10] In 1987, the PCP joined the PLO.

Beginning in 1968, the DFLP, soon followed by the PFLP, began its transformation from a pan-Arabist organization to a Marxist-Leninist organization. These organizations were concerned with fundamental social and political change in Palestinian society, as well as throughout the Arab world. Both groups also initially called for the creation of one secular democratic state in which Christians, Jews, and Muslims would enjoy the same political rights. In the early 1970s, the DFLP began to entertain the idea of creating a binational state that would represent the Palestinian and Jewish communities, and later called for a sovereign state in the WBGS. The Palestinian Communist Party, PCP (later named the Palestinian People's Party, or PPP), on the other hand, limited its struggle to ending Israeli occupation of the WBGS, and the establishment of an independent state in that territory.[11] Although the early record of Fatah's military operations was quite humble, the high losses that they were able to inflict on the Israeli military during the Karameh battle of 1968, further reinforced the strength of the organization.[12] The growth of the guerrilla organization imposed its own logic on the structure of the PLO. By the fourth Palestine National Council (PNC) meeting in 1969, it was a foregone conclusion that Fatah, because of the seats allotted to it, and the support it enjoyed from independents, would be able to elect the leader of its choice to head the PLO. During that meeting, the delegates elected Yasir Arafat as chairperson of the organization.

During the 1970s, the internal organization of the PLO was rationalized, enlarged, and consolidated, and beginning with the Lebanese civil war until its expulsion from Beirut (1975–82), the economic and social functions of the PLO were dramatically expanded. Among the divisions of the PLO established were the Palestine National Fund, the Department of Education, the Red Crescent Society for Health Services, Departments of Information, Popular Mobilization, and the Occupied Homeland, a research center, an economic development center, and a social affairs institute.[13] By the mid-1970s, the PLO had developed the structures of a de facto government in exile.[14]

The decisive shift in terms of mass mobilization and associational activity in the WBGS took place in 1972. The PLO's defeat in Jordan in 1970 culminated in the Palestine National Council's 1972 decision to shift the locus of attention to the occupied territories and to incorporate the masses into the struggle.[15] Hence, at the tenth session of the PNC, the members passed resolutions calling for new trade unions, student groups, women's groups, welfare organizations, and other mass-based organizations that could mobilize the population in the territories under the auspices of the PLO.[16] By the end of the 1970s, an alternative strategy had emerged that involved supporting grassroots efforts in the WBGS.[17] Following the example of the PCP, then not part of the PLO but an early pioneer of mass mobilization efforts in the WBGS, the leftist factions of the PLO, the DFLP and PFLP, and later Fatah, followed suit in the latter part of the 1970s.[18] In time, the Palestinian population began recognizing the establishment of grassroots organizations as the new standard mode of sociopolitical organizing. They also began to identity this grassroots expression as proof of the strength of the political factions and as a reaffirmation of their presence on the ground.

In the 1980s, activists in the WBGS founded a number of political organizations that would come to play a significant role in Palestinian contemporary politics, and amass significant followings. Although Muslim Brotherhood activities in the Palestinian territories date back to the 1940s, Islamist associations, unions, and organizations became increasingly prevalent in the early 1980s following the Iranian Revolution. In the mid-1980s, Islamic Jihad splintered from the Muslim Brotherhood, and established itself as a separate organization. Most notably, the Islamists founded the Harakat al-Muqawama al-Islamiyya (Islamic Resistance Movement, Hamas), in 1988, shortly after the outbreak of the first Intifada. Following the initiation of the Madrid peace process, a schism emerged in the DFLP between those who supported the peace process and those who opposed it. Subsequently, supporters of the Madrid peace process broke away from the DFLP, and founded the Palestinian Democratic Union (FIDA), a splinter faction of the DFLP that supported the Oslo Accords.

The Rise of the Salvadoran Organized Opposition

El Salvador too has a rich history of political parties, but here I focus only on those institutions, including the Catholic Church, that would come to play a critical role in mass movement mobilization, and later in the establishment of NGOs, effectively laying the groundwork for a future civil society in El Salvador.[19] One of the oldest political forces in El Salvador is the PCS, whose roots date back to the late 1920s.[20] As a result of the economic recession of the period, international coffee prices crashed and social unrest ensued in El Salvador. Rising rural unemployment fueled strikes and protests. Although members of the Salvadoran oligarchy ruled the country directly until 1931, they were incapable of controlling the unrest. It was during this period that El Salvador's long history of struggle against socioeconomic inequality assumed the ideological framing of the PCS's Marxism-Leninism. The Salvadoran government outlawed the PCS in 1932. During that year, the government violently suppressed the insurrection led by the Communist leader, Farabundo Martí. By the end of the *matanza* (massacre or slaughter), the Salvadoran government was responsible for the killing of over 30,000 *campesinos* (farmers). Many regard the 1932 *matanza* as a culmination of another settler-colonial project also reflecting bitter indigenous resentment against Spanish land-owning usurpers.[21] The magnitude of the 1932 conflict molded the repressive nature of subsequent government regimes that would have little tolerance for dissent.

Between 1931 and 1979, a series of military dictatorships ruled over El Salvador. In 1960, well-to-do middle-class professionals founded the Partido Demócrata Cristiano (Christian Democratic Party, PDC), an anti-Communist party that upheld social Christian principles.[22] By 1972, the PDC had amassed a substantial following and became a key target of the military dictatorship's oppression.[23] Meanwhile, the military institutionalized its political participation through the creation of political parties; two main parties were the Partido de Reconciliación Nacional (Party of National Reconciliation, PRN) and the Partido Revolucionario de Unificación Democrácia (Party of Revolutionary Democratic Unification, PRUD). The political-military organizations would emerge from a tactical disagreement within the PCS in the late 1960s. Disagreement within the party regarding the legitimate means of struggle and whether or not the party should adopt armed struggle resulted in proponents of armed struggle breaking away and establishing the first of the military political organizations—the FPL in 1969 and the Ejercito Revolucionario del Pueblo (Revolutionary Army of People, ERP) in 1972. Subsequent divisions would result in additional political military organizations, each of which would play an important role in establishing popular organizations.

One of the key tactical differences that distinguished the political-military organizations from one another was their approach to armed struggle. Although both the ERP and the FPL advocated armed struggle against the regime, the FPL upheld a political-military strategy. The ERP's constituencies extended to the young Communists, youth from the PDC, and radicalized sectors of the Salvadoran bourgeoisie.[24] By the mid-1970s, another schism emerged in the ERP regarding the need to accompany military struggle with a political program. Roque Dalton, also El Salvador's national poet, advocated a more moderate line, insisting that the party adopt political as well as military strategies. The hardliners in the ERP charged Dalton with treason, tried him in absentia, and condemned him to death. In May 1975, extremists in the ERP killed Dalton. Due to these tactical disagreements and the murder of Dalton[25] by Joaquín Villalobos and his faction, Dalton's followers left the ERP and established the Resistencia Nacional (National Resistance, RN) in May 1975. Villaloboso and his followers retained the ERP label.[26] In 1976, regional activists founded the Trotskyist Partido Revolucionario de los Trabajadores Centroamericanos (Revolutionary Party of Central American Workers, PRTC) in Costa Rica. The PRTC's conception was more regional in scope, though it maintained separate national units.[27] Popular mobilization by the political-military organizations began in the mid-1970s, and became a central component of their work.

The dearth of political openings, mounting repression, and the deterioration of socioeconomic conditions propelled people to affiliate with the emerging revolutionary organizations in ever-increasing numbers. By the 1970s, the majority rural population did not have access to land or employment opportunities. The military and oligarchy continued to prosper, as the majority of the population was further impoverished. The mechanization of agriculture after World War II, and the introduction of export crops such as cotton and sugar cane put further pressure on cultivable land and reduced employment opportunities for Salvadoran *campesinos*. The military, as defender of the interests of the oligarchy, left little room for democratic participation. The ruling parties, supported by the oligarchy, prevented reformist political parties such as the Christian Democrats and the Social Democrats from electoral victory and access to the government in the 1972 and 1977 elections. The military regime exiled political leaders, and persecuted and dismantled their grassroots organizations.[28] José Napoleón Duarte, one of the leaders of the PDC and the presidential candidate of the National Opposition Union, won the 1972 election; subsequently, the ruling regime captured Duarte and deported him to Guatemala. Center and more radical opposition groups became more radicalized and began to advocate armed revolutionary struggle as the only solution to end repression in the country. The fraudulent elections of 1977 further exacerbated the conflict, convincing the opposition that they should employ more forceful means.[29]

The year 1979 was a turning point. A group of reform-minded military men overthrew the regime and installed a joint civilian-military junta composed of center-left opposition leaders. The conservative wing of the military persisted in its wave of terror, as internal disputes developed among the junta members. The PCS turned into a political-military organization in 1979 following the 1977 Plaza Libertad massacre[30] and the events surrounding the coup in 1979; it too came to the conclusion that the situation required armed struggle.[31] After the 1979 junta, the more left-leaning contingents of the PDC broke away and established the Movimiento Popular Social Cristiano (Popular Social Christian Movement, MPCS).[32] By the end of 1980, over 15,000 had been killed.

Among the political-military organizations, the RN—at that point only a tendency in the ERP and not yet an independent organization—was the first to initiate popular movement mobilization. In 1974, the RN began working with the *campesinos* of Suchitoto, and quietly helped establish the Frente de Acción Popular Unificada (United Popular Action Front, FAPU) with Christian community activists. By 1979, each of the political-military organizations had founded its own umbrella organization with a number of affiliated popular, grassroots-based organizations.[33] Each political-military organization also established a "wartime chain of command" and controlled a given territory, with its mass-based organizations and other affiliated NGOs.[34] In January 1980, the political military organizations created an umbrella structure, Coordinadora Revolucionaria de las Masas (Revolutionary Coordinating Council of the Masses), which unified all their affiliated popular organizations. Then in October of 1980, the five political-military organizations united and formed the FMLN.

In 1980, the Coordinadora Revolucionaria de las Masas and the Frente Democrático Salvadoreño (Salvadoran Democratic Front), a more leftist branch of the Christian Democrats and two small Social Democratic parties, came together, forming the Frente Democrático Revolucionario (Revolutionary Democratic Front, FDR), one of the most organized opposition coalitions in El Salvador's history.[35] This coalition also included the Movimiento Nacional Revolucionario (National Revolutionary Movement, MNR), the Movimiento Popular Social Cristiano (Popular Social Christian Movement, MPCS), and a coalition of professional and technical small business organizations, the National University, six unions and union federations, and a student association, with the Universidad Centroamericana "José Simeón Cañas" (José Simeón Cañas, Central American University, UCA), and the Catholic Church as observers. The FDR became the official umbrella organization of all leftist and center-leftist forces in the country.

In January 1981, the FMLN launched the "general offensive" that marked the official beginning of the civil war. Four days later, the FMLN and the FDR joined forces and created the Political Diplomatic Commission, the body that would represent these organizations in the international arena. In 1981, right-wing constituencies who wanted to ensure their own socioeconomic standing in El Salvador and to guarantee the neoliberal, free market development of the country founded ARENA. Exacerbating the country's polarization, by late 1981, the thrice-reconstituted junta had moved to the right-of-center, headed by José Napoleón Duarte.

The US-backed Salvadoran establishment tried to defeat the FDR-FMLN coalition through different means. The PDC tried to resolve the conflict with the help of US-sponsored programs and reform, and the armed forces with the help of US military support aimed to destroy the FMLN.[36] As the international community called for peace negotiations to resolve the conflict, the United States and Duarte insisted on presidential and legislative elections to lend legitimacy to Duarte's government. Duarte managed to win the 1984 presidential elections and to stay in power until 1989, after which the more right-wing ARENA came to power. The election of Duarte, however, provided activists with new opportunities to reestablish associations and organizations dismantled by military repression in the late 1970s and early 1980s. By 1989, the armed forces and the FMLN had reached a military stalemate.

With the heightening of the Salvadoran Civil War in the early 1980s,[37] most of these mass organizations were forced underground or into exile, or became clandestine.[38] After 1984, the government began to decrease its repression and legalized associational activity, and as a result, those organizations repressed in the early 1980s reemerged with new names and with different leaders but still politically affiliated. With the help of European private aid agencies, both secular and church-related grassroots leaders founded a few hundred popular organizations that organized workers, peasants, students, displaced persons, and women, and delivered health, education, housing, and other services. These institutions effectively laid the foundation for rebuilding civil society after the end of the Civil War. As the Salvadoran Civil War drew to a close in 1989, over 400 mass-based popular organizations existed in the country.[39] Meanwhile, pro-government groups also established worker and *campesino* organizations supported by US aid programs. NGOs also became polarized, mirroring the polarization between the government and the opposition political organizations.

Laying Foundations for Mass Movement Mobilization

In both the Palestinian territories and El Salvador, the political organizations played a pivotal role in establishing mass-based organizations. These mass-based organizations supported different communities and laid the groundwork for civil society. The establishment of these organizations was not a simple response to challenging circumstances, but more accurately a complex process involving constantly evolving dynamics of oppression, adaptation, and resistance. Three phases characterized associational life in both contexts. Starting in the 1920s and 1930s, there was a proliferation of charity organizations in both cases, and especially unions in El Salvador. In the 1960s through the early 1980s, there was a steady increase in mass-based organizations whose objectives were more political. And then in the mid to late 1980s, many of these organizations began to professionalize their operations and became increasingly reliant on foreign funding. These mass-based organizations, especially in the Palestinian territories, were more or less autonomous and capable of functioning without the directives of a party. This point would have important implications for the extent to which these formations could shape the nature of the future emergent civil society. The divergent trajectories that emerged and the extent of the weakening in the Palestinian case are even more puzzling given the foundations put in place. They also shed light on the not so clear distinction between political society and civil society. This analysis builds on Frances Hasso's work, which links opposition movements to the interaction between local "political fields," that is, "the legal-cultural-historical-political environment within which a protest movements exists," and globalized shifts.[40] Although the political settlements were local developments, they cannot be assessed as separate from the end of the Cold War and the emergence of the United States as the main superpower.

The Nationalist Movement and Associational Life in Palestine: From Charity to Resistance and Mass Mobilization

In the absence of a full-fledged state, limited local government structures, and weak social service institutions, the various political organizations in the WBGS perceived the founding of mass-based organizations and more professionalized NGOs, and other social institutions more broadly defined, as necessary support for the national liberation stage.[41] NGOs have played a crucial role in the mobilization of Palestinian society, in the provision of social services, and in the interest representation of various constituencies. By 1993, Palestinian NGOs accounted for 60 percent of primary health care services, 49 percent of secondary and tertiary health care, 100 percent of disability care, 100 percent of preschool programs, and a large proportion of tertiary education, agricultural extension, welfare, housing, and other services in the WBGS.[42]

Associations and civic organizations in the Palestinian territories date back to the Mandate period. During this period, Palestinians from the urban upper-middle and middle class established a number of charity organizations. Fifteen percent of NGOs that existed in 2000 were established before 1967, 12 percent between 1948 and 1967, and 3 to 4 percent in the Mandate period.[43] Additionally, different sectors of Palestinian society, including the Communists, initiated efforts to organize the working class.[44] Despite the various efforts of groups and individuals to establish some institutions during this time period, however, these organizations were urban-based and did not extend to all sectors of society. In the late 1960s and throughout the 1980s, associational and union activity increased dramatically, growing most rapidly after 1978.[45] The rise of associations during this period extended to grassroots-based organizations, including charitable societies and cooperatives,[46] professional associations and syndicates, and Islamist groups, including zakat committees.[47] The DFLP initiated much of the associational activity during this period, especially after 1978.[48] In the late 1980s and early 1990s, a number of NGOs—but, importantly, not all—began to access Western foreign donor funding and to professionalize and institutionalize their operations. Then after the establishment of the PA, associational actors in the WBGS struggled to reconcile their relations with the incipient government and to shift their priorities to accommodate the burgeoning state-building phase.[49]

A number of factors coalesced to instigate these changes, especially related to mass mobilization in the territories. Most notably, the realization began to take root that Israeli military occupation would not be ending any time soon. The entrenchment of the Israeli military occupation and the myriad ways in which it would come to dominate the lives of Palestinians living in the WBGS were becoming more and more apparent. By 1974, approximately 45 percent of the employed West Bank residents and 50 percent of employed Gazans were working in Israel.[50] Meanwhile, the continued confiscation of Palestinian lands, building of illegal Israeli settlements, and increased repression resulted in activists in the WBGS developing their own political agenda, which focused on resisting Israeli military occupation, and empowering Palestinian communities.

The increasing realization that only the Palestinians themselves, and not outside "benevolent" actors, could improve their daily living conditions extended across the Palestinian political polity more generally. In 1978, Israel and Egypt signed the Camp David peace accords, which included arrangements for the autonomy of the WBGS. The PLO, along with Arab countries, opposed these agreements, especially those components related to autonomy. To avoid "strategic marginalization," the PLO recognized the necessity for a more systematic mobilization campaign in the occupied territories.[51] A more organized presence of groups affiliated with the PLO would minimize chances that external actors, particularly Arab countries such as Egypt and Jordan, would come to determine the fate of the Palestinians. Few if any of the individuals involved in the grassroots organizations were actively involved in armed resistance against the occupying power, and many members were not necessarily official members of the parent political organizations.

Associational and union activity that took place after 1975 often reflected factional competition, especially between Fatah and the Communist Party.[52] Groups competed not only over who would control these associations and unions, but also over who would distribute the funds received from various Arab states.[53] Recruitment to the mass-based organizations often started in high schools, and initiated activists into joining one of the different political organizations. Marwan Barghouti, a founding member of Fatah's youth wing, *Al-Shabibeh*, and later student body president at Birzeit University, and one of the leaders of the first and second Intifadas, explained:

> The late 1970s through the 1980s was the golden age of Palestinian popular, mass mobilization. The reception was amazing. In addition to our nationalist activities, we led critically important social initiatives. *Al-Shabibeh* (the Fatah youth branch), which recruited members from high schools, colleges and universities, for example, organized numerous volunteer campaigns, including anti-drug campaigns in the refugee camps. Our volunteer work involved cleaning and repairing streets, cleaning and restoring grave yards, painting schools, helping in the villages with the

harvest of olives and other crops, and restoring and cultivating lands that are in threat of being confiscated by the Israeli military occupation authorities for lack of use.

Our structures were so extensive that the arrest of numerous *Al-Shabībeh* leaders could not undermine the movement. Leading up to the first Intifada, we had 8000 elected youth leaders representing *Al-Shabībeh* throughout the West Bank and the Gaza Strip. An individual who was a formal member of Fatah or of *Al-Shabībeh* could organize a group if s/he had a minimum of fifteen members in the particular town or village.[54]

Indeed, the social dimensions of this work paved the way for the hundreds of thousands of recruits who would carry out the first Intifada.

As a result of the Iranian Revolution, Islamist associations, unions, and organizations also became more prevalent in the Palestinian territories, especially in the Gaza Strip, in the early 1980s. Much of the activity of Islamist organizations focused on social and cultural issues and community development. Islamist institutions play an important and very visible role in the provision of services in areas related to relief and charity work, preschool and primary education, rehabilitation of physically and mentally challenged persons, primary and tertiary health care, women's income-generating activities, literacy training, the care of orphans, and youth and sports activities.[55] It is important to note that these organizations differ vastly in the extent to which they are linked to one of the Islamist political organizations.

Though these organizations were affiliated with the political factions, for the most part they maintained varying degrees of autonomy. The organizations affiliated with the PCP, the DFLP, and the PFLP had Marxist-Leninist structures organized on the basis of democratic-centralism. Although these organizations were autonomous from the "outside" political organizations, they were often much closer to the respective political organization in the occupied territories. Often, these organizations maintained close contact with the grassroots, which allowed for input from these constituencies. Because of the sheer distance between the members and supporters of the political organizations in the occupied territories and their leadership in exile, most Palestinian factions accorded a flexible degree of autonomy to their associations, unions, and affiliated committees in the WBGS. Despite the overlap in membership of factions and grassroots organizations, there tended to be a lot of disagreement between the two. Leaders in the grassroots organizations, especially in the labor unions, played key roles and maintained that "they were the ones who really knew what was happening or were truly in touch."[56] Even more so was the degree of autonomy of the popular committees established during the first Intifada. As Ali Jaradat explained, "The decision to create the popular committees came from the grassroots committees themselves, and not from the political organizations. The grassroots committees had more democratic organizational structures than the political organizations themselves, and the more sophisticated members wanted to increase their autonomy."[57] The leadership of the political organizations in exile did not control these associations, unions, and other mass-based organizations, though there was more interaction with the respective leaderships in the occupied territories.

Civic Traditions and Associational Life in El Salvador: From Charity to Revolution, and New Forms of Organizing

The transformation of associational life in El Salvador reflected political developments and attempts to cope with these changes.[58] Following the establishment of charities and unions in the 1930s, there was a dramatic increase in the grassroots organizing by the Salvadoran Catholic Church. By the late 1960s, and throughout the 1970s and early 1980s, these organizations were predominately affiliated with the broader opposition movement, either with the PCS, the Christian communities, or later with one of the parties of the FMLN.[59] Then, from the mid-1980s to the present, many of these organizations began to professionalize and rely on foreign donor assistance, but this would not undermine mass mobilization to the same extent as in the Palestinian case.

In the late 1960s, the Salvadoran Catholic Church, influenced by liberation theology,[60] underwent a massive transformation, emerging as a radicalized force in Salvadoran politics; this transformation would have momentous consequences for Salvadoran political life in the 1970s. The Catholic Church in El Salvador came to be known as the Iglesia popular (Popular Church). At the parish level, priests initiated the mass popular organizations, or Comunidades Cristianas de Base (Christian base communities). The Christian base communities initially consisted of small

groups organized by the parishes that would meet to discuss social issues and possible community strategies to address some of these daily
challenges.[61] The result was an explosion of community activity in rural
areas, leading to the establishment of hundreds of Christian base communities. Although priests or nuns led the initial courses and sessions,
the groups were encouraged to develop their own leadership. According
to some estimates, the Church trained over 15,000 leaders during the
1970s.[62]

The Catholic Church also played an important role in forging alliances with other opposition movements. Most notably, along with other
organizations, the Catholic Church in El Salvador played a critical role
in the founding of the first mass-based organization, FAPU, in Suchitoto
in 1974. By 1977, *campesinos* constituted most of the rank-and-file and
much of the leadership of the mass movements, including the Christian
base communities. FAPU had two factions, one oriented toward the RN
and the other toward the FPL. The organization split in 1975, and activists founded a new organization oriented toward the FPL called the
Bloque Popular Revolucionario (Popular Revolutionary Bloc). In 1978,
ERP sympathizers founded the third of the popular organizations, Ligas
Populares 28 de Febrero (28 February Popular Leagues, LP–28 1978).
Finally, in 1979, the PRTC spawned the Movimiento de Liberación Popular (Popular Liberation Movement). The PCS had created the Unión
Democrática Nacionalista (Nationalist Democratic Union, UDN) in
1967. The PCS also historically played a leading role in the teacher, stu-
dent, and labor organizations. Although the UDN was not a formal mass
organization, it played a comparable role in Salvadoran society.

The sectors affiliated with these mass-based movements included
rural workers, teachers, students, women, and repopulated and war displaced persons.[63] Despite the shared goals among the mass-based organizations and the level of coordination between these groups, important
differences and disagreements existed. In particular, FAPU and the Bloque Popular Revolucionario differed regarding strategies, tactics, and
the constituencies on which to focus.[64]

Similar to the Palestinian case, the degree to which the mass movements were autonomous is unsettled. Michael Foley, for example, argued that although there was considerable variation among the mass
movements, "The logic of organization, especially once communities

were reestablished in what were still combat zones, was 'vertical,' approximating a 'war communism' in which community decision-making, though founded on participatory principles, was subordinated to the exigencies of the war effort."[65] Mario Lungo Uclés, on the other hand, argued that an autonomous relationship does not mean complete separation, and that there was a mutually influencing relationship. Problems associated with vertical decision-making had more to do with individual leadership styles, according to him.[66] In the latter part of the 1980s, there was growing autonomy of the mass movements from the FMLN because as the FMLN expanded its military influence from the "controlled zones" to the "expansion zones," it loosened its control on organizations in the former. The FMLN also recognized that more autonomy served the mass-based organizations well.[67] Although the degree to which these mass movements were autonomous is not settled, a sole focus on autonomy as the measure of associational efficacy obfuscates the real determinants of citizen participation and empowerment.

PLO- and FMLN-Affiliated Women's Movements: Power in Numbers and Reach

The women's sectors would emerge as integral sectors of the PLO and the FMLN's mass-mobilization efforts. These sectors would share similar historical trajectories, goals, and objectives. Especially in the Palestinian case, the women's mass-based organizations were careful to involve members in expressing their needs, and in establishing and running committees in the various locations. Much of these major achievements in the Palestinian case, however, would be reversed by the early 2000s.

Palestinian Women's Organizing

The Palestinian women's sector metamorphosed from a number of charitable societies founded in the 1920s,[68] into an integral component of nationalist resistance during the late 1970s and early 1980s, and later to a community of institutionalized feminist organizations. In 1965, 139 women delegates convened and established the General Union of Palestinian Women, a mass-based organization affiliated with the PLO. After 1967, these societies expanded their purview from traditional welfare functions to place greater emphasis on education, health, and vocational training. These organizations were predominately run by middle-class Palestinian women and were located in Palestinian urban centers, and therefore inaccessible to the majority of Palestinian women who lived in the rural areas.[69]

By the early 1980s, the major Palestinian political organizations had established their respective mass-based women's organizations. In March 1981, women affiliated with the PCP founded the Union of Palestinian Working Women's Committees (UPWWC) with branches throughout the WBGS. Later that year, women affiliated with PFLP established the Union of Palestinian Women's Committees (UPWC). In 1982, women affiliated with Fatah founded the Union of Women's Committees for Social Work (WCSW). In 1989, the WWC was renamed the Federation of Palestinian Women's Action Committees (FPWAC).[70] The women who were involved in establishing the women's committees were relatively young, educated, and activists in their own right. Many of them were also political cadres in their respective political factions. These women were committed to articulating women's issues both in relation to and separate from the broader national movement.

Goals

For the most part, the women's committees shared the same goals: to enhance the status of women by empowering them to improve their daily living conditions, and to lend support to the broader national struggle,[71] though the WCSW was not as progressive as the others, and did not espouse an agenda of societal transformation. The founders of the committees were also interested in addressing women's status in Palestinian society-at-large, including the promotion of women's economic self-sufficiency.

Most of my interviewees, including founders of the women's committees, talked about the increasing realization that women's lives needed to be improved. Each committee wanted to increase support for its political faction, and eventually to recruit more members. In turn, by strengthening women's role in the national movement, they hoped they would be able to realize women's full potential in Palestinian society. The UPWWC, the UPWC, and the FPWAC stood out as more willing to address socially contentious issues relating to the status of women, such as early marriage and polygamy, and more willing to promote less traditional roles of women, including employment outside the home. But, generally, the committees focused on addressing women's immediate practical needs, as well as their economic, political, and social consciousness, while providing them with greater economic opportunities by establishing self-help and productive ventures. There was also particular focus on addressing the needs of working women and women in rural areas.[72]

Organization, Membership, and Decision-Making

In the pre-Madrid and pre-Oslo period, the most important and uncontested achievements of the Palestinian women's committees were their ability to recruit large numbers of women from different sectors of Palestinian society, including remote villages, and to involve them effectively in decision-making structures. These committees had radical democratic structures, in which the members were directly involved in choosing their immediate leaders and the types of projects and programs that they implemented. The ability of the various women's committees to forge horizontal links with grassroots constituencies and directly involve them in decision- making laid the groundwork for what could become an effective civil society that could contribute to democratic development in Palestinian society.

By the mid-1980s, all four women's committees had amassed a substantial following, with a visible presence in terms of projects and activities in the public realm. Despite the fact that the exact membership of these committees was difficult to verify, all four committees claimed to have a membership base in the thousands, covering most geographic locations of the West Bank and later the Gaza Strip. By 1986, the members of the FPWCA claimed to have over 5,000 members.[73] At the height of the Intifada at the end of the 1980s, one organizer estimated that their membership had reached 15,000 individuals.[74] Also, there was a high level of participation, as demonstrated through the daily activities of the Intifada such as sit-ins, marches, and neighborhood committee meetings. The UPWC estimated to have about 5,000 members up until 1994,[75] and by 1990 the WCSW estimated that its membership had reached 12,000.[76]

The official policy of these committees, especially those in the leftist-leaning organizations, was to recruit members from all geographic locations, especially rural areas, which were considered the most in need of organizational support. One entry strategy into the villages was to establish nursery schools and kindergartens.[77] Other activists initiated collective recruitment drives in which organizers would meet with women in a village. A representative from the steering committee of an organization would visit an area and help set up a local committee. The women would discuss some of the activities they wanted to initiate and then they would hold an election. Although each committee was responsible for its own local projects, it was also part of a nationwide network in which it participated by electing a representative to a regional committee, which in turn elected a national executive and steering committee. The women in the village would continue to meet on a regular basis, and regional organizers would visit the respective location every three to four months

Most of the women I spoke to discussed the consensus decision-making approach used in the various locations. When women were not able to reach a decision by consensus, they would often vote on the particular issue. One grassroots coordinator explained, "We used to meet with women in the villages every two weeks. We would put together a needs-assessment list based on what the women wanted. Then we would vote to prioritize what they wanted to see accomplished."[78] Though the respective political organization might have had some general suggestions regarding the types of programs being implemented, the women also had a direct say in the projects and programs that were being carried out. Another grassroots women's committee organizer explained, "When we met, the women told us what they wanted. There was a lot of autonomy in decision-making and in choosing events."[79] Moreover, the political organizations knew that increasing membership in these women's committees was contingent on satisfying the women's demands and needs.[80] Hence, ideas and initiatives flowed both ways between the local committees and the executive. The WCSW differed in this respect because it never aspired to organize the masses per se, but rather sought to gain their support through charisma and patronage.[81]

Although there was some competition and political disagreement among the different women's committees, there was also a degree of cooperation. In 1984, the women's committees set up a mechanism to facilitate informal coordination, especially related to consciousness-raising programs, and in the activities to protest Israeli occupation.[82] The lack of overt and acrimonious competition between the different women's committees facilitated their ability to recruit members in such high numbers.

In reminiscing about this period, all of the activists recalled with nostalgia their commitment to the committees and the important roles they played in shaping their programs and in meeting the needs of women in Palestinian society. In "Feminist Generations," Frances Hasso traced the impact of women's previous involvement in these committees on their later life choices, and demonstrated how the activists had developed a higher sense of self-efficacy and were differentiated by their gender egalitarian ideology.[83] Indeed, women who were involved in the committees were likely to make life choices that reflected their greater sense of self-empowerment.

Programs

Although the specific programs and activities tended to vary from one region to another, especially between the rural and urban areas,[84] many of the programs dealt with women's practical needs such as literacy classes, health education, small-scale vocational training, the provision of childcare, and the establishment of ventures, such as cooperatives, for producing goods.[85] Consciousness-raising was also central to the activities of the women's committees in both the rural and urban areas. The members usually chose the committees' topics for the consciousness-raising programs. Health-related topics were also very popular and included family planning, prenatal and postnatal care, and preventive medical treatment for children, such as the importance of immunization.

All the committees were involved in enhancing women's economic self-sufficiency, especially through the development of productive ventures such as co-operatives. Some of the goods produced in the co-operatives included baby food, engraved brass, embroidered clothes or linens, hand-woven rugs, knitted sweaters, concentrated fruit juices, frozen vegetables, and bakery products. Members of the FPWAC even established a carpentry factory. At one point, the UPWC managed ninety cooperatives in the Ramallah area alone.[86] Most of the committees also took part in the organization of annual cultural bazaars. These activities had two goals: to promote women's productive capacity[87] and to increase reliance on Palestinian domestic goods in place of Israeli and other foreign imports.[88]

To facilitate women's integration into the public sphere, the committees also established nursery schools and kindergartens. By the late 1980s, the FPWAC managed between thirty and thirty-five nursery schools and kindergartens,[89] the UPWC managed eighty-six nursery schools and kindergartens, and the WCSW managed fifty kindergartens[90] throughout the WBGS. Along with Islamist institutions, the women's committees were among the main providers of nursery schools and kindergartens in the WBGS.

The types of program and the related goals espoused by the women's committees played an important role in the empowerment of its members. By incorporating women and providing them with fora to identify their immediate needs and the opportunity to develop programs to address them, women's committees helped to equip its members with the skills that are critical for the development of an effective civil society that can contribute to democracy.

Resources and Funding

The various committees supported their activities primarily through membership fees, small income-generating activities, occasional seed money from solidarity organizations, and funding from the parent political organization. Because all the committees had more or less the same access to resources, especially through their membership fees, they operated on a more or less equal playing field. The funding discrepancies between the different committees were not significant. Few, if any, of the activists were paid for their involvement in the women's movement; this ensured that the spirit of voluntarism was the driving force behind civic and political participation.

The committees created a number of income-generating activities and programs. They all hosted annual bazaars and earned profits from the products they sold. The UPWC hosted occasional fund-raising dinners, and also sold agendas, planners, and calendars for profit. Some of the women's committees also ran cooperatives in the hope they would generate income for some of the women involved. In most cases, however, the cooperatives were not very successful or economically viable.

The women's committees also received minimal funding from different donors, including Western foreign donors, often in the form of seed money for specific projects. During the mid-1980s, for example, the UPWC received seed funding to help in the establishment of a baby food production facility.[91] Until 1992, the FPWAC received some funding from Oxfam-Netherlands (NOVIB) for the salaries of kindergarten and nursery school teachers, and for teacher training.[92] During the 1980s, FPWAC also received funding from al-Najdeh North America, a Palestinian women's organization based in the United States.[93] The women's committees also received occasional funding from their respective parent political organizations; this was especially the case for the WCSW. Dynamics between the different women's committees, however, began to sour once certain committees and some members began to receive preferential treatment in terms of access to higher amounts of foreign funding and to political institutions and decision-makers.

Salvadoran Women's Organizing

Salvadoran women's organizations date back to the 1930s.[94] From the 1930s to the late 1960s, Salvadoran women founded a number of charitable organizations, as well as more political organizations. From the late 1960s to the mid-1980s, the existing political organizations founded a number of affiliated mass-based women's organizations that were quite successful in incorporating and mobilizing women in large numbers from all parts of El Salvador. During the latter part of the 1980s and early 1990s, these organizations began to professionalize their operations, but unlike in the Palestinian case, all the mass-based organizations had access to donor funding, and grassroots incorporation was often a precondition for the receipt of foreign donor funding.

In 1957, women established the Fraternidad de Mujeres Salvadoreñas (Fraternity of Salvadoran Women), which became one of the first organizations to attempt to incorporate women into the political opposition by addressing their specific needs. Although the organization accepted women from all political backgrounds, it was loosely affiliated with the PCS. The organization produced a monthly magazine called *Fraternidad* (Fraternity), and also carried out a number of cultural, political, and social activities. In addition to providing secretarial and sewing classes, they started a school for members' children. The group was also active in the protest movement that supported trade unionists and political prisoners.[95] The Fraternidad de Mujeres Salvadoreñas would serve as a model for all women's organizations founded in the 1970s.[96]

During the late 1960s and early 1970s, mass-based opposition organizations, known as popular organizations, emerged in El Salvador. These groups were predominately affiliated with the Christian communities or with the PCS. During the latter part of the 1970s and early 1980s, women's organizations emerged that were more closely affiliated with one of the existing political organizations; these included right-wing organizations in San Salvador, as well as leftist opposition-affiliated women's organizations that sought to mobilize and address the needs of women in the controlled zones. Finally, during the mid-1980s, more professionalized women's organizations that were also closely linked with one of the political organizations were established in San Salvador.

During the late 1960s through the early 1970s, the Popular Church and the broader leftist opposition established a number of women's groups, and encouraged women to participate in non-women's groups, often targeting laborers. Of particular concern to the Salvadoran Popular Church was the promotion of women's equality. The Church leaders encouraged women in different communities to join Christian base communities and self-help groups or trade unions. Women became active in a number of organizations established at that time, the most notable of which were the Federación Cristiana de Campesinos Salvadoreños (Christian Federation of Salvadoran Farm Workers)[97] and the Comité de Madres y Familiares de Presos, Desaparecidos y Asesinados de El Salvador "Monseñor Romero" (Committee of Mothers and Relatives of the Disappeared, Assassinated and Political Prisoners, COMADRES). COMADRES was established in 1977 by women who were looking for information about relatives who had disappeared, were imprisoned, or killed.[98] Among the first of the organizations targeting women in the labor force was the Asociación Nacional de Educadores Salvadoreños (National Association of Salvadoran Teachers), which was founded in

1968. Although not solely for women, approximately 90 percent of the group's members were women.[99] By the early 1980s, Asociación Nacional de Educadores Salvadoreños claimed to represent 20,000 of the 23,000 teachers in El Salvador, of whom only 10,000 were official members since open affiliation carried tremendous risks. In 1969, labor activists founded the Comité de Mujeres Sindicales (Committee of Women Trade Unionists), followed by the Asociación de Mujeres Progresistas (Association for Progressive Women of El Salvador) in 1975. Asociación de Mujeres Progresistas claimed direct continuity with the Fraternidad, and its leadership also concentrated on recruiting women workers in cooperation with the PCS trade unions. In 1978, the FPL founded the Coordinating Committee of Market Women, "Luz Dilian Arévalo," which organized market women on issues relating to their rights, and set up political meetings to denounce the government. Women also founded the Asociación de Usuarias y Trabajadoras de los Mercados (Association of Market Workers) in 1979, which specifically addressed market women's working conditions by campaigning against the corrupt market administration.

The organizing during this period concentrated on recruiting women to the unions and helping them organize around their working conditions. Following the crackdown against and persecution of popular organizations in the late 1970s, many of these organizations went underground and were reestablished in the controlled zones in 1981. Unlike the previous generation of women's organizations, these groups did not target specific populations of women, but rather were concerned with broader mass mobilization. Right-wing groups also founded a number of women's organizations during this period.

In 1978 and 1979, the FPL established the Asociación de Mujeres de El Salvador (Association of Women of El Salvador, AMES). AMES was one of the largest women's associations and operated in Nicaragua and Honduras as well as in El Salvador. (See table 5.3, which lists the year in which each of the political organizations established its respective women's association.) The PRTC and ERP founded women's organizations along the same lines. In 1982, forty-seven women combatants of the PRTC and members of the popular organizations founded the Asociación de Mujeres Salvadoreña (Association of Salvadoran Women, ASMUSA). By 1984, the persecution of opposition groups made it almost impossible to organize as ASMUSA in El Salvador, so PRTC members founded a new front organization, the Asociación por Mejorar de la Mujer y el Niño (Association for the Improvement of Women and Children).[100] During that same year, members of the RN founded the Asociación de Mujeres Lili Milagro Ramírez (Association of Women—Lili Milagro Ramírez), for women in the FAPU.[101] Then following the seizure of power by the 1979 Junta, right-wing women's organizations appeared on the political scene, including the Cruzada por Paz y Trabajo (Crusade for Peace and Work), a broad organization that united all women to the right of the Christian Democrats, and the Frente Femenino Salvadoreño (Salvadoran Women's Front), which was unofficially affiliated with the right-wing ARENA party.[102] Although these organizations were not as involved in mass organization, they did launch high-profile media campaigns through paid advertisements in daily newspapers.[103]

Following the election of Christian Democrat José Napoleón Duarte in 1984, there was increased political opening in El Salvador. As a result, many of the political-military organizations of the FMLN and the Christian communities were able to operate more openly, and they established their own women's mass-based organizations, many of them in San Salvador. Most of the women's mass-based organizations that emerged during this period were founded between 1985 and 1988. The first of these was the Organización de Mujeres Salvadoreñas (Organization of Salvadoran Women, ORMUSA), which was founded in 1985 and affiliated with the MPCS. In 1986, the Instituto de Investigación, Capacitación y Desarrollo de la Mujer "Norma Guirola de Herrera" (Institute of Research, Training, and Development of Women "Norma Guirola de Herrera," IMU), and the Movimiento Salvadoreño de Mujeres (Salvadoran Movement of Women, MSM) were founded. The IMU was established by university women, and was affiliated with the PCS.[104] MSM was created by the midranking PRTC cadre and incorporated its previous organization, ASMUSA. That same year, the FPL founded the Asociación de Mujeres de las Zonas Marginales (Association of Women of the Marginalized Zones), a group dedicated to helping women to access public services and become economically independent.[105] In 1987, a group called Christian Mothers, along with women's committees of the north of San Miguel and Morazàn, founded the Asociación para la Autodeterminación y el Desarrollo de Mujeres Salvadoreña (Association for the Self-Determination and Development of Salvadoran Women,

AMS); the organization became affiliated with the ERP.[106] Subsequently, in 1988, the PCS founded another women's organization, the Asociación Democrática de Mujeres (Democratic Association of Women, ADE-MUSA). During this period women also founded the first association for indigenous women in El Salvador, the Asociación de Mujeres Indígenas Salvadoreñas (Association of Indigenous Salvadoran Women).

These organizations were more formal and also in a better position to access foreign funding than their predecessors, especially from Western solidarity groups and foundations. Given the high levels of repression of the late 1970s to the mid-1980s, most of the mass-based organizations worked in the FMLN-controlled zones, and not in the capital city, San Salvador. By 1985, however, these women's organizations were predominantly openly based in San Salvador.

Goals of the Mass-Based Women's Organizations

In general, the FMLN's five political organizations shared the same goals in establishing the mass-based women's organizations: These were to address women's basic needs, including literacy; to raise their awareness and consciousness; and to incorporate them into the struggle. As with the founding of other associations and organizations during this period, each respective political organization also sought to gain mass support. One of the main distinguishing features of the newer women's organizations was that they were more likely to incorporate feminist gender analysis into their work.[107] Moreover, the last wave of women's organizations differed from the previous waves in that they also sought to gain the support of and to mobilize women in the urban center, San Salvador, while continuing to work with their grassroots communities in the FMLN-controlled zones.

Organization, Membership, and Decision-Making

As with the Palestinian women's sector, the most important and uncontested accomplishment of these women's organizations was their ability to recruit and organize women in large numbers from the remotest parts of El Salvador. When the security situation permitted, there was an attempt to develop radical democratic structures in which the local community organizations elected their own representatives, and then the elected representatives would meet on a regular basis to coordinate the activities of the organization.[108] In most instances, however, much of the organizing was very discreet. As Carmen Medina explained, "Everything was dangerous, so the approach was very low profile. Even in the association, the meetings were not open."[109] For the most part, women in each community decided on their priorities when the situation allowed.

Although the membership of these organizations was in the thousands, exact numbers were difficult to come by given the clandestine nature of much of the work. In many cases, leaders did not keep official records of the exact membership. Some of the organizers, however, were able to provide rough estimates of their membership. For example, by 1982, AMES was estimated to have approximately 8,000 members—most of whom were members or supporters of the FPL.[110] Similarly, by March 1988, AMS claimed to have enrolled nearly 4,000 women in literacy and self-help training,[111] and, by 1985, ORMUSA was estimated to have 2,000 members.[112]

Programs

The programs and projects of these organizations addressed women's practical needs, but were sometimes distinguished by the particular needs of women in a given region. As Yanera Argueta succinctly explained, "We [AMS] addressed three systematic demands: health services for women, literacy, and sustenance."[113] Many of the women's organizations also ran literacy classes, health workshops, and nurseries. The newer women's mass-based organizations were more likely to set up programs that went beyond practical gender interests, especially in the 1990s. The geographic demarcation of territory between the different groups ensured that there was less replication of programs and projects.

Consciousness-raising was central to the programs of the various women's organizations. In addition to running literacy courses, they provided workshops on health issues, such as first aid, hygiene, prenatal health, and childcare. Some of the organizations also provided ideological and political training, as well as lectures and discussions on domestic violence. Azucena Quintera further elaborated, "A number of the comrades beat up their wives, so we tried to address that problem."[114] ORMUSA, for example, organized consciousness-raising sessions and reflection groups in which the women discussed issues pertaining to labor, violence, and political participation.

Many of the organizations also focused on improving the material conditions of women by addressing their most basic needs, as well as providing material support to women combatants. As Jeanette Urquilla explained, "The main concern of our members was not to die of hunger during the war."[115] Accordingly, various political organizations distributed food through the women's organizations. Women in ASMUSA, for example, cultivated beans and corn in the various communities. The women's organizations also attempted to improve women's economic conditions by providing them with more opportunities to produce goods. ORMUSA, for example, had a clothing production center in one of the communities, and AMES provided sewing classes for its members. They also provided women combatants with boots, clothes, sanitary napkins, and spending money; food was also provided for their children.[116] Moreover, women members of the FPL leadership began demanding that the FMLN-FDR adopt a "Minimum Women's Program"—a program of basic women's demands.

Resources and Funding

During the war, most of the funding to mass-based women's organizations was predominantly from committees of women's organizations based abroad, from solidarity organizations, and from women's organizations based in other countries, especially in Europe.[117] Most of the popular women's organizations in El Salvador had committees or women members who were responsible for fundraising. ASMUSA representatives, for example, fundraised in Nicaragua, Mexico, and Costa Rica.[118] Similarly, the FPL set up a committee to organize solidarity work and raise funds in Nicaragua and Mexico for their women's groups.[119] These organizations also received funding from abroad, especially from solidarity NGOs whose primary raison d'être was to fundraise or lobby for the Salvadoran left. Among these solidarity NGOs were the Committee in Solidarity with the People of El Salvador and the Salvadoran Humanitarian Aid, Research, and Education Foundation.[120] These solidarity groups seldom distributed the funding directly to the women's organizations, but rather funneled it through their affiliated political organizations.[121] Besides the payment to women combatants, almost all women's work in the organization was voluntary, and therefore members were not paid for their work.

Conclusion

As in the Palestinian case, among the important accomplishments of the different Salvadoran women's organizations during the 1980s was their ability to recruit women from all walks of life and locations, including the remotest parts of El Salvador, and to address their most basic needs, while involving them in decision-making when the situation allowed. By the early 1990s, the Palestinian and Salvadoran women's sector shared substantial similarities in terms of their social and political organization, their functions, their social reach, and their relationship to political organizations. Ultimately, the unfolding political settlements in these two societies, and the mediating role of Western donor assistance that was introduced to buttress these processes, resulted in dramatically different outcomes for the women's sectors in these two contexts. In what follows, I discuss the contrasting political settlements that emerged in the Palestinian territories and El Salvador.

3

Political Settlements and the Reconfiguration
of Civic and Political Life

Life, Works
. . . Discovering,
deciphering,
articulating,
setting in motion:
the old works of liberators and martyrs
that are our obligations now . . .
—Timoteo Lue, pen name for Roque Dalton, student of
law and Salvadoran poet; born in Suchitoto in 1950

In the early 1990s, the Palestinian territories and El Salvador began their conflict-to-peace transitions. A key difference between the evolving settlements in the two cases was the level of inclusivity. This distinction would have important implications for how the political organizations would develop in the postaccord period, especially related to their patterns of professionalization of their mass- based organizations, their relationship to mass movements, and the creation of national and local government institutional openings. Understanding the variation in mass movement activity in postsettlement cases requires an appreciation of how these agreements came to shape associational and civic life.

Palestinian Territories: From the Madrid and Oslo Accords to the Post-Oslo Era

On 13 September 1993, the PLO and the state of Israel signed the historic Oslo Accords. Fatah, as the leadership party, negotiated these agreements on behalf of the PLO. Although, these accords were only meant to serve as interim agreements and their authors emphasized that their contents would not "prejudice" the outcome of permanent status agreements,[1] the accords failed to meet minimal Palestinian nationalist aspirations. Ultimately, the Oslo peace process and initiatives related to this process would enjoy narrow support in Palestinian circles, and would marginalize important sectors of Palestinian political life. The establishment of the PA, and its associated institutions, would serve to reinforce these dynamics.

Palestine: Negotiations from a Point of Weakness

The circumstances under which the negotiating parties came to the table in many ways portended the outcome. Three factors decisively propelled the PLO to begin negotiations with Israel at a less than opportune time, when conditions were not in favor of the Palestinian bargaining position: (1) the PLO's military defeat in Lebanon; (2) international geopolitical changes, specifically the demise of the Soviet bloc in the early 1990s; and (3) the PLO's near bankruptcy after it was estranged from Egypt and the Arab states of the Persian Gulf following the Gulf War of 1991. By the end of the summer of 1982, Israel had destroyed the PLO in Beirut—not only its military potential, but also the entirety of its administrative and political apparatus in Lebanon.[2] The PLO's military defeat in Lebanon and its expulsion to Tunisia thereafter made clear that a military solution to the conflict was not a feasible option. Then, in 1988, during the PNC's nineteenth session, the PLO made two momentous decisions that would forever alter the course of the Arab-Israeli conflict: a renunciation and rejection of armed struggle, and a declaration of a willingness to negotiate "directly" with Israel on the basis of UN resolutions 242[3] and 338.[4] These decisions tacitly implied acceptance of both Israel's right to exist and a two-state solution. The shift in international public opinion and the new urgency that the international arena assigned to the conflict obliged the United States to turn its attentions to the region. With the end of the Cold War and the demise of the Soviet Union, many Arab regimes, particularly Syria, lost the economic, political, and diplomatic support they had previously received from the Soviets. Effectively, this was the end of an era for a Middle East that had previously been one of the Cold War's most active playing fields.

Iraq's defeat in the 1991 Gulf War asserted the United States as an uncontested hegemonic power in the region.[5] A deeply divided Arab world and an end to Soviet involvement in the region created an environment conducive for new US policy initiatives in the Middle East."[6] In the aftermath of the Gulf War, President George H. W. Bush announced to Congress that he would pursue new strategic goals in the region, including a just settlement to the Arab-Israeli conflict. Then Secretary of State James Baker maintained that the Madrid Peace Conference was a necessary part of President Bush's "new world order" after the fall of Communism.[7]

Accompanying these changing regional dynamics was a weakened PLO. The PLO's ill-fated decision to support Saddam Hussein's invasion of Kuwait cost the PLO US$120 million in annual donations from Saudi Arabia and Kuwait. Confiscation of Palestinian deposits in Kuwaiti banks brought the PLO's losses to about US$10 billion. As punishment for Arafat's solidarity with Saddam Hussein, Kuwait summarily expelled 400,000 Palestinians. These financial losses completely undermined the organization's ability to sustain itself, and by 1993 the PLO had closed a number of its offices in Tunis and elsewhere because of lack of funds.[8] The grassroots Intifada, which had commenced in the WBGS at the end of 1988, and the ascendance of the local PLO leadership, also challenged the continued relevance of the exiled PLO leadership to developments in the occupied territories.

At the Madrid peace conference, the Palestinians did not attend as an independent delegation under the auspices of the PLO, but as part of a joint Jordanian-Palestinian delegation. The conference set in motion bilateral negotiations between Israel and its neighboring countries, including the Palestinians. Simultaneously accompanying the ten rounds of negotiations between Israel and the PLO in Washington, DC, was a second track of negotiations: Israel and the PLO were secretly negotiating in Oslo.

The Oslo Accord's Inadequate and Problematic Provisions

The fourteen meetings in Oslo culminated in the 13 September 1993 signing of the Declaration of Principles. The DOP began:

> The Government of the State of Israel and the PLO team (in the Jordanian-Palestinian delegation to the Middle East Peace Conference)

(the "Palestinian Delegation"), representing the Palestinian people, agree that it is time to put an end to decades of confrontation and conflict, recognize their mutual legitimate and political rights, and strive to live in peaceful coexistence and mutual dignity and security and achieve a just, lasting and comprehensive peace settlement and historic reconciliation through the agreed political process.[9]

The DOP was not a peace treaty, but rather an agenda for negotiations covering a five-year "interim period" that would lead to a permanent settlement. The agreements outlined the principles that would govern relations between Israel and the PLO for the five-year period. They were nonbinding, and they stipulated that "nothing in the interim would prejudice the outcome of final status negotiations." After the first two years, final status negotiations would begin on the most critical issues related to the Israeli-Palestinian conflict—namely, Israeli settlements in the occupied territories, the status of Jerusalem, the fate of Palestinian refugees, water rights, borders, and security arrangements.

The main provisions of the DOP included the establishment of a "Palestinian Interim Self-Government Authority"—what would become known as the Palestinian Authority, or PA—for Palestinians residing in the WBGS, an elected legislative council, withdrawal of the Israeli military from parts of the WBGS, and a final permanent settlement within five years from the signing of the Interim Agreements. The DOP also stipulated that the permanent settlement would be based on UN Security Council Resolutions 242 and 338. Within the first two months of the DOP's implementation, the Israeli military would commence redeployment from Gaza and Jericho, and would be replaced by a Palestinian police force responsible for Palestinian "internal security and public order." At a later point Israel would redeploy from the major Palestinian population centers—Ramallah, Nablus, Jenin, Qalqilya, Tulkarem, Bethlehem, and Hebron. Shortly after the Israeli military redeployment, Palestinians in the WBGS would hold elections for a Palestinian Legislative Council. In the interim, Israel would control the borders. Finally, the agreement called for the establishment of a joint Israeli-Palestinian Economic Cooperation Committee to carry out economic development programs for the WBGS.[10]

In many ways, the DOP resembled previous proposals relating to Palestinian autonomy, such as in the Allon Plan and Camp David

Agreements, but for the notable exception of the PLO's participation. Supporters of the DOP pointed out that the agreement de facto implied Israel's formal recognition of the PLO, allowed the Palestinians to administer their own affairs, and addressed the Palestinians inclusively "as a people."[11] Critics pointed out that the Palestinians had not received any guarantees for a future independent, sovereign, viable state, as well as no guarantees for a halt to Israeli settlement expansion in the occupied territories. The DOP also failed to address Israel's illegal claim to the "occupied territories"; rather, the DOP identified the territories as "disputed territories."[12] One of the most damning critiques of the PLO was that it had allowed itself to be transformed from a liberation movement into a governing body in the WBGS.[13] Key Palestinian leaders pointed out that the Executive Committee and other representative bodies of the PLO—"the sole and legitimate representative of the Palestinian people"—were absent from the negotiations, and that unknown names of little relevance to the organization's structure and their advisors were negotiating on behalf of the Palestinian people.[14]

Absent from the DOP and all the implementation agreements that followed was any recognition of the Palestinians' historic grievances. The ambiguity enshrined in the political settlement was not unique to these agreements. This lack of precision, often referred to as "constructive ambiguity," is a common feature of political settlements that address substantive causes of the conflict.[15] The most striking feature of the DOP's constructive ambiguity, however, was that it compromised the lowest common denominator of consensus among different Palestinian groups and political organizations: the demand for Palestinian sovereignty.

Not surprisingly, then, the Oslo peace process and related initiatives did not receive solid support from the Palestinian leadership and Palestinians in the territories and diaspora. According to a Center for Policy Research poll, 38 percent of Palestinians in the WBGS opposed the DOP and 20.4 percent were not sure how they would evaluate the agreement.[16] On 3 September 1993, Arafat convened the PLO executive committee in hopes of ratifying the DOP. Some of the most prominent members of the PLO, such as Mahmoud Darwish and Shafiq al-Hout, resigned and a number of members abstained. The cabinet resolution in favor of the DOP passed by only one vote, compared to sixty-one in favor and fifty opposed in the Israeli Knesset.[17] Prominent Palestinian intellectuals, as well as political organizations such as Hamas, Islamic Jihad, and the leftist PFLP and DFLP, opposed the DOP. Even former PLO negotiators, most notably Haidar Abdel Shafi,[18] and to a lesser extent Hanan Ashrawi, were vocal in their opposition to Oslo. The PPP did not outright reject the Oslo Accords, but adopted more of a wait and see approach.

A series of agreements followed that effectively outlined the nature of implementation after the DOP. Among the most important of these agreements was the Paris Protocol,[19] Gaza-Jericho First Agreements, the Oslo II Agreements, and the Protocol concerning redeployment from Hebron. The two parties signed the Paris Protocol in April 1994; this agreement outlined the economic arrangements between the two parties, including issues related to the customs union, import tariffs, trade taxes, import licensing regulations, and trade standards. One month later, in May 1994, the two parties signed the Gaza-Jericho First Agreement, also known as the 1994 Cairo Agreement. These agreements gave the Palestinians autonomy in the Gaza Strip and the West Bank town of Jericho and established the Palestinian self-governing entity, the PA.[20] On 27 August 1995, the parties signed the Protocol on Further Transfer of Powers and Responsibilities, which put the PA in charge of labor, commerce and industry, gas and petroleum, insurance, postal services, local government, and agriculture.[21]

The two parties then signed the Interim Agreements on Implementation of the DOP, Oslo II, on 28 September 1995. The Oslo II Agreements fully detailed the interim arrangements between the two parties during the next five years and the transfer of certain powers to the PA. These agreements established institutions of self-government including a legislative council and an elected "President," and also elaborated on redeployment arrangements outlining how the WBGS would be divided into three distinct areas—A, B, and C—each with different security and civil power arrangements. There would be four different phases of Israeli military redeployment from the WBGS. By the third military redeployment, Area A would consist of approximately 17.2 percent of the West Bank. In this area, the PA would be responsible for internal security and civil affairs, and Israeli checkpoints would surround each of these areas. Area B would consist of 21.8 percent of the West Bank, over which the PA would have civil control over Palestinians and maintain a police force to protect "public order for Palestinians," and Israel would maintain overall security control. Area C would consist of 60 percent of the territory where Israel would retain full territorial jurisdiction, and the PA would have functional jurisdiction over Palestinians and "only in matters not related to territory."[22] The two sides, however, did not agree on the territorial size of the fourth and final redeployment. Once the Israeli military redeployment from any area was complete, the Israeli government would transfer the civil powers for education and culture, health, social welfare, direct taxation, and tourism of that area to the PA. These agreements would come to supersede the Gaza-Jericho Agreement and the Protocol on Further Transfer of Powers and Responsibilities. On 15 January 1997, the two parties signed the Protocol concerning redeployment from Hebron, which outlined the nature of Israeli withdrawal from this Palestinian town.[23]

Formidable Undertakings

The PA became responsible for public sector functions in the WBGS under substantial adversity in a conflict situation. The body was expected to build public sector institutions and assume responsibility for these functions while promoting good governance, democratic political institutions, a robust civil society, security (both internally and for Israel), and a free market while lacking key requisites such as jurisdiction over the land for whose population it would be responsible, or control over water resources. Moreover, it was expected to build a fiscal administration and guarantee fiscal stability without control over monetary policy or its own currency.[24] A substantial portion of the PA's budget would rely on the value-added tax (VAT) and other fees transferred from Israel. From the onset, it would be confronted with the challenge of Israeli closure policies that disrupted the movement of goods and labor, dealing an immense blow to the economies of the WBGS.[25] Israel would retain control over the external borders, airspace, water, and the electromagnetic spheres of the WBGS.[26] Despite these challenges, the PA succeeded in establishing functioning state institutions.[27] From the onset, however, the founding of these institutions privileged certain groups and political organizations.

Opposition to the unfolding Oslo Accords was by no means limited to extremists. The implementation agreements would draw mounting criticism, as each stage increasingly appeared to address Israel's security concerns at the expense of Palestinian nationalist aspirations. The negotiation of these agreements did not expand beyond the initial narrow participation of the DOP,[28] further entrenching the noninclusivity of these agreements. The institutions that historically represented all Palestinian political organizations, such as the PNC and the Executive Committee of the PLO, were not included in this process. An overriding criticism revolved around the PA's lack of control over jurisdiction. The unfolding agreements also did not bring an end to settlement expansion; on the contrary, settlement expansion would continue unabated as negotiations were under way.[29] The issue of Israel's control over almost every land aquifer in the West Bank was also absent from these agreements and postponed to final status negotiations. Moreover, the subsequent agreements of the Oslo Accords did not move beyond the autonomy framework, with no guarantees toward sovereign statehood.[30]

The Paris Protocol, Annex IV of the Gaza-Jericho Agreement, established the transitional framework that would govern economic relations, including policies related to trade, specifications, taxation, and banking between Israel and the PA for the next five years, until 1999. The agreement extended control to the PA in some areas, such as the authority to collect domestic taxes, set its own industrial policy, and resume limited imports from Arab countries. The agreement also stipulated a gradual elimination of export restrictions on agricultural products, and it allowed for the establishment of an autonomous Palestinian Monetary Authority for the interim period. The Monetary Authority would perform limited central bank tasks, such as financial sector supervision and regulation; this would not include the issuing of a national currency.[31] As the permanence of the agreement took hold, and its disadvantages to the Palestinians became increasingly apparent, it would draw damning condemnation from many quarters. One of the overriding criticisms centered on the creation of a "Customs Union," and the aligning of Palestinian customs tariff rates, procedures, and taxation policies with those of Israel.[32] This arrangement reinforced Israel's economic control over external borders. Moreover, the alignment of the Palestinian economy with a more advanced, industrial outward-looking economy would not help equip the Palestinian economy to become more competitive in international markets. Since Israel would be required to transfer import taxes and VAT pertaining to revenues collected for goods and services sold in Israel and destined for the WBGS, the overdependence on the Israeli economy facilitated fiscal leakage. According to a 2011 United Nations Conference on Trade and Development (UNCTAD) study, over US$300 million was "leaked" or not transferred to the Palestinian economy, as a result of weak customs control, dated clearance arrangements, and tax avoidance on the part of Israel.[33] Control over these transfers also provided Israel with additional political leverage to penalize the PA if it deemed necessary. Initially, proponents rationalized that the arrangements would allow Palestinian labor free access to Israeli markets. Israel, however, unilaterally and gradually limited the entry of Palestinian laborers into its markets.

The Hebron Agreements of January 1997 divided the city into H1 and H2 zones; H1 was handed over to the Palestinians, and H2, the Old City, where 450 Israeli Jewish settlers would remain, would continue to be under complete Israeli security control. Provisions for H2 were designed to separate Arabs and Jews, dividing the city with barbed wire and privileging the Jewish settlers with bypass roads and extra security arrangements. After the Hebron Protocol was signed, Israel issued a "Cabinet Communique" elaborating on its understanding of the Oslo Accords and declared that "details of the further stages of the redeployment in Judea and Samaria will be determined by the Government of Israel."[34] These gestures were not simply symbolic but reaffirmed Israel's insistence that it would unilaterally shape the final outcome. Benjamin Netanyahu's term as prime minister, like his subsequent terms, further pushed Israel's unilateralism.

Twenty years after the signing of the DOP, the Israelis and Palestinians were no closer to peace: no progress had been made in terms of final status negotiations. In terms of military presence, the Israeli military had simply redeployed around Palestinian towns and was still very present. According to a number of Western mainstream narratives, the two sides were close to reaching an agreement at the Camp David negotiations of 2000. Palestinian accounts, however, maintained that the negotiating positions of the two sides were unbridgeable. By the close of 2017, Israel's policies of institutionalized separation between the occupied territories and Israel had created a mental chasm that blinded and prevented the Israeli establishment, and perhaps even the public, from grasping the extent to which Palestinian lives had deteriorated and their circumstances had become unsustainable.

The Post-Oslo Era and the Reconstitution of Palestinian Political Life

The noninclusivity of the Oslo Accords and subsequent implementation agreements further polarized the Palestinian political landscape. In general, three political tendencies emerged in relation to the Oslo accords: Fatah and its clientelistic networks, the Opposition, and the Liberal Moderates. These tendencies included the relevant political organization, as well as loosely affiliated individual and groups—affiliations based on various forms of group membership, political beliefs, or sometimes even shared labels, such as "Islamist."[35] They (the tendencies) vis-à-vis the accords remained relatively unchanged over time, albeit with minor shifts in tone or degree in various periods; the changes were often tactical and not fundamental in terms of how they related to the accords. Each of these tendencies initially adopted a different strategy in relation to the peace accords that was often conditioned by their ability to access Western foreign donor funding or other sources of funding. Because of the interests of Western foreign donors, especially state-sponsored donors, they were more likely to fund groups that supported the peace accords and were in a better position to promote a "post–Cold War liberal order."[36] The availability of Western foreign donor assistance, hence, played a critical role in mediating relations between these different groups.

Members and groups affiliated with Fatah, the leadership party of the PA and the broker of the Oslo Accords, were the staunchest supporters of the Oslo peace process. Although groups and individuals affiliated with Fatah were eligible to receive foreign donor funding, often these groups did not seek Western foreign funding because of their more steady flow of funding from Fatah and the PLO. After the Oslo Accords, Fatah was better able to consolidate its financial base in the territories, and therefore enlarged its clientelistic networks, including those involved in its affiliated volunteer and grassroots organizations. Fatah institutions have become the backbone of the PA. As the governing body of the PA, all groups affiliated with Fatah sought to expand their grass-roots bases so as to maintain Fatah's primacy in Palestinian society.

The Opposition tendency broadly included groups and individuals affiliated, loosely or otherwise, with the radical left of the PLO, namely the DFLP and the PFLP, or with Islamist organizations, Hamas, or Islamic Jihad, or simply individuals who identified as Islamist. The Opposition tendency included those groups that more ardently opposed the Oslo Accords, as well as groups and individuals directly and indirectly, perceived or otherwise, affiliated with these organizations.[37] Often, the level of affiliation with these political organizations was limited to the political affiliation (former or current) of the founders of the respective group or grassroots organization. Groups associated with this tendency adopted a clear position against the Oslo Accords; for example, refusing to run candidates in the 1996 Palestinian Legislative Council elections for fear that the elections would serve to legitimize the Oslo Accords.[38] Conversely, those associated with this tendency did participate in local government elections from the beginning, as local responsibilities involved the day-to-day affairs of Palestinians in the WBGS, as opposed to direct negotiations with Israel. These groups would run candidates in the subsequent 2006 legislative elections. And even when these groups and organizations did not run candidates, however, their members and supporters did vote.

Though the grassroots organizations associated with the Opposition tendency varied in their willingness to articulate a position for or against the Oslo Accords, most were unable to access state-sponsored Western donor funding. Western foreign donors were reluctant to fund these groups for fear that they might undermine the peace process. Moreover, even those groups that were more Western in their cultural and social orientation were less willing to embrace a liberal market approach to democracy. In the case of groups perceived as Islamist, Western foreign donors were even less inclined to provide funding because they also were not in a position to promote the "post–Cold War liberal order," especially in relation to its pro-Western cultural and social orientation. Despite the apolitical nature of many of these Islamist groups, their overriding concern with charity, and the extensive networks and social services they provided to various constituencies in Palestinian society, Western donors feared that they might be connected to more political Islamist organizations, and that they also were too anti-Western in their social outlook. Similarly, although the leftist groups that fell under the purview of the Opposition were in a better position to promote aspects of the "post–Cold War liberal order," they were not eligible to receive funding from Western foreign donors because of their opposition to the peace accords.

Individuals formerly associated with the more leftist groups of the Opposition were able to access Western foreign funding if they no longer displayed any ties with political groups associated with the Opposition, or any strong ties to grassroots constituencies; such a display might indicate that these individuals are still important political players affiliated with the actual political organizations. Therefore, when individuals such as Riad al-Malki[39] and Waleed Salem, former members of the PFLP, established the Palestinian Center for the Dissemination of Democracy and Community Development (PANORAMA), they did so without incorporating any previously active grassroots constituencies.

The Liberal Moderates involved those groups and individuals who did not necessarily support the peace accords, but were willing to adopt a wait and see approach.[40] These groups were in a favorable position to promote a "post-Cold War liberal order" because of their more Western social orientation and greater willingness to support the ideals of liberal market-democracy. Of the three tendencies, the Liberal Moderates had the most consistent access to Western donor funding and as a result spearheaded the establishing of professionalized NGOs. These individuals and groups were more willing partake in the national and local elections, both in terms of voting and running candidates, and in filling key government positions in hopes of influencing certain outcomes related to the Oslo Accords. The Liberal Moderate tendency was most closely associated with the PCP (later the PPP), the FIDA, a splinter organization of the DFLP that supported the Oslo Accords, and subsequently broke away. These groups and individuals were in a position to promote a "post-Cold War liberal order" given their more Western cultural and social outlook. Because individuals and groups associated with this tendency also did not adamantly oppose the Oslo Accords, especially in the case of FIDA, they were in a good position to receive Western foreign donor assistance.

In the post-Madrid era, groups and individuals within this tendency had the most consistent access to Western donor assistance, and hence adopted NGO professionalization of their grassroots committees to facilitate their political transition in the post-Madrid era; the new professionalized NGOs (often sans grassroots) would provide these factions and their leaders employment prospects and opportunities to remain involved in the political life of Palestine without being wedded to the Oslo Accords. Among the former leaders of the PPP who were able to professionalize their organizations and maintain some of their grassroots constituencies are Ismail Dueik, head of the Palestinian Agricultural Relief Committees (PARC), and Amal Khreisheh, head of the Palestinian Working Women's Society for Development (PWWSD), and to a lesser extent Mustafa Barghouti, head of the Union of Palestinian Medical Relief Committees, to name but a few. Later, prominent members of the DFLP established new professionalized organizations, including the Women's Study Center and the Women's Center for Legal Aid and Counseling (WCLAC). Most of the DFLP members who were involved in the founding of these organizations, later broke off and joined FIDA, the new splinter organization of the DFLP. Because the founders of these organizations formerly affiliated themselves with the Opposition tendency, and because of the tenuous nature of the split in the organization, these new NGOs did not incorporate or maintain their grassroots constituencies. Initially, foreign donors were more reticent to fund an NGO that was headed by members (or former members) of the DFLP (an Opposition group), who still maintained a strong relationship with their former grassroots constituencies. Subsequently, after the schism in the DFLP, FIDA (the new Liberal Moderate group) did not seek and was not able to garner the same support among its former grassroots base.

The Professionalization of Politics in Palestine

Beginning in the late 1980s, but especially after the initiation of the Madrid peace process in 1991, various NGOs began seeking out Western foreign donor assistance. The noninclusive nature of the Madrid peace process and the Oslo Accords caused increasing polarization among these associations, unions, and organizations—specifically, between those who supported or did not oppose the peace process, and therefore were eligible to receive foreign donor assistance, and those who opposed the peace process, and were less likely to receive or have access to foreign donor assistance. Consequently, the organizations and members affiliated with the Opposition became the recipients of services or training sessions from those organizations affiliated with the pro-peace accords or nonopposition groups. In some cases, this political chasm also overlapped with existing social divisions between those who were more Western-oriented and English-speaking, and those who were not. The increased polarization among the various associations, unions, and organizations resulted in increased tension, animosity, and mistrust among the various groups. The emergent Palestinian civil society became more elitist in nature, addressing the needs of a narrower population base, and devoid of the principles of voluntarism that were so central to previous modes of sociopolitical organizing. As Marwan Barghouti elaborated, "The spirit of voluntarism was gone . . . The PA left people disappointed, and the Left turned to NGOs . . . It was not only about the increase in donor assistance, but the poor performance of the PA, politically, practically, and on all levels, left former activists seriously demoralized."[41] The combination of these factors negatively impacted the development of Palestinian civil society.

As Western foreign donor assistance became more readily available to the WBGS after 1991, many of these NGOs became dependent on this source of funding. Accompanying this reliance on Western foreign donor assistance were new standards for NGO professionalization.[42] Although there might have been a decrease in overall funding to NGOs in the WBGS, the structure of this aid shifted from being more Arab and solidarity-based in character, to being from state-sponsored bilateral donors. Increased reliance on Western foreign donor assistance, as opposed to reliance on membership fees and voluntarism, meant that NGOs were no longer accountable to the constituencies they served, but rather to the donors who funded them. Therefore, the program and project priorities of the emergent professionalized NGOs began to shift from self-help initiatives and other programs reflecting the needs of the membership base to advocacy, human rights monitoring, civic education, and democracy training. Professionalized NGOs engaged in activities as diverse as medical relief, agricultural relief, and women's empowerment adopted these program priorities. According to the Palestinian Economic Policy Research Institute, NGOs in the WBGS increased by one-third in the post-Oslo decade alone.[43] At the end of the decade after the Madrid Peace Conference, one Palestinian organization estimated that there were twenty professionalized NGOs focusing on "democracy and civic education," and eighteen dealing with human rights (including labor rights) in the Jerusalem-Ramallah area alone.[44] These figures are especially significant if one considers that the projected total population of the WBGS in 2005 was less than 3.7 million, and only reached 4.8 million in 2016.[45]

The Disconnected NGOs

Even more significant, however, was how disconnected these NGOs were from the overall Palestinian population. Despite the prevalence of these professionalized organizations, few Palestinians outside of elite circles ever heard of them or had contact with them. According to one 1999 Jerusalem and Media Communication (JMCC) public opinion poll, only 19.2 percent of those polled were members of any type of organization,[46] and only 0.4 percent were members or participated in the activities of a human rights organization.[47] Trends remained more or less consistent into the next decade. Many of these new professionalized NGOs served as political platforms for their directors and were known by the name of their directors, as opposed to the actual name of the organization. Among the Palestinian elite who established professionalized organizations are Hanan Ashrawi,[48] Mustafa Barghouti,[49] Ghassan Khatib,[50] and Ziad Abu Amar.[51] One commentator aptly noted: "Palestine is probably the only place where you give up your job as a minister in order to establish an NGO."[52] Because these individuals can rely on their professionalized organizations for publicity, as well as financial support in the form of salaries, they are not reliant on any political party to provide a political platform. Mustafa Barghouti's example perhaps best illustrates this point. Mustafa Barghouti left the PPP in 2002 and established the Palestinian National Initiative for which, as of 2017, he served as secretary general. Barghouti also founded at least two professionalized NGOs, and as of 2014 served as the director or president of both. The new political organization, as well as the professionalized NGOs he established, did not have grassroots constituencies. In the 2005 presidential election, Barghouti was the main political opponent of Mahmoud Abbas, who was elected president of the Palestinian Authority.

Foreign donors were not oblivious to these dynamics in Palestinian society. One director of a foreign donor agency stated that Western foreign donors were willing to fund professionalized NGOs that served as personal platforms for their directors in hopes that an alternative leadership would emerge from the NGO sector. Ghassan Khatib elaborated, "There was the idea that NGOs could replace political parties. Although NGOs may help in the promotion of democracy, only the political parties can play a real role in putting democracy into practice and pushing for pluralism. Civil society is only effective in the context of a well-functioning and vibrant political society."[53] The directors of these professionalized NGOs may have been critical of the Oslo Accords, and some initially adopted a wait and see approach. But crucially, most did not dismiss the accords and they thus remained relevant, often assuming important positions in the PA.

Although the Liberal Moderates participated in the PA, many were often critical of PA policies, especially those pertaining to corruption, human rights abuses, and authoritarian tendencies—though this was criticism that did not question the very basis of the Oslo Accords. In the initial years after the establishment of the PA, sectors of the NGO community and the PA competed intensely and repeatedly over mandates and funding, especially in the agriculture and health sectors. In the case of the agriculture sector, for example, PARC initially had a larger operating budget than the Ministry of Agriculture.

PA Attempts to Control NGOs and the Laws Governing Them

The PA went to great lengths to control the emergent civil society, and especially the Opposition tendency affiliated NGOs. This relationship, however, was not static, and, in general, four different phases can be ascertained. The first period, approximately 1994 to 2000, coincided with the establishment of the PA and the ensuing power struggle between the governing body and the emergent civil society as the two camps sought to stake mandates and shape the contours of the relationship. Dynamics stabilized in 2000 after the promulgation of the NGO Law. During the second phase, approximately 2000 to 2004, and most notably after the start of the second Intifada, sanctions against Islamist NGOs and Opposition tendency affiliated NGOs more broadly took effect. Western donors, especially USAID, become much more aggressive in their crackdown. Relations stabilized between 2004 and 2006, and it appeared that the PA and NGOs in particular had worked out a modus vivendi. After Hamas's election victory in 2006, a fourth phase congealed, and the PA and the international community launched a vicious crackdown against Opposition-tendency groups, and especially Islamists.[54] Although different phases represented variation in the degree of exclusion of the Opposition, especially Islamist opposition groups, the constant was the promotion and inclusion of supporters or potential supporters of Oslo, and the noninclusion and sidelining of any credible opposition.

During the first phase, among the mechanisms the PA attempted to enforce was a requirement that all NGOs register with the PA. The NGOs worried that such a move would invite more PA direct control, further curtailing NGO autonomy. The PA responded by drafting a Palestinian NGO Law that would help rein in this third sector. Ultimately, the PA was not entirely successful in this endeavor. Previously, the exiting NGO law was a combination of Ottoman, British Mandate, Jordanian, and Israeli law. The Palestinian NGO community considered this law too intrusive, not yielding enough autonomy to NGOs. According to this draft of the NGO law, NGOs would have to receive PA approval before receiving funding from donors, and register with the Ministry of Interior to receive approval for their operations.

Bowing to pressure from the Palestinian NGO community, as well as from foreign donors, the PA agreed to redraft the NGO law. The new NGO law was similar to the first, with a few important modifications: NGOs would no longer require approval for their operations, and they would have to report funding to the PA, but not seek their approval. After substantial discussion and debates between the NGO community, the PA executive, and the Palestinian Legislative Council, the law was promulgated and accepted by Arafat in January 2000 without incorporating many of the cabinet's recommendations and amendments. Ultimately, both the PA and the NGO community considered the new NGO law a victory. Although NGOs were still required to register with the Ministry of Interior, they were not required to seek permission for their operations from the PA, nor request approval for their funding.[55] The NGO community proudly conceded that the Palestinian NGO law was the most "progressive" in the Arab world. Similarly, the PA executive was satisfied, since the NGOs were required to register with the Ministry of Interior.[56]

Legislative Council and Local Government Development and the Creation of Institutional Openings

The institutions that emerged in the post-Oslo era reflected the noninclusive nature of the settlement that governed political relations in this era. Where these institutions were nonrepresentative and opportunities to engage the state were limited, disarticulated spaces resulted, further undermining the quality of civil society and the longer term prospects for democratic development. As the governing party of the PA and the main signatory of the Oslo Accords, Fatah needed to ensure the PA's predominance in the face of mounting opposition. Fatah and the PA essentially depended on one another for their continued existence. New opportunities and challenges emerged through a constrained process of government-related institutional development. On the one hand, a sense of optimism in terms of the prospects for peace, the availability of more resources, and new openings in the institutional setting all coalesced to provide various political actors enhanced opportunities for political participation. As part of the Oslo accords, Palestinians would have the opportunity to hold legislative and local council elections in the WBGS. However, because of the noninclusive nature of the peace accords, and because it possessed the power to do so, Fatah crafted mechanisms and strategies to ensure its predominance in relation to each of these sites of power; it could also dictate the timing of these elections and when they could be held.

At the level of the legislative council, Fatah imposed constraints that limited the representative nature of this body, increasing chances of its electoral victory. In turn, the limitations of this body constrained civil society's ability to interact with it; a more representative body would have provided the different civil society actors with greater openings and opportunities to interact and make demands on the state. From the onset, the electoral law discouraged party competition.[57]

In spite of the constrained institutional setting, opposition groups, the Opposition tendency, namely Hamas, prevailed at the local government level, and later in the 2006 legislative elections. This ascendance was in spite of institutions designed to privilege included groups, and a direct result of Fatah's badly calculated decisions and disastrous election campaigns, and the leftist and secular opposition's organizational blunders. Notwithstanding Hamas's legitimate electoral victory, the sanctioned noninclusion of the political settlement resulted in Fatah's unwillingness to accept the electoral outcome, and it facilitated the international community's brutal backlash against Hamas and the Gaza Strip. These developments would doom prospects for civil society and democratic development more generally for decades to come.

Fatah designed and redesigned the electoral system to increase its likelihood of prevailing at these levels of government. According to the 1995 Election Law, which governed the 1996 Palestinian legislative elections,[58] the Palestinian territories (including East Jerusalem) were divided into sixteen districts in which the winning party would take all the seats allotted to the district. The council was comprised of eighty-eight seats—fifty-one in the West Bank and thirty-seven in the Gaza Strip. Some seats were reserved for minority representation: six seats were reserved for the Christian population and one for the Samaritans. The system, and in particular the lack of proportional representation, provided smaller parties such as FIDA and the PPP—groups affiliated with the Liberal Moderates—less opportunity to win seats in the legislative council. The Opposition tendency demanded that the electoral commission change the electoral law so that the WBGS be treated as a single constituency with proportional representation as opposed to the majority-take-all district system. The Opposition tendency's discontent with the electoral system surely was another reason they did not run candidates in the 1996 election.[59]

In 1996, the Fatah official list won fifty-five seats (62.5 percent), independent Fatah members won seven seats (8 percent), and other independents and other groups won twenty-six seats (29.5 percent). Although leading critics of the Oslo Accords and of Arafat's policies also won, such as Haydar Abdel Shafi, Abdul Jawad Saleḥ, Abbas Zakī, ad Salah Ta'amarī, they did not actually represent established opposition parties, but won on the basis of their individual popularity. Fatah went to painstaking efforts to prevail in the elections, including the initiation of vote recounts in some districts, and according to some analysts, such as Lamis Andoni, worked out special arrangements with Israel to allow scores of Fatah members to cross from Amman to the West Bank days before the election.[60] Although Fatah did not win a majority of the vote, the electoral system enabled a resounding victory in terms of seats won.

In another attempt to maximize its presence in the 2006 elections, the Fatah-dominated PLC amended the elections laws and adopted a mixed electoral system according to which 50 percent of the total 132 PLC seats would be elected under the majority system in the sixteen districts, and the remaining 50 percent (sixty-six seats) would be contested nationally through proportional representation lists. By then, the participation of Opposition tendency affiliates in future legislative elections had become more likely. Fatah was noticeably weaker and plagued by its internal divisions, and the strong showing of Hamas and PFLP affiliates in local government elections foreshadowed the strong performance of Opposition–tendency in future legislative elections. The election reforms increased Fatah's chances of gaining seats at the national level because of the substantial recognition that some of its members enjoyed. The new law also guaranteed representation for women, and annulled the 1995 election law.

Despite Fatah's maneuvering to ensure its preeminence, Hamas won seventy-four of the 132 legislative seats, compared to Fatah's forty-five. Fatah lost in spite of its institutional design efforts, which ultimately could not withstand its disastrous electoral campaign. Mahmoud Abbas, incumbent Palestinian president, believed that inclusion of Hamas would moderate the organization. Accompanying this rationale was the belief that Fatah could maintain its preeminence at the political helm in the face of political challenge; this led to a self-assurance that would delay Fatah's much needed internal reform. As a result, Fatah did not seriously embark on rebuilding the organization or organizing a competitive electoral campaign. In protest against Abu Mazen's decision to suspend Fatah's primaries, members of the "insider new guard"—the WBGS Fatah leadership that had not spent most of their lives in leadership positions in Amman, Beirut, and Tunis—decided to run in opposition to the official Fatah list. Hence, days before the election, Fatah was running on two lists—one representing the Fatah "old guard" and another representing the "insider new guard." On the eve of final list submissions, Abu Mazen managed to fuse the two lists, a move that outraged as many Fatah loyalists as it satisfied. From the onset, Fatah's election campaign was fraught with problems on all fronts. The party put little effort into coordinating its campaign tactics, electioneering in Palestinian villages, or formulating a winning election strategy.[61] The Opposition and Liberal Moderate tendencies also performed quite poorly. The PFLP, another group that is part of what I describe as the Opposition tendency, ran as the Popular Front slate and won three seats. And individuals and groups that could be labeled as part of the Liberal Moderate tendency ran on three separate slates: Mustafa Barghouti's Independent Palestine, Salam Fayyad and Hanan Ashrawi's The Third Way, and the PPP and FIDA (joined by the Opposition group, the DFLP), as the Alternative List —and collectively they won six seats, none of which were at the district level.

In contrast, Hamas waged a very organized election campaign, buttressed by years of long-term strategizing in terms of gaining support among fellow Palestinians and a meticulous, careful reading of the Palestinian electoral system. Running as the Party of Change and Reform, Hamas promised what seemed like a real alternative. According to Khaled Hroub, its fourteen-point electoral platform represented the broadest vision that Hamas had ever articulated concerning all aspects of Palestinian life.[62] The emphasis on reform permeated the entire document, and it paid special attention to "pluralism" in Palestinian political life. Hamas's public relations experts ensured that each town had a three-member election committee that focused on fundraising and campaign mobilization. Hamas also provided media and public speaking training to all its candidates, and in the weeks prior to the elections, it ran five single-issue radio programs addressing corruption, women's rights, education, the Oslo Accords, and internal change and reform.[63] To ensure that its vote was not divided, Hamas also ran only the number of candidates for which there were seats, and was thus able to secure an impressive forty-four out of the total sixty-six seats at the district level.

As a result of the 2006 election results, Abbas again amended the election law in 2007 by presidential decree.[64] According to the new election law, the entire election would take place through the proportional representation list system at the national level, and the district level elections were eliminated.[65] All candidates would have to accept the PLO as the sole and legitimate representative of the Palestinian people, in addition to upholding the Declaration of Independence Document and the Basic Law, and submit an affidavit endorsing this recognition with the application for their candidacy.[66] This regulation de facto increased the likelihood of Hamas candidate exclusion since the party/political organization is not a member organization of the PLO.

Similarly, by shaping institutional design, as well as being in control of the timing of elections, Fatah constrained the development of local government structures in the WBGS, and in turn the Opposition–affiliated civil society's potential to interact with it. In the case of local government elections, however, it was more difficult for Fatah to determine outcomes. Palestinian local election laws did not require candidates to indicate partisan affiliation. Most candidates ran as independents, so the outcome of the elections were (and remain) considerably more fluid. The timing of the elections, however, is a tool at the disposal of the PA, and as a result, it held elections when it felt better positioned to win.

In early 1997, the PA Ministry of Local Government appointed "transition" mayors in the WBGS for the interim period until the elections; most of these mayors were either members of Fatah or supporters of the party. Subsequently, in the interim period, which spanned eight years, the PA did not hold municipal elections, further disempowering this level of government. In the wake of President Yasir Arafat's death, the PA decided to hold presidential, legislative council, and local elections. The local government elections, however, would be held in five phases, which would help the PA ensure that the Opposition did not prevail at this level of government. The PA held the first round of municipal elections in December 2004, a second round in May 2005, a third round in September 2005, and fourth round in December 2005, and the fifth and final round was never held. By the third round of elections, Fatah had won 712 seats, compared to 418 for Hamas, and single digit percentages were gained by the PFLP, PPP, and independent affiliates. Realizing again the extent of Fatah's weakness, on 13 August 2005, before the completion of that year's local government elections, Abbas amended the Local Council Elections Law No. 5 of 1996. He replaced the winner-take-all system with the Local Council Elections Law No. 10 of 2005 according to which each electoral list that received 8 percent or more of the vote would be allocated seats in the local council proportional to the number of votes it received.[67] By the fourth round, Hamas had won the absolute majority of seats in three of the largest WB towns of Nablus, Jenin, and El-Bireh, again exposing the weakness of Fatah. The fifth and last phase was not held; this round was cancelled right before the close of the nomination period as it became apparent that Fatah would be unable to produce candidate lists.[68] Local elections were subsequently cancelled in 2010 and postponed in 2011. Following Hamas's 2007 take-over in Gaza, many councils led by Hamas were removed from office. Many international donors also suspended assistance to municipalities headed by Hamas affiliates or supporters.

The PA finally held local elections in 2012 because it knew Hamas would be boycotting the elections. Hamas cited harassment of its members and the need for national reconciliation as reasons for this boycott.[69] As a result of Hamas's call for the boycott of the elections, only 54 percent of the 50 percent registered to vote participated in the elections compared to the approximately 77 percent in the 2006 legislative elections. The defining feature of this election was its lack of political pluralism. Of the 354 local government localities, contested elections took place for ninety-three councils.[70] In 179 localities, only one list was submitted or was valid for the elections, and in the remaining eight-two localities, no valid candidate list was submitted. In the latter, elections were postponed until November of that year. Ultimately, the majority of electoral contests in the ninety-three municipalities were between Fatah members, former Fatah members, or independent Fatah members who ran on independent lists, and other candidates who were independent or leftist-affiliated. Ultimately, Fatah failed to receive the majority of seats in five of eleven major towns. Having won the majority in six towns- Hebron, Qalqīliya, Jericho, Ṭūlkarem, Salfīt, and El Bīreh, they still declared it a victory for Fatah. The PA held elections in the West Bank in May 2017. Reaffirming democratic development in noninclusive contexts, these elections were only held in the West Bank, and only took place in 145 out of 361 councils. In the remaining councils, no electoral lists were registered, or lists simply did not exist.

The Oslo Accords presented a number of new opportunities and constraints for the reconstituted civil society. The Fatah-dominated PA went to great lengths to ensure its preeminence in Palestinian political life. This maneuvering included the development of electoral laws to enhance its prospects at the polls, as well as restricting the timing of elections. Western democracy promotion efforts seeking to produce a post–Cold War liberal consensus sanctioned this exclusion, despite its undermining of Palestinian civil society and democracy more generally. Chapter 6 discusses in more detail the Western donor response to Hamas's election victory in the 2006 legislative elections. The manipulation of local governments, however, further constricted the potential for citizen participation and circumscribed the work of civil society since its various constituent parts, especially those that were affiliated to the Opposition tendency, were limited in their potential interactions with this level of government. Such maneuvering effectively obstructed the articulation between society and the state. The discontinuation of Western donor funding to local councils dominated by Opposition tendency affiliates further undermined these representative institutions and perpetuated the disarticulation of these spaces. The significance of this disadvantage should not be underestimated given that historically it is at this level of government that the poor and marginalized have often been able to attain citizenship gains. The initial noninclusion of the political settlement hence had longer term consequences that extended well beyond the initial post-Oslo period.

El Salvador: From the Chapultepec Accords to the Postwar Era

The circumstances leading to negotiations and to the eventual political settlement in El Salvador lent themselves to greater inclusivity. By 1989, both the Salvadoran government and the FMLN realized that neither side would achieve a clear military victory and that only negotiations could achieve a resolution to the conflict.[71] First, and perhaps most importantly, the FMLN's 1989 offensive underscored that the two parties had reached a military stalemate; second, the changing Cold War context resulted in declining US support for the Salvadoran government and loss of Soviet support for the FMLN; and third, mounting criticism against the government led to a quantitative (if not qualitative) decline in government human rights abuses that resulted in political openings not present previously.[72] The Salvadoran agreements built consensus on the different issues and culminated in a comprehensive final framework agreement that included agreements reached over the two preceding years.

Negotiations as an Outcome of Stalemate

The sustained insurgency of lower class actors in El Salvador made clear to the elite establishment that although the insurgency could perhaps be militarily contained, it could not be defeated.[73] The 11 November 1989 FMLN military offensive reminded all parties that they had reached a military stalemate, and that a logical resolution to the conflict could only be attained by a negotiated settlement. The trigger to the offensive was the government's bombing of the National Union Federation of Salvadoran Workers' headquarters.[74] In response, the FMLN infiltrated 2,000 combatants into the capital, San Salvador, with the intention of unsettling the status quo and restarting the stalled political negotiations. More ambitious proponents hoped that a popular insurrection in the urban center would follow.[75] During the two week offensive, over one thousand civilians were killed, and members of the high command of the armed forces assassinated six Jesuit priests and two of their assistants at the UCA, sparking an international outcry. The government recognized that despite its massive and indiscriminate bombardment of popular neighborhoods, it would not be able to wipe out the FMLN militarily. The FMLN, for its part, came to realize that a popular uprising would not ensue, and, despite substantial sympathy and solidarity with the FMLN, the Salvadoran people wanted an end to the war. Meanwhile, El Salvador's wealthy elite began to push for negotiations as fears that the army would no longer be able to protect them intensified.

The changing Cold War context presented new priorities for the former patrons, the United States and the Soviet Union. Especially after the 1989 offensive, the United States could no longer justify its unconditional support for the government of El Salvador and its military. The army's human rights abuses, including the slaying of the Jesuit priests, and the army's bombing of poor neighborhoods were blatant abuses that the United States could no longer defend. In the face of mounting criticism, the Bush administration could not obtain congressional approval for renewed aid to El Salvador. The left in El Salvador no longer constituted the same geostrategic threat to the United States, especially after its invasion of Panama in 1989, and the victory of Violetta Barrios de Chamorro in Nicaragua in 1990.[76] By 1988, the Soviet Union's Mikhail Gorbachev administration had begun scaling back its support for military conflicts around the world, and, by 1990, it urged the FMLN to negotiate with the government under UN auspices. Meanwhile, support from the Soviet Union and other leftist countries was on the wane. The collapse of

Communism in many parts of the world forced leftist leaders to rethink their strategies.

During the late 1980s there also was a noticeable decrease in the extent of the human rights abuses by the government of El Salvador, which led to relatively more relaxed political participation. Much of this change was also attributed to increased US pressure. Although groups such as Amnesty International, among others, continued to document the persistence of extensive human rights abuses in the form of torture, extrajudicial killings, and imprisonment, these abuses had declined in number. State violence was responsible for the killing of approximately 100 individuals per month in the late 1980s compared to the early 1980s, when the Salvadoran state killed 12,000 to 16,000 individuals annually.[77] As a result, the FMLN began to establish front organizations that could operate in the country and refugees returned in highly organized groups.[78] The leaders of the FDR, Rubén Zamora and Guillermo Ungo, returned to the country and participated in the 1989 elections as part of the Democratic Convergence's party ticket.[79] The FDR's involvement demonstrated the election's credibility as a route to political participation. Moreover, ARENA's shift toward relatively more moderate leaders such as Alfredo Cristiani contributed to their legislative, mayoral, and presidential win in 1989. Their electoral success convinced wealthy Salvadorans that their interests could be safeguarded by means other than the military.[80]

After the offensive, the presidents of the five Central American countries, as well as the FMLN and the government of El Salvador, requested UN mediation.[81] On 4 April 1990, the two parties signed a framework agreement that delineated the stages of future negotiations and secured a commitment from both parties not to abandon the talks unilaterally. Over the next two years, the two parties negotiated the procedural, constitutional, and institutional framework that led to the final agreement.[82] On 16 January 1992, the government of El Salvador and the FMLN signed peace agreements in Chapultepec, Mexico—a conclusion that became known as the "negotiated revolution."[83] After twelve years of civil war, the stalemated conflict came to an end with no clear victors: 75,000 people had been killed, one-fourth of the population had been displaced, and the economy was in complete shambles. The accords signed at Chapultepec concluded six separate sets of agreements.[84]

The first two sets of agreements, the Geneva and the Caracas Accords of April and May 1990, concerned procedural matters. In July 1990, the two parties concluded the San José Accord on Human Rights, followed by the Mexico Accord on constitutional reforms in April 1991. Finally, in September 1991, the two parties concluded the New York Accord concerning the basic understandings that would be elaborated in the final Chapultepec Accord.

Inclusivity despite Unsatisfactory Socioeconomic Terms

In contrast to the Oslo Accords, the Salvadoran peace accords enjoyed high levels of political inclusion and societal support despite their limitations related to socio-economic change. The FMLN created a negotiation commission that included the members of its General Command: Schafik Handal (PCS), Leonel González (FPL), Francisco Jovel (PRTC), Joaquín Villalobos (ERP), and Eduardo Sancho (RN), and a representative from each of the political commissions of the Front's five organizations: Joaquín Samayoa (FPL), Ana Guadalupe Martínez (ERP), Roberto Cañas (RN), Nidia Díaz (PRTC), and Dagoberto Gutiérrez (PCS).[85] Although groups such as the Christian Democratic and Social Democrats did not sit at the negotiating table, they were part of the Inter-Party Commission that endorsed the accords and were not marginalized by the terms of the agreement. To broaden the base for the implementation of the agreements, the parties created the Comisión Nacional para la Consolidación de la Paz (National Commission for the Consolidation of Peace), which was responsible for overseeing the implementation of the agreements. The Comisión Nacional para la Consolidación de la Paz was composed of two representatives from the government, two representatives of the FMLN, one representative from each of the parties or coalitions represented in the Legislative Assembly, and representatives of the Catholic Church and the UN.

The UN's role in brokering the peace accords was unique. This was the first time in the organization's history that it was involved in resolving an internal, rather than international, conflict.[86] UN representative Alvaro de Soto spent three years mediating the final Chapultepec Agreements signed in Mexico City.[87] The UN dispatched a peace building mission to facilitate and then verify the two parties' compliance with the agreements.[88] Subsequently, this mission, the Observadores de las Naciones Unidas en El Salvador (United Nations Observer Mission in El Salvador, ONUSAL) intervened to facilitate implementation on a number of occasions regarding issues such as land transfer and the government's reluctance to dissolve security bodies like the National Guard. When ONUSAL's mandate was terminated in 1995, a small political office, the Misión de las Naciones Unidas en El Salvador (United Nations Mission in El Salvador), was left, on the Secretary-General's recommendation, to provide further assistance and follow up on implementation and outstanding obligations in cooperation with other UN agencies and donors.[89] ONUSAL is largely regarded as one of the most successful post–Cold War peace operations.

The peace accords represented a clear compromise in that the FMLN agreed to participate in a democratic system as a way to attain its economic goals, and the right agreed to the FMLN's participation in democratic elections. Similar to how the DOP legalized the PLO's status in the occupied territories, the Salvadoran peace agreements legalized the status of the FMLN as a political party and allowed for the right of return of its members. The FMLN backed away from its previous position that it would only take part in democratic elections if the government guaranteed it power sharing arrangements. In regard to the institutionalization of democratic practices, the peace accords stipulated reform of the armed forces, accountability for past human rights violations, the founding of a new police force, and restrictions on the arbitrary exercise of state power. The accords provided a detailed agenda for the dissolution of the security services, as well as the gradual demobilization of the FMLN. In addition to narrowing the military's mandate, the accords also included the dissolution of the civil defense patrols, the regulation of private security forces, the institutional separation of intelligence services from the Ministry of Defense, the suspension of forced conscription, and the restructuring of reserve services. The accords also mandated the establishment of the new civilian police force under the Ministry of the Interior, completely separate from the armed forces chain of command, and they established an ad hoc commission to address human rights violations. This body would be responsible for investigating the human rights records of the officer corps of the armed forces and making necessary recommendations—including, if necessary, the dismissal of officers. The accords reaffirmed the commitment of both the FMLN and the government to the existing Truth Commission.[90] The peace accords also reformed the constitution in relation to the selection of the Supreme Court magistrates, and established a new Supreme Electoral Tribunal to supervise voter registration and election. The underlying goal here was to break the traditional dominance of the ruling party over the judicial system.

Although the peace accords clearly institutionalized the democratic rules of the game, the socioeconomic aspects of the agreements were far less concrete. Provisions that addressed socioeconomic conditions in the country did little to alter the structural causes of this inequality. The agreement's agenda of socioeconomic reform was limited to land transfer to ex-combatants and civilian supporters of the FMLN, the creation of channels for the flow of external aid to communities in the former conflict zones, and the drafting of a National Reconstruction Plan (NRP).[91] Two principal reasons accounted for the focus on political, as opposed to economic, goals: the FMLN made an explicit decision to pursue political goals that would make democratic politics possible, and more importantly, the government refused to discuss any modification of its economic policy.[92]

Per the peace accords, land redistribution was limited to some land transfer that required ex-combatants to purchase the land, as well as landlord agreement. The Programa de Transferencia de Tierras (Land Transfer Program, PTT) involved 10 percent of El Salvador's rural land, and offered "land for arms," and help with the reintegration of ex-combatants of the FMLN and Salvadoran military and civilian supporters of the FMLN known as *tenedores* (landholders), most of whom had farmed land in the conflict zones throughout the war.[93] Most land transfers would take place in the ex-conflict zones, and therefore would not threaten the political and economic base of ARENA in the coffee areas. The land to be transferred through the PTT included properties belonging to the state, properties exceeding the 1983 constitutional limit of 245 hectares,[94] and private properties in the conflict zones that were voluntarily offered for sale by their owners. Transactions would be through a Land Bank for a thirty-year repayment period, with a four-year grace period, and an interest rate of 6 percent. Considerable ambiguity existed regarding the amount of land to be transferred and to whom.

By 1992, the FMLN halted the third of five phases of demobilization to protest the amount and quantity of land that was received, and the government's lack of political will to proceed.[95] In October 1992, the UN directly intervened and presented the terms to both parties to ensure the implementation of the PTT, effectively saving the peace process from the most serious impasse it had confronted to that date. The FMLN managed to expand the target areas that would be addressed in the NRP, and by 2000, 36,000 individuals had received land through the PTT.

The peace accords did address some socioeconomic issues by including provisions related to housing, microenterprise assistance to small business and agriculture, poverty alleviation programs to ex-combatants, as well as foreign donor funded development programs to communities. But, overall, the accords failed to address several key economic concerns, such as agrarian reform legislation, wage increases, and union organizing.[96] A number of issues such as working conditions pertaining to wages, labor laws, and regulations, as well as the social impact of structural adjustment policies, were left to the Foro para la Concertacíon Económica y Social (Forum for Economic and Social Negotiation).[97] As critics pointed out, the lack of prioritization of socioeconomic issues was exacerbated by the macroeconomic stabilization policies pursued by Bretton Woods institutions, and the conflicting goals of peace implementation and IMF and World Bank structural adjustment policies.[98] These initial omissions, however, were especially significant given that socioeconomic inequalities had been key underlying factors contributing to El Salvador's troubled history.

Despite these limitations in the socioeconomic realm, the Salvadoran conflict to peace transition was considered one of the most successful examples in the post–Cold War era. In terms of institutional development, the military was removed from politics, resulting in a realignment of their relationship with landlords, and security institutions were restructured and put under civilian control.[99] Electoral laws for fair competitive elections were established, resulting in peaceful transitions of power to the FMLN.

The Postpeace Accord Era and the Reconstitution of the Political Arena

The conflict to peace transition in El Salvador did not create the types of disjunctures that emerged in the Palestinian transition.[100] The more inclusive transition allowed many of the NGOs affiliated with political organizations to maintain contact with and incorporate their grassroots bases in the transition process. The transition afforded the various associations and NGOs more or less the same resources and opportunities. Although USAID initially attempted to exclude the FMLN-affiliated opposition NGOs from the NRP, other donors, especially Canadian donors and European private aid agencies, supported the opposition NGOs. Even when groups such as the ERP and the RN left the FMLN in 1994, their members remained with the FMLN. The coherence of the professionalization process of most NGOs also did not lead to the marginalization of grassroots constituencies as it did in the Palestinian case, and although some social movement sectors experienced some demobilization, grassroots constituencies remained intact as political forces that could continue to mobilize for the expansion of citizens' rights. The Salvadoran case led to electoral institutional development that allowed for genuine competitive elections and, in turn, equitable institutional access to the various political groups, NGOs, and grassroots constituencies.

This is not to say that disputes did not exist between the different political organizations of the FMLN. Despite these differences, however, there was no forced exclusion and the international donor community did not work to reinforce and mediate this exclusion. The smaller organizations, namely the RN and ERP, objected to the decision-making process of the FMLN that advantaged the larger political organizations. They also pushed for the organization to abandon Marxism-Leninism and adopt a social-democratic platform. Unable to reach a compromise, the two parties left the FMLN in 1994 and 1995, respectively. Subsequently, the PCS, the FPL, and the PRTC dissolved and formed the FMLN as an integrated political party.[101] Despite these differences and the reconstitution of the FMLN, no parties were outright excluded from the emergent political landscape or penalized by Western foreign donors.

Initially, ARENA tried to undermine FMLN-affiliated NGOs by enacting a strict NGO law, but international donors opposed it and forced the government to draft a more liberal NGO law. Donors threatened to leave the country en masse if the government did not back down.[102] The government, however, did not back down from its request that all NGOs had to register with the Ministry of Interior. This demand outraged the

NGO community given the Interior Ministry's reprehensible association with death squads. By 2014, although little had been done to reform this law, there was satisfaction with the government's discretion to deny or delay registration.[103] Very importantly, unprecedented levels of insecurity and social violence became pervasive defining features of postwar El Salvador.[104] As I will explain in chapter 7, the more inclusive context, however, allowed for cooperative approaches to stemming this problem.

The Professionalization of Politics in El Salvador

NGO professionalization and the reconstitution of the NGO sector led to the emergence of two markedly different civil society tendencies. The first tendency involved the mass-based organizations that were affiliated with the FMLN; the NGOs of this tendency varied in the extent to which they had severed their ties with the former FMLN political organizations. The second tendency included nongrassroots organizations that were not affiliated with political parties. Because these organizations did not have grassroots constituencies, Western donors were less willing to fund them. Many of the new professionalized NGOs with mass-based constituencies still focused on production-related or economic-development-related activities. Many foreign donors would only support NGOs that maintained grassroots bases; therefore, many of these NGOs professionalized, incorporating their grassroots constituencies in the process. Moreover, the institutional setting in relation to the legislative and local government provided NGOs, and civil society more specifically, with more institutional openings to interact with the state. Since the mid-1980s, but especially after the signing of the peace accords, the number of officially registered, professionalized NGOs in El Salvador had increased considerably. Some estimates indicate that this number increased from twenty registered NGOs in 1979, to thirty in 1983,[105] and over 1,300 in 1998.[106] According to government estimates, by January 2014 there were 2,944 registered organizations in the country.[107]

Although there was an increase in funding to Salvadoran NGOs in this initial period after the accords, these amounts were still relatively low compared to other developing contexts. The majority of funding to NGOs came from European private aid agencies. Most of these NGOs still worked in "production-related" areas, and were relatively small in size, with twenty-seven staff members on average. In general, multilateral donors only worked with production-oriented NGOs—66 percent had a relationship with United Nations Development Program (UNDP), 60 percent with USAID, and 46 percent with the Inter-American Development Bank.

Following the end of the war, FMLN-affiliated NGOs had to transition from being "opposition NGOs" to "development NGOs"—a transition that was not always easy.[108] Western donors to El Salvador were more interested in production-related programs, or economic development-related programs, as opposed to more political objectives such as the promotion of certain leaders in the NGO sector as in the Palestinian case. Moreover, in addition to development or production-related activities, 75 percent of these NGOs worked in the area of *incidencia política* (political advocacy) at the municipal level, and not the national level.[109] Although political advocacy projects were also popular with Palestinian NGOs, the institutional limitations, especially at the level of local government, severely undermined the full potential of this work.

By the early 1990s, although there was a decline in mass movement activity, there was substantial variation among the different sectors.[110] In general, some popular movement activists were disillusioned after the signing of the peace accords, especially since the accords did not improve socioeconomic conditions for the majority of El Salvador's poor. Moreover, the unified front of the opposition also began to break down. Many popular movement organizations were simply incapable of making a transition to accommodate the new political situation, particularly because of their lack of technical capacity and experience in implementing development projects.[111] By the early 2000s, however, various social movements had regrouped to fight the neoliberal policies gripping El Salvador, with a particular focus on health care privatization.[112]

Legislative Assembly and Local Government Development and the Creation of Institutional Openings

From the onset, the Salvadoran electoral system was not designed to exclude any parties from the election process. The FMLN entered elections as a unified party. Since it had entered the formal political arena, its affiliated groups developed access to the Legislative Assembly and the municipal councils. Even after the RN and ERP broke away from the FLMN in 1994, they still supported the peace accords and fully participated in the elections. Similarly, all parties involved—namely, Western donors, the FMLN, and the government—pushed for the development of local government, though perhaps motivated by different goals.

Few will dispute the institutionalization of a genuinely competitive electoral system in postwar El Salvador. Throughout El Salvador's troubled history, the military party, PRUD, or its clone, the Partido de Concertación Nacional (National Conciliation Party) prevailed in every election up until the 1980s, often through corruption and distortion of the election results. With US backing, the Christian Democratic candidate, José Napoleón Duarte, won the 1984 presidential elections, and the party attained a majority during the 1985 Constituent Assembly elections.[113] El Salvador's leftist opposition parties, however, did not participate in elections until the late 1980s. The FMLN formally competed as a political party only in the postwar elections, establishing itself early on as a serious political electoral contender in all presidential, legislative, and local elections.[114]

Competition and smooth turnover became defining features of El Salvador's elections. Indeed, the degree of political competition and the smooth shift of power from ARENA to the FMLN in presidential and legislative elections reflect the vigor of political life in the country as well as the possibilities for democratic development in inclusive contexts. After two decades of ARENA presidential victories, the FMLN won both the 2009[115] and 2014 presidential elections, marking the first presidential turnovers of power to the opposition.[116] In the 2009 presidential election, Mauricio Funes, a popular television commentator who was not a former combatant or left-wing activist, and his vice presidential running mate, Sánchez Cerén (Commandante Leonel González of the FPL), a former FMLN leader, won, becoming the first winning left-of-center presidential ticket in El Salvador's history. Sánchez Cerén subsequently won the 2014 presidential election. Similarly, in the period between 1992 and 2001, the FMLN established itself as the second largest group in the legislature, and in both the 2003 and 2009 elections, the FMLN won the majority of legislative seats.[117] The new wave of social movement activity that emerged in the late 1990s and early 2000s, and the FMLN's continued work with the popular sectors, helped it develop its electoral base.[118] Moreover, after 1997, it established itself as the second largest political force in terms of municipal elections, steadily increasing its share of municipalities in more recent years. Although in the January 2009 local elections, the FMLN lost the capital of San Salvador to ARENA, it had won in ninety municipal governments and gained thirty-five legislative seats, its largest gains in any previous elections. Eighty-four deputies, elected for three-year terms, make up the unicameral Legislative Assembly. In the first postwar election of 1994, sixty-four candidates were elected through departmental (district) lists and twenty through national lists. Starting in 2006, all candidates were elected through departmental lists,[119] and beginning in 2012, the electoral law eliminated closed lists and introduced open lists in which one could vote for a party list, one or more candidates in a single list, or one nonparty candidate. The inclusivity of the political settlement in El Salvador also facilitated the strengthening of the party system.

In El Salvador, all parties involved supported the development of local government.[120] At this level of government, especially in municipalities governed by the FLMN, important initiatives were implemented, successfully narrowing the gap between the electorate and the government.[121] USAID and the right-wing groups in El Salvador initially pushed for the strengthening of local government so as to facilitate decentralization and lessen the burdens of the state. The promotion of local government by USAID was not new. In 1986, USAID, with the support of the Duarte regime, established the Municipios en Acción (Municipalities in Action, MEA) initiative to finance infrastructure projects through local government rather than government ministries. MEA, however, became tainted and shared a historical connection with the counterinsurgency efforts of the Comision Nacional de Restauracíon de Areas (National Commission for the Restoration of Areas). Following the end of the war, the FMLN negotiated with USAID and the Secretaría de la Reconstrucción Naciónal (National Reconstruction Secretariat), to ensure the participation of the opposition in local government. The negotiations resulted in two mechanisms to ensure participation of the local opposition: expanded municipal assemblies, which include local NGOs; and municipal reconstruction committees intended to enable opposition input in priorities.[122] Local mayors and councils remained in charge of local funding and MEA programs were the principal avenue for local development.[123] Both European donors and the FMLN became strong proponents of local government initiatives, especially after the FMLN prevailed at this level of government in the 1997 elections.

The institutionalization of these sites of power—the national legislature and local government—took place in a highly coherent fashion, fully incorporating the former opposition into this process. Postwar aid was not as politicized in El Salvador as in the Palestinian territories, and did not have the same marginalizing impact. In fact, Western donors played an important role in pushing for the full incorporation of the FMLN and opposition groups at the local government level. They also played an important role in promoting a liberal NGO law. In turn, civil society groups, including formerly affiliated opposition civil society groups, attained greater access to the state. Because of the more inclusive political settlement, the process of state institutionalization, mediated by foreign funded programs, resulted in the development and institutionalization of a more "articulated space" between the state and civil society, allowing for the more effective participation of civil society.

Conclusion

Much of the extant literature that examines the impact of donor assistance on civil society treats donor assistance as the main explanatory factor driving outcomes. Departing from this approach, this chapter has taken a step back and highlighted how the levels of inclusivity of the respective political settlements shaped institutional access and the nature of competitive elections in these two cases, and contributed, in turn, to future patterns of civil society organization. Foreign donor assistance mediated these outcomes, but by no means did it solely determine them. In both cases, the post-peace accord period ushered in opportunities for the reconstitution of political and affiliated organizations, enabling many to become more autonomous from their parent political organizations; this would lay the groundwork for a future civil society. In the Palestinian territories, however, not all organizations had the same opportunities—not only in terms of resources, but also in terms of continued access to former constituencies and opportunities to engage the state. These differences ultimately produced significant variation in citizen participation. How donor funding to the Palestinian territories and to El Salvador differed and how it shaped these divergent outcomes is the subject of the next chapter.

4

Foreign Donor Assistance and the Political Economy
of Settlement Outcomes

This chapter comparatively examines funding patterns to the Palestinian territories and El Salvador,[1] specifically illustrating how these
patterns were often shaped by the prevailing political settlement in each
case. It begins with a brief comparative discussion of donor funding to
the Palestinian territories and El Salvador before the respective conflict-
to-peace transitions and then addresses the key changes that took place
after the start of the transitions, focusing on funding patterns after 1991.
Given the geostrategic interests of many state-sponsored donors and
their goal of promoting the Oslo Accords, the WBGS received much
more assistance than its middle-income status would have suggested.[2]
Ultimately, the Palestinian territories became one of the world's highest per capita recipients of foreign aid. Moreover, the composition of
funding to the Palestinian territories prioritized programs related to
democracy and civil society, in contrast to program priorities in El
Salvador, which focused on economic development and local government. The chapter then turns to the types of channels and coordination
mechanisms put in place in both contexts. It illustrates how the higher
amounts of funding because of the geostrategic importance of the
Palestinian case during this period led to more complex channels
and coordinating mechanisms, and greater opportunity to promote
included groups. The next section discusses changes in sectoral priorities, and it pays particular attention to funding to civil society
development and democracy promotion, and comparative funding
patterns from USAID to the two cases in the area of Democracy and
Governance. The more detailed discussion of USAID funding to the
two cases illustrates how state-sponsored funding intervened to shape
political outcomes, conditioned by the political settlement. The chapter
concludes with comparative examination of funding to NGOs, local
government, and the women's sectors.

My analysis challenges a number of existing works that treat foreign aid, and democracy promotion assistance in particular,[3] as a key independent variable.[4] Alone, foreign aid could not determine outcomes, but, rather, it heightened the impact related to the degree of exclusion and inclusion.[5] This was facilitated by the consensus between dominant political groups and the pervading "post–Cold War liberal order"; this consensus ensured that an alliance between dominant political groups and Western donors could marginalize groups that did not align with similar objectives.[6] Very importantly, this is not to say that state or donor agency policy, or personnel working in these institutions do not matter, but, rather, that the pervading political settlement shaped the broader parameters of these institutions' interaction with each context. This discussion is less relevant to Arab donors because, for the most part, they provided relief and budget support to the PA, including funding to infrastructural development, and seldom addressed democracy promotion in particular. In the post–Cold War era, Western donors have had a monopoly over democracy promotion (as opposed to Arab donors who have not concerned themselves with this programmatic area), and a post–Cold War liberal consensus ensured an understanding of what democratic outcomes should look like.

Although this book focuses on democracy assistance, I also examine more general aggregates of donor assistance to each case. In the post–Cold War period, donor objectives shifted from a sole focus on socioeconomic development to one that addressed development and democracy as compatible, as well as desirable, objectives. Hence, donor agencies introduced democracy assistance. The linking of aid to political reforms and democratization outcomes became more acceptable.[7] Democracy aid was a low-budget way to boost the image of foreign aid,[8] as well as the soft power of the donor. Since the late 1980s, democracy aid evolved from a specialized niche into a well-institutionalized donor program area that has been introduced to nearly every country in the world.[9] Although the two program areas of development and democracy assistance became demarcated, the division between these two program areas is not always clear-cut. In many instances, democracy assistance programs may incorporate a development or socioeconomic dimension and vice versa. Similarly, CSOs that are able to attract assistance for citizen empowerment may also be well positioned to attract development assistance. Hence funding to civil society cannot be easily typologized as development or democracy related. For example, project areas related to citizen empowerment often include both development and democracy related components.

Shifting Geostrategic Significance and Presettlement Foreign Donor Assistance

During the earlier periods of their conflicts, much of the assistance received in the two cases was oriented toward relief, becoming increasingly political in the 1980s, especially in the Salvadoran case. In the Palestinian territories, Arab states, and regional and Arab and Islamic organizations, played an important role in promoting the PLO and its affiliated organizations. The PLO gave some funding to the various political organizations, and the leftist political organizations received additional funding from the former Soviet Union and its allies. After the Madrid peace conference in 1991 and the influx of Western donor assistance, Western state-sponsored donors became the main donors to the WBGS, supplanting the Arab countries and regional organizations that had previously been the primary donors.[10] The change in the profile of donors meant less funding directly to the PLO and its affiliated groups, and greater funding to the newly established PA and greater involvement of state-sponsored donor agencies in the occupied territories. It also meant an increase in the polarization of aid as groups that supported, or did not strongly oppose the Oslo Accords, and were in a position to promote a "post–Cold War liberal order" became the primary recipients of aid. In El Salvador, donor aid was also highly polarizing during the conflict. The political polarization among donors, however, which was shaped by Cold War politics, mirrored the same polarization in society and ensured that all groups and organizations would receive funding and support and hence would remain important political players. USAID funded the economic elite and the right-wing Salvadoran government, and actively marginalized the Salvadoran opposition, which was supported financially by solidarity groups and European aid agencies. After the start of the conflict-to-peace transition, the political settlement led to less polarized aid and more equitable distribution among the different groups.

Foreign Donor Assistance to the Palestinian Territories
in the Presettlement Period

Foreign donor assistance to the Palestinian territories has a long complex history, which can be traced back to 1948, following *al-Nakbah*.[11] During its earlier stages, the assistance was predominately relief in nature, shifting to more development assistance after the 1967 war, and becoming expressly much more political, and involving more Western state-sponsored donors after the start of the Madrid peace conference. The introduction of state-sponsored funding often required Israeli approval, even when the funding was from some Arab counterparts such as Jordan. Prior to the Madrid Peace Conference, foreign aid to the WBGS was primarily from Arab countries and targeted relief and development. After 1991, Western donors also become major players, and the key objective of the assistance was to promote the peace process with Israel. I identify four different phases of foreign donor activity to the Palestinian territories. Between 1948 and 1967, funding to the Palestinian territories was relief-oriented in nature, predominately from United Nations Relief Works Agency (UNRWA), and a number of Western relief organizations. Following the 1967 war and to the early 1980s, funding to the Palestinian territories was predominately from other Arab countries and regional organizations, and from the PLO. In 1975, the United States also began a program of development assistance to the WBGS. The third phase of funding to the Palestinian territories began in the early 1980s, especially after the 1982 massacres of Sabra and Shatilla, and continued until the late 1980s. During this period, Palestinians and other Arabs in the diaspora established various charity organizations to funnel funding to the WBGS, as well as to Palestinian refugees living in other parts of the world. Moreover, after the start of the Intifada in 1987, there was an increase in Western solidarity funding, as well as UN multilateral funding. The fourth phase of foreign donor activity began after the start of the Madrid peace process, and heightened after the signing of the Oslo Accords in 1993. During this period, foreign donors introduced official bilateral funding to Palestine.

Following the 1948 war, but especially after the 1967 war, Arab countries and the Arab League became the main donors to the Palestinian territories. After 1974, a 3 to 6 percent income tax was imposed on

Palestinians residing and working in the various Gulf countries; this was then given to the PLO's Palestinian National Fund.[12] A substantial portion of this funding was then diverted to the WBGS. A number of Arab and Islamic regional organizations also began sending funding to the occupied territories.[13]

Western countries, especially the United States, introduced more political aid during the second phase. In the aftermath of the October 1973 war, the US introduced a US$100 million Middle East Special Requirements Fund "whose objective was to identify 'targets of opportunity' which would encourage a resolution to the Middle East conflict" and promote an Arab-Israeli rapprochement.[14] In 1975, USAID allocated 1 percent of the total fund, US$1 million, to the WBGS. An unprecedented feature of the program was its bilateral American-Arab character.[15] Although this assistance was supposed to remain independent of Israeli government control, ultimately the Israeli government had to approve all projects. The US assistance program to the WBGS required that the private volunteer organizations (PVOs) submit their projects to the Israeli Ministry of Labor and Social Affairs, which were then channeled to the Office of the Coordinator of the Occupied Territories in the Ministry of Defense, which had the final say on project implementation.[16] The funds were monitored by the Department of State, and channeled through one Palestinian organization and the five American PVOs that were active in the occupied territories. The American PVOs, some dating back to 1948, were: the American Near East Refugee Aid, American Mideast Education and Training Services, Catholic Relief Services, Save the Children Federation, and the Cooperative Development Program.[17]

In 1978, the Arab League created the "Jordanian-Palestinian Joint Committee for the Support of the Steadfastness of the Palestinian People in the Occupied Homeland."[18] The purpose of this fund was to alleviate the daily hardship of Palestinians by providing them with better access to basic services such as water and electricity; to build education, health, and social service institutions; to build houses; to support local municipalities; and to provide economic support to disadvantaged families. This fund disbursed between US$417 million to US$463 million to the occupied territories during this period.

Remittances from Palestinians in the diaspora also became more readily available, as did donations from charity foundations, especially after the 1982 Sabra and Shatilla massacres in Lebanon. In 1983, a group of wealthy Palestinians founded the Welfare Association, or what came to be known as Al-Ta'awun[19]—one of the most notable organizations founded during this period. Other charity organizations established during this period were the Jerusalem Fund and the United Palestine Appeal in the United States, the Holy Land Foundation for Relief and Development, and Medical Aid for Palestine in Canada and the United Kingdom.

In 1983, US Secretary of State George Schulz announced a "reinvigorated" assistance program for the WBGS, dubbed the "quality of life initiative." As with previous USAID initiatives, all programs had to be approved by Israeli authorities. As official USAID policy shifted toward longer-term economic development, as opposed to mere welfare projects, tensions heightened between American PVOs and the Israeli government. Despite these tensions, US assistance to the occupied territories increased in the 1980s from US$6.5 million in 1983 to US$22 million in 1989.[20]

In 1986, King Hussein of Jordan announced a five-year development plan for the occupied territories; the objective of the plan was to provide and improve the quality of economic and social services to the residents of the WBGS. Like the USAID funded projects, Israel would also have to approve all projects that would receive funding under this plan. Jordan's five-year development plan was brought to a halt in July 1988; eight months after the start of the Intifada, King Hussein severed Jordan's ties to the occupied territories, which also meant an end to the development plan.

With the onset of the Intifada in 1987, there was a substantial increase in funding from Palestinian individuals and groups in the diaspora, as well as from solidarity organizations, many of them European in origin. In 1986, the UNDP also began operations in the WBGS. The character of funding to the WBGS was dramatically altered after 1989. Funding associated with the Baghdad Summit was discontinued.[21] Then, following the PLO's stance in support of Saddam Hussein's 1991 invasion of Kuwait, both Kuwait and Saudi Arabia discontinued their funding to the PLO, US$24 million and US$72 million, respectively.[22] This halting of funds dealt a debilitating blow to the PLO, seriously putting into question whether or not it could continue to exist. Subsequently, as the

Madrid peace process got under way, funding from Western donors, especially from state-sponsored organizations, became more available to the Palestinian territories. In 1992, Western donors disbursed US$173.9 million to the WBGS; this amount increased to US$262.8 million by 1993.[23] These changes meant greater involvement by Western state-sponsored donors.

Foreign Donor Assistance to El Salvador in the Presettlement Period

Aid patterns to El Salvador during the Cold War reflected its geostrategic significance to different parties. More exactly, the prevailing political settlement then also shaped donor involvement, which mirrored the Cold War polarized domestic politics of the country. Throughout the civil war, most, if not all, political groups and their affiliated bodies had access to foreign donor funding: USAID supported more right-wing elements, as well as the business class in El Salvador, while solidarity groups and European private aid agencies supported more left-wing elements. El Salvador was the third largest recipient of foreign aid from USAID following Egypt and Israel.[24] This distinction between USAID and solidarity and European private donors decreased in the latter part of the 1990s following USAID's change in policies and personnel in San Salvador, which resulted in a greater willingness to support all sectors of Salvadoran society.

Between 1970 and 1979, El Salvador received approximately US$1.172 billion in Official Development Assistance (ODA),[25] and US$6.398 billion from 1980 to 1990,[26] in addition to military assistance. US assistance of approximately $4.66 billion between 1980 and 1989[27] represented the bulk of this assistance, representing 73 percent of total funding to the country during this period. During El Salvador's civil war, US assistance to El Salvador played a critical role in sustaining the Salvadoran government, and in promoting right-wing groups and organizations.

During the 1980s, the United States also funneled funding through local municipalities and a number of more right wing-oriented, Salvadoran NGOs.[28] In 1986, the US initiated the MEA program, whose goal was to pacify rural areas and incorporate displaced persons into rural civic action programs coordinated by the army.[29] Meanwhile, USAID also funded organizations like Fundación Salvadoreña para el Desarrollo

Económico y Social (Salvadoran Foundation for Economic and Social Development, FUSADES). FUSADES was created by a group of Salvadoran businessmen in 1983,[30] quickly becoming one of the most influential right-wing think tanks in El Salvador. During the 1980s, FUSADES received US$150 million over a ten-year period.[31] The foundation promoted nontraditional exports and investment, and became recognized as the main drafter of the structural adjustment plan that served as the basis for the ARENA's economic program in 1989.[32] The organization, along with USAID, also helped create a number of right-wing organizations.[33] As Michael Foley explained:

> the very configuration of the NGOs spun off by FUSADES, under the tutelage of USAID, bespeaks a concept of civil society in which economic elites play the leading role . . . the NGOs created under USAID auspices draw on business elites almost exclusively for their board members and executive personnel. Not only do these arrangements make use of considerable talent and influence of these individuals, but they also reinforce their social and political position . . . Board members give elites access to politicians and US officials, as well as control over considerable sums of money with which USAID has chosen to endow the new institutions.[34]

One group of its minifoundations became known as Project Fortas; the goal of these minifoundations was to carry out social services in the rural areas. A local coffee baron headed each foundation, with the participation of a few wealthy property owners or business people in the area. With the help of USAID, right-wing groups established other organizations such as the Industrial Foundation for Prevention of Occupational Hazard, Habitat Foundation, and the Business Foundation for Educational Development. Such initiatives helped maintain the status quo and strengthened old alliances between USAID and El Salvador's oligarchy.

The solidarity groups and European aid agencies that channeled funds to opposition groups began to organize their aid more systematically as the conflict persisted. In the early 1980s, a small group of churches and older NGOs came together to form an ecumenical consortium called Díaconia to manage relief and support for refugees.[35] The Dutch cofinancing agencies—Bilance, Humanistisch Instituut voor Ontwikkelingssamenwerking (International Humanist Institute for Co-operation with Developing Countries, HIVOS), Interkerkelijke Organisatie voor Ontwikkelingssamenwerking (Dutch Interchurch Organization for Development Co-operation- ICCO), and NOVIB were the main funders of Díaconia throughout the war.[36] By 1985, because of increased levels of foreign donor assistance, the FMLN had founded a number of mass-based organizations that could also carry out the same functions as Díaconia. The new organizations were often community-based and dedicated to providing services—developmental, educational, and health-related—to refugees. According to Foley, these NGOs served as local counterparts to international organizations, often European in origin.[37] They played a critical role in channeling material goods and funds to these communities. Among the donors who funded these NGOs were: solidarity organizations in the United States and Canada; governments including Canada, the Netherlands, Belgium, and the United Kingdom, and NGOs like Díakonia (Sweden), and Médecins Sans Frontières (Doctors Without Borders).[38] In particular, the FPL was successful in acquiring funding through solidarity networks in the United States, as well as in Europe. Although the ERP was more successful in raising funds in Europe compared to the United States, it still was not as successful as the FPL.[39]

Funding patterns to the various parties in El Salvador underscored the inherently political nature of foreign donor assistance. Although foreign donors were selective about which parties they would fund, the polarization among donors, which also mirrored the same polarization in society, ensured that all groups and organizations received funding and support and would remain important players in the political landscape.

Foreign Donor Assistance to the Palestinian and El Salvador in the Immediate Postsettlement Period

In general, the postwar foreign donor involvement in El Salvador was a much smaller operation than that in the Palestinian territories, involving less complex coordinating mechanisms, and less funding. The presence of donor agencies, as well as field staff in the Palestinian territories, was far more extensive than in El Salvador. The difference in the scope of operations illustrated foreign donors' more significant geostrategic considerations for the Palestinian territories.

TABLE 4.1. Donor Assistance to the Palestinian Territories and El Salvador from 1992 to 2001

	Palestine	El Salvador
Disbursements($)[a]	$6.37 billion	$3.4 billion
Disbursements per capita ($)	$1,820[c]	$523[d]
Commitments to government and civil society[b]	$471.05 million	$463.52 million
Commitments to strengthening civil society	$91.34 million	$54.10 million

[a]All disbursements in constant prices 2006 USD (OECD data: Development Assistance Committee-DAC2a, ODA Disbursements).
[b]All commitments constant prices 2005 USD (OECD data: Creditor Reporting System).
[c]Based on a population of 3.5 million.
[d]Based on a population of 6.5 million.

Foreign donor commitments and allocations to the Palestinian territories were among the highest in the world in per capita terms. This is especially significant given that Palestine did and does not qualify as a lower income country, and therefore was not eligible for development funding from states like the Netherlands, Norway, Sweden, and Switzerland, which reserve their development funding for lower income countries. Nonetheless, in each of these states, special provisions were made to allow funding to the WBGS.[40] Disbursements to the WBGS had reached US$6.37 billion by 2001, for the period between 1992 and 2001 (see table 4.1). Disbursements to El Salvador, on the other hand, for the period between 1992 and 2001 were US$3.4 billion.[41] In per capita terms, the WBGS received US$1,820 per capita (based on a total population of 3.5 million) for this period, compared to El Salvador, which received US$523 per capita (based on a total population of 6.5 million) for this same period. Of these total disbursements, loans represented over 40 percent of allocations to El Salvador between 1992 and 2001.[42] Conversely, in the Palestinian case, loans represented approximately 3 percent of total aid for the same period.[43] The donor funding profile, both in terms of amounts and political exception, underscored the geostrategic significance of the Palestinian case and the need to promote the prevailing political settlement and a "post–Cold War liberal order."

In many of my interviews in the WBGS, directors of donor agencies or program officers acknowledged the greater geostrategic importance of the Middle East as compared to Latin America after the end of the

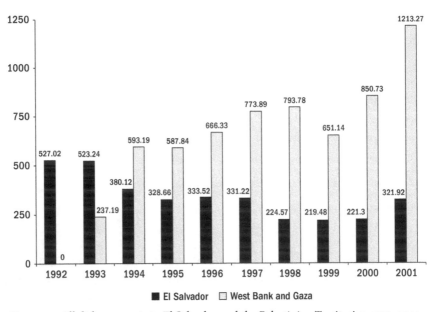

Figure 4.1. All disbursements to El Salvador and the Palestinian Territories, 1992–2001 (in USD million)
Source: OECD data, DAC (constant 2006 USD)

Cold War. This was especially the case for USAID and one of the German foundations that perceived the promotion of the peace accords and the development of the WBGS as necessary for Israel's stability.[44] This also was the case for some European donors who considered the Middle East as part of "their backyard," and that a more stable Middle East meant fewer immigrants and refugee asylum seekers to their own countries.[45] The discrepancy between what the EU gave to the occupied territories in contrast to El Salvador reflected this point. With the end of the Cold War, El Salvador was no longer as geostrategically important for many donors, especially the United States. Moreover, because of the end of the conflict to peace transition, many foreign donors decreased their funding to El Salvador, and many predicted funding would continue to decrease.[46]

The provision of funding to the Palestinian territories by foreign donors was contingent on some level of support for the peace accords, or, more precisely, non-opposition. Some representatives from the foreign donor agencies explained that although they did not inquire about the political or ideological positions of their recipients, they did expect them to share their values, especially in terms of democracy and human rights, including women's rights.[47] This point aligns with my argument about donors requiring their recipients to be in a position to promote the "post–Cold War liberal order." Other donors pointed out that although there was no written policy regarding recipients having to support the Oslo Accords, those who opposed the Oslo Accords, especially Islamists, did not approach them for funding.[48] A number of the representatives further explained that funding to Palestine itself was very political, since it was a middle income country and did not qualify for the amounts of assistance it received.[49]

Foreign Donor Assistance to the Palestinian Territories in the Immediate Postsettlement Period and the Promotion of the Oslo Accords

Immediately following the signing of the Oslo peace accords in 1993, representatives from over forty-three countries met in October of that year in Washington, DC, to pledge support to the WBGS. They pledged US$2.49 billion for the period from 1994 to 1996, of which US$2.3 billion was committed to actual programs and projects in the WBGS. By 2001, the amount of total pledges to the WBGS had increased to US$6.9 billion, of which US$5.16 billion was committed to programs and projects for the period between 1993 and 2001.[50] Approximately 23.9 percent of this total amount was from multilateral organizations.[51] Of total commitments between 1993 and 2001, US$817.9 million (15.8 percent) were in the form of loans.[52] By 2001, donors had disbursed US$459.93 million in loans, with the largest contributors being the World Bank and the European Investment Bank (EIB); disbursing 45 percent and 22.2 percent respectively of the total loan amount. By June 2001, donors had disbursed US$3.4 billion, or 65 percent of total commitments. This contrasted with El Salvador, which received a far higher percentage in loans.

From the onset, both the United States and the EU vied for greater influence in the Israeli-Palestinian peace process and the related peace-building initiatives. During the first Consultative Group (CG)[53] meeting in 1993, the European Union (EU)—including the EIB and other EU member bilateral donors—was clearly the largest contributor to the donor effort to Palestine. The total EU and EIB contribution amounted to 19.8 percent of total commitments (excluding EU states' bilateral contributions). The United States was the second largest contributor, committing the equivalent of 10 percent of the total aid effort, followed by Japan, Norway, and the Netherlands, contributing 9 percent, 6 percent, and 4.9 percent, respectively, to the total aid effort. During this period, the EU repeatedly demanded or required that its financial contribution to peacebuilding efforts be matched in terms of their political and diplomatic clout and ability to influence the peace process, often causing friction between the EU and the United States.

Despite some of the political differences and competition between the EU and the US, the objective of their funding was to promote the post-Oslo political order. At the civil society level, these two parties funded the same types of civil society groups—large, nonopposition professionalized NGOs that were in a position to promote the "post-Cold War liberal order." In this case, "competition" and increasing amounts of funding further exacerbated the tension between the Opposition and the Liberal Moderate groups and affiliates. For example, between 1996 and 1999, both the EU, through its MEDA Democracy Program, and USAID, through its Democracy and Governance Program, predominately supported Liberal Moderate tendency–affiliated large NGOs. Between 1994 and 2000, USAID provided US$27 million to eight Palestinian NGOs, in addition to US$9 million for the strengthening of the Palestinian Legislative Council. Similarly, between 1996 and 1999, the EU provided the bulk of its funding to Liberal Moderate, nonopposition NGOs, in addition to some assistance to media and university research centers. In 1999, of the total 2.02 million euro budget of the MEDA Democracy program, the EU allocated 657,455 euros to the program secretariat at Birzeit University's Institute of Law, and disbursed the remaining amount to five Liberal Moderate tendency–affiliated professionalized human rights organizations.[54]

By 2001, the configuration of major donors had slightly changed: underscoring its political influence, the US had become the single largest donor to the WBGS, with commitments totaling US$987 million (19 percent of total commitments) for the period between 1994 and 2001.[55] In sum, the US contributions of aid to the occupied territories had increased 287 fold, from US$1 million in 1975 to US$287.9 million in 2001. By 2001, although the EU and EIB were still major contributors (with commitments totaling US$740.9 million, 14.34 percent of total commitments, excluding bilateral contributions), its contributions were more closely matched by the United States. The United States' commitments were followed by the contributions of: Japan, US$509.9 million (9.9 percent of total commitments); Germany, US$381 million (7.4 percent of total commitments); the World Bank, US$319.6 million (6.2 percent); Norway, US$242.5 million (4.7 percent of total commitments); and Saudi Arabia, Spain, and Italy. As the United States took a more prominent role in the aid effort, the contributions of Norway and Netherlands decreased substantially. Arab countries, most notably Saudi Arabia, also increased their commitments. In general, however, although the Arab contribution was smaller in dollar terms, in most instances the commitments represented a higher percent of GDP in comparison to their Western counterparts.[56]

With the outbreak of Al-Aqsa Intifada in October 2000, official bilateral assistance to the occupied territories decreased drastically, from US$711 million in 2000 to US$408 million in 2001.[57] Donors countered this decrease in official bilateral assistance by increasing emergency funding to accommodate the deteriorating political situation. Despite this shift, the objective was to continue to bolster the political settlement. Donors allocated much of the emergency assistance to the WBGS to the PA for budget support or employment generation projects, or to disadvantaged populations in the form of food and other assistance. Western foreign donors often chose Liberal Moderate NGOs as conduits to disburse this emergency funding, further enhancing their profiles in Palestinian civil society. By 2001, contributions from Arab countries alone totaled US$381.5 million.[58] Although the amount of aggregate donor flows remained constant in 2001, many of the programs and projects being implemented were either halted or altered to accommodate the emergency situation, especially after the reinvasion of Areas A (areas that were fully under the control of the PA) by the Israeli military in late October 2001.

Foreign Donor Assistance to El Salvador in the Immediate Postsettlement Period and the Promotion of a Conflict to Peace Transition

As the peace accords became imminent in El Salvador, the international community, led by the United States, rallied to support El Salvador's conflict to peace transition. The US's 1989 invasion of Panama and the 1990 victory of Violeta Barrios de Chamorro in Nicaragua had already foreshadowed the extinction of any perceived threats to the United States before the Cold War formally ended.[59] Moreover, the United States found it more difficult to justify its support for the Salvadoran military given its blatant human rights violations, most notably the slaying of the Jesuit priests and the army's bombing of poor neighborhoods in El Salvador. In March 1992, two months after the signing of the Salvadoran peace accords, the CG met in Washington, DC.[60] In general, the international community was forthcoming in its support for El Salvador's conflict to peace transition. Unlike the Palestinian case, the majority of funding came from multilateral organizations.

Between 1992 and 1997, the international community committed US$2.47 billion to El Salvador,[61] of which approximately US$1.09 billion was from bilateral resources, US$1.33 billion was from multilateral sources, and US$55.3 million was from NGOs.[62] Thirty-one percent of total funding made available to the country was from the Inter-American Development Bank, 17.3 percent was by the United States, 9.5 percent was by the Central American Bank for Economic Integration, and 9.4 percent came from the World Bank.[63] Although the US's share of foreign aid disbursements had dropped to 46 percent between 1992 and 1995, the United States still accounted for 71 percent of all grants, making it El Salvador's biggest donor of grants until 1995. In addition to the United States, the IDB, the World Bank, the European Commission (EC), Germany, and Japan were major donors to El Salvador.[64]

As in Palestine, aid to El Salvador was initially very politicized, promoting certain groups over others during the first years after the signing of the peace accords. However, unlike in Palestine, aid to El Salvador subsequently became less selective; smaller amounts of aid also meant less leverage. After 1994, foreign donors, including USAID, became less politically selective regarding whom they would fund and not actively marginalizing individuals or groups because of their political backgrounds or former affiliations. By then, Cold War politics had dissipated, and the political settlement had taken form and was set. The politics of USAID personnel vis-à-vis El Salvador during this post-1994 period had not been shaped by the Cold War, but rather shaped by the new prevailing inclusive political settlement.[65] After 1997, following what many considered to be the end of the conflict to peace transition in El Salvador, the structure of aid to El Salvador fundamentally changed. With the end of the Cold War and the end of the war, many bilateral donors no longer considered El Salvador an important priority. In general, there was a substantial decrease in net flows to El Salvador, including a decrease in concessional lending.[66] Meanwhile donors, especially the World Bank, substantially increased nonconcessional lending.

It is estimated that loans to El Salvador represented 40 percent of total peace-related programs in the postwar period.[67] By 1992, El Salvador's debt had risen to US$2.34 billion, with US loans representing 34 percent of the total, and, by 1994, an increase in multilateral lending raised the county's total debt to US$2.497 billion.[68] From 1998, annual disbursements to El Salvador were almost halved compared to their 1992 and 1993 levels. Less aid to El Salvador also meant less foreign donor involvement in determining political outcomes, including in the realm of civil society.

Coordinating Mechanism and Channels

In the Palestinian territories and El Salvador, donors and the recipient governments established channels and mechanisms to coordinate the aid effort. In both contexts, the mechanisms sought to promote certain actors, giving them greater ownership over the reconstruction and transition process. In the Palestinian territories, the uncertainty of the political situation associated with noninclusion, and the higher amounts of assistance led to more complex and centralized coordinating mechanisms, which allowed for more foreign donor involvement, and greater opportunity to shape political outcomes. Very problematically, the coordination mechanism also put Israel on equal footing, or, in some respects, on superior footing, relative to the Palestinians.[69] The mechanisms established affiliates of the Fatah and its clientelistic network tendency as the counterparts to all Western donors; the Opposition tendency affiliates had no role in these mechanisms. The centralized coordinating mechanisms reflected the greater consensus among donors about the actors and political outcomes they wanted to promote.

In El Salvador, the coordination mechanisms were less complex and less centralized. Although in its first incarnations, the coordinating mechanism in El Salvador excluded the FLMN, many pro-FLMN donors simply chose to bypass the more right-wing, government controlled mechanism and channeled their funding through the more neutral UNDP. Moreover, a number of donors initially lacked confidence in the NRP, because many of its programs were funded almost exclusively by USAID. Hence, they channeled funding through other ministries and through the UNDP.[70] This initial polarization, however, decreased after the first couple of years after the signing of the peace accords, as different foreign donors became more willing to fund different parties. No such remediation took place in the Palestinian case.

The entirety of the coordination mechanism in the Palestinian territories was put in place to bolster the Oslo Accords. The PA, along with the donor community, initially founded the Palestinian Economic Council for Reconstruction and Development as the counterpart to the World Bank. Since the Council's inception in 1994, its mandate has undergone a number of changes; it now works more specifically in the area of infrastructural reconstruction, serving as an implementing agency. The Ministry of Planning and International Cooperation (MOPIC) became the key coordinator of foreign donor assistance on the Palestinian side. The donor community also created two main bodies: the CG and the Ad Hoc Liaison Committee, the principal coordination mechanism on political matters related to the donor development effort, as well as on the economic aspects of the 1993 DOP.[71] In 1994, the Ad Hoc Liaison Committee created the Local Aid Coordination Committee, which reports back to the World Bank, the United Nations Special Coordinator's Office to the Occupied Territories (UNSCO), and Norway, and the Joint Liaison Committee, which reviews the budgetary performance of the PA, and monitors the implementation of the Tripartite Action Plan.[72] Additionally, the Local Aid Coordination Committee created twelve sector working groups;[73] for each group, a UN agency serves as a secretariat, a donor serves as a shepherd, and the relevant PA ministry serves as the gavel holder. The unfolding mechanisms, especially after Hamas's election victory in 2006, would work to further marginalize the Opposition.

In El Salvador, the postwar donor coordination structures were not as centralized as those in Palestine. From the onset, a struggle ensued between the government of El Salvador and USAID, on the one hand, and the FMLN and the European donors, on the other, regarding which channels and organizing mechanisms donors should use to implement the NRP, as well as to disburse aid to the FMLN ex-conflict zones. Initially, the Salvadoran government and USAID insisted that the National Commission for Restoration of Areas, a counterinsurgency development agency, should coordinate aid efforts related to the NRP. The FMLN and a number of donors, however, felt that the UNDP should coordinate the aid effort.[74] Until 1993, a number of European countries boycotted the Secretariat and channeled funds through the UNDP, leaving USAID as the principal donor to the Secretariat. Although, during the initial years after the signing of the peace accords, postwar reconstruction remained under the purview of the government, including municipalities, ultimately, some funding was channeled through the UNDP, namely from some European countries and other UN agencies.

Similarly, the two parties initially disagreed over which bodies should distribute the aid, especially to the ex-conflict zones. The Salvadoran government and USAID believed that aid should be channeled through the government, minimizing any possible power-sharing with the FMLN,[75] or the possibility that the FMLN would be strengthened in any part of the country. Other donors, especially state-sponsored European donors, maintained that aid to the ex-conflict zones should be channeled through nongovernmental organizations that were familiar with and had previously worked in those areas. A number of donor countries, most notably the Netherlands, Norway, Spain, Sweden, Canada, and Spain, chose to bypass the Salvadoran government and relevant parties. According to UNDP's 1997 report, these countries channeled as much as 60–75 percent of their total funding through NGOs, multilateral projects, or their own agencies, in contrast to the United States, the EU, and Germany, which delivered approximately 90 percent of their total funding through the government.[76] Although in the first couple of years after the signing of the peace accords, the NRP channeled less funding through the opposition NGOs, these NGOs still received substantial funding from solidarity groups and European donors.[77] Kevin Murray estimated that, between 1992 and 1993, the total amount of funding channeled by opposition NGOs to ex-conflict zones was approximately US$30 million.[78]

Initially, though there also was little coordination between those managing the peace process and those involved with the international financial institutions and implementing economic reforms, the polarization among donors was later redressed by the more inclusive nature of the peace accords, which better enabled donors to unify their goals and support all groups in society. Alvaro de Soto and Graciana del Castillo referred to the dichotomy as the "two-track process"[79] in which the international financial institutions had little regard for how their policies would affect the peace process. For example, to expedite the disbursement of funding, and to ensure that the government had greater control of the funding being received, the Salvadoran government requested that foreign donor assistance be channeled through the World Bank's second structural adjustment loan program (SAL II). The government's rationalization was that they had little power to reassign previously earmarked funding to other priority sectors, and that funds were being disbursed at too slow a pace. The World Bank strongly supported the position of the Salvadoran government. The Scandinavian countries, Denmark, Finland, Norway, and Sweden, adamantly opposed such a move on the grounds that the purpose of aid was to support peace and reconciliation. These countries requested that peace conditionality be included in the SAL II.[80] Ultimately, none of these issues were incorporated into the SAL II, and although the government was provided with greater flexibility, there were no new pledges in 1993; with the exception of Germany, all donors simply reaffirmed their previous pledges. A situation to accommodate all political tendencies did not transpire in the Palestinian case.

Foreign Donor Sectoral Priorities

In both cases, social infrastructure and services related projects and programs, which included water and sanitation and government and civil society, received the lion's share of donor funding. Important priorities for the international donor community also included postwar reconstruction and the promotion of the private sector. Moreover, budget support in the Palestinian case,[81] and debt forgiveness in the Salvadoran case,[82] figured prominently in the early years following the peace accords in each case. But it was political considerations, or more specifically, the parameters of the political settlement in each context, that guided foreign donor priorities; this was most evident in Government and Civil Society related program areas.[83] Given the political sensitivity and more precarious levels of support for the Oslo Accords, Western donors were more intent on funding more politically visible projects and program that could bolster the prevailing political settlement and contribute to the emergence of a "post–Cold war liberal order."

Although foreign donors were reluctant to fund those sectors that they considered politically contentious, the level of uniformity among donors significantly affected what happened. In Palestine, because of the greater uniformity among Western foreign donors, especially regarding which recipients or sectors they perceived as more politically contentious, such as agriculture and local government; these sectors were underfunded by all Western donors. In El Salvador, on the other hand, foreign donors were less uniform about which sectors they perceived as politically controversial, therefore increasing the likelihood that all sectors would receive some funding. Moreover, there was greater emphasis on economic development and local government, in contrast to the Palestinian case where these sectors were not regarded as important, and local government was addressed with hesitancy and wariness for fear that Opposition tendency–affiliated groups and individual might prevail at this level of government.

Given the unstable nature of a noninclusive political context, the agriculture sector was not regarded as pressing a priority as budget support, emergency employment creation, and selective institution building for the PA. For donors, the agriculture sector did not provide the visibility and expediency that most donors seek and appreciate. Moreover, developments in the agriculture sector, especially those involving water, irrigation, and land reclamation, were more likely to ignite political tensions with Israeli authorities. In El Salvador the more politically contentious programs initially included land transfers and the reintegration of ex-combatants. There was less consensus, however, about which sectors were controversial, and therefore no sector was marginalized by all donors. For example, two program areas that were critical to the implementation of the peace accords, the creation of a civilian police force, separate and distinct from the armed forces, and the transfer of land to former combatants,[84] were underfunded by non-US foreign donors. Nonetheless, the United States was willing to fund these sectors. Other donors were willing to fund other contentious sectors such as the reinsertion of ex-combatants into civilian life.

Funding to Local Government, Civil Society, and NGOs in Palestine and El Salvador

In the immediate postsettlement period, donors committed nearly the same amount of funding to the Government and Civil Society-General sector in both contexts (US$463.52 million in El Salvador and US$471.05 million in the Palestinian territories). Despite the similarity in this amount, funding to the subsectors within this category reaffirms my argument about how the political settlements shaped the priorities of Western donors (see figure 4.2). In particular, funding to Government and Administration,[85] which included local government and decentralization, was considerably higher in El Salvador than to the WBGS, and funding to the Civil Society sector was considerably higher in the Palestinian case than in El Salvador. For this period, El Salvador received US$292.67 million for Government Administration, compared to US$176.16 million in the WBGS in the Palestinian context, and $54.10 million for Strengthening Civil Society[86] in El Salvador compared to $91.34 million in the Palestinian case. Similarly, in the Human Rights subsector,[87] which is more likely to involve funding to professionalized NGOs, donors committed US$70.70 million to the WBGS, compared to US$19.90 million to El Salvador. Given the historical particularities of the Palestinian case, and the weak or nonexistent state institutions, there was urgent need for programs related to government administration and the strengthening of government institutions, including local government. However, in this noninclusive political settlement context, the promotion of state institutions, especially at the local government level, could provide an opening that might allow the Opposition tendency to prevail at this level of government, thus undermining the political settlement. When Western state-sponsored donors introduced funding for local government development in the Palestinian territories, most bypassed municipalities controlled by Opposition affiliated groups. Moreover, funding to civil society, most often to professionalized NGOs, provided donors with the opportunity to help promote the NGO sector and an opportunity to promote the prevailing political settlement. In the Palestinian territories, the immediate political objectives of supporting the implementation of the peace accords trumped other concerns such as democratic development. Relative to other cases, there seemed to be a greater willingness among foreign

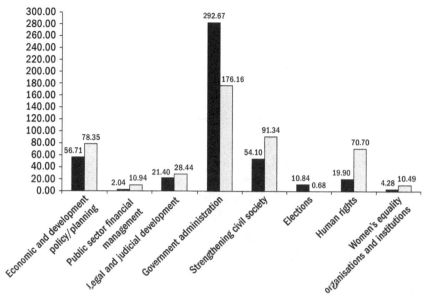

Figure 4.2. Commitments to government and civil society, 1992–2001 (in USD million)
Source: OECD data, CRS (constant 2005 USD)

donors to support professionalized NGOs that were not rooted in society, or did not have grassroots bases. A number of my interviewees from donor agencies told me that they were cognizant that they were supporting professionalized NGOs that served as political platforms for certain individuals and often did not have much contact with the grassroots or the broader Palestinian society. These representatives, however, explained that they were interested in promoting certain discourses in Palestinian society, especially in relation to the peace accords, democratic process ideas, and consciousness-raising about the status of women and civic education—projects that do not require these organizations to maintain a long-term relationship with the recipients.[88] As one director of a donor agency explained, "[Sometimes] it is more important to promote an idea or an agenda than have a grassroots constituency."[89] A number of NGOs play an important role in developing future leaders.[90] Hence, according to these representatives, professionalized NGOs did not need to have grassroots constituencies, or be able to forge horizontal linkages. In 2000, USAID introduced an aid model that targeted community-based groups that could help with service delivery. Funding to these groups did not replace funding to the professionalized NGOs and was still selective about not funding Oslo Opposition groups.

The impact of "Government Administration" funding, especially in developing local government and decentralization, was an important development in the Salvadoran context. Donor programs related to decentralization included the channeling of services and the organization of economic projects through local governments, and the promotion of civic education and lobbying at this level. Although a discussion regarding the exact impact and assessment of decentralization in El Salvador is beyond the scope of this book, foreign donors played a critical role in shaping decentralization agendas in developing countries such as El Salvador. Moreover, these types of programs illustrated how donors promoted certain civil society development activities, depending on the "articulated" or "disarticulated" space between society and the state, which was influenced by the political settlement.

Since in noninclusive contexts, foreign donors have a greater incentive to promote certain groups over other groups, they committed higher amounts of funding to professionalized NGOs in the Palestinian territories than in El Salvador. These organizations often serve as political platforms for their directors. In the WBGS, the NGO sector received US$20–50 million a year, compared to US$25–30 million a year in El Salvador.[91] Despite complaints from the NGO sector about the diversion of funding to the PA, official funding to Palestinian NGOs remained substantially high, especially in comparison to other cases of conflict to peace.[92] Between 1994 and 2001 US$402.9 million was committed to the NGO sector (representing 8 percent of total commitments). Since service provision shifted to PA institutions, funding to the NGO sector fell from over US$94 million in 1994, to US$20–50 million per year between 1999 and 2001[93] Notwithstanding this net decrease in funding to the NGO sector after 1993, the number of NGOs in the WBGS increased by a third during this period. According to more conservative estimates, the number of local NGOs in the WBGS increased from 617 NGOs in the late 1980s to 926 NGOs after 1993.[94] Less conservative estimates put the number of NGOs in the WBGS at between 1,200 and 1,500 in the post-Oslo period; this figure included unions, cooperatives, and youth clubs.[95]

The World Bank also created an NGO trust fund, the first of its kind, with allocations of US$14.9 million, for the WBGS. The goal of this fund was twofold: (1) to provide services for the poor and disadvantaged; and (2) to develop the NGO sector.[96] The World Bank chose the Welfare Association, a pro-*Fatah* institution to administer the fund. The World Bank's rationale was that a pro-PA institution would face fewer challenges from the PA. Relatedly, though not explicitly stated, such an organization ensured that this aid would not support those organizations that opposed the Oslo Accords.

Although foreign aid contributed to the increase of Salvadoran NGOs from 20 in 1979, to 31 in 1983,[97] to over 1,300 registered civil associations in 1998,[98] official funding to Salvadoran NGOs was generally consistently lower compared to the Palestinian case. Although data regarding total funding to the Salvadoran NGO sector is difficult to come by, existing studies estimated that the annual turnover of the entire "social development" sector of NGOs was approximately US$25–30 million.[99] A 1995 survey of Salvadoran NGOs indicated that the average budget of a Salvadoran NGO was US$300,000, of which two-thirds was allocated to development projects.[100]

In El Salvador, much of the funding to NGOs was from private aid agencies, as opposed to state-sponsored donors, which are more likely to uphold the political considerations of their respective states. Private aid agencies, on the other hand, often have more flexibility.[101] Among the very active aid agencies in El Salvador that channeled their funding through NGOs were the Dutch cofinancing agencies—Bilance, HIVOS, ICCO, and NOVIB—and other German, British, and Scandinavian private aid agencies.[102] This situation contrasted to the Palestinian territories in which NGOs also received substantial amounts of more political funding from state-sponsored donors agencies.

A Comparative Examination of USAID's Democracy and Governance Programs

A comparison of USAID activities in its program area of Democracy and Governance in the Palestinian and Salvadoran contexts illustrates how donors were circumscribed by the existing institutional settings, which were shaped by the prevailing political settlements. Moreover, the tailoring of the general programs also shows how foreign donors targeted different recipients so as to further their political goals. Between 2000 and 2002, for example, the Democracy and Governance program in El Salvador had a US$14.96 million budget, compared to US$40.49 million in the Palestinian territories. In the Palestinian context, although USAID prioritized strengthening the legislative council, it also focused on promoting certain NGOs, especially during the first six years of the program. In the Salvadoran context, USAID focused on strengthening government institutions, including those at the local level, and allocated only a small percentage of its Democracy and Governance funding to NGOs.[103] More funding to Palestinian NGOs meant a greater discrepancy between the Fatah and Liberal Moderates haves and the Opposition tendency have-nots in civil society.

USAID established the Democracy and Governance program in the Palestinian territories in 1994. The program included three different components. The first component involved a US$27 million grant for the period between 1994 and 2000, to develop an "effective civil society." In actual terms, this meant funding for eight Palestinian NGOs that were involved in advocacy, education, citizen participation, opinion polling, policy analysis, and women's issues. These NGOs were large professionalized organizations, headed by affiliates of Fatah or the Liberal Moderates.[104] The second component involved a US$9 million grant to strengthen the elected Palestinian Legislative Council to help fulfill its legislative and constituency responsibilities. The third component was a five-year program that began in 2001, and involved a US$33 million grant for a program called Tamkeen.[105] Tamkeen was specifically responsible for assisting a wider variety and larger number of NGOs, especially in service delivery, in more remote geographic locations.[106] Although Tamkeen targeted smaller groups, it also targeted non-Opposition groups.

In El Salvador, the Democracy and Governance program involved five program activities: judicial training and implementation of new criminal and penal codes; strengthening municipal governments; working with legislatures to establish constituent outreach offices; expanding the use of mediation centers and other alternative dispute resolution mechanisms; and collaboration with NGOs to encourage greater participation in public policy formulation.[107] USAID allocated 35 percent of the total budget to strengthening municipal governments.[108]

These different approaches had varying impacts on civil society. In the Palestinian territories, because of the noninclusive settlement and the resultant institutional setting, USAID could contribute to the shaping of political outcomes by promoting certain actors in civil society through certain professionalized NGOs. Although USAID funding played a role in strengthening selected NGOs, it ultimately contributed to the polarization between the haves and have-nots in civil society, which also coincided along non-Opposition and Opposition tendency–affiliated NGO lines. Moreover, for fear that Opposition tendency–affiliated groups and individuals might gain a foothold in local government, USAID initially did not prioritize the strengthening of local government. Later, when USAID introduced local development programs, they bypassed those municipalities that were controlled by Opposition tendency–affiliated individuals or groups. In El Salvador, USAID was able to focus on the development and strengthening of government institutions, including local government, without worrying that unwanted opposition would prevail at this level. Therefore, USAID allocated a considerable amount of its Democracy and Governance budget to the strengthening of local government.

Local level development programs in inclusive contexts such as El Salvador elucidate the potential of articulating spaces between state and society, and how this contributes to the enhancement of citizen engagement with this level of government. Although earlier programs in El Salvador such as the MEA and the Social Investment Fund, both local level interventions associated with the NRP, favored non-FMLN groups over others, the Program for Refugees, Displaced, Repatriated in Central America was much more inclusive in its approach. It created an institutional framework that absorbed different polarized groups and served as a structure to facilitate development as well as social and political reconciliation.[109] This institutional framework endeavored to develop new political relations in which the different groups were on equal footing. Moreover, unlike the Social Investment Fund, Program for Refugees, Displaced, Repatriated in Central America promoted regular patterns of civic engagement with local government, focusing on developing linkages between government and formally excluded groups.

Foreign donor civil society promotion programs in El Salvador often institutionalized regular patterns of interaction between NGOs and government institutions. Donor initiatives to strengthen civil society therefore took place in a more articulated place, allowing for greater interaction between CSOs and the relevant national and local government institutions, thus further articulating these spaces.

Funding to the Palestinian and Salvadoran Women's Sectors in the Postaccord Period

In what follows, I examine all foreign aid directed to the women's sectors. Hence, I attempt to capture the impact of specific civil society and democracy assistance, while also taking into account development assistance more generally. As Thomas Carothers explained, there has been a "half-way" synthesis of these two domains of development and democracy aid.[110] According to OECD-Creditor Reporting System (CRS) data, between 1992 and 2001, US$10.49 million was committed to women's equality organizations and institutions in the Palestinian territories, compared to US$4.28 million in El Salvador.[111] This information, however, is incomplete because not all donors reported funding to the CRS. Although exact information about the amounts of funding to the Palestinian and Salvadoran women's sectors in the postaccord period is difficult to obtain, important trends are discernible from material provided by donor agencies, professionalized women's NGOs, members of the women's grassroots organizations, and government agencies. In general, this sector was an important priority for many donors. A comparative examination indicates that the Palestinian women's sectors was an especially important priority for state-sponsored donors in contrast to the Salvadoran case where private aid agencies and solidarity groups were the main donors to the women's sector. Moreover, in the Palestinian territories, Western state-sponsored donors prioritized the funding of professionalized NGOs regardless of their access to grassroots constituencies,[112] more so than in El Salvador, where donors prioritized mass-based women's organizations.

In general, this has been a well-funded sector in the Palestinian territories. According to MOPIC, US$19.943 million was committed to the women's sector between 1994 and 2000. Although, this figure does not include all funding committed to the sector, especially to the professionalized NGOs, it is relatively higher than commitments to other sectors.

According to MOPIC, for example, donors committed US$15.457 million to the children's and youth sector, and US$3.768 million to the telecommunications sector for that same period.[113] Professionalized NGOs in the women's sector received a high percentage of this funding. For example, according to the MOPIC's 2001 First and Second Quarterly Monitoring Report, between 1994 and 1998, foreign donors committed US$697,000 to one professionalized NGO, the Women's Affairs Technical Committees (WATC), compared to US$10.234 million committed to the whole women's sector during that same period. Between 1991 and 2001, USAID's Democracy and Governance program funded six CSOs, of which WATC and PWWSD were two key recipients. Among the foreign donors who funded the women's sector were the Canada Fund, Díakonia, the EU, Friedrich Naumann Foundation, Heinrich Böll Foundation, the Netherlands Representative Office, the Norwegian Representative Office, Save the Children, the Swedish Representative Office, UNDP, United Nations Development Fund for Women, USAID, and World University Service.

The profile of USAID's funding to the Palestinian women's sector reflected many of these trends. Between 1994 and 2000, USAID was one of the main donors to the WATC and the PWWSD.[114] Although, the PWWSD did have a grassroots-base of approximately 300 registered members, neither NGO was as rooted in society as other grassroots-based organizations, or as the women's committees. Both organizations were founded by individuals who are well known in the Palestinian political scene and were not in opposition to the Oslo Accords. Both the WATC and the PWWSD were active in providing workshops and training seminars on civic literacy, democratization, and women's rights. The relationship that ensued between these organizations and the recipients of these training sessions was more hierarchical and vertical between the two parties and not necessarily conducive to the strengthening of civil society.

The pattern of USAID's funding contrasted with smaller donor agencies, such as Canada Fund, which was more likely to support smaller, grassroots-based community projects and organizations, and to be less stringent regarding the political background and credentials of their recipients. The majority of Canada Fund's recipients were small community initiatives located in marginal or remote areas, especially refugee camps. As of 2001, among Canada Fund's recipients in the women's sector were: the Women's Center in Jalazone Camp, the Women's Center in Al-Amal Camp, the Qualandia Refugee Camp Co-op, and the Women's Center in Bureij Camp.[115]

The type of aid that donors made available to the Salvadoran women's sector was markedly different from the type of assistance that was made available to them in the previous period, as well as also from the type of aid that donors made available to the Palestinian women's sector. As previously mentioned, foreign donor assistance to the Salvadoran women's organizations was predominantly from solidarity groups. Increasingly, as the peace accords became more imminent, funding from foundations and state-sponsored donors also became more readily available, although to a lesser extent than in the Palestinian case. The smaller donor operations afforded the women's organizations greater control over their allocations, as opposed to larger donor operations, which were more likely to require more stringent accounting and administration.[116] A number of the directors of women's organizations indicated that they focused on funding from solidarity groups and foundations, which were more flexible with project implementation and not as stringent in terms of accounting.[117] In general however, foreign donor assistance was no longer as readily available as it had been in the years immediately after the signing of the peace accords.

The foreign donor agencies that funded MSM during the first twelve years of its operations were representative of the types of donors that funded other women's organizations in El Salvador. These foreign donors predominately included solidarity groups and municipal assemblies, such as Comité de Padova (Italy), Desarrollo y Paz (Spain), and Pelupessi de Holanda, and foundations and state-sponsored donors such as the Council for International Development (United Kingdom), HIVOS (Netherlands), and so on. The relatively high number of donors who funded MSM also suggested that these donors provided smaller grants to the organization.[118]

Most, if not all, professionalized women's organizations did not receive funding directly from USAID. For the most part, USAID in El Salvador no longer worked with NGOs. Rather, USAID channeled funding to NGOs through implementing organizations such as Creative Associates International, Inc. (CREA International). The amounts of funding channeled to these projects were considerably less than those channeled to the Palestinians territories.[119]

Conclusion

By examining general funding patterns (including to the women's sector in both cases), as well as through closer scrutiny of program allocations as reported by the OECD, and through USAID's funding to both cases, this chapter showed how the political settlement shaped the impact of Western donor assistance in three fundamental ways. First, it shaped Western donor selectivity and thus influenced who received funding and who did not. Second, the degree of inclusivity of the settlement and the associated political objectives tied to the settlement influenced the types of programs that donors prioritized in these two contexts. And, third, it also illustrated how the institutional setting (as a result of the political settlement) influenced the types of projects and programs that donors promoted in that context. The political context remained critical in determining outcomes, and foreign donor assistance served to mediate these outcomes.

5

Beyond Professionalization

Foreign Aid and the Transformation of the Women's Sectors

Through an analysis of the women's sector with its constellation of women's committees, NGOs, and gender-related projects and programs, this chapter demonstrates how the level of inclusion of the political settlement in each case shaped the impact of assistance to this sector in the first decade after the political settlements. Moreover, this chapter illustrates how institutional professionalization explanations are inadequate to account for the divergent trajectories in the two cases. Adopting a feminist approach, this chapter puts women activists and their experiences at the center of the analysis.[1]

Following the peace accords in each case, the leaders and organizers of the women's committees in both the Palestinian territories and El Salvador felt that the programs of the committees needed to accommodate the burgeoning peace process stage, and, in the Palestinian case, the new state-building stage. This realization coincided with the increased availability of Western donor assistance. The transition strategy adopted by the women's grassroots committees was determined by their ability to access Western donor funding. The political settlement shaped donor selectivity in terms of who received funding and who did not,[2] as well as the types of projects donors implemented, both in terms of the extent to which they prioritized the promotion of the peace accords and how they intervened to shape relations between civil society and the existing political institutional setting. In what follows, I show how the projects and programs promoted by foreign donors (which were shaped by the settlement) intervened to affect new patterns of interaction between different tendencies of the women's sector, and, in turn, how this affected the longer term prospects for the development of civil society.

In the Palestinian case,[3] given the noninclusivity of the political settlement, the ability to access funding was determined by the expressed political position of the committee or its leaders vis-à-vis the Oslo Accords.

Hence, foreign donor support for the formalization, institutionalization, and professionalization of the women's sector took place in a fragmented manner, and a bifurcated sector of civil society developed. Western donors also lacked an understanding of the women's movement's strength and reach, and failed to appreciate how unequal access to resources and selective support for certain individuals and components would undermine the women's sector as a whole. More politicized Western donor interests in the Palestinian case sought to promote the peace accords, specifically and implicitly (or explicitly, in some cases), as a "post–Cold War liberal order." Many of the programs sought to transform the women's movement's collective struggles into individual cases that could be tackled with "proper" training, often discounting the military occupation's ongoing violations against women, and the Palestinian population more generally. Donors often promoted individuals or organizations, or both, that could promote certain ideas and norms associated with the peace process, ignoring their ability to incorporate and interact with broader grassroots constituencies. Moreover, fearful that Opposition tendency–affiliated groups would prevail at the local level, donors did not promote programs that encouraged regular interactions with this level of government. Instead, donor programs emphasized gender-related empowerment and civic engagement in the abstract,[4] and through their selective funding engendered new forms of tension and animosity within the women's sector.[5]

In contrast, given El Salvador's more inclusive political settlement, aid was not as discriminatory, and Western donor-funded programs were less political and free to focus on economic development and the institutionalization of regular patterns of interaction with local government. Implementation of these goals actually required that the women's organizations be able to reach and incorporate grassroots constituencies, and regular patterns of interaction and engagement with state institutions were encouraged.

The higher amounts of foreign assistance allocated to the women's sector in the Palestinian territories relative to the Salvadoran case was intrinsically linked to Palestine's greater geostrategic importance to Western donors and not to the poorer status of women in that context. Indeed, Palestine is categorized as middle income and thus did not actually qualify for the high amounts of assistance it received from certain donors. And as some of the following indicators (see table 5.1) illustrate, Palestinian women did not necessarily lag far behind in terms of most

TABLE 5.1. Comparing Women's Status in El Salvador and the Palestinian Territories

	El Salvador	Palestinian Territories
Gender Development Index (GDI)[a]	.965 (2013)	.974 (2013)
Female youth literacy (15–24 years)	92.3% (2004)	98.9% (2004)
Percentage of women aged 20–24 years old who were married or in a union before age 18	25.4% (2008)	20.6% (2010)
Share of female science, engineering, manufacturing and construction graduates at tertiary level	32.92% (2002)	43.79% (2001)
Proportion of seats held by women in national parliament	10.7% (1994)[b]	5.7% (1996)[c]
Labor force participation rate for persons aged 15+	44.5% (2001)	10.4%(2001)

Source: UN Gender Statistics (United Nations, 2015).
[a]GDI measures gender gap in human development achievements in three basic dimensions of human development: health, measured by female and male life expectancy at birth; education, measured by female and male expected years of schooling for children and female and male mean years of schooling for adults ages twenty-five5 and older; and command over economic resources, measured by female and male estimated earned income.
[b]In the first post-accord election in 1994, women won eight of the eighty-four seats. El Salvador Parliamentary Chamber: Asamblea legislative, http://www.ipu.org/parline-e/reports/arc/2099_94.htm.
[c]In the first post-Oslo election, women won five out of eighty-eight legislative seats. Central Election Commission, "The 1996 Palestinian and Legislative Elections," 1996.

socioeconomic indicators. In fact, they surpassed Salvadoran women in most indicators related to educational attainment. The most obvious area of discrepancy between Salvadoran and Palestinian women was labor force participation—the area most neglected by donors to the Palestinian territories. The remainder of the chapter examines the unfolding of these developments in the Palestinian and Salvadoran women's sectors in the postaccord periods. In each case, the discussion pays particular attention to the types of horizontal and vertical relationships that transpired, the extent of polarization that resulted, and the broader impact on the development of civil society and democracy.

The Reconstitution and Fragmentation of the Women's Sector in the Palestinian Territories

In the Palestinian case, the politicized processes through which various women's organizations came into existence and the mediating role of

Western donor funding impeded their ability to contribute to a stronger civil society. Though some professionalized organizations became known in international networks and better positioned to demand women's rights, their inability to engage and incorporate mass constituencies and forge horizontal links resulted in the marginalization of previously active women and fostered new divisions and hierarchies within the women's sector.[6]

As in other sectors of Palestinian civil society, three broad tendencies emerged, which included pertinent political organizations as well as loosely affiliated individuals and groups (see table 5.2). Fatah-affiliated grassroots women's committees consolidated their clientelistic relationship with the PA. An Opposition tendency of grassroots women's committees and women's organizations that did not support the Oslo Accords and therefore could not access Western donor funding also emerged; this tendency attempted to maintain and carve out a space for itself, bound to the professionalized organizations for resources and restricted in its access to the PA. And, finally, a Liberal Moderate–affiliated, Western-funded. and professionalized circuit of women's organizations became prevalent.

In this new hierarchy of relations, the Liberal Moderate tendency–affiliated professionalized organizations provided lectures and training sessions, while Opposition tendency–affiliated grassroots committees were often the recipients of these services.[7] The Fatah and its clientelistic network tendency, meanwhile, had the most consistent access to the PA. The privileging of certain groups of the women's sector over others in terms of access to both resources and institutions resulted in the creation of hierarchies in the women's sector, which exacerbated the existing polarization. Because this new hierarchy coincided along political lines, it further exacerbated existing tensions and decreased the likelihood of generating the kind of cross-cutting collaboration needed for the development of social capital, thus weakening the overall fabric of civil society. Depoliticized NGO programs often addressed the empowerment of women as separate from the broader economic and political context related to Israel's ongoing military occupation.[8]

Table 5.2. Inception of Women's Organizations in Palestinian Territories–Jerusalem Ramallah Access Area (1978–2001)

Palestinian People's Party (PPP)	Democratic Front for the Liberation of Palestine (DFLP)	Popular Front for the Liberation of Palestine (PFLP)	Fatah
Union of Palestinian Working Women's Committees (UPWWC) 1981	**Working Women's Committees (WWC) 1978**	**Union of Palestinian Women's Committees (UPWC) 1981**	*Union of Palestinian Women's Committees for Social Work (WCSW) 1982*
Gender Desk, Palestinian Agricultural Relief Committees 1986	**renamed Federation of Palestinian Women's Action Committees (FPWAC) 1989**		*Women's Affairs Technical Committees (WATC)* 1992*
Women's Center for Legal Aid and Counseling (WCLAC)‡ 1991	(Pro-Fida Cadre)		
Gender Desk, LAW- Palestinian Society for the Protection of Human Rights and the Environment 1991	Women's Center for Legal Aid and Counseling (WCLAC)‡ 1991		
Palestinian Working Women Society for Development (PWWSD)* 1991	Women's Studies Center 1991		
Women's Affairs Technical Committees (WATC)* 1992	Women's Affairs Technical Committees (WATC)* 1992		
Jerusalem Center for Women 1994			

Islamist Women's Organizations:
al-Huda **(1996)**
al-Khansa' **(1997)**

Note: All italic text = Fatah and its clientelistic networks; bold text = Opposition; no bold or all italics text = Liberal Moderates.

*PWWSD was founded by a few branch members of the Ramallah committee of the UPWWC, against the will of the Palestinian People's Party.

*Women's Affairs Technical Committee was founded by women from the UPWWC, FPWAC, UPWC, and WCSW are now among its member organizations.

‡WCLAC was founded by women from the UPWWC and the pro-Fida cadre of the FPWAC.

Source: This table is slightly modified from the original that first appeared in Manal A. Jamal, "Democracy Promotion, Civil Society Building, and the Primacy of Politics," *Comparative Political Studies* 45, no. 1 (January 2012): 3–31. Reprinted by permission of SAGE.

Fatah and Its Clientelistic Networks

"We helped a lot of members of the WCSW gain employment in the PA ministries and public schools. Rabiha or Nuha (leaders of the WCSW and prominent members of Fatah), would send letters to the various ministries or public schools on behalf of these women, requesting that employment opportunities be made available."[9]

"We were able to have a lot of our committee members appointed in the different ministries . . . I see this as an achievement."[10]

The tendency associated with Fatah, the leadership party of the PA and the broker of the Oslo Accords, and its clientelistic network included the WCSW and the General Union of Palestinian Women (GUPW)—an umbrella grassroots women's organization in which all the women's committees are represented. Because of WCSW's financial support from Fatah and other pro-Fatah institutions such as the Welfare Association, the WCSW was less in need of Western donor assistance than other women's committees. The WCSW adopted a new strategy of heightened mobilization that often involved payment to members and employment provision, thus solidifying clientelistic networks.[11] By 2001, the WCSW appeared to have fared much better than the other women's committees in terms of membership and visibility, as well as activity levels according to a number of office visits.[12]

In general, the WCSW was distinguished from other committees in its clientelistic networks, its ability to provide employment for some of its members, and its access to the PA more generally. Although it may have experienced a decrease in membership and funding from Fatah,[13] it still maintained a relatively strong membership base compared to other grassroots women's committees.[14] According to some members, they did not experience the same decrease in membership because they sometimes were able to pay or compensate their members,[15] though they were not able to give an exact number. The WCSW also expanded its operations by setting up offices in various locations.[16] As one member explained, "With money from the

Union [referring to WCSW], we bought furniture, sewing machines, curtains, chairs, and couches for our office . . . We also have a computer center now."[17] They were quite candid about their clientelistic networks.

In 1993, the GUPW was reactivated in the WBGS as an umbrella grassroots women's organization. Women activists had initially founded the GUPW under the auspices of the PLO in 1965 as an umbrella organization for all Palestinian women's organizations. In 1967, the Israeli authorities outlawed the union in the occupied territories, prompting the general secretariat of the organization to move its base abroad. By 2001, organizers were trying to reactivate the organization as the umbrella grassroots women's organization in which members from all the women's committees and professionalized women's NGOs would be represented. In the process of developing their programs, they received a modest monthly stipend from the PLO for their recurrent costs, and some funding from the Welfare Association.[18,19] Although, activists in the women's movement recognized the GUPW as a legitimate, umbrella organization, they were wary of the extent to which it was controlled by Fatah.

The Opposition

"It is shameful that the salaries of some of the directors of these NGOs are approximately US$4,000.00/month at a time when some Palestinian laborers cannot even earn enough money to buy food."[20]

"These projects and programs are not sustainable, but they now provide salaries and funding to former leaders of other committees."[21]

"They expect us to volunteer while they get paid."[22]

Opposition tendency–affiliated grassroots organizations were far from uniform, but they shared a relative inability to access state-sponsored Western donor funding. Not only were the leftist opposition factions excluded from the formation of the PA, but they were incapable of affecting a coherent transition strategy, especially in terms of defining a clear relationship with their grassroots organizations[23]—shortcomings that were also apparent in their women's committees. Women's organizations in this tendency included the FPWAC and the UPWC, affiliated with the DFLP and PFLP, respectively, and Al-Huda and Al-Khansa', two Islamist women's organizations founded in 1996 and 1997, respectively. Of these women's groups, FPWAC and UPWC were more liberal and Western in their cultural orientation; however, along with the Islamist organizations, they too were shunned by Western donors because of their opposition to the Oslo Accords.

All the organizers from the FPWAC and UPWC confirmed undergoing a dramatic decrease in membership after the Oslo Accords, though most were unwilling to provide actual membership numbers.[24] Although not technically Oppositon tendency-affiliated, the UPWWC also experienced decline in its membership.[25] An organizer of the FPWAC estimated a membership of approximately 1,000 members by 2001.[26] According to Maysoun Ahmad al-Ramahi, the organization's director, Al-Khansa' had approximately ninety members by the early 2000s, with only some paying full membership, and others working as paid or unpaid volunteers.[27] These decreases in membership were reflected in the committees' decreased visibility in the public realm, especially in terms of project implementation. The organizers rationalized the losses, noting various factors such as raised expectations that, after the signing of the Oslo Accords, Israeli military occupation would soon end; waning interest in voluntarism given the initial promise of improved economic conditions and more employment opportunities; and higher paying jobs with the professionalized NGOs in the initial post-Oslo period. Others stressed that some members ended their volunteer work with the committees because of their disappointment with the overall political and social conditions, and that the political appointments after Oslo had little to do with one's individual political contributions in the previous period.[28] After the start of Al-Aqsa Intifada, most of these committees tried to reactivate their membership bases, though this proved difficult given the noninclusive political landscape for Oopposition affiliates and the apathy and disappointment this engendered.[29]

These organizations also experienced economic decline. Decreased membership meant fewer membership fees, and thus less revenue for the committees. Many of these committees had to close their offices and nursery schools in various locations.[30] They could no longer turn to their affiliated political organizations—the DFLP and PFLP—for financial support because the political organizations themselves were also undergoing financial crisis.[31] Not only did the DFLP and the PFLP lose their funding from the PLO because of their opposition to the Oslo Accords, but they also lost their funding from the former Soviet Union and other Socialist bloc countries.[32] Though the Islamist women's organizations claimed to have no affiliation with any political group, they too could not access Western donor funding.[33] According to the elected director of Al-Khansa', "We have approached certain Western foreign donors with a proposal, but I felt that our *hijab* (headscarf) dissuaded them. They immediately turned down the proposal. We also met with the Welfare Association, but they needed us to be members of their organization for two consecutive years prior to receiving funding. We will try to approach them again in two years."[34] Instead, these Islamist women's organizations relied on funding from membership fees, zakat, community donations, and donations from Islamic NGOs based abroad, including from the Gulf countries.[35] Membership fees and community donations, in particular, figured prominently in sustaining their activities. The members of Al-Khansa' pay the equivalent of forty Jordanian dinars per year, then equivalent to US$56 a year, in membership fees. Because Israel maintains tight control over official financial transfers into the territories, the amounts transferred from other Islamist organizations appeared to be less than amounts disbursed by Western donors.[36]

A number of foreign donor agencies claimed that they could not fund these committees because they lacked the required levels of institutionalization and professionalization to receive foreign donor funding.[37] Foreign donors addressed the lack of institutionalization and professionalization among the women's committees by funding the establishment of a new professionalized organizations, the WATC—a non-opposition organization that was to serve as a conduit between the women's committees and the foreign donors. As I explain in a later section, this decision, however, was far more political than is at first apparent.

The Liberal Moderates

"We did not anticipate that these NGOs would become so distant from the grassroots. An important link between the women former political cadres who run these NGOs and the grassroots has been lost."[38]
—Zahira Kamal

A founding member of the FPWAC and a force behind the founding of the WCLAC and the Women's Studies Center, Zahira Kamal, acknowledged that these professionalized NGOs had not served their intended goals.

Of the three tendencies, what I describe as the "Liberal Moderates" had the most consistent access to Western donor funding and thus spearheaded the process of establishing professionalized NGOs (see table 5.2). As I explained in chapter 3, this tendency was not adamant in its opposition to the Madrid Peace Conference and Oslo Accords, and was more liberal and Western in its cultural orientation. Its organizations, in short, were seen by foreign donors as more promising partners in the establishment of the post-Oslo, "post–Cold War liberal order." This tendency became best associated with the fraction within the FPWAC that supported the peace accords and was loosely affiliated with FIDA, and women in UPWWC, which were affiliated with the Palestinian People's Party (PPP). FIDA and the PPP did not oppose the Madrid Peace Conference and Oslo Accords and were more liberal and Western in their cultural orientation. Historically, as Frances Hasso explained, these groups, especially the older FPWAC, symbolically represented "the modernity" of the Palestinian struggle within international networks.[39] The FPWAC, however, was more leftist in its socioeconomic and political orientation. Both these political organizations adopted NGO professionalization of their former grassroots committees in order to facilitate their political transition in the post-Madrid era; the new professionalized NGOs (sans grassroots) would provide these factions and their leaders employment prospects and opportunities to remain involved in the political life of Palestine without being wedded to the Oslo Accords.[40] In order to appeal to Western donor priorities, many professionalized NGOs adopted programs that addressed democratization, human rights, the "empowerment" of women, and civic education. As Hammami (1995) explained, "democratization" of Palestinian society became the rallying call of the former leftists after the Oslo Accords.[41]

Western donor agendas generally did not require organizations to incorporate grassroots elements when they professionalized; indeed, strategic delinking was encouraged in some cases. Most of the organizations established by PPP and FIDA did not incorporate their grassroots constituencies and decided to distance themselves from their grassroots bases so that the organizations would not be "politically labeled." In 1991, cadre from the PPP, along with pro-FIDA cadre of the FPWAC, established the WCLAC.[42] Pro-FIDA cadres from the FPWAC also established the Women's Studies Center.[43] Although the UPWWC was regarded more favorably by donors because its affiliated PPP was not as adamant in its opposition to the Oslo Accords, some of its members were reluctant to professionalize their committees.[44] A few of the leaders of the UPWWC, however, took over the Ramallah membership base and established a professional women's NGO in the Jerusalem-Ramallah area, the PWWSD;[45] this decision was reached against the will of other organizers of the UPWWC and PPP.[46] In 1994, other members of the UPWWC went on to establish the Jerusalem Center for Women and two gender desks in PPP-affiliated NGOs: the Palestinian Society for the Protection of Human Rights and the Environment (LAWE) and PARC.[47] Of the new eight professionalized organizations, the PWWSD and PARC's gender unit were among the only organizations that incorporated their grassroots constituencies into the structure of their organizations.[48] In 2000, Hanan Ashrawi, the founder of MIFTAH—the Palestinian Initiative for the Promotion of Global Dialogue and Democracy—also established a gender desk for the organization.

Meanwhile, in 1992, a number of women cadres from Fatah and the Liberal Moderate affiliates founded the WATC to assist the Palestinian negotiators in preparing for negotiations with Israel.[49] Once the work of the technical committees ended in 1996, WATC reevaluated its role and decided to professionalize the institution in which women's committees could serve as institutional members.[50] Initially, only women's groups and committees that did not oppose the Oslo Accords participated in the WATC. Within the next couple of years, the work of the institution expanded, and women's committees that opposed the Oslo Accords also joined. Despite the intended inclusivity of the WATC, nearly a decade after its establishment some felt that for the most part it was still controlled by pro-Fatah members, or at least was not as inclusive of women associated with the Opposition tendency.[51]

Western donor agencies provided professionalized NGOs generous aid packages in hopes of buttressing support for the post-Oslo order. The general funding patterns to the WATC and the PWWSD were illustrative, especially concerning bilateral donors' preference for funding professionalized NGOs that did not oppose the Oslo Accords. Most of the donor agencies that funded both of these organizations include larger bilateral or state-sponsored donor agencies, including USAID.[52] The main donors to WATC were the EU, the Norwegian Representative Office, USAID, the Canada Fund, the Friedrich Ebert Foundation, and Díakonia.[53] With the exception of the Italian organization and Díakonia, all the donors were either state-sponsored donor agencies or the state-affiliated foundations that work with NGOs (when their representative offices only worked with bilateral partners, and did not work directly with NGOs). The member states of the first three donors listed were also heavily involved in Israeli-Palestinian negotiations, at one point or another.[54] Funding to the PWWSD fit a similar profile; among its donors during this period were the EU, the Netherlands Representative Office, and USAID.[55]

The Transformation from Active Political Participants to the Recipients of Skills and Services in Need of Awareness Raising

The new programmatic priorities of the Palestinian women's sector in the post-Oslo period reflected the postoccupation, state-building phase for which the Oslo settlement aspired. In this same vein, Western donor priorities reflected their version of the burgeoning post-Oslo state-building phase. The professionalized NGOs focused on workshops and training sessions that endeavored to foster citizen engagement norms in the post-Oslo period, including an enhanced focus on women's rights: advocacy, legislation, and lobbying pertaining to women's rights, civic education, and democracy. Popular topics in workshops and training sessions also included domestic violence, gender sensitivity and gender empowerment training, computer classes, promotion of women in the media, and government lobbying. A number of organizations also provided counseling services. As noted above, the WCLAC provided women with counseling, as well as legal services. The PWSSD also provided counseling services to women, teenage support groups, and educational lectures dealing with labor rights, domestic violence, and decision making.

Although at least in theory, grassroots women's committees in each geographic location chose their own programs, it was hardly coincidence that the activities most popular with the professionalized NGOs also became popular with the women's committees. The availability of resources and the readiness on the part of the professionalized NGOs to coordinate around those issues facilitated the work of the committees in these areas, especially in the face of their decreased funding. In most instances, the professionalized NGOs provided the services, and the grassroots women's committees were the recipients. Although many of the programs of the WCSW were a continuation of earlier programs pertaining to consciousness-raising and skills training, they too adopted programs that were also more popular with professionalized NGOs, especially pertaining to civic education. According to some organizers, at the end of the decade after the start of the Oslo Accords, the WCSW was still running between sixty-eight and eighty kindergartens in the WBGS,[56] but previous mainstays of the women's committees, such as cooperatives and the types of programs that addressed women's challenges of living under military occupation, had noticeably declined.

Because Al-Huda and Al-Khansa' did not rely on donor funding, they were more autonomous in terms of formulating their own program priorities. The women in the organization decided on the topics of their weekly discussions and lectures, which included lectures on women's role in society, early marriage, women's rights, and women and Islam more generally.[57] The founders of these organizations were also keen to provide employment for women in economic need. Women employed by Al-Khansa' either worked in the organization's kitchen or were commissioned to embroider certain articles; the foods produced in the kitchen and the embroidered pieces were marketed, and profits were used to subsidize the organization's expenses, including salaries to these women. Al-Khansa' employed three women in the organization's kitchen, and commissioned thirty women in different areas to embroider articles that were later sold by the organization. The organization also helped some women market the items they produced. Al-Khansa' also had a gym to which all its members had access.

To better meet the professionalization criteria of Western donors, projects that lent themselves to quantifiable outputs and implementation within established funding cycles became more prevalent. Those organizations that were in a position to access Western donor funding were also clever in adapting their programs to meet donor objectives. Invariably, the programs shifted toward short-term and individually oriented goals, thereby compromising the longer term developmental objectives of many organizations that had intended to address the most pressing needs of women in the grassroots committees. These professionalized organizations were successful in terms of the number of seminars and training courses they held and the number of reports they produced. Although these outputs met important criteria for the donors who funded them, the impact of this work was less appreciated by fellow activists. Most of these programs promoted a post-Oslo landscape that provided little room, if any, to register fundamental disagreement with the Oslo Accords and the new political order.

Reframing Women's Participation and Priorities in the Palestinian Territories and the Impact on Civil Society and Democratic Development

Whereas the previous section focused on changes in the structures and relations of the groups themselves and their relation to funders, here I turn to how changes in the organization of the women's sector and the substantive content of their programs affected the nature of interactions between the different tendencies of the women's sector and their capacity to make demands on the state at the national and local levels.

Operating in Institutional Vacuums: Horizontal Linkages between the Different Tendencies and with the Grassroots

The new structure of relations in which nonopposition, or Liberal Moderate, professionalized women's organizations, especially umbrella organizations such as the WATC, received most of the Western foreign funding created new animosities and tensions between the different tendencies. In effect, these developments bifurcated the women's sector between organized grassroots committees and professionalized women's NGOs. The newly professionalized organizations tended to be the major recipients of state-sponsored Western donor funding. Given the more generous donor packages, donors were more stringent about the political backgrounds of their recipients. Ultimately, many women conveyed that the creation of organizations like the WATC lessened the likelihood that the grassroots women's committees would be the direct recipients of foreign donor assistance.[58] Moreover, the hierarchical, vertical relationship that transpired between the Opposition tendency–affiliated committees and the Liberal Moderate professionalized NGOs was at odds with the horizontal and inclusive relationship needed for the strengthening of civil society and the development of democracy.

Although the grassroots committees remained crucial for implementing many of these programs and provided the necessary social conduits for reaching women in various locations, especially more remote villages, they felt that since they were not associated with pro-Oslo political groups, they could not receive the financial assistance they needed to effectively promote or sustain their work. When invited to training sessions, individuals from these grassroots committees, often the leaders, received transportation costs and meals if they participated in WATC events. A grassroots coordinator explained how the grassroots committees were willing to forgo funding from an organization to ensure that the WATC did not receive additional funding in their name.[59] Although this particular USAID funded program no longer exists, the activists' sentiments toward the program were illustrative of the dynamics that had transpired. Often only leaders of the grassroots committees were invited to events in the hope that these women would relay the contents of the events to their constituencies. In effect, the same women attended most of the different events and lectures. Many of the activists, especially those not affiliated with Fatah and its clientelistic networks or the Liberal Moderates, felt increasingly alienated from these organizations. On the part of donors, such a strategy ensured that, although they might be promoting individuals who are affiliated with the opposition, they were not promoting entire organizations.

Tensions were exacerbated too by new incentive structures. Many of the activists in the women's committees were particularly disturbed that the prevailing incentive structure no longer reflected one's previous political involvement in terms of impact or influence. Moreover, individuals affiliated with certain political groups were now paid for the same work that activists had engaged in for years without compensation. These developments departed from ordinary professionalization outcomes in that those individuals who were not paid employees could not simply plan to acquire the necessary training and join an organization. Rather, in this noninclusive political context, these individuals would have to sever their ties with, and in many cases renounce, their previous political affiliation. Many women expressed their dismay that the whole concept of volunteer participation no longer existed in Palestinian society—in part because of the work of the professionalized NGOs and because many Fatah activists were now on payroll.[60] Many activists felt that social disparities in society were heightened by these newly created overlapping schisms: between those who could work in NGOs and are therefore eligible to earn high salaries and those who could not; those who were part of the accepted post-Oslo political landscape and those who were not. The relatively higher salaries of professionalized NGO staff—sometimes four to five times higher than the average salary in the public sector—exacerbated these tensions.

Although at face value these complaints may seem to represent only the grievances of unsalaried activists, they encapsulated an emerging divide shaping post-Oslo Palestinian political life: an emergent political elite able to navigate through the post-Oslo political landscape, and an Opposition tendency not afforded the same resources, and whose continued attention to local political dynamics and Israel's military occupation hindered its ability to do the same. The polarization that resulted was not simply between contending parties vying for influence; rather, it reflected a new political terrain, shaped by Western donors that afforded political inclusion only to certain groups, while marginalizing others.

With the bifurcation of the women's sector between an organized grassroots movement and a professionalized women's NGO sector came a significant reconfiguration of what it meant to "empower" women and a redefinition of what their priorities were (or should be). This programmatic shift could be seen in the roles accorded to the women now marginalized within the new organizational hierarchy. The members of the grassroots women's committees were effectively transformed from active political participants involved in their own organizations to recipients of skills and services in need of "awareness raising," often with little opportunity to apply their skills. Underlying this was a transformed approach to women's empowerment that no longer entailed political and social organization and increased economic independence and production, but rather something to be effected through "consciousness-raising" and individual relief. Aside from PARC's gender unit economic development program, most of the professionalized NGOs did not focus on the actual living conditions of Palestinian women and their productive role, but rather disproportionately focused on changing gender stereotypes, "consciousness raising," legislative reform when possible, and sometimes the provision of individual relief.

A key grievance raised by many of the activists in 2001 pertained to the high levels of replication and repetition in the programs of the professionalized NGOs. Additionally, they felt that there was often little follow-up to ensure that this "knowledge" was being put to practical use. The disarticulated spaces that existed between the state and civil society reinforced these dynamics and did not contribute to citizen engagement with state institutions. Keen to promote potential political leaders and pro-Oslo discourses and norms, by the end of the decade after the Madrid Peace Conference all five of the new women's NGOs and three gender desks in the Jerusalem-Ramallah access area provided educational training sessions: six of the organizations provided training in the area of women's rights, human rights, and democracy.[61] Hadeel Qazzaz's more recent research on women's NGO and election literacy training further corroborated my earlier findings.[62] According to Qazzaz, recipients of the training complained that they had received the same training from a number of different NGOs. As one organizer explained, "There are a lot of workshops, training sessions, and conferences, but everything is left there."[63] Another UPWC coordinator complained, "We are saturated with training sessions. . . . that's why the only programs I like involve transportation costs for students in need."[64] Similarly, another grassroots coordinator explained, "There are far too many events, workshops, and lectures. . . . We need follow-up . . . But everyone just wants to give training sessions and lectures."[65] According to most of my interviewees, these workshops were a waste of time. Many of the activists I interviewed continued to go to such activities because of the nice lunches and the opportunity to socialize with other activists. The professionalized NGOs, however, became accountable to their donors and not to the constituencies they were supposed to serve.

Many women in the grassroots committees felt that a defining problem was that the newly established Western donor-funded NGOs had begun addressing issues pertaining to women's rights as if they existed in a vacuum. As one activist succinctly put it, "These NGOs began to work as if they existed in an independent Palestine."[66] Another activist ironically referred to the establishment of a hotline for domestic abuse by one of these new professionalized NGOs: "Don't these women or the donors who fund them understand that most Palestinian villages still do not have phone lines, or running water for that matter?"[67] Fatah affiliated activists of the WCSW did not share the same extent of grievances. Of my WCSW interviewees, one expressed dismay with the political appointments of Fatah returnees versus locals of the WBGS, and three discussed the diminished focus on work in the villages.

Previously, many of the members of the women's committees were involved in choosing the projects and programs of their respective committees. Economic projects, although not always very lucrative, often figured prominently in these programs. As Western donor priorities shifted to promoting the Oslo Accords and the associated state-building phase, women's most pressing economic and political problems, often intimately associated with the persistence of Israel's military occupation, were no longer priorities.

Because of Israel's closure policies, which restricted Palestinian movement, many families lost their main breadwinner, which necessitated that more women seek paid employment. Accordingly, many activists pointed out the need for more skills training that could enhance women's employment opportunities. As one coordinator explained, "Many of our members are disappointed with the current programs [of the WATC]. . . . We talk about lobbying, advocacy, and democracy, but this does not address many women's real problems, which are related to the lack of employment and poverty and are directly an outcome of the current political situation."[68] Another coordinator complained: "Most professionalized NGOs only focus on educational programs and lectures. Very few focus on the productive role of women."[69] Another coordinator added: "One set of WATC training sessions in Hebron cost approximately US$4,000; this money could have been used more constructively for more sustainable projects."[70] Programs that emphasized skills training, they argued, would yield the greatest returns to society, instead of training sessions and workshops that were not sustainable in the absence of donor support.[71] One organizer lamented: "I feel much of this funding is for nothing. When we criticize these programs, the response is that the donors want this, or this is the donor's plan."[72] Many of the activists shared the view that foreign donor funding could have been put to better use. Not surprisingly, such views were disregarded.

My objective here is not to paint the work of the grassroots committees as positive and that of the professionalized NGOs as negative or counterproductive. Rather, I seek to highlight how the configuration of relations that transpired adversely affected the longer terms prospects for the strengthening of civil society. Some of the programs implemented by the professionalized NGOs are commendable. The WCLAC is a case in point: when pushed, all the activists I interviewed acknowledged that they had referred women to the organization, and that its legal and counseling services benefited many women. In 2000, the WCLAC provided individual counseling to 347 abused women, and legal assistance to 544 women.[73] A sole focus on some of the services of an organization, however, does not capture the political dynamics that transpired. Although many of the activists spoke favorably of the impressive work of the WCLAC, this was colored by their resentment that it was former leadership of the women's movement who became FIDA members and established this organization. These schisms between the grassroots women's committees (excluding the WCSW) and the professionalized women's NGOs (including the WATC) coincided along political lines, which further exacerbated existing polarization.

Engaging the PA through Disarticulated Spaces

In the post-Oslo era, the women's sectors engagement with the PA was also obstructed by the emergent disarticulated spaces between civil society and the state in which national and local government institutions discriminated against certain groups by not allowing them the same access. From its inception, the legislative council was not instituted to be fully representative of the Palestinian political spectrum and has been controlled by Fatah. Similarly, local government has remained quite weak. As a result, Fatah and its clientelistic networks tendency, including the Fatah-affiliated women's groups, have had the most consistent access to the PA. Non-Fatah women's groups, without the same direct access to members of the legislative council or to ministerial representatives, have channeled their demands through organizations, such as the WATC.

In general, the women's sector as a whole has attained some legislative gains through the WATC and the various gender units of some ministries.[74] For example, shortly after its establishment, the WATC attained key victories in terms of administrative regulations, including the drafting of the Palestinian Women's Charter. The Palestinian Women's Charter addressed a woman's nationality and her right to travel or move freely. According to the charter, "[Legislation] must grant women her right to acquire, preserve, or change her nationality. . . . Women should also be guaranteed the right to give citizenship to her husband and children, and be guaranteed the full freedom to move, travel and choose her place of residency."[75] They also changed regulations that allowed women to be issued passports, either for themselves or for their children, or register children on their passports without the approval of a male guardian.[76] Although these were significant legislative victories, they were not as appreciated by women in the Opposition tendency, and this in many ways was attributed to the political coloring of the WATC.

The WATC was perhaps the most political women's organization established in the post-Oslo period, with the specific objectives of enhancing women's participation in the Oslo process. Despite the attempt to incorporate women from all political backgrounds, the political tensions that existed hampered or undermined the work of the organization. Members of the WCSW were candid about their control of the WATC. As one member of the WCSW bluntly explained, "We [Fatah] dominate the WATC. . . . it is our organization."[77] Similarly, they were also frank about their clientelistic networks connecting them to the PA. Although many of the women acknowledged that the WATC was more effective than other professsionalized NGOs in reaching grassroots constituencies, they felt that the WATC exacerbated the schism between volunteer activists from the opposition grassroots women's committees and the pro-Oslo, or Liberal Moderate, salaried activists of the women's sector.

In the emergent organizational structure of the women's sector, organizations affiliated with the Opposition tendency were merely organizational members and recipients of services from the WATC. Many felt that, ultimately, the creation of the WATC ensured that the grassroots women's committees would no longer be the direct recipients of foreign donor assistance. Since a pro-Oslo, professionalized NGO like the WATC exists, foreign donors worked through that organization instead. Most of the funding to the WATC was to support the running costs of the coordinating mechanism, as well as the salaries of its employees.

Many, especially opposition-affiliated groups, felt that the legislative priorities of the WATC often reflected the "post-Israeli occupation," depoliticizing concerns of donors and of those who had benefited from post-Oslo developments at the expense of those who remained disadvantaged by the continuation of Israeli military occupation. They also felt that they did not represent women's most important priorities, and that they did not "own" these reforms. However, many of the members of the WCSW—the Fatah women's committee—did not have the same grievances since many of their practical concerns about employment and material help were more likely to be met directly through Fatah or the PA. Although the women's sector as a whole attained important legislative victories, the activists' discontent with these achievements could be attributed to the lack of inclusion and the politicized schism that defined the sector.

Engaging Local Government through Disarticulated Spaces

Teaching about democracy and citizen engagement in
Palestine is like teaching children to play football without a
football field.[78]
—Ghassan Khatib

Because of the politicized considerations associated with a noninclusive institutional setting, foreign donor programs seldom involved regular interactions between civil society and government institutions. This area of work certainly had not reached its full potential. In general, very few of the Western donors that funded the women's movement that I had interviewed had regular or ongoing programs involving local government; among the professionalized women's organizations, only the WATC had programs that involved local government. As I have explained, this was in many ways attributable to the disarticulated space in which they operated, a space in which groups and individuals affiliated with the Opposition tendency of the women's sector were a step removed from state institutions. Sanabel, a rural women's empowerment project established by the WATC in 1997,[79] is illustrative of the limits of building civil society in politically noninclusive contexts, in which "disarticulated spaces" result. The stated aim of the project was to

> support the strategic goals of women through helping them address their practical needs. Targeting twenty villages in Hebron and Gaza, the project involves selecting two women from each village and training them in empowerment skills so that they could lobby for their human rights and reach out to women of their village. A total of 400 women were reached with the aim of empowering them and raising their awareness of the concept of full citizenship in an attempt to improve their environment and daily conditions.[80]

The two women chosen for this project were often the designated coordinators of the established women's committees, and were the link between the professionalized NGOs and women in the villages. This project was renewed for another cycle.

Another WATC project that sought to address local governance was the Women and Elections for Municipal and Village Councils Project.[81] The project endeavored to raise women's awareness about the importance of their participation in municipal and village council elections. Its end of cycle outputs included the holding of a number of training sessions, workshops, and lectures about women and elections and meeting with decision makers and officials to encourage the appointment of women to these bodies. In addition to the political dimension of who is providing these workshops, who are the recipients, and who is paid and who is not, the impact of such programs was limited given the "disarticulated spaces" of political institutional development. In respect to both of these programs, participants did not apply any of their acquired skills in the first several years since local elections were not held until 2004, and the last round of the final phase of elections was postponed indefinitely because Opposition tendency affiliated groups attained majorities in a number of councils and were projected to perform strongly in the last round. Most Western donors then bypassed those municipalities or village councils with Opposition tendency–affiliated majorities. These outcomes were not simply a by-product of donor priorities, but a consequence of a noninclusive political settlement to which dominant political groups and Western foreign donors were committed.

The Model Parliament: Noninclusive, Hierarchical Organizing in the Making

I close this discussion with another illustrative example. The Model Parliament: Women and Legislation project reflected, in many ways, the outcomes of noninclusive, hierarchical, vertical civil society organizing. A few years after the signing of the Oslo Accords, the WCLAC and a coalition of professionalized women's NGOs spearheaded the model parliament—an initiative to begin discussions on women's rights and legal reform concerning all laws that relate to women's status in the WBGS.[82] A number of women and organizations affiliated with the Opposition tendency also participated. The stated goal of the Model Parliament was "to pass legislation that ensures equality and women's human rights for Palestinian women, as well as their participation in building a civil society based on justice, equality, respect for human rights and the rule of law."[83] What started out as a (donor-funded) modest initiative by women activists to begin a debate on legislation and women's rights in Palestinian society spiraled into a highly polarized debate that "propelled model parliament activists, and the women's movement as a whole, into real political activity within a highly contested public space."[84] The Model Parliament provoked a critical national debate regarding the rights of women in Palestinian society.

Initially, the Islamist movement instigated opposition to the Model Parliament, but they quickly gained support from broad sectors of Palestinian society, including non-Islamists. Although many analysts attributed the backlash against the Model Parliament activists to the inherent contradictory nature between *shari'a* laws and their primacy in Palestinian society and women's rights premised on equality (as understood in the West),[85] many of my interviewees (who were not religious or Islamist) referred to the Model Parliament project to illustrate the problematic nature of interactions between the grassroots women's committees and the professionalized NGOs.[86]

My interviews indicated that the primacy of *shari'a* laws in Palestinian society was only one dimension of the controversy that surrounded the Model Parliament. The dispute that transpired was just as much a result of the noninclusive nature of the Model Parliament, and the attempt of women from professionalized NGOs to speak on behalf of all women in Palestinian society regarding such a critical issue. A number of the women I interviewed, who were affiliated with the leftist Opposition tendency and considered themselves secular, also opposed the Model Parliament. According to these women, the Model Parliament was simply another exercise by this group of women, affiliated with Liberal Moderate–affiliated professionalized NGOs, to speak on behalf of the Palestinian women's sector as a whole. A survey conducted by the Center for Palestine Research and Studies in 2000, which sought to determine which legitimate bodies should decide on reform, supported these findings. According to the results, 33 percent of respondents (the highest percentage for this question), believed that society should decide on social reform issues. This was followed by 26 percent who believed that *shari'a* court should decide, and 17 percent who believed that the legislative council should decide.

Although the critiques of women associated with the Islamist Opposition–affiliated tendency movement were more religious in nature, many were upset that they were not consulted about the Model Parliament or included from the outset.[87] In a newspaper interview, an organizer from Al-Khansa' Society for Women explained that they were not entirely against the Model Parliament, but that they were opposed to the marginalization of Islamist women in the parliament.[88] In line with the noninclusive nature of the professionalized women's sector, a committee was put together to continue advocacy to change the personal status laws. A recognized figure in the women's movement, Islah Jad, developed a new strategic plan for this endeavor in which she proposed that future campaigns should be less open and of lower public profile, to avoid a confrontation with Islamists.[89] In essence, it was this noninclusive approach that further ignited the attack. Despite the backlash, the subject matter, which most simply preferred to ignore, was put into a national spotlight, and an important legal recommendation was realized: the legal age of marriage was raised to eighteen. One could imagine, however, more positive outcomes had the tensions associated with noninclusivity not colored these deliberations.

Inclusivity and the Reconstitution of the Women's Sector in El Salvador in the Postwar Period

In El Salvador, the more inclusive transition afforded the various associations and NGOs more or less the same resources and opportunities. As a result, all the women's organizations were able to professionalize their operations (see table 5.3) and maintain contact with and incorporate their grassroots bases during the transition.[90] The greater consensus among the political organizations vis-à-vis the peace accords reproduced itself in the affiliated organizations; this led to less polarization among these groups and more opportunities for effective cooperation. Moreover, because of the greater inclusivity of the Salvadoran peace accords, there was less foreign donor wariness regarding the reestablishment and institutionalization of local government, and hence the institutional setting was more conducive to the creation of "articulated spaces" between civil society and the state. Western donors promoted programs and projects that encouraged and often required regular interaction with grassroots constituencies and coordination with local government. The combination of these factors led to greater opportunities for political participation.

Most, if not all, of the women's organizations also pushed for the founding of the government body Instituto Salvadoreño para el Desarrollo de la Mujer (Salvadoran Institute for Women's Development; ISDEMU) in 1996.[91] The organization's mandate was to represent women's interests in the implementation of the peace accords and in the formulation and implementation of national policies toward women. Unlike the WATC, however, ISDEMU did not serve as an intermediary body but worked with other professionalized NGOs as an equal partner. As a result, a broad-based coalition of women's groups that were also strongly tied to various grassroots constituencies developed.[92] In general, two different tendencies in the women's sector emerged in the period following the signing of the peace accords (see table 5.3 for details).[93] The first tendency involved the mass-based women's organizations that were affiliated with the FMLN. Although all women's organizations in this tendency claimed to have severed their ties with the former FMLN factions and to have become entirely autonomous, the various women's organizations differed in their degree of actual autonomy from the FMLN. The second tendency included nongrassroots organizations, such as Flor de Piedra and Mujer Joven, which were not affiliated with political parties (see table 5.3 for more details). Because these organizations did not have grassroots constituencies, Western donors were less willing to fund them. Moreover, following the end of the Cold War, El Salvador was no longer as geostrategically important, especially to the United States. Foreign donors were more concerned to utilize these organizations to help improve the economic conditions of the impoverished population, including women, in the remotest parts of El Salvador.

The Mass-Based Organizations in the Post-1989 Period: New Mandates and Names but the Grassroots Remained

"After the peace accords, women returned to the cities
and there was a new space for organizing. . . . There was
a systematic reorganization of society, and we needed to
organize according to the new needs."[94]
—Azucena Quintera

As a negotiated settlement became more imminent, the various leaders of the FMLN began to devise strategies to accommodate the new political reality. Issues pertaining to elections, the reintegration of ex-combatants, and the status of the mass-based organizations all came to the fore. For the most part, the leaders of the FMLN factions agreed that more institutionalized and professionalized NGOs would be in a better position to access foreign donor assistance. Consequently, all political organizations of the FMLN decided that their respective women's organizations should re-create themselves as more institutionalized

TABLE 5.3. Inception of Women's Organizations in El Salvador—San Salvador, 1978 to 2001

Fuerzas Populares de Liberación (Popular Forces of Liberation, FPL)	Partido Comunista de El Salvador (Communist Party of El Salvador-PSC)	Ejercito Revolucionario del Pueblo (Revolutionary Army of People, ERP)	Partido Revolucionario de los Trabajadores Centroamericanos (Revolutionary Party of Central American Workers, PRTC)	Resistencia Nacional (National Resistance, RN)	Movimiento Popular Social Cristiano (Popular Social Christian Movement-MPSC)	Salvadoran Right-Wing+	Non-Affiliated, Non-grassroots-based
Asociación de Mujeres de El Salvador (Association of Women of El Salvador-AMES) 1978	Fraternidad de Mujeres Salvadoreñas (Fraternity of Salvadoran Women) 1956	Asociacion para la Autodeterminación y el Desarrollo de Mujeres Salvadoreña (Association for the Self-Determination and Development of Salvadoran Women-AMS) 1987 1991*	Asociacón de Mujeres Salvadoreña (Association of Salvadoran Women-ASMUSA 1982	Asociación de Mujeres Lili Milagro Ramirez (Association of Women-Lili Milagro Ramirez) 1984	Organización de Mujeres Salvadoreñas (Organization of Salvadoran Women-ORMUSA) 1985 1990*	Cruzada Pro Paz y Trabajo (Crusade for Peace and Work) 1979	Centro de Orientación Radial Para la Mujer Salvadoreña (Training Center for Salvadoran Women on Radio-CORAMS) 1988
Movimiento de Mujeres 'Mélida Anaya Montes' (Melida Anaya Monte Women's Movement-MAM) 1992*	Asociación de Mujeres Progresistas de El Salvador (Association of Progressive Women of El Salvador-1975) AMPES		Asociación Por Mejorar de la Mujer y el Ni~no (Association for the Improvement of Women and Children 1984	Mujeres por la Dignidad y la Vida (Women for Dignity and Life-Las Dignas 1990 1996*		Frente Femenino Salvadoreño (Salvadoran Women's Front) 1979	Instituto de Estudios de Mujer "Norma Virginia Guirola de Herrera" (Institute of Women's Studies "Norma Virginia de Herrera" –CEMUJER) 1990
	Instituto de Investigación, Capacitación y Desarrollo de la Mujer 'Norma Guirola de		Movimiento Salvadoreño de Mujeres (Salvadoran				Iniciativa de Mujeres

	Movement of Women- MSM) 1986 1988*	*Cristianas* **(Initiative of Christian Women) (1990–1993)**
		Grupo de Mujeres Universitarias **(Group of University Women) (1990–1993)**
		Flor de Piedra **(Flower of the Stone) 1994**
		Mujer Joven **(Young Women) 1996**

Herrera' (Institute of Research, Training, and Development of Women 'Norma Guirola de Herrera-IMU) 1986 1994*

Asociación Democrática de Mujeres (Democratic Association of Women- ADEMUSA) 1988 1992*

Instituto Salvadoreño para el Desarrollo de la Mujer (Salvadoran Institute for Women's Development- ISDEMU) 1996§

Note: bold text = non-grassroots-based NGOs; no bold text = mass-based organizations. The line designates incorporation of organizational membership into a new organization.

*Organization leaders officially registered and licensed the respective NGO during the indicated year.

†Of these organizations, the Crusade was a broad-based organization that united all women to the right of the Christian Democrats, whereas the Front was unofficially affiliated with the right-wing ARENA party. Neither of these organizations, nor the successor ARENA women's organization, amassed a substantial grassroots following.

§ISDEMU is not an organization but a government institution established in 1996 to ensure that the ministries are addressing women's interests in the formulation and implementation of national policies. ISDEMU works with other women's professionalized NGOs as an equal partner. The various directors of the women's organization participate as members of the ISDEMU board; therefore, the women's organizations coordinate and implement the policies and programs of ISDEMU and are not simply the recipients of its services.

Source: This table is slightly modified from the original that first appeared in Manal A. Jamal, "Democracy Promotion, Civil Society Building, and the Primacy of Politics." *Comparative Political Studies* 45, no. 1 (January 2012): 3–31. Prepublished online 27 April 2010, doi:10.1177/0010414010365998.

and professionalized organizations. The decision adopted by the various organizations calling for this change was directly influenced by the greater availability of foreign donor assistance in general, including from state-sponsored donor agencies.

As a result, after 1989, all the existing FMLN women's mass organizations became officially registered and further institutionalized and professionalized their organizations to facilitate access to Western donor funding. As Carmen Medina candidly explained, "When the war was winding down, all groups wanted to access foreign donor funding; the women's groups were no exception."[95] Others emphasized that the domestic changes facilitated for better institutionalized NGOs. The professionalization of these organizations was also intrinsically tied to various women's groups' desire to secure a position in the newly reconstituted civil society. Western donor funding was also more readily available for such institutions, provided that they had grassroots constituencies and were in a position and willing to implement economic development programs.

Because of the uniform consensus of the various political leaders vis-à-vis the imminent political settlement in El Salvador, there was less variation in the strategies adopted by the various leaders and political factions. Unlike in the Palestinian territories, work with the grassroots-based communities persisted and remained a central organizing principle. This task was facilitated by the very demands of, and actual support received from, foreign donors. As happened in the Palestinian territories, the professionalization of the Salvadoran women's movement contributed to the waning sense of voluntarism in Salvadoran society, as well as the emergence of hierarchies in the women's sector, between those who were now paid professional employees of the movement and those who are the actual stakeholders or members.[96] The vertical and hierarchical relations that emerged in the Salvadoran women's movement, however, did not coincide along political lines.[97] Also, the resentment that Palestinian organizers of the grassroots women's committees felt against their former leadership existed to a lesser degree in El Salvador since, in most cases, the leaders of the organizations did not abandon their constituencies.[98]

The more equitable organizational access to resources led to less tension and polarization and more cooperation, and thus to a stronger basis for civil society development. Political groups, especially those on the left, were party to the peace accords, and therefore undergoing the same process of transformation. The women's organizations became officially registered: the PRTC-affiliated MSM in 1988; the PCS-affiliated IMU in 1994; the ERP-affiliated AMS in 1991; and the Popular Christian Social Movement-affiliated ORMUSA in 1990. Meanwhile, the RN founded a mass-based women's organization, Mujeres por la Dignidad y la Vida (Women for Dignity and Life, Las Dignas) in 1990, and the FPL followed suit and founded Movimiento de Mujeres "Mélida Anaya Montes" (Melida Anaya Monte Women's Movement, MAM) in 1992. Some of the political factions, such as the RN for example, supported the founding of the women's organizations because they expected to be given a percentage of the funding that was received by the women's organization.[99]

A number of the directors of women's organizations indicated that they tried to focus on funding from solidarity groups and foundations, which are more flexible with project implementation and not as stringent in terms of accounting.[100] Funding from the Canadian International Development Agency (CIDA) to the women's sector in the immediate postsettlement period, however, illustrated how foreign donor assistance did not need to exacerbate competition between the different organizations. CIDA did not outright exclude any grassroots-based women's organization, but more or less treated the different organizations equally by not privileging certain organization over others. During this period, for example, CIDA funded the Instituto de Estudios de Mujer "Norma Virginia Guirola de Herrera" (Institute of Women's Studies "Norma Virginia de Herrera," CEMUJER), COM, MSM, and IMU for programs on citizen participation and leadership training. In the immediate period after the accords, CIDA also funded the AMS, IMU, and ORMUSA for programs on citizen participation and leadership training with a focus on women's leadership in the reconstruction efforts. CIDA also provided funding to Las Dignas for a program addressing economic opportunities for women. CIDA basically provided funding to all the major professionalized grassroots-based women's organizations, with the exception of MAM.[101] By funding different women's organizations for the Citizen Participation and Leadership Training Program, CIDA was able to reach a larger number of women in the different communities.

The programmatic priorities of foreign donors included local development as well as economic development projects;[102] these programs often required the recipients to work and maintain contact with grassroots constituencies. These organizations all maintained some sort of contact with their former grassroots constituencies, and therefore were in a good position to implement many of the foreign donor agendas that included local development and decentralization, and to serve as conduits in the implementation of economic development projects. Although these organizations were not necessarily better institutionalized than the Palestinian grassroots committees, they were part of an inclusive civil society development process, and therefore better positioned to access foreign donor funding given donors' priorities.

Although these groups continued to meet with their grassroots constituencies, the regularity of these meetings differed from one group to another. It was often difficult to ascertain the exact changes in membership given that many of these organizations did not maintain records during the war. In general, however, some of the organizers acknowledged that there was a decrease in their membership, and that they are no longer in contact with as many women as they were during the war. Moreover, some of the organizers claimed that they no longer maintained an official body of members and therefore did not require formal membership; instead, the role of these organizations was to help coordinate committees for their local development programs.

Nonetheless, despite the different strategies of the various FMLN-founded women's organizations, grassroots constituencies remained central to their work. In contrast to the reconstitution process of the Palestinian women's sector in which the heads of the grassroots women's committees became intermediaries between grassroots constituencies and professionalized NGOs, each of the Salvadoran women's organizations professionalized, incorporated its membership in the process, and independently maintained direct contact with its communities. MAM and MSM perhaps maintained contact with the largest number of women. As of 2002, MAM had an eighty-five-member General Assembly, with work divided between nine departments. The organization also had ninety-six affiliated committees, each composed of ten to twenty members; these members were not official members of MAM, but rather affiliates of MAM. MAM had roughly 1,800 affiliates, in addition to 352 women who were involved in the economic credit program.[103] Similarly, MSM had 150 delegate members in the General Assembly, and worked in eight *municipios* (municipalities) in twenty-six different communities. Isabel de Gevara of the MSM estimated that approximately 5,000 women participated in their national assembly.[104] AMS did not have an exact count of their affiliates, although organizers indicated that it had 125 members in its General Assembly. Moreover, AMS estimated to reach an average of 2,500 women per year through prenatal, postnatal, and reproductive health care programs.[105] OR-MUSA had 75 members in its General Assembly, and 300 affiliates.[106] And Las Dignas, whose General Assembly decided in 1994 that it is no longer a grassroots organization per se, worked in eleven *municipios* in its former communities, and had 450 affiliates involved in its local development programs.[107]

Autonomy

In the process of institutionalizing and professionalizing the Salvadoran women's sector, the various mass-based women's organizations eventually attained greater levels of autonomy from the political organizations that had established these women's groups. The women's organizations, however, underwent different routes to "autonomy" vis-à-vis their respective political organizations prior to the FMLN's merger. The mass-based women's organizations also differed in their eventual degree of autonomy from the FMLN political organizations, and the extent of their affability with the FMLN.

Of the mass-based women's organizations, Las Dignas had the most acrimonious break with its parent political organization, the RN, in 1993. Although relations between Las Dignas and the RN were tense from as early as 1991, Las Dignas received some funding through the party until its split in 1993. After the break, the RN no longer funneled resources to Las Dignas, and launched a public defamation campaign against the members of the women's organization, claiming that they were untrustworthy and that "they worked for the interests of the upper classes." The RN also targeted foreign donor agencies in the hope of dissuading them from funding Las Dignas.[108] The AMS also experienced a tense break from the ERP in 1991. At the time, women in AMS protested against Villalobos's undemocratic policies, women's lack of participation in the party's decision-making structures, and the unequal distribution of benefits to women following guerrilla demobilization at the end of the war.[109] Subsequently, seventy-eight women were expelled from the party; the expulsion served as a catalyst for demanding greater autonomy from the political party.

Other groups, such as MAM, MSM, ORMUSA, and IMU, had less tense breaks with their respective political organizations. As Irma Maya explained, "The reactions from the FPL were mixed; some felt that we did not respect the party. Others assumed that MAM was still one of their organizations since there was an overlap in membership and leadership."[110] Although some members of these tendencies were critical of the women's calls for greater autonomy, other party members were quite supportive.

The delineated geographic distribution of territories among these groups also ensured less project replication in the same region. The professionalized mass-based women's organizations predominantly worked in the communities of their respective organizations. Even at the time that these organizations separated from their parent political organizations, many of the women who founded them remained active in the ranks of their organizations, either as leaders or as members at large.[111] Irma Maya further explained, "The thirty-five of us who established MAM decided to work where the FPL was active; it was often difficult to establish where the FPL ended and where MAM began. At our first public meeting of MAM, there were 1,500 members. Now we laugh that all the women were members or supporters of the FPL."[112] As of 2002, many of the women who ran these organizations were previous cadres in the parent organizations, and still affiliated with the FMLN. For others the relationship became more informal. "Our relationship is now personal and not official," Isabel de Gevara explained.[113] Moreover, after the FMLN won the elections in some municipalities, many of the mass-based women's organizations were keen to coordinate and strengthen their relationship with the municipalities in the regions of their operation. In many instances, however, these organizations also worked in communities with ARENA mayors. Naturally, because of the varying dynamics at play, the degree of affability between the mass-based organizations and the FMLN party varied. For the most part, the women's professionalized mass-based organizations were still considered supporters of the FMLN, and shared many of the same ideological and political positions.[114]

The New Nongrassroots-Based Organizations

I think they only want to support the political organizations. It seems that we can only get funding if we are conducting research. Donors are not really interested in other projects, especially if you are not a political organization. In the future, we are thinking about selling services, but this is difficult.[115]
—Sophia Delgado

In parallel to the professionalization of ORMUSA[116] and FMLN-affiliated women's mass-based organizations, other women founded a number of new unaffiliated, nongrassroots-based organizations in San Salvador (see table 5.3 for more details). The programs of these various organizations were eclectic and included raising gender awareness through the mainstream press and lobbying on behalf of sex workers. The founders of the new nongrassroots-based organizations had the clear and distinct character of being independent of any political organization or tendency. Despite the innovative work of some of these organizations, all complained that they had difficulty accessing foreign donor funding. In El Salvador, foreign donor agencies were more keen to fund the FMLN-affiliated organizations because of their relationship with grassroots constituencies.

Among the new groups founded in this period were CEMUJER, the Centro de Orientación Radial Para la Mujer Salvadoreña (Training Center for Salvadoran Women on Radio, CORAMS) in 1988, Flor de Piedra (Flower of the Stone) in 1994, Mujer Joven (Young Women) in 1996, Iniciativa de Mujeres Cristianas (Initiative of Christian Women), and Grupo de Mujeres Universitarias (Group of University Women). An ARENA-affiliated women's organization was also founded in 1992, but never became very active or very present in the Salvadoran women's sector. The founders of CORAMS established the organization to bring more light to gender issues and to promote sustainable development.[117] Alba America founded CEMUJER as a feminist organization that would specifically address issues pertaining to women's rights and discrimination against women.[118] The founders of Mujer Joven established the organization to address the needs of younger women,[119] and the founders of Flor de Piedra wanted to formalize the rights of sex workers. Some women also founded other organizations such as Iniciativas de Mujeres Cristianas and Grupo de Mujeres Universitarias to address the issues of certain constituencies of women. These organizations did not have a membership base, though Flor de Piedra had an assembly. Among these organizations, CEMUJER reached the largest number of women, despite the fact that it did not have an official membership base.

In this tendency, CEMUJER was the most successful in accessing foreign donor funding from various UN bodies, foundations, or solidarity groups, such as the United Nations Children Fund (UNICEF), UNDP, Catalan Association for Lawyers, Rights and Democracy (Montreal, Quebec), NOVIB, and the Norwegian Agency for Development Cooperation, albeit in more limited amounts. In part, this was related to CEMUJER's ability to reach a large number of women. Although CEMJUER was able to access funding from various solidarity groups and foundations, the organization was initially founded without any donor assistance. As Alba America explained, "My family supported me morally and financially; my father let me use the house. I then invited other women to join me. . . . It was very difficult because we started during the war, without a political party. International donors did not trust us, and we did not receive assistance. . . . It is still very difficult."[120] Both CEMUJER and CORAMS also had to rely on private funding, either from businesses or from an individual in the case of CORAMS.[121]

Meanwhile, Flor de Piedra and Mujer Joven had to limit their activities, or in the case Mujer Joven, simply halt its activities altogether, because of its inability to access funding.[122] As Sophia Delgado explained, "We were not able to receive any funding, and now we have no activities."[123] Flor de Piedra initially received funding from the Lutheran World Federation and from HIVOS. In 1996, these organizations stopped funding the group. For a whole year, a customer of one of the members paid the organization's rent. Various members of the organization tried to generate income for Flor de Piedra by selling drinks in a makeshift *tienda* (small shop). The organizers, however, had to close down the shop because the law prohibited an NGO from owning a business. The organization started selling condoms to generate income.[124] Despite the various efforts and the constructive work carried out by these nongrassroots organizations, foreign donors were more willing to fund organizations that had broader access to segments of the population, especially in the more remote communities.

Programmatic Changes in the Salvadoran Women's Sector in the Postwar Era: Local Development, Political Advocacy, and Economic Development Take Center Stage

As a negotiated settlement became imminent, war-related survival was supplanted by other programmatic priorities, which included coordination with local government, *desarrollo local* (local development), *incidencia politica* (political advocacy), and economic development, including microfinancing. Gender related issues, such as reproductive rights and women's health more generally, paternal child-care support, domestic violence, and the condition of women workers in the *maquilas* (factories producing goods for export), also assumed a stronger presence in the program priorities of these organizations. As Yanera Argueta explained, "In general, during the war, our programs focused on basic necessities. Then in 1992, we began addressing women's practical needs, and in 1997 and 1998 we started incorporating a feminist agenda in our local development work."[125] A number of organizations also began to incorporate more gender analysis in their programs. Later, disaster prevention also became popular with foreign donors, and therefore with the women's mass-based organizations as well.

Of the women's organizations under examination, all had programs for *incidencia politica* and *desarrollo local*. The political participation programs involved training that encouraged women's political engagement and were accompanied by local development programs.[126] Moreover, of the women's NGOs I examined, all but the IMU had some form of economic empowerment programs. Eleven of the seventeen donor agencies I surveyed considered economic development to be one of their program priority areas.[127] By 2002, MAM had the most comprehensive economic development program, which involved microfinancing, administrative training, and vocational training.[128] Similarly, MSM's economic development programs involved support for home agricultural production, as well as a number of shrimp cooperatives.[129] ORMUSA's programs included computer classes and support for women's agricultural and dairy production.[130] Although AMS and Las Dignas did not organize productive ventures for women, they provided skills training in a number of areas: AMS provided technological training for women involved in agriculture,[131] and Las Dignas provided support to women training in nontraditional sectors.[132]

Initially, Las Dignas expended considerable effort in maintaining contact with its communities, and tried to channel resources to women in the former RN zones. Through the assistance of foreign donors, Las Dignas helped to organize small microfinance projects such as bakeries, chicken farms, and shops. In 1994, Las Dignas reevaluated the productivity of these microfinanced projects and concluded that, given their limited economic returns, they were not successful ventures. In turn, Las Dignas turned its attention to skills training in nontraditional technical areas.[133]

Many of these organizations also provided consciousness-raising workshops on women's rights and domestic violence. These workshops involved the same themes as those covered in the Palestinian context, such as leadership training, civic education, and women's rights. Las Dignas, for example, organized feminist consciousness workshops, through what they called Escuela de Debate Feminista (School for Feminist Debate). These workshops were often attended by members of other women's NGOs, and were open to anyone who was willing to pay the modest registration fee. Other workshop themes were women's health, domestic violence, and women's rights, especially for those working in the *maquila* sector. A few of the organizations also provided counseling, especially for victims of domestic violence.

In general, these programs were more comprehensive in addressing women's needs. The more "articulated space" between civil society and the state allowed for greater opportunity to apply the knowledge gained, and a greater likelihood that the work would be sustained once donor funding was discontinued. The programmatic priorities of the women's sector evolved from first addressing basic, practical needs, to incorporating greater gender consciousness. Despite this evolution of these priorities, all organizations still had programs that addressed women's practical needs.

The programs of the various nongrassroots-based organizations were eclectic in nature and varied from publishing in the mainstream press to lobbying on behalf of sex workers. Both CEMUJER and CORAMS were involved in communications; CORAMS provided training for women in the media, as well as in gender issues and in sustainable development, and CEMUJER worked on the production of alternative radio, video, and audiovisual programs dealing with gender issues. CEMUJER also worked on legal issues, including the promotion of alternative understandings of the law as it affects marginalized groups, and provided legal counsel to women. Flor de Piedra's programs in 2002 centered on providing health and psychological services to sex workers. The organization also lobbied the various municipalities regarding rezoning and the expelling of prostitutes from certain areas. By 2002, Mujer Joven no longer had any activities. Although the members of the organization stopped meeting two years ago, Sophia Delgado continued to volunteer for the organization and wrote articles for *La Prensa Grafica*.[134]

Reframing Women's Participation and Priorities in El Salvador and the Impact on Civil Society and Democratic Development

Following the peace accords, the reconstituted women's sector enabled its organizations to focus on programs that addressed women's practical and political needs, and contributed to the strengthening of civil society and democratic development. The more inclusive political settlement enabled a more positive role for foreign donor funded programs, especially those that encouraged grassroots-based women's organizations to interact with local government. Not only did the number of women mayors and council members increase considerably in the postwar period, but various women's organizations systematically pushed municipalities to incorporate gender-sensitive components in their local development plans.[135] Although foreign-funded programs tended to differ, they almost always included some level of coordination with local municipalities, regular meetings with municipal authorities, the provision of meeting space, and thus the establishment of more regular patterns of interaction with this level of government. These regular patterns of partnership ensured that coordination between the women's organizations and the municipalities was more likely to continue once donor funding was discontinued. As in the previous section on the Palestinian women's sector, I assess the quality of this emergent civil society sector by examining the level and patterns of interaction between the different tendencies of the women's sector and the state, and local government specifically. I conclude with an illustration of a Western-funded *desarrollo local* program to elaborate on the dynamics that transpired.

Solid Horizontal Linkages between the Different Professional NGOs and the Grassroots Take Root

Although a number of Salvadoran women's organizations experienced some decrease in membership, the Salvadoran women's sector as a whole became represented by a number of strong, foreign donor-funded professionalized NGOs that maintained access and strong relations with their grassroots constituencies. The more inclusive settlement provided the main political parties and their affiliated groups with relatively equal opportunities (including access to Western donor assistance) to shape the reconstitution of civil society, and it allowed for a more "articulated" space relative to the Palestinian case between the state and civil society. Given these combined factors, Western donor programs encouraged the incorporation of grassroots constituencies and cooperation between the different organizations, as well as the institutionalization of more regular interactions with state institutions.

Many groups in El Salvador had long-standing relationships with certain solidarity groups or donors that preceded the creation of the professionalized NGOs; this relationship often continued after the peace accords. Therefore, NGOs access to certain funding sources was more assured and hence minimized the competition with other organizations. Moreover, because of the geographic distribution of territories among groups and their established relationship with certain donors, the replication of programs in the same region was minimal.[136] As Michael Foley explained, "The wartime chain of command—which assigned each FMLN party its own territory of operation, each territory its community organizations, and each organization its NGOs" was still more or less intact despite the professionalization and distancing from the various political parties.[137]

Grassroots organizing remained central to the organization of the women's sector. As Isabel de Gevara explained, "This [our structure] is very similar to the structure of organization during the war. . . . We have basically maintained our relationship with the grassroots in a particular [geographic] area."[138] Foreign donors also played a direct role in increasing levels of coordination between different women's groups by requiring them to participate in these coordinating mechanisms. The fact that Las Dignas continued its role in grassroots organizing, despite its decision to stop doing so, emphasizes how foreign donors can play an important role in promoting certain patterns of interaction between NGOs and other parties, including grassroots constituencies. Similarly, IMU was initially founded as a research and training institute, and not a mass-based organization, but shifted its work to also engage with various grassroots constituencies.

Both during the war and after the peace accords, women created a number of organizing mechanisms to coordinate the different women's organizations. Many of these networks were also initiated by the FMLN.[139] In the postwar period, women set up new organizing mechanisms to address specific issues such as domestic violence, women's health, and elections. Among the most active networks created in the postwar period are the Concertación Feminista Prudencia Ayala (Prudencia Ayala Feminist Coalition), Fora de Ciudadanas (Women Citizens' Forum), Red por la Salud de las Mujeres (Network for Women's Health), Red 25 Noviembre (25 November Network Against Violence Against Women), and Mujeres' 94, to name but a few. Mujeres '94 was perhaps one of the most important coalition-building exercises of the Salvadoran women's sector. COM initiated this effort to increase the participation of Salvadoran women in electoral politics, and to develop a women's political platform for the 1994 elections. Foreign donors strengthened these horizontal linkages by encouraging women's organizations to participate in these networks. For example, as Isabel de Gevara explained, "Most donors, especially European donors required that we be part of a network. Often the funding is distributed through the network, and then the funding is distributed equally among us. I do not think this is necessary."[140] These networks were sometimes distinguished from ordinary networks in that funding was distributed through them to the member organizations. Moreover, the equal distribution of funding to the member organizations ensured that less of a hierarchical relationship would develop between these organizations.

Engaging the State through More Articulated Spaces

Interactions between the Salvadoran women's sector and the state predominately took place through the various ministries, ISDEMU, and local government structures. In El Salvador the more representative Legislative Assembly, the more institutionalized and developed structures of local government, and the types of projects foreign donor have promoted provided women with more direct access to the state, especially at the local government level.[141] A number of women's organizations also worked directly with specific ministries; for example, both ORMUSA and AMS coordinated directly with the Ministry of Health, often facilitating the work of the ministry by providing access to grassroots constituencies.

Many of the directors of the women's organizations with whom I spoke considered the founding of ISDEMU to be one of the major achievements of the women's sector. As Palestinian women had done with the WATC, the various Salvadoran women's organizations founded ISDEMU to represent women's interests in the implementation of the peace accords. The various directors of the women's organization participated as members of the ISDEMU board; therefore, the women's organizations coordinated and implemented the policies and programs of ISDEMU, and were not simply the recipients of its services. ISDEMU worked in ten areas including employment, family, violence, agriculture, local development, citizen participation, and health, and its programs include a national campaign against domestic violence and training and technical assistance to various government bodies, especially related to domestic violence. In each of these areas, ISDEMU worked with the relevant ministry or ministries in coordination with various NGOs or private groups.

The Salvadoran women's sector has made important legislative gains since the signing of the peace accords in 1992. The women's success in implementing legislative reforms was attributed to the formation of a broad-based coalition, including women from across the political spectrum, to push for women's demands.[142] As Michelle Saint Germain explained, "A difference in the Salvadoran case from other Latin American (or Eastern European) cases was the widespread adoption of a gender perspective by many diverse types of women's groups, from some women deputies elected to the national legislature to university women to communal and grass-roots groups."[143] The women's sector was inclusive of women from different backgrounds; specifically, it was not only the intellectuals or elite leaders of the movement who were part of the movement and advocated for the incorporation of women in democratization and national development, but women at the grassroots were also included and actively embraced such visions.[144] Most notably, the women's sector pushed for the passing of legislation against domestic violence, and a reformed Family Code. With the support of other groups, La Asociación de Madres Demandantes (Association of Mothers Seeking Child Support), an organization founded by *Las Dígnas*, passed a series of laws relating to *cuota alimenticia* (child support payments).[145] These laws included regulations requiring candidates to fulfill all child support obligations before assuming office. Through MAM's Iniciativas Ciudanas en Favor de las Mujeres (MAM's Citizens' Initiative for Women), its multidisciplinary team—which included two legislative deputies[146]—worked on legislative reform proposals, including labor laws in the free-trade zones. Individual organizations have had to work extensively with other groups in the women's sector to pass these laws.[147] Moreover, women from diverse sectors felt that they owned these reforms.

Engaging Local Government through More Articulated Spaces

By 2002, eleven of the seventeen donor agencies I examined in El Salvador were involved in some aspect of local development programs.[148] Professionalized organizations' access and regular interaction with grassroots constituencies continued to facilitate the work of foreign donors in these program areas. Local development programs encouraged the newly professionalized women's organizations to maintain and attempt to consolidate their relationship with grassroots constituencies.[149] These regular patterns of interaction ensured that coordination between the women's organizations and the municipalities would be more sustainable if or when the donor funding was discontinued.

Many of the NGO organizers who were involved in organizing local development initiatives also felt that this was an area where important gains can be achieved. As the director of IMU explained, "After the FMLN won some seats in the municipal elections in 1994, there was an opportunity for us to expand our work."[150] Sonia Baires elaborated: "Local development is important because it is where civil society has more space to organize, and it is at this level that we can impact democratization; it is where you see more results. Donors are also interested in local development."[151] Similarly, Jeanette Urquilla explained, "It is important for us to coordinate with the municipalities . . . in this process of democratization, and in this new economic context, municipal governments have an important role to play in developing these areas. They can also promote citizen participation."[152] These women felt that local development programs ensured that the women's committees were able to make demands and seek support from the local municipality.

Some, however, were more critical of *desarrollo local* and argued that the impact of local development schemes should not be exaggerated. For example, Hector Dada-Hirezi, director of Facultad Latinoamericana de Ciencias Sociales (Latin American Faculty for the Social Sciences, FLACSO), explained:

> [A] systematic approach to the concept does not exist, and there is little consensus regarding what local development exactly is. . . . There is also variation between the different municipalities, and the programs that donors promote. . . . Therefore, one should not always assume that a focus on local development is going to yield positive outcomes.[153]

He further explained, "With an excessive focus on local development, mayors focus on the development of 'their territory,' disregarding the national picture."[154] David Holiday also pointed out that "although donors are more focused on local development, on the negative side donors compete for model communities, such as Bajo Limpa and Suchitoto, because they have very organized citizen structures and mayors."[155] In effect, donors were sometimes less likely to address poorly organized communities in their local development programs, despite the need. Isabel de Gevara further explained, "Although MSM has a local development program, the actual level of coordination between the MSM's affiliated women's groups and their respective municipalities was quite low. In general, we do not coordinate much with the municipalities—the *compañeros* [comrades] in the mayor's office sadly do not take advantage of resources and work with the different organizations."[156] It is important, therefore, not to romanticize local development programs, but to recognize the possible opportunities and limitations.

Although the nature of the relationship and level of cooperation between the various municipalities and the women's groups might have differed from one case to another, and despite the criticisms regarding the overemphasis on local development, these women were now closer to local government, and in a better position to make demands on the state at this level. Moreover, regular patterns of interaction ensured that sustained coordination between the women's organizations and the municipalities was more likely once the donor-funded projects ended. This discussion illustrates how civil society development in more articulated spaces allows for a range of development possibilities that would not be available otherwise.

Local Development and an Attempt at More Horizontal Organizing

I close this discussion of the women's sector in El Salvador by discussing the particular example of local development programs that illustrate how, in the context of more inclusive political settlements and more articulated spaces, the promotion of civil society by foreign donors can yield more positive outcomes. Most notably, these positive outcomes included outlets that facilitated civic engagement. The establishment of regular patterns of interaction between the committees and the municipalities also better ensured the sustainability of the work once the funding was discontinued.

Local development programs took several forms, but often included some sort of regular pattern of interaction between the communities and the municipalities. Often, a *promotora* (promoter or organizer) was the link between the community and the professionalized women's NGO. The community elected the *promotora* and she became a salaried employee of the NGO. The *promotora* met with women in the community, as well as other *promotoras* at the NGO headquarters, on a regular basis. These women formed a committee and then maintained contact with the local municipality.

Local development programs could include the formation of committees to interact with the municipality, as well as training for municipal employees. For example, in relation to MAM's local development programs, Isabel Fabean explained:

> We carried out a diagnostic meeting with the women during which we asked about their needs. Then we arranged a meeting with the mayor, and decided on the program and how the mayor was going to help us. . . . We administered and funded projects, and the municipality facilitated the process, and sometimes also provided resources. In some cases, the municipality provided the physical space and the furniture and paid the salary for one employee.[157]

Local development could also be conceived more broadly and include gender-sensitivity training for municipal employees in hopes that they will focus on gender concerns in their work with youth and health clinics. For example, Deysi Chaine explained:

> We wanted mayors to become more gender conscious. Therefore, we also created a group to involve municipal personnel in gender-training sessions. We had ten groups in different areas for training through municipalities. Municipalities also supported us in implementing these projects. For example, they provided us the room for training.[158]

Members of the municipal council, or the mayor, met with the women's committee regularly; the frequency varied from one municipal area to another. During these meetings, the women raised many of their concerns and demands to the municipal officials.

This organizing took place in the former communities of the respective political organizations. As Sonia Baires explained, "Much of this work was in our [RN] old zones. We helped in the creation of women's groups at the local level, and then we supported their work and initiatives to cooperate with the municipalities."[159] The continuation of work in the community where an established relationship already existed between the NGO and the community often ensured a higher level of trust between the parties. Many of the directors of the women's NGOs maintained that, although political participation and local development were new titles, these women's organizations have always had these types of programs but under different titles.

Although there were vertical aspects to the relationship between the professionalized NGOs and the committees, the pattern of regular interaction between the professionalized NGO, the committees, and the municipality also ensured a horizontal dimension to the relationship. Moreover, women in the committees had input pertaining to the issues they wanted to address with the municipalities. The more articulated space also guaranteed that women who participated in these projects had increased access to resources or networks through the municipalities; in turn, this increased access facilitated citizen participation.

Conclusion

Professionalization alone cannot explain the impact of Western donor assistance. Rather, the inclusivity of the political settlement figures much more prominently. The inclusivity of political settlements has important implications for the nature of the political institutionalization that emerges, and by extension the extent of articulated space between the state and society. Appreciation of these factors elucidates how foreign aid will figure in. Moreover, reconfiguration of this sector of civil society, and women's position in it, will have important implications for gender related legislative reform.[160] Some have argued that the quality of democracy is important for women's rights.[161] My argument takes this analysis a step back and emphasizes the degree of inclusion that emerges from the political settlements is important for the quality of civil society and democracy. The quality of civil society has important implications for women in their struggles for expanded rights.

In the Palestinian case, there was also resentment against the paid employees of the professionalized NGOs, and against the Fatah-affiliated members who had more access to PA institutions. Crucially, these divisions coincided along political lines. Despite the increase in associational density, the noninclusive configuration of the emergent civil society and the hierarchies created, as well as the disarticulated spaces, led to its weakening, adversely affecting prospects for the development of democracy. Even when the women's sector attained legislative victories, the configuration of this sector contributed to the lack of ownership that many women felt vis-à-vis these reforms.

These developments in the women's sectors in both cases extended beyond the first decade. In the Palestinian context, the women's grassroots committees have become even weaker and less able to mobilize or engage in broader national politics. In the Salvadoran context, the women's grassroots organizations have remained active in reaching grassroots constituencies and in national politics. By no means is this an attempt to romanticize civil society development or women's achievements in El Salvador, or to overlook the increased factionalization, disillusionment, and violence[162] in society, the challenges women face,[163] or the many weaknesses of the Salvadoran left. My goal is to illustrate how a more inclusive political settlement allows for more equal distribution of foreign funding and the development of more articulated spaces, which may contribute more positively to the strengthening of civil society.

6

Hamas after Electoral Victory

Fatah and the Western Donor Community Respond

Did we have to fall from a tremendous height so as to see our blood on our hands . . . to realize that we are no angels . . . as we thought? . . . To be friendly with those who hate us and harsh on those who love us—that is the lowness of the arrogant and the arrogance of the low. . . . He asked me: does a hungry guard defend a house whose owner traveled to spend his summer vacation at the French or Italian Riviera . . . no difference?
—Mahmoud Darwish, "You, from Now On, Are Not Yourself"

Hamas's 2006 legislative election victory was a watershed moment in the study of Middle East democracy, and especially relating to Western democracy promotion efforts in noninclusive political contexts. The developments that transpired were not simply the result of the international embargo and Western donor cessation of funding. Rather, the noninclusive settlement, in this case one defined by the Oslo Accords and the dominant Palestinian groups who upheld these accords, could not accommodate these election results. Although the international embargo and Western donors' refusal to accept the results exacerbated prevailing dynamics, mayhem would have transpired regardless. Hamas won the 2006 election with a landslide victory, securing seventy-four out of a total of 132 legislative seats (68 percent at the district level and 44 percent at the national level); certainly, the outcome was a surprise to all parties, not least to itself.[1] Within days of the election, the Palestinian polity was in crisis. Fatah, the dominant Palestinian political party and signatory of the Oslo Accords, refused to accept the election results, and with the international community virtually paralyzed the

Palestinian polity. Effects extended beyond Hamas and its leadership and severely polarized Palestinian political life, inflicted what may have become an irreversible divide between the West Bank and Gaza Strip, and undermined years of government institutional development. Later, these developments undermined humanitarian efforts and any semblance of civil society related cooperation between Islamists and Fatah in the Palestinian territories.

Hamas's initial efforts to establish a unity government failed miserably. Fatah refused to join a coalition government for fear that it would compromise its political position at the helm of Palestinian leadership, which it had occupied for almost forty years.[2] The Liberal Moderates also refused to join a coalition government because they opposed Hamas's political program, and were concerned that Hamas would digress from its more moderate electoral campaign. Moreover, Fatah, the Liberal Moderates, and the PFLP were also concerned that Hamas had not explicitly recognized the PLO as the "sole and legitimate representative of the Palestinian people," and that such a move would undermine this long-held position of the Palestinian nationalist movement. With no partners in sight, Hamas established its government on 29 March 2006, led by Ismail Haniyeh, the new prime minister. As a result of Fatah's intransigence, as well as the international community's backlash, Hamas would not be able to continue to rule. Throughout, the international community's position was inflexible; it refused to accept a unity government that did not meet the conditions of the Quartet, that is Russia, the United States, the EU, and the UN. The Quartet maintained that the new Palestinian government had to uphold the principles it outlined on 30 January 2006: renunciation of violence, recognition of Israel, acceptance of all previous agreements and obligations, including Oslo and the Road Map.[3] Moreover, the United States warned that unity government partners would also be subjected to a boycott by the international community. Meanwhile, the various parties, and especially Fatah, bargained that Hamas's lack of political experience, a Western embargo, and cold reception by the Arab world would doom the political organization and discredit it in the eyes of the Palestinian population.[4]

Ultimately, Hamas was unable to continue its rule. In February 2007, Fatah and Hamas signed the Mecca Agreement,[5] which led to the establishment of a new coalition government. Tensions continued to mount, and the agreement broke down in June 2007 following a spate of all-out armed conflict between the two parties, which lasted a few days. In a preemptive move, Hamas forcefully seized power. Immediately thereafter, Abbas dissolved the unity government, and appointed a government headed by Salam Fayyad in the West Bank. The international community's response was a brutal lockdown of the Gaza Strip, and a heightened diplomatic, economic, and political embargo with debilitating humanitarian consequences. From the moment that Fatah conceded to a unity government, it failed because of the already established Oslo parameters, which left little, if any, room to maneuver in the political landscape.

In what follows, I elaborate on these unfolding events. Although the chapter will not focus on microdevelopments in associational life, it will discuss the macro, broader changes in Palestinian political life, and how Western donors worked to promote included groups and to marginalize excluded groups. Departing from standard explanations that focus on the role of external actors as a key independent variable, it will show how the political settlement, in this case the Oslo Accords, shaped the impact of Western donor assistance.

The Days after "Democracy"

Shortly after the election results, the Quartet welcomed President Abbas's call for the new Palestinian government to commit to a platform of peace. When the Abbas government approved the new Hamas-led government, the international community was dismayed that they had not committed to the principles spelled out on 30 January 2006. The Quartet reiterated its view that future assistance to any new government would be reviewed by donors based on the said government's commitment to the principles it had outlined. It emphasized that direct assistance to Hamas's government and ministries would be halted under the given circumstances.[6] Western donor assistance to the Palestinian people therefore became conditioned on Hamas's adherence to post-Oslo terms, which included the Quartet's conditions.[7]

Initially Hamas did not reject these conditions outright, and it was willing to work around them. Hamas's leaders in the WBGS responded that they would be willing to adhere to a ten year *hudna* (cease-fire) provided that Israel withdraw to the 1967 borders. For Hamas, the *hudna* was proof that they regard Israel as a reality they are willing to work with on day-to-day matters. The *hudna*, however, was far removed from the Quartet conditions because it entailed reciprocal obligations on the part of Israel, and did not go as far as recognizing Israel's right to exist. Moreover, Hamas promised to respect and to not obstruct the PLO's negotiations with Israel on condition that the final agreements would be put to a national referendum. Although Hamas was not willing to unconditionally accept the Quartet's conditions, they put forth alternative (though related) proposals. In 2008, Hamas's leader, Khaled Mashaal, reiterated these assurances to former US president Jimmy Carter who relayed them to the White House; both the US administration and the Israeli leadership dismissed these proposals. Ehud Barak, then Israeli prime minister, refused to meet with Carter to ensure that the meeting would not be misinterpreted as part of negotiations with Hamas.

Fatah and the Western Donor Community Retaliate

Fatah's inhospitality was exacerbated by international pressure. In particular, Fatah refused to cooperate in terms of its transfer of power, especially at the security and lower ministerial levels. Intent on not relinquishing power to Hamas, Abbas expanded the powers of the presidency, limited existing ministerial areas of control, and reasserted control over security forces.[8] Shortly after the election, Abbas transferred control of official media, namely PA news, TV, and radio from the Ministry of Information to the Office of the President. He also reactivated the formerly consultative PA National Security Council as a body that would oversee all security forces and would report to him directly.[9] Furthermore, he stripped the Interior Ministry of control over all border crossings, including the Rafah crossing, which is the Gaza Strip's main land passage to Egypt, and brought them under the control of the "presidential guards" who reported directly to the presidency.[10] Abbas also appointed nine ministerial undersecretaries, all Fatah members, none of whom were technocrats, who would report directly to him.[11] The formerly Fatah-dominated civil service also refused to abide by the new Hamas-dominated cabinet directives.

The combination of obstacles severely restricted the ability of the Hamas government to supply basic public services to citizens of the WBGS. In particular, Hamas was unable to deliver salaries to approximately 160,000 public sector employees. Exploiting the volatility of the situation, Fatah mobilized widespread strikes among civil servants, especially teachers.[12] The civil servants received their first full salaries in July 2007, and Hamas affiliates or supporters were excluded from these arrangements. Moreover, several Fatah-controlled security forces remained outside the control of the Hamas's interior ministry, especially in the Gaza Strip.[13] The United States permitted the redirecting of Arab funds to the Office of the President for the salaries of security personnel.[14] Despite Fatah's attempts to discredit Hamas for this sad state of affairs, the majority did not fault Hamas but rather the international community for facilitating Fatah's actions, and what translated to collective punishment of the Palestinian people. Friction continued to mount.

Encouraged and fostered by US assistance to Fatah, the security situation continued to decline after Hamas's electoral victory. Fatah and Hamas armed skirmishes became commonplace, and Fatah security officials refused to take orders from the new Hamas government. Fatah-controlled preventive security and intelligence units kidnapped and assassinated a number of Hamas members and its affiliates. Meanwhile, internal divisions in Fatah were festering. Palestinian political prisoners intervened to end the mounting conflict between Fatah and Hamas. Headed by the former leader of Fatah's West Bank civilian organization, Marwan Barghouti, they coauthored the Prisoners' Document. This document departed from international community demands and was premised on inclusively reconciling the different political tendencies. The key authors of the document were affiliated with Fatah and the Opposition tendencies, which included Hamas, Islamic Jihad, the PFLP, and the DFLP. The document consisted of eighteen points, key among them the end of Israel's military occupation of the West Bank (including East Jerusalem) and the Gaza Strip, and the establishment of a Palestinian state on lands occupied in 1967, the right of return of all Palestinian refugees, and the release of all Palestinian political prisoners, and was meant to serve as the basis of an agreement between Fatah and Hamas. Israel and the West, however, disregarded the agreement and actively worked to undermine such a step in the direction of Palestinian national reconciliation. Recognizing an opportunity to gain control over the government and to make Hamas appear counterproductive, Abbas issued an ultimatum that he would hold a national referendum on the document if Hamas did not accept it and if the two parties could not reach reconciliation agreements. The agreement also authorized Abbas to negotiate with Israel on behalf of the Palestinians, provided Hamas was properly integrated into the national movement, and that any agreement must be properly ratified, either through a national referendum or a vote by "legitimate Palestinian institutions" (that is, the PLO Executive Committee or Palestinian National Council that would include Hamas). The agreement was not a response to the international community as much as it was an endeavor to dislodge the Palestinian polity from its existing impasse. Israel dismissed the document as meaningless because it did not fulfill Quartet demands, which required the explicit recognition of Israel's right to exist, acceptance of all previous agreements reached by the PLO and Israel, and official renunciation of the use of violence. The agreement was never implemented, and became effectively irrelevant following the capture of Israeli Corporal Gilad Shalit on 25 June 2006. Israel refused to negotiate a prisoner swap in return for Shalit's release, and arrested over sixty Hamas officials in the West Bank—detainees include two dozen members of the PLC and nine cabinet ministers—a third of the standing Hamas cabinet.[15] Israel's attacks against the Gaza Strip increased, while armed clashes between the military arm of Hamas, the Qassam Brigades, and the PA Preventive Security continued to mount.

Throughout, Western donors attempted to tilt the political balance by making the Hamas government dependent on Abbas for funding. The EU, for example, pledged funding to Palestinian hospitals that would be routed through Abbas.[16] In early September 2006, Fatah incited civil servants to begin a strike to protest the salary payment irregularities despite Haniyeh's request that all employees return to work.[17] Abbas and Haniyeh announced an agreement to form a national unity government on 11 September, 2006, but the prospects for implementing any agreement between the two parties remained far-fetched. Armed clashes continued, and in October Abbas retracted preliminary unity government arrangements.

The Imposition and Consolidation of an International Boycott

The international community imposed sanctions against Hamas, the PA, and the entirety of the Gaza Strip following the Palestinian Legislative Council's endorsement of a Hamas-led government. Officially, the international boycott went into effect after Hamas assumed power on 29 March 2006. By then, the boycotting parties included the members of the Quartet—Russia,[18] the United States, the EU, and the UN—and the United States also pushed for a tertiary boycott that would penalize any third party, including banks, that dealt with the PA.[19] Diplomatic ties with the PA were suspended, international assistance was cut off, PA ministries were disregarded, and VAT revenue transfers from Israel were halted. Israel's general closure and restrictions surrounding travel in and out of Gaza was eventually consolidated as a complete blockade of the Gaza Strip after the Hamas takeover in June 2007. This closure would apply to individuals traveling in and out of the Gaza Strip, and to almost all imports and exports.[20]

By the end of April 2006, the United States had formalized the tertiary boycott by deeming the entirety of the PA areas as terrorist sanctuaries.[21] The US tertiary boycott had far-reaching implications, ushering a fiscal crisis that virtually paralyzed the Hamas-led PA. By threatening all third parties or international banks from dealing with the PA, the United States managed to successfully implement the boycott and draw in unanticipated observers such as Iran and the League of Arab States.[22] Although the League of Arab States had suspended budgetary support to the PA, it initially planned to bypass the boycott by depositing salaries directly into public sector employee bank accounts. Ultimately, however, they were unable to execute their plan since it required bank transactions with the Palestinian territories. Commercial banks in the Palestinian territories also withheld services to the PA. In effect, the PA's ability to operate an internal payment system was crippled.[23] Under these circumstances, Hamas eventually would not be able to continue its rule and would renew its call for a unity government.

In an effort to appear that the United States was only interested in isolating Hamas, and not the Palestinian people, the United States initially committed US$40 million to the UN to finance relief projects in the Gaza Strip. As Secretary of State Condoleezza Rice explained, "We will not have one and a half million Palestinians at the mercy of a terrorist organization."[24] This assistance, however, served to further polarize the Palestinian polity since it was directed toward Fatah and its supporters and the Liberal Moderates, and explicitly bypassed Islamists and the Opposition tendency more broadly.

To alleviate the stress on the Palestinian population, the EC, in collaboration with the World Bank established the Temporary International Mechanism (TIM) at the request of the Quartet. The objective of this new mechanism was to bypass all PA government institutions—in effect, severely undermining years of government institutional development. The TIM allowed for the delivery of fuel, essential supplies to hospitals and health care centers, and social allowances to the most vulnerable segments of the Palestinian population.[25] The United States channeled its funding through UNRWA, or directly to NGOs. Previously, the PA had embarked on an ambitious program of institutional reform in hopes of formalizing and institutionalizing revenue transfer mechanisms. These reforms included the establishment of the Central Treasury Account through which all government revenue, including donor transfers to the PA, would be collected and disbursed. As part of the embargo, donors rerouted funding from the Central Treasury Account to the Office of the President, undermining these previous institutionalization efforts.

Israel followed suit, suspending transfers of new Israeli shekel banknotes and VAT revenues to the PA and terminating relations with all Palestinian banks.[26] Per the 1994 Paris Protocol of Economic Relations between the Government of Israel and the PA, Israel was obligated to transfer all Palestinian related VAT to the Authority. In the past, when Israel suspended VAT transfers to the PA, the EU would step in to help the PA meet its payroll obligations and avoid collapse; this time, however, the EU did not step in.[27] The interruption in VAT transfers catapulted the PA into an unprecedented fiscal crisis. In 2005, the PA received approximately US$757 million in VAT transfers annually; after Hamas assumed power, the cessation of this transfer resulted in an approximate US$63 million shortfall in PA revenue per month.[28]

The economic impact on the Palestinian territories was considerable after the elections, and even before Hamas assumed office; according to the World Bank, PA revenue fell by 44 percent between the quarter beginning October 2005 and that beginning January 2006. Revenue contraction as a result of Israel's withholding of VAT transfers, the cessation of donor funding from Western and Arab League states, and the hesitancy of local commercial banks to lend to the new government resulted in an average US$130 million decrease per month, compared to earlier 2005 levels.[29] Palestinian Investment Fund dividends were also in short supply since the PA had already used them for advances or committed them as guarantees for bank loans.[30] By March 2006, the wage bill was over three times total revenues:[31] the monthly wage bill was estimated at approximately US$93 million,[32] and monthly domestic revenue was a maximum of US$25 million per month. The absence of a banking system through which this revenue could be distributed impaired the overall fiscal system.[33] At that point, an already unsustainable fiscal situation was exacerbated by Fatah policies and the international boycott. The PA was already running a monthly deficit of US$60 million—60 percent over its average monthly revenues by 2005.[34]

The impact on the average Palestinian was considerable. By conservative estimates, approximately 30 percent of the Palestinian population was affected by the PA's fiscal crisis. According to the World Bank, 71 percent of government employees technically fell below the poverty line, with poverty defined as an income level of $460 or less for a six-member household.[35] Between March 2006 and January 2007, the PA was unable to pay full salaries to most of PA public sector employees. On average, PA employees received 40 percent of their ordinary salaries. Palestinian employment in Israel also decreased by 12 percent during the first six months of 2006, dropping from 40,000 in 2005 to 35,000 by June 2006.[36] Unemployment disproportionately affected Gazans, who were categorically barred from entering Israel. By the third quarter of 2006, unemployment rates were at 36.3 percent in the Gaza Strip, compared to 19.1 percent in the West Bank.[37] By the summer of 2012, the Gaza embargo had still not eased, and the population was severely afflicted. By June 2012, 34 percent of the population was still unemployed, and GDP per capita had stabilized at 17 percent below 2005 figures. Forty-four percent of Gazans were food insecure and 80 percent were recipients of aid, and a severe fuel and electricity shortage resulted in twelve-hour outages per day. Also, eighty-five percent of Gaza schools ran on double shift.[38]

In an attempt to bolster included groups and constituencies and to marginalize the Opposition tendency and their affiliates, Western donors reduced development aid and stepped up emergency and humanitarian assistance to the West Bank (and not the Gaza Strip) and through channels outside of the government. IMF estimates indicated that US$349 million was provided to budget support in 2005, compared to US$700 million in 2006.[39] Given that this assistance was more selective and not distributed through government institutions, its impact was more limited in developmental terms, but polarizing in political terms. Although exact estimates to emergency and humanitarian assistance are more difficult to measure, some institutions such as UNRWA received an increase of 15 percent in their emergency pledges in 2006 compared to 2005. In particular, US assistance to UNRWA increased from US$108 million in 2005 to US$137 million in 2006, and to US$154.2 million by 2007.[40] The World Bank estimated that this increase in budget support cushioned the actual decline in GDP as each US$100 million prevented a decline in GDP by 2 to 3 percent.[41]

Measures to Overthrow the Hamas Government

Meanwhile, the promotion of noninclusion extended to coup support. The United States advocated more drastic measures that would entail the overthrow of the Hamas government. US policy in support of regime change was straightforward: bolstering Fatah while maintaining the boycott against Hamas would force the Hamas-controlled PA to fail, and would require a new Palestinian election. This assistance extended to additional arms to the Fatah-controlled PA. After the elections, with the coordination of Egypt and the West Bank PA, Israel allowed the transfer of light weapons to the PA presidential guards in hopes of bolstering Fatah.[42] Security assistance to the PA was initially more bilateral, ad hoc, and clandestine, and hence not reported transparently.[43] An important dimension of this strategy was to deny the new Hamas government control over security forces while bolstering Abbas's control.

US direct interference to affect political outcomes was by no means new; the United States had channeled approximately US$42 million to the National Democratic Institute, the International Republican Institute, and other contractors[44] to support Fatah and Liberal Moderate candidates. These institutions alleged that the aid was primarily directed toward campaign training. Palestinian observers, however, noted that the actual campaigns in terms of publicity materials, posters, gimmicks, and so forth were extravagantly lavish and must have been supported by substantial Western donor assistance. Moreover, the US and EU donors had penalized pro-Opposition tendency groups in the past; in particular, after Hamas made a significant showing in the 2004–2005 municipal elections, the US and EU donors imposed a donor embargo against all Hamas-dominated municipalities, Islamist social welfare organizations, or organizations that had Hamas or Islamist-affiliated individuals on their boards or among their employees.[45]

The US promotion of the Fatah and its security sector also was not new. Following the Road Map Agreement in 2003 and the death of Yasser Arafat in 2004, the United States initiated the creation of the US Security Coordinator for Israel and the Palestinian territories team with the intent of bolstering and aiding PA president Abbas in developing the security sector. This assistance was provided through the State Department's US Bureau of International Narcotics and Law Enforcement Affairs (INCLE).[46] The INCLE historically was involved in Latin American and in places like Afghanistan and Pakistan countering narcotics trafficking, and its initial mandate was to reduce the entry of illegal drugs into the United States and to minimize the impact of international crime on the United States and its citizens. Since 2005, however, INCLE has expanded beyond counternarcotics missions to internal security assistance in Middle Eastern countries like Iraq and Lebanon and to the West Bank.[47] The introduction of INCLE missions to the Middle East entailed a reconceptualization of this assistance by intentionally linking a country's domestic, internal security to international crime and its impact on the United States and its citizens. This link was arbitrary, and broadened the US's reach in perpetuating the US's desired outcomes in the region.

Breakdown of the Mecca Agreement and the End of the Unity Government

The post–Mecca Agreement unity government, established in March 2007, would not be able to overcome two major obstacles that had paralyzed the Palestinian polity: the lack of unity of the internal security forces, and the continued embargo by the West.[48] The agreement also did not outline how the parties would reform the structure of the PLO. Western donors extended the embargo against the unity government because of Hamas's inclusion and its failure to endorse Quartet conditions, and again effectively undermined the unity government and any prospects for national reconciliation.

The United States, as well as European countries, received the agreements coldly. The United States and Israel in particular were clear about their intent to bring down the unity government. The agreement fell short of the Quartet's demands in that Hamas did not explicitly recognize Israel or renounce the use of violence. Although the Quartet stipulated that it respected Palestinian democracy and the Mecca Agreement, it reiterated its priorities and reaffirmed its earlier position that any Palestinian government must renounce the use of violence, recognize Israel, and accept all previous agreements and obligations, including the Oslo Accords and the Road Map.[49] The international community's response would undermine the agreement and play a pivotal role in further exacerbating the existing polarization between Fatah and Hamas. Javier Solana, then EU commissioner for external relations, made it clear that he would not meet with Hamas members of the unity government, and Chancellor Angela Merkel, then EU president, warned that any new government would have to officially recognize Israel if aid was to be resumed through normal "channels." Hamas's position was clear: they recognized that Israel was a reality and were willing to deal with it on day-to-day matters, but that formal recognition would not be forthcoming (especially in light of continued military occupation),[50] and that they would not be involved in any negotiations with Israel, but were prepared to submit any agreements reached between the PLO and Israel to a national referendum.[51] Hamas maintained that mutually satisfactory arrangements could be reached on the issues of violence and previous agreements, and the *hudna* proposal had been put forth prior to 2006.

International donors bypassed the government and continued their support of all parties that did not oppose the Oslo Accords, especially Mahmoud Abbas's President's Office at the helm. With the help of Egypt, the United States and Israel continued the military support of Fatah, ensuring that the security situation would not be consolidated. In April 2007, for example, the Israeli government transferred 375 rifles of its own stock to the presidential guard, while Washington committed US$59 million in security equipment and training.[52] Led by Lieutenant General Keith Dayton, US security coordinator for Israel and the PA, this security intervention undertook to strengthen Abbas's presidential guard and prepare them for a possible confrontation with Hamas, strengthen the PA Office of National Security, and upgrade security infrastructure at the Palestinian side of the Karni crossing point between the Gaza Strip and Israel "to address Israel's legitimate security concerns." The US's overt bolstering of Fatah while pushing for the marginalization of Hamas dealt a serious blow to any prospects for national reconciliation between the two parties.

By May 2007, US officials were unambiguous about their aspirations to bring down the unity government and explicitly voiced their desire to intervene to punish those who had supported Hamas. In testimony to a congressional subcommittee on 23 May 2007,[53] C. David Welch, the assistant secretary, Bureau of Near Eastern Affairs, U.S. Department of State, explained:

> Through this comprehensive assistance strategy, our goal is to help create conditions conducive to advancing Israeli-Palestinian peace via the Road Map—that means supporting security, stability and prosperity in the Palestinian territories, and empowering Palestinian moderates as a counterbalance to radical and rejectionist groups like Hamas.

Western donors were intent on using any assistance to bolster Fatah and the Liberal Moderates with the objective of moving the political settlement forward while undermining the Opposition tendency. Their definition of radical and rejectionist groups extended to groups that basically opposed the terms of the Oslo Accords.

David Welch candidly explained:

> Since the election victory by Hamas in January 2006, we had to undertake a full scope redirection of our assistance programs to the Palestinian people so that they would not benefit in any way by a government that was led by Hamas or in which Hamas had the sort of representation it does today.
>
> The EU did an excellent job ensuring a broad swathe of Palestinians were included in the TIM, coordinating payments with the Office of President Abbas in an effort to accrue political credit to Abbas, and ensuring

adequate oversight through direct deposit payments and superb on the ground management. The great challenge in this, as in much of our assistance, is ensuring that it is provided in a way that benefits President Abbas, and not the Hamas-led PA government. We continue to work with the EU to improve the coordination of all support with President Abbas, and to provide assistance in ways that provide a political boost to Palestinian moderates.

We will not work with Hamas or any other foreign terrorist organization, but we should continue to support, as you said, moderate institutions and elements of Palestinian society, whether in the private sector, moderate municipalities, civil society, or independent media, to counterbalance extremist views and positions.

Buttressing Fatah and the Liberal Moderates dominated the American agenda; the driving objective was to promote the prevailing political settlement, in tandem with Israel's interests. In the same hearing, Welch further explained:

At the same time, we are working to advance political and economic reforms and to strengthen Palestinian moderates in support of our diplomatic efforts for peace. We have a number of programs through both USAID and the Middle East Partnership Initiative, working with local, U.S., and international implementers, focused on developing important organizational skills and structures of moderate Palestinian organizations, to generate grassroots political activism, and to support reform both within Fatah and other moderate political parties, as well as within certain elements of the PA government, including security forces under the authority of President Abbas.

The aims of US assistance in particular, however, were not limited to bolstering Fatah and Liberal Moderates, but also aimed to punish those who had supported Hamas, or opposed the Oslo Accords more generally, and disregarded any distinction between the political organizations, armed wings, and CSOs. Representative Gary L. Ackerman, chairman of the House of Representatives Subcommittee on the Middle East and South Asia of the Committee on Foreign Affairs, was unambiguous about this objective:

When the Palestinian people chose to empower Hamas they implicitly and perhaps unknowingly sent a number of messages to the rest of the world, messages about the acceptability of terrorists and terrorism, about the durability of past commitments, and about their relationship with the world.

Mark Ward, the senior deputy assistant administrator, Bureau for Asia and the Near East, US Agency for International Development, elaborated on US objectives, especially related to how US assistance would shape democratic outcomes.

On the democracy front, it is critical that we remain engaged with and support Palestinians who reject Hamas and other extremists. We are working with Palestinian leaders, particularly those elected to municipal councils, to provide much-needed assistance to their communities. Currently, we are working with 20 communities to help municipal leaders assess and meet the needs of their communities. . . .

Our assistance program has found him or her [a mayor of community who is not Hamas] and is providing direct assistance to that community. . . . There is a community next to that community that is not run by a moderate Fatah member. It is run by the other guys. One of the hopes of our program . . . is that the people in that community, if everybody talks to each other, are going to see what is going on in the community next-door that is receiving help from the United States or maybe from the TIM, and they are going to see that their community was involved in how decisions are made and that their community leaders are accountable.[54]

Ward's statement, like the policies it embodies, reflected the political motivations that informed US democracy promotion in the Middle East. A noninclusive political settlement facilitated this type of intervention. Polarization would still have transpired without external involvement, but Western donor assistance served to merely exacerbate these dynamics. The non-Fatah or non-Liberal-Moderate tendency– controlled municipalities were often aware of the more calculated political motivations behind US assistance, and were loath to embrace them. These municipal leaders were also democratically elected by individuals aspiring for greater political voice and inclusion. Municipal representatives were therefore well aware that successful office and possible reelection were contingent on serving and representing their constituencies. Funding certain municipalities over others, however, exacerbated the political rift, not because of competing models of representation and accountability among different municipalities, but rather because some municipalities were seen as complicit and benefiting from the post-Oslo order, and others were summarily excluded.

Near Civil War and Hamas's Gaza Takeover

The unity government lasted a mere three months. By early June 2007, military confrontations between Fatah and Hamas had taken the character of a near civil war. Throughout May, Fatah's security maneuvers and US and Israeli overt support portended a coup against Hamas. US officials promised to increase their security assistance to the PA and continue extending the US$84 million aid package to Abbas. Meanwhile, Israel allowed the transfer of light arms to Abbas's presidential guard, and arrested over thirty Hamas members in the West Bank.

By mid-June 2007, aware that a coup was imminent, Hamas went on a relentless offensive and managed to take over Gaza in a matter of days. Fatah retaliated in kind. Within five days, over one hundred Palestinians had been killed. On 15 June, Abbas unilaterally dissolved the unity government, stripped Hamas of its representation in the National Security Council, and set up an emergency government to be headed by Salam Fayyad as prime minister. The United States strongly supported Abbas's actions and on 16 June announced that it would lift its ban on aid to Abbas's new emergency PA government in the West Bank, initiating the end of the Western boycott against the now Fatah-controlled West Bank.[55] The EU followed suit and announced its plans to resume direct aid to the PA, and then Israeli prime minister Ehud Olmert announced that Israel would release PA tax revenues that Israel had held since Hamas's election victory.[56] The thirteen-member new PA emergency government was sworn in on the 17 June 2007. Abbas reappointed a new emergency government within thirty days, although according to the PA Basic Law, any emergency government not approved by the PLC could only remain in power for sixty days. The appointment of the emergency government was challenged on constitutional grounds. The initial drafters of the Palestinian Basic Law,

Anis al-Qasim and Eugene Cotran, argued that although the Palestinian president could dismiss a prime minister, he did not have the power to appoint a new government or call for new elections without PLC approval. Moreover, according to the Basic Law, Haniyeh's unity cabinet should remain the caretaker administration until Abbas could secure parliamentary approval for a new government.[57] On 11 July, the PLC session was suspended because of lack of a quorum; by then, Israel had arrested forty-two Hamas-affiliated PLC members, and the remaining members decided to boycott given the assault on Hamas.[58] The United States supported these measures. In justifying US policy, US Secretary of State Condoleezza Rice responded, "I think we will leave to the Palestinians issues of how they work through their own constitutional issues. . . . Our view, very strongly is that what President Abbas has done is legitimate and it is responsible and we're going to support that action."[59] Despite the lack of legitimacy of the new government, it remained instated.

The International Boycott and Heightened Security Assistance to the West Bank PA

Following the Hamas takeover, most state-sponsored Western donors implemented a "no contact policy" that forbade any contact with Hamas authorities, often also on a technical level. According to the "no contact policy," Western donors, such as the United States and Canada, would no longer have any dealings with the political leadership or appointments of the Hamas government. Although the United Nations did not adhere to an official "no contact policy," it too would not deal with the political leadership or appointments of Hamas, but would deal with technical counterparts, which included ministerial department heads and engineers, among others.[60] A number of donors rechanneled their assistance to ensure that Islamists would not accrue any political capital from donor-related socioeconomic improvements. The "no contact policy" severely hampered development coordination, as a minimum exchange of information was and is necessary to implement the most basic development projects. Needless to say, this maneuvering served to further undermine Palestinian government institutions, particularly any cohesiveness bridging the West Bank and Gaza Strip, and reversed important institutional developments, especially related to public financial management. Moreover, these measures, beginning in 2006, undermined the existing consolidation of revenue in the Treasury Account and more routinized annual budget planning and implementation. At a more fundamental level, these policies resulted in a partial return to cash payments in the public sector, severely damaging Ministry of Finance oversight of payroll-related issues, and more generally weakened transparency throughout the system.[61]

The US Treasury Office of Foreign Assets forbade USAID from engaging with any PA institutions connected to the Hamas-led government. USAID therefore shifted its funding from PA institutions in Gaza to NGOs and international organizations such as UNRWA. In the health sector, "USAID funding was re-routed from the Hamas run ministry of health clinics to NGO run clinics and shifted from more development-oriented programs to small-scale, labor intensive programs."[62] Many of these "substitute" institutions lacked the societal reach that government institutions possessed, and as a result the number of individuals who could be reached was considerably restricted.

After Hamas's 2007 takeover of the Gaza Strip, the United States substantially augmented its security support to Fatah. Up until 1996, the United States provided a little over US$5 million to security, and this was allocated to police salaries and nonlethal weaponry (specifically, trucks and boots from surplus stocks). In 2007, the US Congress appropriated its first direct project funding to the US Security Coordinator team.[63] By 2012, this assistance had increased to US$113 million from the State Department's INCLE account. Of this amount, US$77 million was allocated to training, nonlethal equipment, and garrisoning assistance to PA security forces in the West Bank, and US$36 million was allocated to the PA Ministry of the Interior and justice sector.[64] Between 2007 and 2012, the US had reprogrammed approximately US$658.4 million from the INCLE account. The US Security Coordinator for the Israel and the PA, supported by staff from the United Kingdom, Canada, and seven other countries, worked to train 1,000 PA presidential guard and 6,000 PA security forces.[65] This security assistance was in addition to other intelligence (covert and otherwise) and security training assistance provided by the EU and other countries.

In additional to security allocations, a substantial amount of the US's bilateral assistance was aimed at promoting the Fatah-controlled PA in the West Bank. Between 2008 and 2012, US bilateral assistance to the WBGS averaged US$600 million annually. Of this amount, approximately US$100 million was allocated to security assistance, US$200 million was allocated to direct budgetary support, and US$300 million to development, governance, and reform programs in the West Bank.[66]

Fatah's Continued Onslaught and Western Donor Support

Fatah implemented a series of policies that further cemented an irreversible polarization between supporters and opponents of the Oslo Accords. In effect, in this noninclusive political context, the interests of Fatah, Israel, and Western powers coalesced to undermine a legitimate democratic exercise, leaving Hamas with few options other than to defend itself in the face of this onslaught. From the outset, Hamas was not allowed or given the opportunity to rule. Fatah's assault was not limited to formal Hamas-controlled government institutions, but extended to individuals who could be identified as Hamas members or labeled as Islamist more generally, as well as Islamist institutions throughout the West Bank. During October 2008, for example, Abbas arrested scores of Hamas cadre, especially in Hebron. By 2010, he had fired over three hundred imams who had delivered anti-PA sermons, or were believed to be affiliated with Hamas.[67] Hardest hit, however, was the education sector; the Abbas government fired over one thousand teachers who identified as Hamas or Islamist. A number of faculty members at An-Najah University were arrested for links to a charity that many believed was tied to Hamas.[68] The Hamas-Fatah tit-for-tat continued throughout 2008. Hamas attacked 152 organizations in the Gaza Strip believed to be affiliated with Fatah, and according to PA news reports abducted 166 Fatah cadre.[69]

Fatah also went after Islamist charities, most of which were zakat committees, in its resolve to destroy Hamas in the West Bank. Over ninety of these organizations were zakat committees, which were by and large not political and not supporters of any political Islamist group, nor instruments of any political organization. Disregarding the existing NGO law, the Fayyad government required all NGOs to reregister, so as to exclude Islamist NGOs in this new round of registration.

According to the Palestinian Center for Human Rights, the Ramallah based PA Ministry of Interior dissolved 103 NGOs that had applied for reregistration, many of them Islamist, on the basis of the decree issued by President Mahmoud Abbas on 14 June 2007 that required all NGOs and charities to reregister. In December 2007, the Fayyad led government closed another ninety-two Islamist charities in the West Bank to penalize Hamas for its rejection of the Annapolis Middle East Peace conference. The justification for closing down these charities was that Hamas had been using these types of organizations to further its political objectives. Fatah closed an additional forty-five Islamist institutions, which included charities, cultural centers, and orphanages, during the summer of 2008, and took over the administration of many others.[70] To replace those charities, the Fayyad government announced that it would establish eleven new charities (one in each governorate) that effectively would be state-controlled new zakat committees.[71] The attack against Islamist charities, however, was not new; Western donors had played a pivotal role in marginalizing and excluding Islamist charities since the start of the Oslo process. Islamist social institutions were an easy target compared to Hamas's military apparatus. These measures, however, were more extreme, subscribing to US and Israeli rhetoric of a war on terror, leading to further polarization.

Civil servants were caught in the polarized mayhem. Shortly, after the Hamas takeover, the Fayyad government ordered all PA employees in the Gaza Strip, approximately 70,000, not to report to work, or to risk losing their salaries if they did so. Medical personnel, however, were exempted from this directive. Although many employees did not abide by these directives, the Gaza-based Haniyeh government had to replace all public sector employees who did. In effect, what transpired were separate governments in the West Bank and Gaza Strip, each with different ministers and agency directors. The issuance of conflicting directives, often annulling decisions that emanated from the rival minister or director, became common practice. Chaos ensued as public sector employees grappled with whose directives to abide by and whether to report to work in the Gaza Strip. Again, foreign donor intervention mediated (and exacerbated) these outcomes, but it did not create them. In 2010, the Ministry of Agriculture in Ramallah and the Ministry of Agriculture in Gaza each released strategic plans pertaining to agricultural development in the Gaza Strip. As a result, donor organizations working in the agricultural sector found themselves attempting to implement different developmental plans, depending on each context.[72]

In an effort to further undermine Hamas, in August 2008 the Fatah-affiliated General Union of Palestinian Teachers alleged that the Gaza Ministry of Education had arrested school teachers and transferred some to different schools, and it called for teachers to strike to protest these policies. By September 2008, 50 percent of teachers (and 48 percent of medical personnel) were on strike. The Haniyeh government adopted an official policy of replacing public sector employees. By early 2010, although the strikes were ongoing, Haniyeh had managed to replace most of the 32,000 striking employees with Hamas sympathizers.[73] The longer term impact of these policies was that Hamas consolidated its control over the social agenda and service delivery in the Gaza Strip.[74] In the longer term, these developments worked in Hamas's favor; by filling ministries and agencies with people who were more supportive, Hamas easily asserted itself and its social agenda in the Gaza Strip. The US/EU resumption of budgetary support to the West Bank PA after June 2007, while supporting (or not intervening against) the Fayyad promoted government employee strike in the Gaza Strip, also reduced the economic burden on Hamas since the West Bank PA was making a substantial, regular contribution to the Gaza economy.

The 2008 Incursion and the Challenge to Rebuild

The daunting challenge of development and humanitarian intervention in light of the "no contact policy" became most evident following Israel's 2008–09 aerial assault against the Gaza Strip.[75] By the end of the twenty-two day incursion, dubbed "Operation Cast Lead," the Israeli military had killed 1,391 Palestinians, including at least 759 civilians, and 318 minors under the age of eighteen.[76] The military assault also resulted in extensive physical damage to homes, industrial plants, and electricity, sanitation, and health infrastructure. Moreover, the UN reported that the homes of 43,000 families had been destroyed, and 20,000 families were left homeless. As a result of damage to water networks, over 32,000 people were left without access to water. According to official Israeli sources, thirteen Israelis, three of whom were civilian, were killed, and 512 Israelis were injured, including 182 civilians.[77] Efforts to rebuild Gaza and convalesce a traumatized population were severely hampered by access constraints and Israel's restrictions on allowing goods and materials into the Gaza Strip. Although the UN and its partners provided humanitarian assistance, early recovery and reconstruction activities remained limited given Western donor conditions that all Hamas run or affiliated institutions, including Gaza PA institutions, must be bypassed. The West Bank controlled PA, along with Israel and Western donors, were also concerned that rebuilding Israeli inflicted damage following the conflict would inadvertently boost Hamas's popularity. Hence, only controlled levels of humanitarian assistance were allowed entry and reconstruction remained limited. As of the spring of 2009, the lack of construction materials, wastewater treatment, and solid waste disposal equipment posed serious public health and environmental concerns. And in the area of shelter recovery activities, only Mercy Corps, along with the UN, had begun their reconstruction. The UNDP and UNRWA also provided alternative housing to approximately 43,000 families whose homes were damaged during the Gaza incursion.[78]

Although in some cases funding was available, reconstruction was severely hampered because of the access constraints to needed materials and equipment. In particular, lack of access to construction materials to rebuild water and sanitation facilities delayed the work of the UN, Islamic Relief, and other relief organizations like Action Contre La Faim (Action Against Hunger), a Canadian organization, involved in these efforts.

The policy recommendations of the Minimum Framework for the Provision of Humanitarian Assistance were uncompromising about the need for access and impartiality.[79] Assistance, however, remained limited to humanitarian intervention in the form of basic food and cash interventions. During the first year after the end of the bombing campaign, little rehabilitation of education and health institutions had taken place.[80] Moreover, as a result of the "no contact" policy, a number of humanitarian organizations also abandoned their needs-based approach in favor of selecting beneficiaries on the basis of political criteria. For example, a number of Western donor organizations decided not to rehabilitate water and sanitation facilities in Gaza public schools since they were administered by Hamas. Most donors refused to fund projects run by the Coastal Municipalities Water Utility, which was the main public water and sanitation utility in Gaza, because a number of the municipal areas it served were headed by a Hamas mayor or had Hamas members on its municipal council. Moreover, humanitarian organizations would not engage in the provision of basic social services that required support from municipal authorities since many of these municipalities were controlled by elected Hamas officials.[81] Health institutions lacked critical materials and drugs: as of July 2009, seventy-seven essential drugs and twenty disposable medical items were out of stock in the Gaza Strip.[82] Throughout this period, development organizations repeatedly voiced concern about the extent of hardship caused by access constraints; all were calling (and continue to call) for better access to the Gaza Strip.[83]

Similar to earlier aid coordination mechanisms, its complexity reflected the challenges and contradictions of the political context. The Ramallah based PA took the lead in putting together the National Early Recovery and Reconstruction Plan for Gaza 2009–10, which was the PA plan based on needs assessment; in practice, however, the UNDP conducted the needs assessment studies for the PA and coordinated the relationship between the UN and the PA. To formulate this document, the UNDP also coordinated with local authorities in Gaza. Although the Hamas-run Gaza PA did not stop or directly impede UNDP's work, they also put in place their own Early Recovery Program and set up coordination committees. UNDP, UNRWA, and other bodies did not work directly with the higher echelons of newly established Hamas institutions, but continued to openly share information.[84] Despite the international community's willingness to develop these complex institutional mechanisms, the impediments to any meaningful development were obvious. According to UNDP official Laurent Marion, "Political issues aside, if we could coordinate with Hamas, it would be more efficient." He rationalized, however, that "it does not have to have a big impact because we are not speaking about high level development. . . . For now, the focus is on waste management, rubble removal, and cash for employment."[85] To ensure the minimum level of information exchange, the United Nations Office for the Coordination of Humanitarian Affairs (OCHA) held biweekly meetings with local authorities. In broader coordination committees, however, Hamas was absent. Development specialists working with UNDP, UNSCO, and OCHA were unanimous in that political constraints restricting the entry of materials to Gaza were the main impediment to recovery in the Gaza Strip.

The United States in particular already had a stringent vetting system in place that ensured that project funding could not be diverted to any unapproved individuals or programs. Following the events of 11 September 2001, President Bush issued Executive Order 13224—"Blocking Property and Prohibiting Transactions with Persons Who Commit, Threaten to Commit, or Support Terrorism," which took effect on September 24, 2001.[86] In August 2003, the WBGS USAID mission established its comprehensive policy for vetting. The new vetting procedures included screening of individuals and organizations to ensure that they are not affiliated with terrorism in any way; requiring recipients to certify that they do not provide support to terrorism before awarding USAID assistance; and requiring the written text of awards to stipulate that US law prohibits any transactions with terrorists. Screening procedures entailed exacting checks of the given organization, its officers, directors, and other affiliated individuals against lists maintained by the Office of Foreign Assets Control within the US Department of Treasury and intelligence community systems. Upfront, USAID required that these organizations furnish information pertaining to their employees: USAID's West Bank/Gaza program would develop the most comprehensive vetting system for foreign assistance throughout the U.S. Government.[87] Subsequent audits ensured compliance with existing procedures.[88] Ultimately, the humanitarian crisis that ensued in the Gaza Strip was manmade—a result of the political situation and political actors shaped by a noninclusive political settlement.[89] Worthy of mention, Hamas was not a passive victim waiting for the resumption of Western donor assistance. It proactively developed its own alternatives.

Fatah was further discredited in the eyes of the Palestinian public because of its level of compliance and coordination with Israel. During the aerial attack against Gaza, the Israeli military ceded direct responsibility to the PA forces, which contained all protests in the West Bank, fulfilling Israeli and US requests. As Dayton recounted,

> The IDF [Israeli Defense Forces] also felt—after the first few weeks or so—that the Palestinians were there and they could trust them. As a matter of fact, a good portion of the Israeli army went off to Gaza from the West Bank—think about that for a minute—and the commander was absent for eight straight days. That shows the kind of trust they are putting in these people now.[90]

Such assessments, however, did not take into consideration Palestinian general sentiment, which saw these entities as delegitimized and beholden to US and Israeli interests at the expense of the Palestinian people.

The West Bank controlled PA led the charge in promoting this noninclusivity by refusing to coordinate with Hamas government institutions in the Gaza Strip. The lack of coordination was especially apparent in the area of health services. Previously, if a patient's medical needs could not be met in the Gaza Strip, and he or she required treatment abroad, they were required to obtain permission from the Palestinian Referral Abroad Department of the Ministry of Health. This permission ensured that the Ministry of Health would pay for the required treatment. The patients would then arrange for the necessary appointments and submit an application to the Coordinator of Government Activity for the Territories, a unit in the Israeli Ministry of Defense that coordinates Palestinian civilian issues between the government of Israel, the Israeli military, international organizations, diplomats, and the PA. When the Hamas government took over the Referral Abroad Department in Gaza, the Ramallah based Ministry of Health refused to approve or fund any applications and a deadlock ensued. On 30 March 2009, the World Health Organization and the UN Office for the Coordination of Humanitarian Affairs issued a joint statement warming of the crisis at hand:

> "We are very worried about the situation," said Tony Laurance, acting Head of WHO in the West Bank and Gaza Strip. "Around 900 patients a month were being referred outside of Gaza for treatment at hospitals in

Israel, East Jerusalem, Egypt, and Jordan in the first half of 2008. Some of the cases are urgent and require immediate treatment. We have already seen referrals affected, and patients will die if they do not receive the treatment they require," he added. . . .

"We need a speedy solution," said Mr. Gaylard, the UN Humanitarian Coordinator. . . . "Whatever difficulties may or may not have existed regarding the procedures, it is not acceptable for essential patient care to be stopped because of an internal political dispute or unilateral steps. We call for a rapid solution to be found among the parties concerned to enable referrals to resume and patients' rights to be protected and for Hamas to reverse their decision so that a way forward can be found."[91]

The conflict was resolved the following month, when Hamas forfeited patient referral authority to the Ministry of Health in Ramallah and to a committee of independent and Fatah-leaning physicians agreed upon by the PA and Hamas.[92] External actors were not acting on their own accord, but perpetuating a noninclusive settlement to which dominant domestic groups were committed.

Fast forward: the 2008 and 2009, 2012 and 2014 violent conflicts were almost rewrites of themselves, with similar unfolding sequences, similar outcomes, similar responses, and similar Western donor involvement.

Hamas's Coping Mechanisms

Hamas instituted new policies in a bid to increase its control over post-assault reconstruction. These policies established greater order, helped develop a functioning public administration, and fortified a "survival economy" bolstered through the underground tunnel routes to Egypt. However, even though these policies entrenched Hamas's control, they further polarized the pervading politics and undermined prospects for civil society and democratic development.

Among these policies, Hamas required all international organizations to reregister with the Gaza PA Ministry of Interior. Moreover, they requested that all organizations provide lists of their employees, beneficiaries, and salaries to the Hamas government. Hamas's rationale for these policies was to ensure that no one was earning a double salary and that the assistance was provided equitably and was not benefiting PA employees who were on strike at the request of the Fayyad government. They also maintained that this was a preliminary measure in instituting an income tax on Gaza residents. Western donors and Fatah countered that the objective of these policies was to manipulate the donor effort, and compel international organizations to work with the new Hamas government. These policies were politically motivated and obviously sought to retaliate against Fatah's policies in the West Bank.[93] International parties refused to comply, and eventually Hamas accepted copies of international organization registration from Ramallah as sufficient to meet this new criteria.[94] Moreover, although international organizations refused to supply the above mentioned lists to the Hamas government, their local Gaza counterparts were already providing this information to the Hamas government.[95] Hamas closed down a number of the local organizations that refused to provide this information and summoned their employees for questioning. Although many subsequently reopened and resumed their activities, oversight remained high.

Hamas instituted stricter disciplinary measures in hopes of installing order, and extended these policies to members of Hamas. Its reform of the security sector included downsizing the number of branches and bringing them under a single, civilian chain of command, reporting directly to the Ministry of Interior.[96] Hamas retreated from its initial commitment to institute the rule of law.[97] It was ruthless in punishing Fatah members and affiliates, and in some cases conducted cold-blooded executions. Hamas also banned any public Fatah gathering, and fired many Fatah affiliates from their jobs in the public sector.[98] Although Hamas initially assured the Palestinian electorate that it would not enforce an Islamist agenda in Palestinian society, individual government authorities increasingly issued "Islamization guidelines." For example, certain officials initiated campaigns to make women's Islamist dress mandatory, to ban male and female mixing on public beaches, and to penalize any organizations that held female/male activities, including the intermixing of boys and girls.

Despite their retreat from democratic principles, Hamas's coping strategies were noteworthy. The tunnel economy flourished in light of the embargo. In a short period after its takeover of the Gaza Strip, Hamas transformed these tunnels into formal, regulated, and taxed institutions. Reliance on access-related rent, however, rather than institutionalized taxation of the citizenry further undermined Hamas's representative legitimacy. Moreover, ultimately the tunnel economy benefitted Hamas, and not necessarily all the citizens of the Gaza Strip. The numbers of these tunnels grew steadily from a few dozen to over 500 in 2008, to approximately 1,500 tunnels by 2010.[99] Shortly after the 2008 incursion, Hamas's Interior Ministry established the Tunnel Affairs Commission to regulate tunnel commercial activity. Hamas introduced safety guidelines and restricted the imports of certain goods, such as alcohol and weapons. The Tunnel Affairs Commission introduced a licensing scheme and comprehensive customs regime that would generate revenue for Hamas. Gaza authorities also imposed a 14.5 percent valued added tax on all imports.[100] Some estimated that tunnel revenue increased from approximately US$30 million per year in 2005 to US$36 million per month on the eve of the 2008 war.[101] The tunnels also emerged as one of Gaza's most lucrative nongovernmental employment sectors by 2010, employing approximately 5,000 tunnel owners and 25,000 employees at $75 a day, according to Nicolas Pelham.[102] Hamas claimed that tunnel revenues accounted for half of the government's US$750 million annual budget.[103] Hamas and its affiliates were the principal beneficiaries of the tunnel economy. Rather than rectifying the structural impairments of a besieged economy, however, it contributed to the increased polarization of the Gaza strip, a polarization that also coincided with political lines.[104]

Conclusion

The outcome of Hamas's election victory in the Gaza Strip is an extreme example of the limits of democracy promotion in noninclusive political contexts. The labeling of organizations based solely on their relationship vis-à-vis pervading political settlements discounts the multifaceted dimensions of these organizations. Ultimately, contrary to the intentions of Western powers, neither the embargo nor international punitive measures seriously dented Hamas's standing.[105] However, Opposition tendency–affiliated groups, especially Islamists more generally, were marginalized regardless of their relationship to Hamas.

As a measure to formalize noninclusion, Abbas issued a decree banning Hamas from running in PA elections unless they embraced the PLO and accepted all agreements between the PLO and Israel. By 2010, the term of the elected parliament had ended with no set date for future elections. Drawing on the Road Map, the US Congress also put in place more stringent conditions to which the PA had to abide in order to continue receiving funding. The updated annual appropriations legislation forbade the granting of assistance to any Hamas-controlled government or entity, or any power-sharing PA government. The legislation further stipulated that any PA government, including all its ministers, must accept the following two principles of Section 620K of the Palestinian Anti-Terrorism Act of 2006, P.L. 109–446: (1) recognition of "the Jewish state of Israel's right to exist" and (2) acceptance of previous Israeli-Palestinian agreements."[106] Congress's new stipulations not only required the official recognition of Israel but that it be recognized as a "Jewish" state—something that even other Palestinian political organizations had not officially accepted.

Against this backdrop, there was a complete polarized breakdown of the political system. Throughout 2010, the humanitarian operation in the Palestinian territories remained one of the largest in the world in terms of international assistance, amounting to US$660 million.[107] As put forth repeatedly by OCHA, these closure and embargo policies impeded the humanitarian community's ability to meet the needs of vulnerable Palestinians whose livelihoods were severely hurt by these ongoing circumstances. OCHA was unequivocal in its call to the international donor community to reevaluate "aspects" of their policies vis-à-vis Hamas so that "humanitarian agencies are able to respond based solely on needs, rather than on considerations about what entity is in control of a particular municipality or school."[108] This discussion also applied to the broader Opposition tendency and their affiliated groups.

Through an in-depth examination of new Western donor policies put in place in the Gaza Strip, this chapter illustrated how the Western donor community's response to Hamas's election victory played a critical role in exacerbating polarization. It effectively dealt a debilitating blow to civil society and democratic development in the Palestinian territories. Although the chapter focused on the marginalization of Islamists more generally and not exclusively on Islamist NGOs, charity organizations, or CSOs, it illustrated the prospects for civil society development and democratization in noninclusive political contexts.

7

Noninclusive Settlements and Democracy's Long Haul in Comparative Perspective

I began this book seeking to answer a fundamental question of concern to comparative politics scholars: Why are Western democracy promotion efforts more successful in some contexts as opposed to others? I found that the answer did not simply lie with the impact of institutional professionalization or different types of democracy assistance, but rather that it was necessary to take the analysis a step back and examine those domestic conditions that shaped the divergent outcomes, and then to understand how donor assistance mediated these processes. My research found that a much more essential issue undermined democracy promotion efforts and this was the noninclusivity of political settlements. Key works in the democratization literature, the peace-building literature, and the conflict resolution literature agree that broader inclusion of different actors and constituencies enhances the longer term prospects for civil society and democratic development. The democracy establishment, however, appears to not fully appreciate this shared understanding.

It is not extraordinary that foreign donors intervene to support certain groups over others. The intervention of external actors to shape various outcomes was also a defining feature of Cold War politics. What is unique about the post–Cold War era state of affairs is that the interests of dominant political groups and Western donors often align to exclude key groups without counterbalance in the democracy arena. During the Cold War, different external camps aided different political groups in their struggle to control the political arena. In the post–Cold War era, however, it is only Western donors who are engaged in democracy promotion efforts involving funding to professionalized NGOs or other advocacy groups seeking to enhance citizen participation, encourage economic development, and so forth. Hence, only certain tendencies are promoted in the civil society and democracy arena. Groups affiliated or identified as Islamist, for example, may receive funding from external actors, but the aid is often related to relief, primary care, or other self-help. These groups are still major actors in the civil society arena, but their involvement is not similar in terms of political engagement. What results is a bifurcated civil society: one that focuses on social service provision and another that works in the democracy realm, or, in areas of political engagement, more specifically. In many instances, the former is systematically pushed away from the democracy arena, and this is facilitated by the disarticulated spaces between the state and society in non-inclusive contexts. New rising donors such as China, Russia, and Turkey are becoming increasingly active. It is unlikely, however, that they will be involved in democracy promotion related endeavors.

Throughout this book, I have illustrated how political settlements and the levels of support they enjoy shape the impact of Western donor assistance to civil society. In the Palestinian context, because of the non-inclusive political settlement, only certain groups were able to access Western donor funding. As a result, a hierarchical relationship developed in civil society between the organizations that were able to access Western donor funding and the Opposition-tendency grassroots committees that could not. In the Salvadoran context, on the other hand, because of the more inclusive settlement and the overwhelming support it enjoyed, Western donor funding played a more positive role in the development of civil society. The more equitable access to Western donor funding allowed for more cooperative relations. In turn, civil society came to mirror this "inclusivity" as well as the agendas of donors as expressed by the political settlement.

In my examination of foreign donor assistance to each case, I argued that the geostrategic importance of the Palestinian territories to many donors translated into higher amounts of assistance. In turn, this meant higher amounts of assistance to professionalized NGOs in civil society, further exacerbating the discrepancy between the haves in civil society (the pro-Oslo and Liberal Moderates groups in civil society), and the have-nots (the Opposition-tendency groups in civil society). Moreover, in the Palestinian territories, donors allocated less funding to the government administration sector, especially in relation to local development and decentralization, than they did in El Salvador. At the end of the war

in 1992 in El Salvador, the local municipal level offered distinct possibilities for involving the former opposing sides in activities to promote reconciliation. The inclusive nature of the political settlement, allowed for
the further strengthening of this level of government, presenting greater
avenues for citizen participation and the development of civil society.

Beyond the Women's Sectors

The trajectory of developments of the women's sector extended to other
sectors, including the labor sector. Like the women's organizations, labor
organizations also emerged from, or became affiliated with the political
organizations. Developments at the civil society level mirrored the more
general state of affairs in both contexts. Ultimately, the labor sector in El
Salvador was far more successful in pushing for labor rights than in the
Palestinian context where the movement became mired by the polarized
dynamics between the different tendencies.

In El Salvador the labor sector, historically, embodied two tendencies:
one affiliated with organizations with rightest leanings, and the second
affiliated with the left. Similar to the popular movements more generally,
unions went underground in the late 1970s because of the increase in
repression. Many of these organizations emerged from the underground
in 1983 onward and different labor union structures were established.
In the mid-1980s, for example, the Coordinadora de Solidaridad con
los Trabajadores (Coordinator of Solidarity with the Workers-CST) was
established. The CST incorporated unions and cooperatives.[1] In 1986,
the Unión Nacional Trabajadores Salvadoreños (National Union of
Salvadoran Workers) was formed, which included all types of worker
organizations. Parallel to these developments was the rise of the coun-
terrevolutionary labor union structures, or what others described as
more moderate unions, such as the Unión Nacional Obrera y Campe-
sina (National Workers and Peasants Union). This period marked a
notable increase in union activity, and more broadly mass-based and
popular movement organization. In the postsettlement period, labor
unions were not marginalized based on their position vis-à-vis the
peace accords. Moreover, foreign aid did not work to discriminate
between the different organizations. After the FMLN's first presidential victory, the progressive and leftist labor unions began to organize

broad-based federations. These efforts culminated in important victories for the labor sector, such as the changes to the minimum wage.[2]

Furthermore, in the postsettlement period, the FMLN leveraged its continued ability to mobilize its mass organizations. In 2002 and 2003, in response to the ARENA government's decision to privatize and out-source medical services, the health care sector and the FLMN, along with labor unions and their allies, organized massive strikes. The FMLN came out en masse, mobilizing its legislative and mayoral deputies and rank and file party members to reverse these decisions.[3] In the end, the government was forced to reverse its decisions on privatization and outsourcing. The FMLN capitalized on this episode of social move-ment mobilization and coordinated closely with leaders of the health care strikes for its successive electoral campaigns. A week before the municipal and legislative elections of 2009, El Salvador witnessed the largest public gathering of its history—the crowd of over 300,000 came out to support the FMLN in a preelection rally. The inclusive terms of the transition and the intervening role of Western donor assistance, in fact, encouraged the FMLN to continue working with the grassroots and popular sectors, allowing for these developments.

This trajectory contrasted with labor union work in the Palestinian territories, which became increasingly ineffectual. The umbrella labor or-ganization, the Palestinian General Federation of Trade Unions (GFTU) was established in 1965. Historically, the labor unions were affiliated with the nationalist forces or with the socialist political organizations, namely the PCP. In sync with the PLO's mass mobilization policies, its different organizations initiated extensive labor union organizing dur-ing the late 1970s.[4] Because of Fatah's insistence that it dominate the GFTU, the organization split in 1981, and it did not reunite until 1990. Mass mobilization and union membership, however, peaked during the first Intifada, despite division in the labor movement. After the start of the Oslo Accords, three tendencies also emerged in the labor movement. The PA subsumed much of the Fatah labor organizations, including the GFTU and the teacher's union.[5] In protest against Fatah's heavy-handed control of the GFTU, FIDA and other union leaders and activists estab-lished the Federation of Independent and Democratic Trade Unions and Workers' Committees in Palestine and other smaller unions. With the help of Western donor funding, the Liberal Moderates also established professionalized labor organizations, such as Democracy and Workers' Rights. Given the increasing polarization between the different tendencies, the labor movement has generally remained weak in effecting any substantial gains pertaining to labor rights.

These divisions played out most significantly in the teacher's strikes following Hamas's election victory. In September 2006, teachers in the WBGS went on strike to protest unpaid wages. The government employees' union, which was aligned with the defeated Fatah party, came out in full support of the strike. Hamas declared the teachers' strike illegal and part of a conspiratorial effort to overthrow a legitimately elected government. The strike ended two months later when teachers received partial salaries and a promise to receive outstanding salaries at the end of the month. Fast forward to 2008: Fatah had overthrown the Hamas-led government, and in turn, Hamas had forcefully taken over the Gaza Strip, leading to a near all-out civil war between the two parties. A teachers' strike was called by Fatah in August 2008 to protest Hamas's take-takeover of the Gaza Strip and its treatment of Fatah-affiliated school teachers. This time, the Fatah-controlled West Bank PA ordered all public sector employees in Gaza not to report to work or risk being penalized by dismissal or the withholding of their wages from the West Bank PA. In an attempt to keep teachers in school, Hamas threaten to fire employees who observed the strike. Ultimately, Hamas replaced many of those who were on strike and transferred others to different schools, and Fatah discontinued the salaries of those who reported to work. By 2016, the ineffectivess of the unions was just as unfortunate. The West Bank witnessed the largest teacher's strike in Palestinian history during February and March of that year. The strike was organized by independents and despite the opposition of the General Union of Palestinian Teachers. Teachers in Gaza were not part of the strike because Hamas did not allow for teacher activism, and West Bank organizers feared that the inclusion of Gaza teachers might imply Hamas affiliation or its involvement in the strike. The PA promised to meet some of the initial demands, especially pertaining to a salary increase. By January of 2018, the PA had not fulfilled its commitments and postponed its timetable. It also had retaliated against many of the strike organizers by firing them, increasing their workload, or transferring them to more remotely located schools.[6] Over a decade later, the Palestinian body politic was still divided with Hamas controlling the Gaza

Strip and Fatah controlling the West Bank, and Western state-sponsored donors worked to promote Fatah and other non-Opposition-tendency groups, and refused the inclusion of Islamists in any unity government. Legislative elections were suspended, and the legislature had not convened since 2007. Very importantly, however, Western donor assistance could only mediate these processes, but by no means determine them.

The situation in El Salvador has not been a flawless ideal, nor has the transition been seamless. Unprecedented levels of insecurity and social violence became pervasive defining features of postwar El Salvador.[7] Between 2002 and 2008, there were no less than thirty homicides per 100,000 residents in any given year.[8] El Salvador's average was three times higher than the Latin American average (which itself is considerably higher than other regions), making this record of nonpolitical violence one of the highest in the world.[9] A key factor contributing to this violence are street gangs, locally known as *maras*. Many of these gangs originated in Los Angeles's immigrant neighborhoods, whose members were subsequently deported, bringing this new gang culture and established networks with them to the country of their birth.[10] In addition to the migration and socioeconomic factors that bred the prevalence of gangs, postwar El Salvador's state institutions had not developed the type of accountability mechanisms to dissuade and help dismantle old institutions that had contributed to these developments.[11] Moreover, internal policing had been inadequate, and it is not clear that the army's intervention helped. It likely exacerbated the problem given its heavy-handed approach. In 2012, the gangs signed a truce with the help of independent mediators (a Catholic bishop and former defense minister advisor included), resulting in a 60 percent decrease in the murder rate.[12] The truce collapsed after two years, and gang violence has remained a problem in El Salvador. An inclusive context, however, enabled the various parties to recognize that the *maras* are a national problem in need of a unified solution and to work toward that solution.

Beyond El Salvador and the Palestinian Territories

The primacy of political settlements in determining the impact of Western donor assistance to civil society extends well beyond the Palestinian territories and El Salvador. In what follows I discuss the generalizability my argument to the cases of Iraq and South Africa. Given that in these cases, as in almost all other cases in the post–Cold War era, Western donors introduced democracy assistance, my study does not illustrate the impact of political settlements in the absence of democracy assistance—per an ideal structured, focused comparison. Rather, I illustrate the generalizability of my argument to other cases by showing how political settlements shaped the impact of Western donor assistance. The discussion of the Iraq case is somewhat more extensive to illustrate that noninclusivity is not limited to Islamist groups. Unlike the initial examination of the Palestinian and Salvadoran cases, I do not trace the evolution of a civil society sector, but rather discuss the broader implications of these dynamics on political life in these two contexts.

Beyond the initial political settlements in these societies, the emergent and evolving constitutions began to define political relations in these contexts.[13] In South Africa, the transition was inclusive of all political groups, and even the groups that were not at the negotiating table did not actively oppose the political settlement. The resultant institutional setting in terms of the representativeness of the national and local governing bodies, and prevalence of CSOs, sought to include political tendencies and organizations across the political spectrum. In Iraq, after the 2003 US invasion, the new political settlement represented by its new constitution, was noninclusive by all accounts. Although not a conflict-to-peace transition per se, Iraq represented the overthrow of a regime, and a foreign occupation resolved to reformulate Iraq's political settlement—understood as the informal and formal rules that govern political relations in a given context. The posttransition settlement disadvantaged Sunnis and anyone affiliated with the former Ba'athist regime. This defining schism shaped (and continues to shape) the mediating role of Western donor assistance to Iraq, including to Iraqi civil society. As the case of Iraq illustrates, noninclusion in the Middle East extends to leftist and secularist political organizations that have historically been at odds with dominant Western geostrategic interests in the region and do not comply with the accepted notion of "post–Cold War liberal order."

South Africa

Developments in South Africa, defined by their inclusivity, differed markedly from the unfolding events in Iraq. At least two dozen political leaders, representing most of South Africa's ethnic and political groups, were represented in the transition talks. This included the National Party of apartheid South Africa, which was included in both the political set-tlement and in the constitutional drafting process that followed.[14] The multi-party forum resulted in a negotiated agreement in 1993, an interim constitution, an election time table beginning in 1994, and an agreement to establish a Government of National Unity that would be in place until 1999. Although Iraq's Ba'ath Party and the National Party of apartheid South Africa were markedly different in terms of what they represented, and the Ba'ath Party was deeply anchored at the societal level in Iraq in a way that the National Party was not, they were both important political actors that represented significant political constituencies. The National Party's willingness to retract previous positions and play by the rules of the game were noteworthy. The agreement also enjoyed extensive lev-els of public discussion and debate, which gave it high levels of public legitimacy.[15] Unlike Iraq or the Palestinian territories, the South African political settlement ultimately enjoyed extensive popular support. In addi-tion to power sharing, the agreement guaranteed property rights, civil service pensions, and amnesty to those who had confessed to politically driven atrocities.

The 1993 interim constitution put forth power-sharing arrangements that sought to avoid a backlash by political spoilers, and hence these groups received concessions and a share of power in the national unity government.[16] A power-sharing national unity government was re-quired for the first five years, and subsequent power-sharing arrange-ments would be voluntary.[17] This sunset clause ensured that initially South Africa would not be subjected to majority rule. Formal power-sharing arrangements ended during the transition, but the ANC con-tinued to run a power-sharing government on a voluntary basis. The voluntary nature of the power-sharing government reflected the po-litical leaders' commitment to an inclusive process.[18]During the 1994 election, both the ANC and the National Party included Inkatha in the national government.[19] The political parties ignored the gross election irregularities that took place in KwaZulu/Natal, Inkatha's powerbase,to ensure that Inkatha would win a province and have meaninful represen-tation in the cabinet [20] Throughout, the ANC was especially sensitive that national reconciliation and a more inclusive coalition went beyond a two-party coalition government.[21] The structural problems that South Africa continued to face were massive, especially those pertaining to the inequalities of apartheid. These challenges will continue to plague the country for decades to come. Moreover, vast sectors of society, and the unions in particular, were adamant in their opposition to the government's embrace of neoliberalism.

South Africa succeeded in extending its power sharing to the informal realm—a necessary measure for successful transitions. Ultimately, power sharing in formal politics was not enough, and civil society actors played an important role in supporting the formal negotiations by providing a platform for contending forces to negotiate their differences. These informal interventions were critical for the managing of ethnic, religion, or racial tensions and problems over time.[22] The Peace Accord committees, which were facilitated by NGOs, operated in the most problematic areas or regions where opposition was concentrated.[23] Power sharing beyond the formal arena became a defining feature of the "New South Africa."

Between 1994 and 1999, state-sponsored and multilateral donors pledged approximately US$6 billion in foreign donor assistance to South Africa. Similar to the Palestinian case, South Africa was categorized as a middle-income country, and technically did not qualify for these quantities of assistance. The EU was by far the largest contributor to the aid effort, contributing over US$1.77 billion, followed by the United States, which contributed approximately $0.9 billion.[24] In October 1994, the EU established a cooperation agreement with the government of South Africa to establish the European Program for Reconstruction and Development. Along with the United States, the EU prioritized the education sector, making it the highest funded sector.

Unlike the Palestinian and Iraqi cases, however, there was a high level of local ownership of the international aid effort. South Africa avoided the Bretton Woods institutions and coordinated the donor effort itself. They also avoided Consultative Group meetings, which were a defining feature of the aid effort in the Palestinian territories.[25] Without sidelining previously active groups, donors favored umbrella organizations over smaller grassroots organizations as a way to centralize the aid effort. Post-1994 patterns of funding to South Africa's CSOs, however, departed from patterns under apartheid-rule. Whereas the influx of

Western donor funding in the 1980s encouraged the proliferation of antiapartheid NGOs, funding in the postapartheid era shifted to the new government.[26] A majority of NGOs that emerged in South Africa were aligned to the antiapartheid struggle. In general, these NGOs were either liberal-oriented organizations or service providers to the mass-based organizations of the national liberation movement (mainly the United Democratic Front and Congress of South African Trade Unions).[27] After the 1994 elections, in which the ANC received approximately 63 percent of the vote, civil society activity shifted from resistance to reconstruction. Many characterized this evolving relationship as a partnership between government and civil society.[28] The dramatic decrease in funding to NGOs, however, reflected donors' preference to formulate bilateral agreements with the new government.[29] The decrease in funding to this sector led many NGOs to turn to the selling of services to the government and the corporate sector. Although this led to greater self-sufficiency in some instances, it resulted in a legitimacy problem since these NGOs were no longer accountable to the grassroots constituencies they once served. These developments also blurred the distinction between for-profit and nonprofit.

Despite the decrease in funding to CSOs, the extent of plurality in civil society and the multitude of state-civil society engagements were a positive move toward the strengthening of civil society and the development of democracy. Developments in civil society pointed to the emergence of three different groupings with different patterns of engagement with the state. In particular, there was a rise in informal, community-based organizations and networks that were survival focused and sought to enable poor and marginalized communities. Adam Habib cautioned, however, that these organizations needed to be seen for what they were: "survivalist responses of poor and marginalized people who have had no alternative in the face of a retreating state that refuses to meet its socio-economic obligations to its citizenry."[30] Alongside these organizations were the more professionalized, advocacy related organizations that sought to counter the state and its policies. And the third group included those organizations that were subcontractors or had entered partnerships with the state. These categories, however, did not coincide with political lines and therefore did not result in the politicized hierarchies that transpired in the Palestinian case.

Many of these developments represented the maturing of South Africa civil society. Under apartheid, civil society was polarized along racial lines: a "white" civil society that had cooperative and collaborate relations with the state, and a majority "black" society that represented a more oppositional mode of engagement. During the transition, this polarization began to blur as "white" civil society began to distance itself from the apartheid regime and its policies. In more recent years, the collaborative and oppositional modes no longer coincided along polarized racial lines but across the entire civil society spectrum.[31]

The inclusivity of the political settlement also contributed to the emergence of more articulated spaces for civil society activity. The South African state instituted effective channels for public participation in policy formulation at the national and provincial levels. During the first post-apartheid administration there was extensive public consultation though formal and informal processes at various stages of the legislative process. South Africa's strong legacy of social movement organization at the local level also continued during the transition where negotiations between the ANC and the National Party were accompanied by local negotiations that involved municipal authorities, unions, parties, and business groups.[32] Subsequently, all political groups supported the empowerment of the local level of government. South Africa's constitution and government policy conceived this level of government as having a key role to play in citizen participation and the empowerment of different groups. The ANC's affiliated unions, in particular, remained active in mobilizing and organizing at the local level. Ultimately, broader governance issues and the relationship between government and political parties, as determined by the political settlement, were decisive in determining the level and efficacy of civil society engagements, and foreign aid mediated these outcomes.[33]

Iraq

After the United States and its allies overthrew the Saddam Hussein regime but failed to find weapons of mass destruction, the promotion of democracy in Iraq and in the region as a whole became a rallying call. The United States carefully managed Iraq's transition to ensure that it met and supported the US's geostrategic interests in the region, and promoted its vision of a "post–Cold War liberal order." Elimination of the old order and the political settlement on which it hinged, and the destruction of any remnants of that regime, were guiding policies. Western donors promoted these political arrangements. These goals were manifested formally in the de-Ba'athification policies put in place after the start of the US occupation and in the constitutional negotiation arrangements and final draft of the constitution, and more informally in the political relations that transpired. The constitution, understood as partly peace agreements and partly frameworks that set up the rules by which the new democracy would operate,[34] came to mirror Iraq's noninclusive political settlement through its exclusion of the Sunni population and anyone associated with the former Ba'ath regime. These policies problematically assumed that elimination of the Ba'ath, including everything it embodied and represented, and quashing any privileges that Iraq's Sunni population enjoyed under Saddam Hussein's regime, would bring a sustainable peaceful and democratic order to Iraq. Moreover, these policies had little consideration for the longer term impact, especially given that membership in the Ba'ath party was a prerequisite for employment in the public sector. Western aid that filtered in perpetuated Iraq's noninclusive political settlement and worsened the existing polarization.

US-initiated de-Ba'athification was among the most ill-thought-out policies implemented in occupied Iraq. World War II Nazi Germany and Japan were upheld as the models to emulate, the rationale being that the key goals of ending the war and imposing democratic rule were attained in both cases. Drawing on Bernard Lewis, Paul Bremer, head of the Coalition Provisional Authority (CPA) in Iraq, argued that the parallels between Nazi Germany and Iraq further justified the model of replication because the origins of the Ba'ath in Iraq and Syria could be traced to Nazi Germany.[35] In the text of Order Number One issued on 16 May 2003, Bremer outlined the "disestablishment" of the Ba'ath Party as the first objective to be met:

> *Noting* the grave concern of Iraqi society regarding the threat posed by the continuation of Ba'ath Party networks and personnel in the administration of Iraq, and the intimidation of the people of Iraq by Ba'ath Party officials. . . .
>
> *Concerned* by the continuing threat to the security of the Coalition Forces posed by the Iraqi Ba'ath Party,

I hereby promulgate the following:

1) On April 16, 2003 the Coalition Provisional Authority disestablished the Ba'ath Party of Iraq. This order implements the declaration by eliminating the party's structures and removing its leadership from positions of authority and responsibility in Iraqi society.

2) Full members of the Ba'ath Party holding the ranks of 'Udw Qutriyya (Regional Command Member), 'Udw Far' (Branch Member). 'Udw Shu'bah (Section Member), and 'Udw Firqah (Group Member) (together, "Senior Party Members") are hereby removed from their positions and banned from future employment in the public sector.

3) Individuals holding positions in the top three layers of management in every national government ministry, affiliated corporations and other government institutions (e.g., universities and hospitals) shall be interviewed for possible affiliation with the Ba'ath Party, and subject to investigation for criminal conduct and risk to security. . . . Any such persons determined to be full members of the Ba'ath Party shall be removed from their employment. This includes those holding the more junior ranks 'Udw' (Member), 'Udw 'Amil (Active Member), as well as those determined to be senior party members.[36]

On 25 May 2003, the CPA issued two additional orders in support of de-Ba'athification: the first order called for the forfeiture and seizure of all assets and property of the Party, and the second order established the Iraqi Higher National De-Baathification Commission, which was composed of Iraqi nationals who were responsible for investigating and issuing recommendations about members of the Ba'ath.[37] These decrees were based solely on party membership and rank (ferqa, or group member, and above, which the CPA designated as senior members) and were built on the presumption of guilt.[38] By addressing the majority of Ba'ath members regardless of the nature of their previous involvement, the initial policy was unnecessarily far-reaching and did not distinguish between those who were simply public sector employees and those who engaged in unlawful activity against the Iraqi population. Very importantly, ferqa members had no decision-making role, and in practice members in training or acting members were also summarily dismissed from their jobs. De-Ba'athification policies also entailed the disbanding of the civil bureaucracy, which had employed hundreds of thousands of civil servants. Moreover, these policies did not take into account the breadth of the party apparatus, its organic ties to Iraqi society, and the institutional knowledge it embodied. Most onerously, de-Ba'athification policies included the dismantling of the existing security sector, which left approximately 400,000 Iraqi soldiers without jobs.

Opponents of de-Ba'athification argued that it would further exacerbate the political tensions, facilitate false accusations against individuals, undermine institutional and economic development, and hamper security restoration. The negative consequences of these policies soon became evident as political polarization mounted. Iraq's Sunnis interpreted and viewed de-Ba'athification policies as "de-sunnification; many felt that these policies were simply sectarian instruments to prevent Sunnis from participating in Iraq's public life."[39] The collective nature of the punishment made it difficult to refute these allegations. The institutional mechanisms that framed de-Ba'athification were devoid of criteria to guarantee minimal standards of due process. The Higher National De-Baathification Commission also had no meaningful oversight.[40] An underlying assumption that guided reconstruction efforts in Iraq was that existing institutions and infrastructure were not worth preserving. De-Ba'athification policies discounted the need for existing human capital and marginalized and dismissed individuals with local knowledge who were needed to run the country. These dismissals dealt a debilitating blow to the public sector and its ability to provide services, extending to critical sectors such as health.[41] Established doctors were fired, and what was left in the Ministry of Health were individuals with technical expertise, but no leadership. It was estimated that 2,367 Ministry of Health employees were dismissed. Moreover, the CPA-appointed health minister in Iraq had no training in public health and had never been involved in postwar reconstruction.[42]

The education sector suffered a similar fate. Initially, an overwhelming majority of Iraq's educators had lost their jobs because Ba'ath membership was a prerequisite for employment in the public education sector. According to the International Center for Transitional Justice, the Ministry of Education was by far the most affected: the ministry had

18,064 senior party members, most of whom were *ferqa* members. By June 2004, 16,149 had been dismissed. Moreover, approximately, 4,361 individuals were dismissed from the Ministry of Higher Education. The education sector as a whole was nearly destroyed. To remedy this situation, the CPA ordered the reinstatement of public school teachers in 2004, but the extent to which this actually took place, especially in Sunni areas, was hard to confirm.[43]

Security institutions that were integral to the Ba'athist regime were also disbanded with no alternative initially in place. The dissolution of the army left hundreds of thousands of troops, who had access to weaponry, unemployed and unable to take part in the development of the new Iraq. Many of these individuals joined the new insurgency.[44] Moreover, a number of individuals were reemployed in the new military or security institutions, defeating the initial objectives of de-Ba'athification.[45] Unanimous consensus obtained that the dissolution of Iraq's army and security apparatus was pivotal in fueling or contributing to the insurgency. De-Ba'athification policies were an evident failure by all accounts.

In due course, there would be a number of attempts to reverse or modify de-Ba'athification policies. As early as 23 April 2004, Bremer acknowledged that the de-Ba'athification policies then in place were hasty and poorly implemented.[46] In September 2004, Ayad 'Allawi, the president of the Governing Council, issued a decree that dissolved the De-Baathification Commission. He ordered that sitting ministers cease any dealings with the former commission and its members, that its members leave their offices, and he imposed barriers restricting the access of its members to the Green Zone.[47] In actuality, however, these policies were not implemented fully, and the institution was not completely dismantled but was reincarnated in the 2008 as Iraq's Higher National Commission for Accountability and Justice, which some believed would be perceived as more legitimate domestically. The Commission retained many of the core features of the old system, though on paper *ferqa* members were permitted to return to their government jobs. Electoral vetting, as well as review of applications for retirement and reinstatement, came to comprise the largest component of its functions.

The transition was implemented with US interests dominating the agenda. As Arato explained, "The democratic transition had to be managed. There were to be elections, but not too early before entirely new forces, presumably friendly to the United States, could really organize themselves. There had to be a new constitution, but the process of its making as well as its contents had to be tightly controlled." The CPA was careful to accord the necessary time to US-friendly groups to organize themselves, and to carefully craft the constitution so that it supported the US's objectives of who should be included and who should not.

Iraq's Emerging Political Settlement: The Constitution

The CPA granted the Interim Government Council the task of drafting the Transitional Administrative Law, which would serve as a transitional constitution and the basis for the Constitution that was drafted in 2005. This body eventually became the Constitutional Commission. From the onset, the Constitutional Preparatory Committee that negotiated the transitional constitution enjoyed little legitimacy in Iraqi society: The occupying power played a very active role and had to approve this body. Moreover, the Sunnis were initially excluded from the constitutional drafting process, and subsequently, when they were eventually included, this was at the behest of the CPA, and hence their inclusion lacked the requisite legitimacy[48] The Constitution also did little to formally include Iraq's Sunni population.[49] Eventually, the Constitution was subject to a national referendum. The majority of Iraq's Sunni population boycotted the interim elections and voted "no" on the October 2005 referendum on the Constitution. Although the draft constitution was eventually approved by a referendum, Sunni support was limited, and for the most part they remained opposed to the provisions relating to federalism. What Sunni support obtained was predicated on a promise that certain clauses could be renegotiated, or, more specifically, that after a four-month review period the Council of Representatives would consider further amendments that would later be subjected to another referendum.[50] These arrangements did not bode well for future developments.

The CPA ensured that de-Ba'athification provisions were very present in the political bargaining process, as well as in the new Constitution. The exclusion was extensive and went well beyond the Ba'ath. As Arato explained, "when the GC [Governing Council] was formed, not only all neo-Ba'athist, but all Arab Nationalist parties were excluded based on the consideration that they, too, could be vehicles for a Ba'ath revival."[51]

The exclusion of Arab nationalists, according to Arato, "was papered over by constructing the GC on the basis of strict ethnic quotas, rather than representatives of viable political organizations, contributing to the ethnicization of Iraqi politics."[52] Moreover, Article 7 of the Constitution outlawed the Ba'ath Party, and Article 135 guaranteed the continuation of the De-Baathification Commission until it had "completed its function," and it banned anyone subject to de-Ba'athification policies from serving on the Presidency Council, as prime minister, in the parliament, and in judicial, provincial, and state positions.[53]

The Constitution not only underrepresented Sunnis, but as a constituency they were not represented distinctly by any political group.[54] Although the National Assembly, the constitutional committee, and the cabinet accepted the principle of increasing Sunni participation, who would actually represent this community was not clearly articulated.[55] In 2005, when the different parties acceded to US demands that Sunni party representatives be included in the Constitutional Commission of the National Assembly, they were not accepted as equal partners since they were imposed by outsiders and did not have electoral legitimacy.[56] Sunnis were eventually also included in the national unity government; they were represented by the Iraqi National Accord, a Sunni bloc overwhelmingly represented by the Iraqi Islamic Party, although Arab nationalists would not be included.[57] Despite formal inclusion of Sunnis, however, they remained in a precarious position given the persistence of official efforts to marginalize them.

Iraq's noninclusive political settlement shaped civil society outcomes in two fundamental ways. First, as illustrated above, the resultant political institutions were nonrepresentative, and their very design was not inclusive of key political constituencies in Iraq; and second, the introduction of Western donor funding, especially from USAID, to strengthen civil society and promote democratization, was political, providing differential access to resources and promoting certain groups and communities over others. Hence, this assistance mediated unfolding outcomes and exacerbated political polarization, undermining prospects for a stronger, more effective civil society and longer term democratic development. Among Iraqi observers, the political outcome of this aid was apparent. As one commentator noted, "the flood of U.S. dollars into the country had fostered a 'triangle of political patronage' among Iraq's political parties, sectarian groups and government officials that sparked corruption and terrorism."[58] Despite this dismal prognosis, Western donor assistance filtered in, perpetuating the noninclusivity of Iraq's new political settlement.

US funding allocations to Iraq were inherently political, and intimately related to its more lofty, political and neoliberal ambitions for the region. Iraq is not a lower income country; by 2012, Iraq had replaced Iran as the world's second largest exporter of crude oil after Saudi Arabia, and despite the weakness of its infrastructural base and development capabilities, it was a solid middle-income country. The largesse of the aid package drew criticism from both sides of the US Congress with frequent demands that Iraq shoulder a greater share of reconstruction. Provisions were introduced that required Iraq to match reconstruction funds; the exceptions were democracy and human rights programs, USAID's Community Action Program, and other NGO-related activities[59]—often because of the political maneuverability and leverage that these programs afforded. The political dimensions of the US's commitment to Iraq's aid effort, especially in terms of bolstering certain political communities, were striking. From the outset, aid allocations to Iraq were drawn not only from standard Department of State and Foreign Operations appropriations, but also from a "Global War on Terror" emergency supplemental. Certain channels were established, such as the Commander's Emergency Response Program (CERP) with the explicit intent of bolstering certain communities in hopes of winning 'hearts and minds." And the various programs of the security and economic tracks also included funding for this objective.

Donor pledges to Iraq were among the highest to a transition context during the post–Cold War era, totaling over US$78.5 billion by September 2012.[60] Of this amount, $60.48 billion was from the United States and the remaining US$18.02 billion was from other donors. Iraq's own contribution (though overseen by the Community Action Plan) to its capital budget was US$138.08 billion.[61] In contrast to Iraq's own contribution, which went toward the capital budget, international assistance, and American assistance in particular, focused on political and security assistance.

In terms of US-related security funding, Iraq was among the highest recipients in the world: based on US FY 2012 appropriations requests,

Iraq received the world's highest budget from INCLE, and the third largest budget for foreign military financing.[62] Similar to new security assistance to the Palestinian territories, aid through the INCLE was tied to the security needs of the United States and was part of the broader framework of the War on Terror. Security funding (including what fell under the Economic Support Fund) also deviated from standard provisions of a public good in that it also provided discriminatory support to certain groups; this included support to Provincial Reconstruction Teams and embedded combat battalions. These teams worked with local Iraqi leaders to identify development projects in certain communities that could be implemented with US assistance.[63] By 2004, the CERP was established; its funding was drawn from Development Fund for Iraq and Department of Defense funds.[64] Its objective was to provide US military commanders with funds to win "hearts and minds." In April 2008, the Iraqi government allocated $300 million to establish an Iraqi CERP that would be managed by the U.S. military.[65] To win support, CERP funds were used to purchase basic items, as well as seed business funding, and to rebuild schools, roads, water and sewer systems, and so forth.[66]

Funding to Iraq was also allocated to political and economic tracks and aid to these tracks was used to bolster certain constituencies. The economic track included assistance to build and maintain infrastructural projects, and the political track was more broadly conceived to include governance, democratization, the rule of law, and overall administration of ministries and local governments. Initial US economic aid programs, which targeted the national level and the building of large scale infrastructural projects, shifted to more local-level assistance programs, such as to the Provincial Reconstruction Teams and Community Action Programs, after 2006. Assistance to the local level focused on technical assistance and local employment initiatives, and also hundreds of community-based projects that were meant to bolster the stabilization activities of the United States.[67] The aid souoght to bolster certain groups. Unlike in El Salvador, it did not endeavor to promote regular patterns of engagement between citizens and this level of government. Other donors programs were also politically selective, exacerbating the polarization of Iraqi society. The Community Action Program, USAID's longest development program implemented between 2003 and 2012, for example, endeavored to help communities address reconstruction needs at the local level and to enhance cooperation between constituencies and local representatives. The program also included the Marla Ruzicka Iraqi War Victims Fund, which provided assistance to Iraqis who were injured or harmed by Coalition forces. According to Mercy Corps, one of the implementing agencies, the initial distribution of this assistance to 122 programs focused on the "Shi'a Heartland," addressing needs related to water, sewage, school rehabilitation, and so forth that had resulted from years of governmental neglect.[68]

As demonstrated above, the different tracks of US assistance included mechanisms to discriminate against or gain the political favor of different constituencies.[69] In particular, the Sunnis were marginalized in reconstruction programming, while certain communities clearly benefited.[70] The more Sunni-dominated regions of Iraq, such as Baghdad and the western areas of the country, voiced grievances about their deteriorating circumstances, as others noticeably benefitted.[71] Sunni demands centered on equal access to basic services, more inclusion in national reconstruction, and rejection of the alleged sectarian political system. US attempts to tackle such grievances, however, involved promoting certain tribes and ensuring they benefitted from US assistance rather than promoting more inclusive policies.[72]

For the most part, democracy promotion and the electoral exercises that took place in Iraq after the invasion did not strengthen civil society, nor cultivate more social capital. Rather, as Adeed Dawisha explained, "they accentuated vertical segmentation of society along ethnic and sectarian divides that led to bloody communal conflicts, including ethnic cleansing; gave birth to administrative and governmental institutions that became mired in corruption; and most dispiriting of all, produced a weak and dysfunctional state that was unable to provide essential services or project power to subdue fissiparous and predatory substate groups."[73] Briefly, around the March 2010 elections, developments appeared less sectarian by some accounts. Nouri al-Maliki's State of Law Party fared much stronger than other Shi'a religious parties, and its main competitor was Al-Iraqiya, a nationalist secularist coalition. Ultimately, the nationalists gained ninety-one parliamentary seats, two more than Maliki's State of Law. Iraqiya owed its position primarily to the Sunni support; 80 percent of the Sunni population voted for it.[74] To Dawisha, the 2010 elections portended a more mature electorate, as

Iraqis were less inclined to simply vote on the basis of sectarian identity. Despite his cautiously positive assessment, he concluded, "Regardless, in the end what won the day was not a federalism based on the territorial boundaries of existing provinces but on wholesale ethno-sectarian considerations."[75] Events surrounding the elections reflected this precarious balance. The Accountability and Justice Commission (the revamped De-Baathification Commission) barred fifteen political groups, representing nearly 500 candidates, from taking part in the election on the pretext that they supported the Ba'ath Party;[76] the majority of these candidates were Sunni.

Subsequently, Iraqiya declined as a political force, and Maliki abandoned the nonsectarian nationalist platform that he had adopted in 2009 and systematically marginalized the senior cadre of Sunni national political parties. During February 2013, hundreds of thousands of Sunnis organized protests against the Shia-dominated government on the grounds that they were systematically marginalized. Protesters alleged that official discrimination tainted antiterrorism laws, along with other policies, as they specifically targeted Sunnis.[77] Prospects for a stronger civil society and a more solid and durable democratic future remained in the balance.[78]

The deteriorating conditions in Iraq also had regional implications. By the summer of 2014, in almost surreal developments, what became known as the Islamic State had come to control large swaths of territory in the northeast of Syria and in the northwest of Iraq, with approximately six million people under its rule. According to many recent reports, former high ranking Ba'ath military personnel made up much of its leadership. For example, at least two members of ISIS's military council, Abu Muhanad al-Sweidani and Abu Ahmad al-Alwani, were former Ba'athist military and intelligence officials in Iraq's army under Saddam Hussein. Similarly, Abu Bakr al Baghdadi and Abu Muslim al Afari al Turkmani, both believed to be members of ISIS's Shura Council, were also high ranking Ba'athist members of the military during the Saddam Hussein era.[79] ISIS's organizational structure included others. The ideological divide that separated Saddam Hussein-era Iraqi Ba'athism and ISIS *jihadism* is not minor. This "marriage of convenience," however, served both parties: ISIS exploited the organizational skills and knowledge of the Iraqi army, and the networks of the former Ba'ath

Party to further militarize and entrench its efforts; and former Ba'athists regained presence and political influence in Iraq (even if temporarily), and worked to restore Sunni political power.

Again, the post-Iraqi political settlement, which the United States, other Western countries, USAID, and other Western donors had stridently worked to uphold and enforce, had created a vicious security vacuum that without doubt contributed to the rise of excluded, marginalized groups in Iraq and beyond. The outcome was a tremendous blow to the region—one that will be felt for years to come.

Concluding Reflections

These additional case studies of Iraq and South Africa further illustrate how evolving political settlements shape democractic outcomes in a given context. Political settlements, broadly understood as the formal and informal political agreements that define political relations in a given context, and the levels of support they enjoy, will ultimately determine the relative effectiveness of democracy promotion efforts. Regardless of how democracy is conceived, or whether aspects related to contestation, participation, or accountability are emphasized, noninclusive political contexts undermine the prospects for the emergent democracy. Moving beyond the "pacted transition" critiques of democratic transition theorists, this book has extended the argument to democracy promotion efforts by Western donors in divided societies, and conflict-to-peace transitions in particular. It makes clear how the impact of foreign donor assistance on civil society cannot be understood without fully appreciating the relevant political contexts, especially the political settlements that define political relations in these contexts, whether in the Palestinian territories, El Salvador, Iraq, South Africa, or beyond. The book also sheds light on the relationship between civil society and political society. In disagreement with conventional understandings that conceive these two realms as separate and comprising actors who are wed exclusively to one realm or another, this work more accurately describes the interactions between these two realms as forever shifting sites of contest, as individuals move from one site to another, inextricably politicizing the link between them. This discussion is especially relevant in conflict-to-peace transitions given the extent to which civil society is born out of political society. Civil society thus becomes increasingly salient given its interconnectedness to political society, and has important implications for the prospects of democratic development in these contexts. And last, the theoretical literature has erred in its overemphasis on the autonomy of civil society. A more autonomous civil society does not connote a stronger one. Groups that emerge from political organizations, especially during conflict to peace, can play a critical role in effectively involving grassroots constituencies in democratic decision-making structures and in building the foundations for democracy.

The contributions of this book speak directly to the promise and peril of external actors shaping democratic outcomes in different contexts. Although Western funded projects and programs cannot alone determine these outcomes, they can play an important role in supporting and facilitating certain dynamics. At the most fundamental level, however, this book highlights the perils of embarking on a mission to shape democratic outcomes while excluding critical actors and promoting political settlements that enjoy minimal support in a given context.

Interviews (Excluding Foreign Donors)

The study draws from close to 150 semistructured interviews with directors and program officers of foreign donor agencies, directors of NGOs, grassroots activists, and political leaders in the Palestinian territories and El Salvador. In both contexts, I began my interviews with the leaders and founders of the women's mass-based organizations. I then traced the development of the mass-based organizations in the post-settlement period. Subsequently, I interviewed all the professionalized women's NGOs in the political centers. In Palestine, I conducted most of my interviews in Arabic, and in El Salvador I conducted most my interviews in Spanish, sometimes relying on the help of an assistant. My interviews focused on the goals behind the founding of the organizations; the nature of their programs and projects and the changes they have undergone; their patterns of interactions with different constituencies; their donors; and their relationship with their funders.

These interviews included six semistructured, open-ended interviews with the initial founders of the four women's committees in the Palestinian territories, and with all the directors or gender desk officers of the eight newly professionalized NGOs in the Jerusalem-Ramallah access area. To further probe the emerging dynamics between these sectors of the women's movement, I conducted twenty interviews with organizers in the women's committees who were responsible for coordinating women's activities in neighboring villages or in other locations in the West Bank, including the director of the GUPW. All the interviewees were active before the political settlement, and especially during the first Intifada. In El Salvador, I focused on the different components of the women's sector centered in San Salvador. In total, I conducted sixteen semistructured interviews with the directors of the newly professionalized NGOs and with the directors of the former FMLN grassroots-based women's organizations. In order to acquire information about the activities of the women's organizations during the civil war, I made sure to interview individuals who had been active in the given organization during that period. Because I conducted my fieldwork in Palestine first, I was significantly more experimental in my interview selection than I was in El Salvador, where I had a much clearer sense of what was required to gather the necessary information.

To ensure that the phenomena this book examines are not limited to the women's sectors, I also examined other sectors of civil society, examining labor, human rights, and civic education NGOs in both contexts. In the Palestinian territories, I conducted nineteen interviews with directors or program coordinators of labor, human rights, and civic education NGOs. Similarly, in El Salvador, I conducted four interviews with directors of labor, human rights, and civic education NGOs. Additionally, in Palestine, I conducted six interviews with political leaders who previously were involved in grassroots organizing during the 1980s. I also had discussions and open-ended interviews with relevant experts or political analysts in both contexts—ten in Palestine and four in El Salvador.

I conducted follow-up research and interviews in the Palestinian territories during the summers of 2006, 2009, and 2013. In 2006, my interviewees included individuals, both activists and political leaders, who were in a position to discuss political organizing efforts leading to the legislative elections. In 2009, my interviews were with members of the donor community who were in a position to discuss international coordination and aid efforts to the Gaza Strip following the 2008–09 Gaza war. My interviews also focused on the boycott of the Hamas-led government. In 2013, my research entailed the collection of primary and secondary sources materials, including reports.

The following list of interviews is organized alphabetically, according to the interviewee's last name. In the case of grassroots activists in the Palestinian women's movement, I do not include the name of the interviewee, but simply refer to the interviewee as Member with a corresponding number if I interviewed more than one grassroots activist from the organization. Included in this listing is the name of the interviewee, his or her title and institutional affiliation, place of interview, language, and date of the interview.

INTERVIEWS CONDUCTED IN THE PALESTINIAN TERRITORIES

Activists and Founders of Women's Organizations and Committees in Palestine
Ahmad al-Ramahi, Maysoun. Director, Al-Khansa'. Interviewed in Ramallah, in
Arabic, on 11 September 2001. Interviewed again, in Ramallah, in Arabic, on 16
September 2006.
Alayan, Thraya. Head of the Women's Program, LAWE—Palestinian Society for the
Protection of Human Rights and the Environment. Interviewed in Ramallah, in
Arabic, on 19 September 2001.
Al-Jayyousi, Nada. President, Al-Huda Development Association. Interviewed in
Ramallah, in Arabic, on 18 September 2006.
Al-Khayat, Maha. Director, WATC. Interviewed in Ramallah, in Arabic, on 9 July 2001.
Al-Kurd, Khawla. Director of the Arab's Women's Union Society: El-Bireh. Interviewed
in El Bireh, on 19 September 2006.
Aweideh, Sama. Director, Women's Studies Center. Interviewed in Jerusalem, in Ara-
bic, on 4 August 2001.
Badran, Amneh. Acting director, Jerusalem Center for Women. Interviewed in Jerusa-
lem, in Arabic, on 15 August 2001.
Barghouti, Nuha. Founding member and member of the Executive Committee, UP-
WWC. Interviewed in Ramallah, in Arabic, on 12 July 2001.
Barghouti, Siham. General director of Agricultural Development in the Ministry of
Local Government and founding member of the WWC, later renamed the FPWAC,
and director of FPWAC-FIDA. Interviewed in Ramallah, in Arabic, on 12 July 2001.
Interviewed again in Ramallah, in Arabic, on 19 September 2006.
Diab, Rabiha. Founding member and president, WCSW. Interviewed in Ramallah, in
Arabic, on 4 July 2001.
Hamad, Iktimal. Director of the UPWC. Interviewed in Gaza, in Arabic, on 31 July 2001.
Kamal, Zahira. Director of the Gender Desk in MOPIC, and founding member of
the WCC, later renamed the FPWAC. Interviewed in Ramallah, in Arabic, on 19
August 2001.
Khreisheh, Amal. Director, PWWSD. Interviewed in Ramallah, in Arabic, on 28 July
2001.
Member 1. Grassroots coordinator, in charge of marketing embroidered items, FP-
WAC. Interviewed in Ramallah, in Arabic, on 5 August 2001.
Member 2. Supervisor of grassroots coordination in the Jerusalem area, FPWAC. Inter-
viewed in Ramallah, in Arabic, on 6 August 2001.
Member 1. Social worker, FPWAC-FIDA. Interviewed in Ramallah, in Arabic, on 10
August 2001.
Member 2. Grassroots coordinator, FPWAC-FIDA. Interviewed in Ramallah, in Ara-
bic, on 12 August 2001.
Member 3. Supervisor of grassroots coordination in Hebron, FPWAC-FIDA.
Member 4. Member of the Executive Committee of the FPWAC-FIDA. Interviewed in
Hebron, in Arabic, on 20 August 2001.

Member 1. Supervisor of grassroots coordination in Hebron area, UPWC. Interviewed in Hebron, in Arabic, on 20 August 2001.

Member 2. Member of Youth Committee, UPWC. Interviewed in Ramallah, in Arabic, on 22 July 2001.

Member 3. Member of the Executive Committee and grassroots coordinator, UPWC. Interviewed in Ramallah, in Arabic, on 24 July 2001.

Member 1. Member of the Executive Committee, WCSW. Interviewed in Ramallah, in Arabic, on 14 July 2001.

Member 2. Member of the Executive Committee and treasurer, WCSW. Interviewed in Ramallah, in Arabic, on 19 July 2001.

Member 3. Grassroots coordinator in the Jerusalem area, WCSW. Interviewed in Jerusalem, in Arabic, on 20 August 2001.

Member 4. Secretary of Salfeet area, WCSW. Interviewed in Ramallah, in Arabic, on 22 July 2001.

Member 5. Administrator, WCSW. Interviewed in Ramallah, in Arabic, on 22 July 2001.

Member 6. Supervisor of grassroots coordination in the Ramallah area, WCSW. Interviewed in Ramallah, in Arabic, on 22 July 2001.

Member 7. Grassroots coordinator, WCSW. Interviewed in Ramallah, in Arabic, on 22 July 2001.

Member 8, supervisor of all kindergartens in Jerusalem-Ramallah, WCSW, and Member 9, grassroots coordinator in the WCSW. Interviewed in Ramallah, in Arabic, on 24 July 2001.

Mohammed, Nihaya. Founding member and member of Executive Committee of the FPWAC. Interviewed in Ramallah, in Arabic, on 29 July 2001.

Naji, Basma. Head of training and education, Women's Department of the PARC. Interviewed in Ramallah, in Arabic, on 22 August 2001.

Nashashibi, Dima. Vice president, WCLAC. Interviewed in Jerusalem, in Arabic, on 4 August 2001.

Nassar, Maha. Founding member and director, UPWC. Interviewed in Ramallah, in Arabic, on 21 July 2001.

Quassem, May. Head of Gender Desk, MIFTAH. Interviewed in Jerusalem, in Arabic, on 7 August 2001.

Shaikh, Naimeh. Director, WCSW. Interviewed in Gaza, in Arabic, on 31 July 2001.

Tarazi, Reema. President, GUPW, West Bank branch. Interviewed in Ramallah, in Arabic, on 14 August 2001.

Labor, Human Rights, and Civic Education NGOs

Abu Awad, Aysheh. Program coordintaor, Palestinian Center for Peace. Interviewed in Ramallah, in Arabic, on 17 September 2001.

Abu Quteish, Ayyed. Program coordinator, Defense Children International. Interviewed in Ramallah, in Arabic, on 20 September 2001.

Arafeh, Abdul Rahman. President, Arab Thought Forum. Interviewed in Jerusalem, in Arabic, on 17 August 2001.

Barghouti, Hassan. Director, Democracy and Workers' Rights Center. Interviewed in Ramallah, in Arabic, on 9 September 2001.

Barghouti, Iyad. Director, Ramallah Center for Human Rights Studies. Interviewed in Ramallah, in Arabic, on 3 September 2001.

Batrawi, Khalid. Board member, Mandela Institute for Political Prisoners. Interviewed in Ramallah, in Arabic, on 5 September 2001.

Eid, Bassem. Director, Palestinian Human Rights Monitoring Group. Interviewed in Jerusalem, in Arabic, on 17 September 2001.

Ibrahim, Ruba. Director, European Affairs Department, MIFTAH. Interviewed in Jerusalem, in Arabic, on 24 September 2001.

Issa, Shawqui. Executive director, LAWE—Palestinian Society for the Protection of Human Rights and the Environment. Interviewed in Jerusalem, in English, on 11 September 2001.

Jabarin, Sha'wan. Human rights officer and program coordinator, Al-Haq Human Rights Organization. Interviewed in Ramallah, in Arabic, on 21 August 2001.

Jaffal, Aref. Executive director, Civic Forum Institute. Interviewed in Jerusalem, in Arabic, on 15 August 2001.

Jarrar, Khalida. Director, Ad-Dameer Association for Human Rights. Interviewed in Ramallah, in Arabic, on 21 August 2001.

Jayussi, May. Director, Muwatin, the Palestinian Institute for the Study of Democracy. Interviewed in Ramallah, in English, on 11 September 2001.

Mu'allem, Nasif. Director general, Palestinian Center for Peace and Democracy. Interviewed in Ramallah, in Arabic, on 14 August 2001.

Nusseibeh, Lucy. Director, Middle East Nonviolence and Democracy. Interviewed in Jerusalem, in English, on 10 September 2001.

Quadi, Iyad. Program coordinator, Palestinian Academic Society for the Study of International Affairs (PASSIA). Interviewed in Ramallah, in Arabic, on 8 September 2001.

Saif, Samir. Director, Palestinian Peace Information Center—Al Jiser. Interviewed in Ramallah in Arabic, on 4 September 2001.

Salem, Waleed. Program director, Palestinian Center for the Dissemination of Democracy and Community Development (PANORAMA). Interviewed in Ramallah, in Arabic, on 22 August 2001.

Zeedani, Said. Director, Palestinian Independent Commission for Citizens Rights (PICCR). Interviewed in Ramallah, in English, on 21 August 2001.

Open-Ended Interviews and Discussions

Ajlouni, Joyce. Program representative, Jerusalem, Oxfam GB, and founding member of the Association for International Development Agencies (AIDA). Interviewed in Jerusalem, in English, on 17 July 2001.

Asfour, Hassan. Minister of state, Ministry of Non-Governmental Organizations. Interviewed in Ramallah, in Arabic, on 7 August 2001.

Barren, Paul. Program coordinator, World Vision. Interviewed in Jerusalem, in English, on 2 July 2001.

Jebayle, Kamal. President, Union of Palestinian Charitable Organizations. Interviewed in Ramallah, in Arabic, on 14 July 2001.

Mansour, Mohammed [Abu Ala Mansour]. General director, Interior Ministry Office in Ramallah, and secretary of Fatah in the Ramallah-Bireh region. Interviewed in Ramallah, in Arabic, on 16 July 2001.

Nakhleh, Khalil. Team member of education, MEDA Team West Bank and Gaza Strip, technical assistance to the EC Representative Office. Interviewed in Jerusalem, in English, on 25 July 2001.

Nue, Tom. Director, American Near East Refugees Assistance (ANERA). Interviewed in Jerusalem, in English, on 5 July 2001.

Qubesh, Renad. Program coordinator, Palestinian NGO Network (PNGO). Interviewed in Ramallah, in Arabic, on 27 June 2001.

Rantisi, Raja. Former member, UPWWC. Interviewed in Ramallah, in Arabic, on 16 July 2001.

Said, Nader. Director, Birzeit Development Center. Interviewed in Birzeit, in Arabic, on 30 June 2001.

Political Leader and Former Grassroots Leaders

Aruri, Mohammed. Member of the Executive Committee of the General Federation of Trade Unions and Politburo member of FIDA. Interviewed in Ramallah, in Arabic, on 1 August 2001.

Assaf, Omar. Former grassroots organizer, school teacher at Friends Boys School, and Politburo member of the DFLP. Interviewed in Ramallah, in Arabic, on 22 July 2001. Interviewed again in Ramallah, in Arabic, on 14 September 2006.

Barghouti, Marwan. Former student leader, member of the Palestinian Legislative Council, member of the Revolutionary Council of Fatah, and general secretary of the Higher Committee of the West Bank, Fatah. Interviewed in Ramallah, in Arabic, on 24 July 2001.

Barghouti, Mustafa. Director of the UPMRC, director of the Human Development and Information Project, member of the General Secretariat of the PPP, formerly the PCP. Interviewed in Ramallah, in English, on 24 July 2001.

Jaradat, Ali. Former grassroots organizer of the first Intifada, editor of *Al-Hadaf* in 2001, head of publicity of the PFLP's Central Committee. Interviewed in Ramallah, in Arabic, on 18 July 2001.

Jarar, Khalida. Elected member of the Palestinian Legislative Council, member of the PFLP (at time of interview), and former director of Addameer: Prisoners' Support and Human Rights NGO. Interviewed in Ramallah, in Arabic, on 18 September 2006.

Khatib, Ghassan. Director of the JMCC, and Executive Committee member of the PPP, formerly the PCP. He has held several positions in the PA, including director of the Government Media Center (2009–12), minister of labor in 2002, and minister of planning (2005–06). Interviewed in Jerusalem, in Arabic, on 5 August 2001.

INTERVIEWS CONDUCTED IN EL SALVADOR

Activists and Founders of Women's Organizations in El Salvador

America, Alba. Director, CEMUJER. Interviewed in San Salvador, in Spanish, on 23
May 2002.

Argeuta, Carmen, psychologist and coordinator of programs for the eradication of
violence, Las Dígnas. Interviewed in San Salvador, in Spanish, on 26 May 2002,
along with Ana Murcia.

Argueta, Yanera. Founding member and director, AMS. Interviewed in San Salvador,
in Spanish, on 10 May 2002.

Ascenio, Isabel. Coordinator from 1997 to 2000, Flor de Piedra (Flower of the Stone).
Interviewed in San Salvador, in Spanish, on 6 June 2002.

Baires, Sonia. President of the board, Las Dígnas. Interviewed in San Salvador, in
Spanish, 23 May 2002.

Chaine, Deysi. Founding member and current director, IMU. Interviewed in San Salvador, in Spanish, on 16 May 2002.

de Gevara, Isabel. President, MSM, and municipal council member of St. Marcos.
Interviewed in San Salvador, in Spanish, on 23 May 2002.

Delgado, Sophia. Director, Mujer Joven (Young Women). Interviewed in San Salvador,
on 3 June 2002.

Fabeán, Isabel. Coordinator of local development and political participation programs,
MAM. Interviewed in San Salvador, in Spanish, on 13 May 2002.

Hernandez, Nora. Secretary of Board of Directors and coordinator of Economic Development Unit, Las Dígnas. Interviewed in San Salvador, in Spanish, on 14 May 2002.

Maya, Irma. Founding member of MAM and deputy member of the Legislative Assembly. Interviewed in San Salvador, in Spanish, on 27 May 2002.

Medina, Carmen. Former member of ASMUSA and founding member of MSM, representative in El Salvador for International Development-England (CID-England).
Interviewed in San Salvador, in English, on 16 February 2002 and 8 May 2002.

Murcia, Ana. Director, Las Dígnas. Interviewed in San Salvador, in Spanish, on 26 May
2002, along with Carmen Argueta.

Quintiera, Azucena. Former coordinator in Nicaragua, AMES, and coordinator in
MAM. Interviewed in San Salvador, in Spanish, on 13 May 2002.

Sales, Dina. Director, CORAMS. Interviewed in San Salvador, in Spanish, on 21 May 2002.

Silva, Zoila. Executive director, ISDEMU. Interviewed in San Salvador, in Spanish, on
11 June 2002.

Urquilla, Jeanette. Director, ORMUSA. Interviewed in San Salvador, in Spanish, on 30
May 2002.

Human Rights and Civic Education NGOs

Aguñada, Sergio. Program director, Consorcio de ONGs por Derechos de Humanos
(Consortium of Human Rights NGOs). Interviewed in San Salvador, in Spanish, on
30 May 2002.

Baires, Victoria Carolina. Program director, Centro para la Promoción de los Derechos Humanos (Center for the Promotion of Human Rights, CPDH). Interviewed in San Salvador, in Spanish, on 7 June 2002, along with Miriam Guzman.

Bernal, Arnoldo. Program director, Consorcio de ONGs por Edución Civica (Consortium of Civic Education NGOs). Interviewed in San Salvador, in Spanish, on 12 May 2002.

Guzman, Miriam. General secretary of the Board of Directors, Centro para la Promoción de los Derechos Humanos (Center for the Promotion of Human Rights-CPDH). Interviewed in San Salvador, in Spanish, on 7 June 2002, along with Victoria Carolina Baires.

Salazar, Armando Peres. Executive director, Comité de Familiares de Victimas de Violaciones de los Derechos Humanos (Committee for the Families of Victims of Human Rights Violations, CODEFAM). Interviewed in San Salvador, in Spanish, on 11 June 2002.

Unstructured and Open-Ended Interviews and Discussions

Eekhoff, Katharine Andrade. Researcher, FLACSO-El Salvador. Interviewed in San Salvador, in English, on 15 May 2002.

Dada, Héctor Hirezi. Director, FLACSO-El Salvador. Interviewed in San Salvador, in Spanish, on 26 May 2002, along with Carlos Ramos.

Doctoroff, Jill. Coordinator, Coordinación de Organizaciones de Mujeres (Coordination of Women's Organization, COM). Interviewed in San Salvador, in English, on 6 June 2002.

Holiday, David. Director, CREA. Interviewed in San Salvador, in English, on 27 February 2002 and 20 March 2002.

Raos, Carlos. Research and seminar coordinator, FLACSO-El Salvador. Interviewed in San Salvador, in Spanish, on 26 May 2002, along with Héctor Hirezi Dada.

APPENDIX II

Foreign Donors

DATA SOURCES SUMMARY AND JUSTIFICATION
To comprehensively capture the mediating role of foreign donor assistance on civil society and democratic development, this book examined democracy promotion related assistance and broader compositions of aid to more carefully determine who received aid and who did not, and for which programmatic priorities. Similarly, the more specific examination of political settlements and the mediating role of donor assistance on the women's sector also required more comprehensive examination of assistance to this sector. To this end, I first examined general flows of donor assistance to the Palestinian territories and El Salvador during 1992 and 2001, and then focused more specifically on donor assistance allocations to the women's sector, which extended well beyond democracy promotion assistance. This more comprehensive approach was necessary since ultimately both democracy assistance and development assistance shaped political outcomes.

I began the research by collecting official donor flow data committed, pledged, or disbursed to the two cases after the signing of the peace accords; in the Palestinian territories, this material was compiled by the MOPIC, and in El Salvador by the UNDP. I then collected data from donor agencies.

I conducted forty semi-structured interviews, eighteen in El Salvador and twenty-two in the Palestinian territories, with the directors of foreign donor agencies that specifically funded programs relating to women, democracy, oe civil society. I conducted these interviews in Arabic, English, or Spanish, depending on the preference of my interviewee. To determine the extent to which the political settlements shaped the impact of foreign donor assistance on civil society, I interviewed directors of foreign donor agencies or program managers in these agencies about the types of groups and organizations they were willing to fund, and whether this depended upon the groups' political position vis-à-vis the peace accords. I also interviewed them about program priorities, their geostrategic considerations and aid activity in the given region relative to other regions, the goals that motivated these programs, their understanding of democracy and civil society, and their follow-up procedures. During these interviews, I also attempted to access summaries of donor flows and other documentation regarding their aid activity. To acquire a more nuanced understanding of donor assistance to the respective women's sector, I interviewed the directors and project managers of the women's organizations about their donors, the donors' programmatic priorities, and their relationship with their donors. I also relied on secondary literature pertaining to the role and impact of foreign donor activity in these two contexts. I also conducted a number of interviews after the 2008–09 Gaza-Israel war to gain a better understanding of the coordination mechanisms and the new considerations that governed donor assistance to the Palestinian territories, and to the Gaza Strip in particular. To prevent the conflation of personal opinions and official agency opinions, I always asked my interviewees to specify whether the given discussion was the official agency policy. Therefore, I cited many of the quotes in this text as personal attributions, rather than official agency positions.

INTERVIEW SELECTION OF FOREIGN DONOR AGENCIES

To select my interviews, I first compiled a list of the foreign donor agencies that were active in each context. My priority was to examine state or state-sponsored foreign donor agencies in order to determine the extent to which donor activity aligned with a state's geostrategic interests, and whether these agencies were more selective about the recipients of their funding. I also focused on donors that funded programs and projects related to democracy, civil society, and women/gender. To ensure that I did not leave out any significant donors in the areas related to democracy, civil society, and women, I cross-checked my list with the matrix of donor flows to the PA compiled by MOPIC. I also cross-checked this list with a number of individuals who were familiar with the activities of foreign donor agencies in the Palestinian territories. When a given state operated through affiliated foundations or nongovernmental organizations, rather than state-sponsored donor agencies, I added those organizations to my list. I also interviewed directors or program directors of women's organizations and inquired about the donors who funded their programs, and added those donors that were mentioned by a number of my interviewees. Following the 2008–09 incursion between Gaza and Israel, I added those UN agencies to my list that were involved in coordinating aid efforts to the Gaza Strip.

Information about foreign donor agencies operating in El Salvador was not as readily available. The UNDP compiled a list of donor flows to the country between 1992 and 1997. Like the list compiled by the MOPIC, this list did not include all funding made available directly to NGOs. Personal contacts who work for foreign donor agencies or for nongovernmental organizations in El Salvador provided me with contact information for the foreign donors operating in the country. After compiling an extensive list of foreign donor agencies, I contacted these agencies, inquiring about whether or not they funded democracy, civil society, or gender or women-related programs. In El Salvador, many foreign donor agencies that operated in the country were based in neighboring Nicaragua or another Central American country, which complicated direct access to these donors.

COMPILATION OF SYMMETRIC DATA

To construct a more symmetric portrayal of foreign donor activity in both contexts, I relied on data from the OECD since compilation methodology and organization would be uniform. OCED data was from two separate databases: the Development Assistance Committee (DAC) annual aggregate database, which provides comprehensive data on the volume, origin, and type of aid and other resource flows; and the Creditor Reporting System (CRS), which provides detailed information on individual aid activities, such as sectors, countries, and project descriptions. These sources, however, are not comprehensive since smaller nonstate donors such as solidarity groups do not report their funding to DAC. Similarly, DAC members do not necessarily report their project breakdowns to the CRS. The completeness of CRS commitments for DAC members has improved from 70 percent in 1995, to over 90 percent in 2000, and close to 100 percent by 2003. CRS disbursements figures, however, are not recommended prior to 2002, though coverage

ratios became near complete by 2007.[1] In assessing OECD-CRS reporting, I focused on commitments to the Government and Civil Society
sector between 1992 and 2001. This comparison allowed me to determine the composition of funding allocations and compare subsectoral
priorities in each context in the immediate postsettlement period. I also
focused on donor agencies that operated in both contexts. Six of these
donor agencies are USAID, the German Heinrich Böll Foundation, the
EC, Díakonia,[2] CIDA, and the German Technical Cooperation Agency
(GTZ), and, in particular, I focused on the work of USAID's Democracy
and Governance program in both contexts. The comparison of USAID
activities allowed me to determine which groups in each case were eligible to receive funding from USAID, sectoral priorities in each context,
the extent to which grassroots constituencies benefited from this funding, and the manner in which the projects promoted by USAID shaped
interactions with other CSOs and state institutions.

Similar to other sources of donor flows, national level reporting had
its limitations, especially pertaining to sectoral categorization and allocations. In some cases, foreign donor agencies did not report their
exact disbursements to these organizations; this is especially the case
with smaller donors, such as NGOs or solidarity organizations. Particularly in the Palestinian case, despite the extensive efforts dedicated to the
coordination and recording of foreign aid, sectoral allocations were not
always clear and exact funding to professionalized NGOs was often not
included in the MOPIC matrices. For example, although commitments
to the women's sector amounted to US$19.943 million between 1994 and
2000, this amount also included funding to the PA institutions and to
development organizations. Moreover, commitments to the Human
Rights and Civil Society sector (which amounted to US$18.719 million
between 1998 and 2001) also included funding to women's NGOs for
civic education and human rights training. Unfortunately, the project
breakdown of funds allocated to the overall sector was not included in
MOPIC's 2001 First and Second Quarterly Monitoring Report. Directors of foreign donor agencies differed in terms of their willingness to
provide detailed information about their recipients.

Information regarding the exact amount of foreign donor assistance to the Palestinian women's sector was difficult to obtain. Different
sources of funding, national and OECD, were often incomplete. In the

case of OECD-CRS funding, not all donors reported their NGO funding to the CRS, and so coverage ratios are estimated at around 90 percent. National level reporting of funding to the women's sector often included all funding that is gender related or involved women and did not distinguish between funding channels or funding to professionalized NGOs or government agencies. Directors of foreign donor agencies and of professionalized NGOs also differed in terms of their willingness to provide detailed information about the aid they provided or received. Despite these limitations, through my interviews with directors of various donor agencies and directors of NGOs, as well as my access to various reports tracking donor assistance to the Palestinian territories and El Salvador, I was able to put together a comprehensive picture regarding the donors who fund the women's sector and the types of organizations and programs they fund.

INTERVIEWS

Foreign Donor Agencies in the Palestinian Territories

Almbaid, Mohammed. Senior CSO specialist, Tamkeen (USAID-Funded Civil Society Project). Interviewed in Ramallah, in English, on 16 September 2001.

Blidelius, Owe, regional representative, and Margoth Sonnebo, program manager, Díakonia. Interviewed in Jerusalem, in English, on 16 August 2001.

Borg, Peter. Acting deputy head, Norway Representative Office to the PA. Interviewed in Jerusalem, in English, on 19 July 2001.

Brenzelius, Anne, head of Swedish International Co-operation Development Agency (SIDA), and Eva-Lotta Gustafsson, Program Officer, Consulate of Sweden. Interviewed in Jerusalem, in English, on 13 September 200.

Buhbe, Mathes. Resident representative, Friedrich Ebert Foundation. Interviewed in Jerusalem, in English, on 18 September 2001.

Clarke, John. Chief of Coordination Unit, office of the UNSCO. Interviewed in Jerusalem, in English, on 4 August 2009.

Claudet, Sophie. Former NGO project coordinator, World Bank. Interviewed in Ramallah, in English, on 10 September 2001.

Fouet, Sylvie. Political officer for Human Rights and Democracy Projects, EC. Interviewed in Jerusalem, in English, on 1 August 2001.

Fröhlich, Fritz. Deputy head, Swiss Agency for Development and Co-operation. Interviewed in Jerusalem, in English, on 11 September 2001.

Gerl, Peter. Head of Economic Co-operation, GTZ, Representative Office of Germany to the PA. Interviewed in Ramallah, phone interview in English, on 18 July 2001.

Malki, Ra'id. Senior development program officer and deputy head of aid, CIDA. Interviewed in Ramallah, in Arabic, on 25 September 2001.

Marion, Laurent. Early recovery advisor to Program of Assistance to the Palestinian People, UNDP. Interview in Jerusalem, in English, on 4 August 2009.

Masud, Wafa. Project coordinator, Hanns-Seidel Foundation. Interviewed in Ramallah, in Arabic, on 20 September 2001.

Muslih, Khader. Team leader of Media and Human Rights, MEDA Team West Bank and Gaza Strip, technical assistance to the EC Representative Office. Interviewed in Jerusalem, in Arabic, on 7 August 2001.

Myers, Martha. Director of Democracy and Governance, USAID. Interviewed in Jerusalem, in English, on 14 September 2001.

Paul, Joachim. Project coordinator and consultant, Friedrich Naumann Foundation. Interviewed in Jerusalem, in English, on 14 September 2001.

Qazzaz, Hadeel. Regional program coordinator, Heinrich Böll Foundation. Interviewed in Ramallah, in Arabic, on 20 September 2001.

Rotinen, Elja. Head, Representative Office of Finland to the PA. Interviewed in Ramallah, in English, on 21 September 2001.

Shadid, Mohammed. Project management organization director, Welfare Association Consortium for the Management of the Palestinian NGO Project. Interviewed in Jerusalem, in Arabic, on 20 June 2001.

Tazelaar, Birgitta. Second secretary, Netherlands Representative Office to the PA. Interviewed in Ramallah, in English, 25 July 2001.

Wright, Kristy. Director, Canada Fund. Interviewed in Ramallah, in English, on 24 July 2001.

Personal interview with OCHA official who asked not to be named. Interviewed in Jerusalem, in English, on 5 August 2009.

Foreign Donor Agencies in El Salvador

Allen, Keith, consul general and deputy of mission, Embassy of Britain, and José Fermán Flores, head of technical cooperation, Embassy of Britain. Interviewed in San Salvador, in English, on 30 April 2002.

Andrade, Oscar. Director of humanitarian assistance and Special Projects Unit, Oxfam America. Interviewed in San Salvador, in English, on 14 June 2002.

Barousse, Francois. Head of technical and scientific cooperation, Embassy of France. Interviewed in San Salvador, in English, on 2 May 2002.

Barrero, Jorge. Program director, Japanese Agency for International Co-operation. Interviewed in San Salvador, in English, on 21 May 2002.

Bohnstedt, Bengt. Project coordinator, GTZ. Interviewed in San Salvador, in English, on 12 June 2002.

Coello, Mauricio Herrera. Director general of Democracy and Governance, USAID. Interviewed in San Salvador, in English, on 22 April 2002.

Conti, Antonio. Director, Italian Co-operation in the Ministry of Foreign Affairs. Interviewed in San Salvador, in English, on 3 May 2002.

Garza, Jorge. Director, Canada–El Salvador Development Fund (FODEC) of CIDA. Interviewed in San Salvador, in English, on 12 April 2002.

Hamer, Dr. Thomas Hamer. Representative to El Salvador, Friedrich Ebert Foundation. Interviewed in San Salvador, in English, on 24 April 2002.

Helfrich, Silke. Director, Heinrich Böll Foundation. Interviewed in San Salvador, in Spanish, on 15 April 2002.

Holiday, David. Director, CREA. Interviewed in San Salvador, in English, on 2 May 2002.

Kerrinckx, Carlos. Consul general, Consulate of Belgium. Interviewed in San Salvador, in English, on 29 April 2002.

López Sanz, Francisco. Deputy assistant, Embassy of Spain. Interviewed in San Salvador, in Spanish, on 10 May 2002.

Paulson, Göran. Regional coordinator, Díakonia. Interviewed in San Salvador, in English, on 25 April 2002.

Quinn, Alan. Project director and legal representative, Canadian Center for International Studies and Co-operation. Interviewed in San Salvador, in English, on 17 April 2002.

Rauda, Marta Elena. Program director, Fundación Practica. Interviewed in San Salvador, in Spanish, on 24 May 2002.

Vanderlinden, Mark. Regional coordinator, EU. Interviewed in San Salvador, in English, on 18 April 2002.

Vital, Consuello. Assistant resident representative, UNDP. Interviewed in San Salvador, in English, on 9 May 2002.

NOTES

Arabic transliteration in this book is based on the general guidelines of the *International Journal of Middle East Studies*.

PREFACE

1   I use Palestinian territories, occupied territories, and West Bank and Gaza Strip (WBGS) interchangeably throughout.

2   The demarcation lines of the pre-1967 borders set out in the 1949 Armistice Agreements between Arab countries and Israel.

3   In 1991, Palestinian representatives attended the Madrid Peace Conference, which ultimately culminated in the 1993 Declaration of Principles (DOP). The DOP and subsequent agreements between the PLO and the state of Israel would collectively become known as the Oslo Accords.

4   A 1997 survey by the Jerusalem Media and Communication Center indicated that only 19.6 percent in the West Bank and 15.2 percent in Gaza agreed that foreign funds were benefiting all sectors of the population.

5   Democracy promotion refers to efforts that contribute to political liberalization, democratic transitions, democratization, or consolidation of political systems, or a combination of these factors. This area of assistance includes funding for the design of electoral systems, the rewriting of constitutions, political party development, teaching party members how to organize and campaign, supporting legislatures, as well as CSOs, and assisting CSOs in lobbying and representing citizen interests, inculcating citizens with "appropriate" civic values and norms, and promoting good governance at the local and state levels.

6   Secretary of State Colin Powell announced the Middle East Partnership Initiative in December 2002.

7   In June 2004, the G8 unveiled the "Partnership for Progress and a Common Future" with the Broader Middle East and North Africa.

8   Through the Millennium Challenge Account, the White House linked significant amounts of foreign assistance to performance on democratic governance (for more on the Millennium Challenge Account, see Windsor 2006).

9   Carothers 2015.

10 Petrova 2014.

11 Carothers 2015.

12 All interviews were conducted by the author. In appendix I, I elaborate on my interview selection, and in appendix II, I specifically explain my selection process

for foreign donor agency interviews and justification for donor funding–related data sources.

CHAPTER 1. THE PRIMACY OF POLITICAL SETTLEMENTS IN DEMOCRACY PROMOTION

1 Robinson 1997, 94. These grassroots committees had relative autonomy from the political organizations. For more on this topic, refer specifically to chapter 5.

2 In the event that Israeli settlers attacked a particular neighborhood or village, the patrol committees were responsible for alerting residents of the neighborhood or village to a possible attack.

3 The women's daily tasks included the mobilization of others, the setting up of units to collect and store food, the creation of popular education committees in the various neighborhoods, and the formation of committees to create local manufactured goods to replace Israeli-made products. The women engaged in these activities in addition to more overt forms of collective action such as protest marches and sit-ins.

4 Taraki 1989.

5 Hiltermann 1991 provides a detailed discussion regarding the Palestinian women's and labor movements.

6 Interview with Siham Barghouti, 12 July 2001. I provide full citation material for an interview—the title of a person or organizational affiliation, or both; the interview location; the language in which the interview was conducted, and the date—in appendix I or II. In the footnotes, I only include the name and date, unless the name is not provided and organizational affiliation is necessary.

7 These are needs that derive from women's living conditions versus demands that seek to transform gender relations. For more on this, see Molyneux 1985.

8 Brouwer 2000, 21–48; Carothers and Ottaway 2005; Challand 2009; Hanafi and Tabar 2005; Le More 2008; Jamal 2012.

9 Hammami 1995, 2002; Jad 2004; Kuttab 2008; Hilal 2003.

10 Markowitz and Tice 2002.

11 Caldeira 1998; and, specifically, Jacquette 1994; and Ottaway and Carothers 2000.

12 Henderson 2003; Edwards and Hulme 1997; Howell and Pearce 2002; Bebbington and Riddell 1995; Sperling 1999; Ottaway and Chung 1999, 107–108; Edwards and Hulme 1996; and, more recently, Bush 2015.

13 Hanafi and Tabar 2005.

14 For a specific discussion of these sociological changes in terms of class formation in the Palestinian case, see Challand 2009, chapter 6.

15 Van Rooy 1998, 51.

16 Bush 2015; Langohr 2004.

17 These were the zones controlled by the FMLN during the war.

18 For a typology of these sectors and types and levels of organizations, see Uclés 1995, 163.

19 For more on the women's mass-based organizations in the Palestinian territories, see Hasso 2005; Hiltermann 1991; and, for El Salvador, see Thomson 1986.

20 In part, more favorable circumstances in the international context following the Decade of Women, which emerged from the UN's 1975 commitment to focus on women and development, influenced the emergence of this "third wave" of women's organizations in El Salvador.

21 Paraphrased parts of this argument have been published in Jamal 2012.

22 Rothchild 2002, 118.

23 Haggard and Kaufman 1997, 270.

24 Karl and Schmitter 1991.

25 O'Donnell and Schmitter 1986, 37.

26 Among the scholars who share this view are O'Donnell and Schmitter 1986, 39; Zhang 1994; and Di Palma 1990, chapter 4.

27 For more on this, refer to Shin 1994.

28 See, for example, Valenzuela 1992 and Hagopian 1992.

29 See, for example, Paris 2004 and Höglund 2008.

30 Belloni 2008; Orjuela 2003.

31 Hagopian 1990; Karl 1992; Karl and Schmitter 1991; Gurr 2000; Walter 2009.

32 Shin 1994; Valenzuela 1992; Hagopian 1992. Others, such as Callaghy 1992 extend the argument to market-democracy transitions.

33 The term "peace-building" came into widespread usage after Boutros Boutros-Ghali announced his "Agenda for Peace" in 1992. He conceived of peace building as: " rebuilding the institutions and infrastructures of nations torn by civil war and strife."

34 Hartzell, Hoddie, and Rothchild 2001; Call 2012; Gurr 2000a; Kovacs 2008; Stedman 1997; Walter 1997; Roeder and Rothchild 2005. Roeder and Rothchild 2005 promote ethnically inclusive majoritarian democracy or power-sharing arrangements, but stipulate that such arrangements may undermine the consolidation of democracy in the longer term.

35 Sisk 1995. In line with his "institutional choice," Timothy Sisk gives priority to the actual bargaining process that leads to the settlement.

36 For more on how electoral system design and timing of elections can impact longer term political outcomes, see Horowitz 2003, and for more recent work with a focus on the timing of various components of elections, see Reilly 2008.

37 Sisk 1996 specifically addresses elite habituation.

38 Sisk 2009; Lijphart 1990; Rothschild 1970.

39 Finkel, Perez-Linan, and Seligson 2007; Kalyvitis and Vlachaki 2010; Scott and Steele 2011; Wright 2009; Dunning 2004; Dietrich and Wright 2013; and Savun, Burcu, and Tirone 2011 specifically examined democracy assistance in conflict contexts and argued that democratizing states that receive high levels of democracy assistance are less likely to experience civil conflict than countries that receive little or no external democracy assistance.

40 Burnell 2002; Sogge 2002; Manning and Malbrough 2013.

41 Knack 2004; Tripp 2013; Gyimah-Boadi and Yakah 2013.

42 Most notably, Henderson 2003; Ottaway and Carothers 2000; Van Rooy 1998; and Bush 2015 have focused on the impact of professionalization. Sundstrom 2006

focused on cultural constraints, and Mendelson 2001 on concentrated support for groups that promote Western-style liberal democracy.

43 Belloni 2008; Orjuela 2003.

44 Sundstrom 2006.

45 Putnam 1993; Van Rooy 1998, 198.

46 For compelling accounts of this argument, see Le More 2008; Belloni 2011; and Snyder and Fariss 2011.

47 Brownley 2012.

48 Challand 2009.

49 On the contrary, they are conspicuous for their similarity. See, for example, Carothers 1999, 12.

50 The only countries with left-leaning leaders in Latin America were Hugo Chavez in Venezuela, who was elected in 1998; Lula de Silva in Brazil, who was elected in 2003; and Evo Morales in Bolivia, who was elected in 2006.

51 Dahl 1971, 2–3.

52 In the Palestinian case, the national level of government is the Palestinian Legislative Council, and in the Salvadoran case, the Asamblea Legislativa.

53 For more on how well-developed institutions of local government will provide more political openings for local participation, and thus facilitate for the emergence of an effective civil society, see Schönwälder 2002, chapter 2.

54 For more on this, see Scott 2002 and Mendelson 2001.

55 Earlier conceptions of civil society arguably owe their intellectual heritage to Alexis de Tocqueville. According to Tocqueville, civil associations such as scientific and literary circles and schools "prevent political despotism and social unfreedom and inequality" (Keane 1988, 61). By participating in these associations, individuals become less selfish and more willing to support others. Ideas pertaining to civil society and the generation of social trust were later popularized by the neo-Tocquevillians, Robert Putnam being a case in point.

56 This concept draws from Jürgen Habermas. For a useful summary, see Baynes 2002, 123–145.

57 Hodgkinson and Foley 2003. For more on the conceptualization of civil society and its contribution to democracy, see Cohen and Arato 1992 and Keane 1988.

58 Civil society theorists did not always recognize this distinction between state and civil society. Early civil society theorists such as David Hume, Jean-Jacques Rousseau, and Immanuel Kant, for example, did not view civil society as distinct from the state, but as coterminous with the state. See Keane 1988.

59 For the purpose of this research project, I use Carrie Meyer's definition of nongovernmental organizations: "not of government, and also not for profit . . . they are independent organizations that receive outside funding to support either staff, programs, or both" (Meyer 1999, 2).

60 Bell and O'Rourke 2007; Belloni 2008.

61 Tarrow 1996; Foley and Edwards 1996; Berman 1997.

62 Weigle 2000, however, cautions that while civil society's role during transitions fosters and relies on solidarity, its role and character during democratic consolidation does not.

63 Putnam 1993, 173–176.

64 Ibid.

65 Edwards, Foley, and Diani 2000, 279.

66 Edwards, Foley, and Diani 2000 (266–280) emphasize access to resources and networks to facilitate civic organization.

67 In addition, the level of legal institutionalization will affect the performance of civil society. The rule of law and an enabling legal framework will encourage civil society organization and activity, and facilitate its development and performance.

68 Schönwälder 2002, chapter 2.

69 Linz and Stepan 1996 (8) define political society as "that arena in which the polity specifically arranges itself to contest the legitimate right to exercise control over public power and the state apparatus."

70 Following the escalation of the Al-Aqsa Intifada in October 2001, the strict imposition of curfews and the intensification of bombing raids on Area A seriously challenged and interfered with the work of NGOs and other CSOs, causing them to focus on emergency relief and international lobbying projects. Therefore, in examining developments between 1991 and 2001, my research focuses on the changes that preceded the outbreak of the Al-Aqsa Intifada.

71 For more on the history, see Quandt, Jabber, and Lesch 1973, and Sayigh 1997.

72 For more on the history, refer to Montgomery 1982 and Baloyra 1982, and on the mobilization of insurgent collective action in El Salvador, see Wood 2003.

73 For example, Doyle and Sambanis 2006 (203–204) argue that it is easier to address conflicts that are not ethnic or religious in nature.

74 For decades, the Palestinians perceived the PLO as a quasi-state governmental structure in exile.

75 Sayigh and Shikaki 1999.

76 Shortly after the signing of the DOP, 38% of Palestinians in the West Bank and Gaza Strip opposed the Oslo Accords and 20.4% were not sure how they would evaluate the agreement (Center for Policy Research, Public Opinion Poll 4, Palestinian Elections and the DOP, 12 December 1993).

77 Bell 2006, 378.

78 Holiday and Stanley 1993; Karl 1992; Sullivan 1994.

79 Karl 1992.

80 Jarstad and Sisk 2008.

81 For more on this, refer to Varas 1998.

82 Many earlier works regarded donor aid programs as unique, and not lending themselves well to comparative analysis. Among the notable exceptions in this regard were the pioneering work of McKinlay 1979; Hook 1995; Nöel and Thérien 1995; Schraeder 2002; and Schraeder, Hook, and Taylor 1998. For a more in-depth

discussion of the dearth of comparative analysis among donors, also refer to Schraeder, Hook, and Taylor 1998.

83 Carothers 2010, 24.
84 In the Salvadoran context, Nidia Diaz and Irma Maya are two of the women who come to mind; in the Palestinian context, Zahira Kamal and Rabiha Diab were important players.
85 For example, Abdulhadi 1998.

CHAPTER 2. THE POLITICAL-MILITARY ORGANIZATIONS AND THE EMERGENCE OF MASS-BASED GRASSROOTS ORGANIZATIONS

1 Reprinted in Tucker 1978, 595.
2 For a succinct discussion of the roots of socioeconomic inequality and unrest in El Salvador, refer to North 1981; Montgomery 1982; Baloyra 1982, 5–14; and Paige 1997.
3 For more on the history of the Arab-Israeli conflict, see Abu-Lughod 1971; Smith 1996; and Tessler 1994.
4 Quandt, Jabber, and Lesch 1973, 68.
5 In the late 1960s and early 1970s, Palestinian political organizations conceived of the "liberation struggle" in strictly military terms. Sayigh 1997, 91.
6 Cobban 1984. Activists established a number of new Palestinian political organizations over the next two decades, although many of these would remain small splinter factions and not play a central role in the occupied territories.
7 For more on the Arab and Jewish Communist Party, see Lockman 1996.
8 Sayigh 1997, 168.
9 Ibid., 476.
10 The Jordanian Communist Party was active in the West Bank, and a separate PCP was active in the Gaza Strip. Unlike other Palestinian factions, the Communist Party made no effort to participate militarily, and initially opposed joining the PLO on grounds that such an action would serve the national struggle at the expense of the class struggle. In the initial years, Jewish and Palestinian Communists worked within the same Communist organizations.
11 Quandt, Jabber, and Lesch 1973, 107.
12 The Karameh battle was fought between the PLO and the Jordanian army against the Israeli military in the Jordanian town of Karameh (Cobban 1984, 44). For more on the Karameh battle, also see Farsoun and Zacharia 1997, 182–183.
13 Farsoun and Zacharia 1997, 187.
14 Ibid., 180–190.
15 Interview with Omar Assaf, 22 July 2001.
16 Kimmerling and Migdal 2003, 286. In 1973, the PNC also founded the Palestine National Front (PNF) as a coordinating mechanism in the occupied territories. Much of the leadership of the PNF came from the Communist Party, as well as from other factions, labor unions, professional associations, and women's groups. As the popularity of the PNF grew, so did the suspicions of the PLO. Because of the organized nature of the Communist Party and the strong base of support it enjoyed in the WBGS, the PLO worried that it would not be able to control the

new organization. In a strange collusion of events, the PLO's reluctant support for the organization and Israel's harsh response to it resulted in its decline and eventual disappearance (ibid., 279).

17 Ibid., 278.

18 For more on this, see Hammami 2002, 30.

19 For more on right-wing political parties, see Montgomery 1997, 64, and Equizábal 1992. For a succinct discussion regarding the political parties in El Salvador from the 1960s to the 1980s, refer to Baloyra 1982, 50–51.

20 Montgomery 1982, 119.

21 Ching and Tilley 1998.

22 During this period, the Movimiento Nacional Revolucionario (MNR) also grew out of a study group that met from 1956 to 1958. The MNR's platform was very theoretical and abstract, and it thus never amassed a substantial following. Guillermo Ungo headed the MNR. Baloyra 1982, 46.

23 North 1981, 73.

24 Ibid., 121.

25 For a more detailed discussion about the break in the ERP, refer to Montgomery 1982, 121–122, and Radu 1985, 676.

26 Radu 1985, 676.

27 Ibid.

28 Quiroz 1982, 4.

29 Biekart 1999a, 14.

30 During a protest against the results of a fraudulent presidential election, security forces opened fire on marchers, killing between sixty and 300 people.

31 Montgomery 1982, 122.

32 Ibid., 133.

33 For an incisive discussion of political mobilization and armed insurgency in El Salvador, see Wood 2003, 87–120.

34 Foley 1996, 82. For a more detailed discussion of the differences among the mass-based organizations, see Montgomery 1982, 125–130.

35 For more on the creation of this coalition, see Radu 1985, 682–684.

36 The civilian-military Christian Democratic junta abandoned efforts to incorporate the political-revolutionary organizations in the reform process and adopted a more traditional counterinsurgency strategy against the civilian population mobilized by the political organizations (Equizábal 1992, 137).

37 For more on the unfolding of the war, refer to Uclés 1996, Gordon 1989, Stanley 1996, and Brockett 2005 (chapter 10), which specifically looks at the cycles of contention and repression beginning in the late 1970s and throughout the 1980s.

38 For more on transformations in the popular movements in El Salvador in the 1980s, see Uclés 1994, 142–157; Murray and Barry 1995; and Almeida 2008, 160–173.

39 Uclés 1995, 159.

40 Hasso 2005, xvii.

41 For more on Palestinian civil society, see Abu 'amr 1995; Salem 1999; and Brown 2003.

42 Zaucker et al. 1995, 17. For more on NGOs in Palestine in the pre-Oslo period, see Clark and Balaj 1994.

43 Challand 2009, 69.

44 Kimmerling and Migdal 2003, 291. Although some activity continued under Jordanian rule, trade unions had declined from forty in 1957 to sixteen in 1961.

45 For an in-depth discussion of the development of Palestinian associational life after 1967, refer to Muslih 1993.

46 The cooperatives engaged in the production and marketing of olive oil production, agricultural produce, handicrafts, and embroidered items.

47 *Zakat*, or mandatory alms giving, is one of the five pillars of Islam. Since the establishment of the PA, the zakat committees have been under PA government oversight. For more on the zakat committees in the WBGS, refer to Brown 2003, 159–161.

48 Interview with Omar Assaf, 22 July 2001.

49 For more on Palestinian associational life post-Oslo, see Brown 2003, 138–190.

50 Pappe 2006, 202–206.

51 Sayigh 1997, 464–465.

52 The most illustrative representation of factional competition between the various factions is the struggle to control the General Federation of Trade Unions. In 1981, a split occurred, and two separate General Federations of Trade Unions emerged—one sponsored by Fatah in Ramallah, and another sponsored by the leftist groups in Nablus. For more on this split, see Muslih 1993, 263–264.

53 Kimmerling and Migdal 2003, 291.

54 Interview with Marwan Barghouti, 24 July 2001. Barghouti was also a Palestinian Legislative Council member and head of Fatah in the West Bank. He was arrested in April 2002, and sentenced to five life sentences by an Israeli military court.

55 For more on this discussion, refer to Roy 2000, 7.

56 Interview with labor union activist affiliated with FIDA, 1 August 2001.

57 Interview conducted by the author on 18 July 2001.

58 For more on cycles of contention, see Murray and Barry 1995, 171, and Almeida 2008, 160–173. On the unfolding of the war, refer to Uclés 1996; Gordon 1989; Stanley 1996; and Brockett 2005, chapter 10.

59 These groups participated in a broad opposition front led by Duarte in the 1972 presidential election. Following the fraud of the 1972 elections, the rank and file of the PDC joined revolutionary parties affiliated with three different revolutionary armed forces. The locus of political organizing also began to shift to the rural areas. For a detailed discussion regarding associational life and the emergence of popular movements in El Salvador, refer to Uclés 1996, 137–176.

60 Liberation theology developed in the 1960s as a Christian socialist philosophy that maintained that it is the obligation of the Catholic Church to adopt the causes of the oppressed, and to strive for social and economic justice, especially in the Third World. In 1968, Latin American bishops met in Medellín, Colombia, and adopted these principles, which later became known as the Medellín documents. The documents condemned poverty and oppressive ruling elites, and

called for agrarian reforms. Moreover, the documents proposed programs based on the method of Paulo Freire's "education for liberation" that "were designed to promote a new sense of community action for change among the poor" (Thomson 1986, 47).

61 The Christian communities in El Salvador were most active during Monsignor Oscar Romero's tenure as archbishop of San Salvador (1977 to 1980).

62 Montgomery 1982, 103.

63 For a typology of these sectors and types and levels of organizations, refer to Uclés 1995, 163, and Foley 1996.

64 For a more detailed discussion of the differences among the mass-based organizations, refer to Montgomery 1982, 125–130.

65 For more on this, refer to Foley 1996, 76.

66 Uclés 1995, 172.

67 Ibid., 171.

68 For more on the history of the Palestinian women's movement, see Fleischman 2003 and Al Khalil 1977 (cited in Abdulhadi 1998).

69 Mayer 1994.

70 For the most comprehensive discussion of the FPWAC, and especially the gendered dimensions of this mobilization, see Hasso 2005.

71 Interviews with Siham Barghouti, 12 July 2001; Maha Nassar, 21 July 2001; Zahira Kamal, 19 August 2001; Member 1 (executive committee member of the Women's Committees for Social Work), Ramallah, 14 July 2001; and Nuha Barghouti, 12 July 2001.

72 Interview with Siham Barghouti, 12 July 2001. The FPWAC, in particular, was heavily involved in organizing women laborers.

73 Interview with Siham Barghouti, 12 July 2001. According to Hiltermann 1991 (141), the FPWAC also had 5,000 members by 1986.

74 Interview with Nihaya Mohammed, 29 July 2001.

75 Interview with Maha Nassar, 21 July 2001. According to Hiltermann 1991 (141), the UPWC had 1,450 members in the 1980s.

76 Interview with Member 1 (executive committee member of the WCSW), Ramallah, 14 July 2001. According to Hilterman 1991 (141), the WCSW had between 3,000 and 4,000 members in 1985.

77 Interview with Member 1 (executive committee member of the WCSW), Ramallah, 14 July 2001.

78 Interview with Member 2 (FPWAC-FIDA coordinator), Ramallah, 12 August 2005.

79 Interview with Member 2 (FPWAC coordinator), Ramallah, 6 August 200; she also stressed this in her interview.

80 Interview with Member 1 (executive committee member of the WCSW), Ramallah, 14 July 2001.

81 Hiltermann 1991, 146.

82 For example, the women tended to coordinate their sit-ins, hunger strikes, and demonstrations.

83 According to the longitudinal study by Hasso (2001), participation in the women's committees resulted in the creation of a "feminist generation."

84 Interviews with Siham Barghouti, 12 July 2001; Maha Nassar, 21 July 2001; Zahira Kamal, 19 August 2001; Member 1 (executive committee member of the WCSW), Ramallah, 14 July 2001; and Nuha Barghouti, 12 July 2001.

85 All the people I interviewed from the women's committees discussed these types of programs and projects.

86 Interview with Maha Nassar, 21 July 2001.

87 Among the items produced by women were dairy products such as yogurt and cheese, sweets and desserts, olives and other pickled vegetables, and embroidered crafts.

88 Interview with Siham Barghouti, 12 July 2001.

89 Ibid.

90 Interview with Member 1 (executive committee member of the WCSW), Ramallah, 14 July 2001.

91 Funding was from a Swiss NGO.

92 Interview with Nihaya Mohammed, 29 July 2001, and Member 2 (FPWAC coordinator), Ramallah, 6 August 2001.

93 Ibid.

94 For a general discussion regarding the evolution of the Salvadoran women's movement, refer to Thomson 1986; Stephen, Cosgrove, and Ready 2000; and Gonzalez 1997. For a more recent study of the mobilization of women into the guerrillas during El Salvador's civil war, see Viterna 2013.

95 For more on Fraternidad de Mujeres Salvadoreñas, see Thomson 1986, 93–95.

96 Ibid., 83.

97 The Federation was not specifically a women's organization, but had a large number of women members.

98 Later, however, COMADRES became aligned with the RN faction of the FMLN. For more on COMADRES, see, for example, Shayne 1999, 90–93.

99 Thomson 1986, 72.

100 Interview with Carmen Medina, 16 February 2002.

101 The mass organization of the RN.

102 Thomson 1986, 87.

103 For more on this, refer to Murray and Barry 1995, 197–198.

104 For a detailed discussion of IMU, refer to Colburn 1993, 43–46.

105 Gonzalez 1997.

106 Interview with Yanera Argueta, 10 May 2002.

107 Interview with Azucena Quintera, 13 May 2002.

108 For example, regarding ASMUSA's meetings and coordination, refer to Thomson 1986, 102.

109 Interview with Carmen Medina, 8 May 2002.

110 Interview with Azucena Quintera, 13 May 2002.

111 WomenWarPeace.org 2000. http://www.womenwarpeace.org (last accessed 25 July 2005).

112 Interview with Jeanette Urquilla, 30 May 2002.

113 Interview with Yanera Argueta, 10 May 2002.

114 Interview with Azucena Quintera, 13 May 2002.

115 Interview with Jeanette Urquilla, 30 May 2002.

116 Interview with Carmen Medina, 8 May 2002.

117 Azucena Quintera, however, explained that in the early years of these organizations, the women sometimes resorted to less sophisticated means of fundraising. Among these means was stealing animals from large farms. Interview on 13 May 2002.

118 Thomson 1986, 102.

119 For example, in 1987, the FPL founded Unión de Mujeres Melida Anaya Montes (Union of Women Melida Anaya Montes) in Mexico.

120 Both Committee in Solidarity with the People of El Salvador and the Salvadoran Humanitarian Aid, Research, and Education (SHARE) Foundation are Salvadoran solidarity NGOs based in the United States.

121 Interview with Carmen Medina, 8 May 2002.

CHAPTER 3. POLITICAL SETTLEMENTS AND THE RECONFIGURATION OF CIVIC AND POLITICAL LIFE

1 For more on the legal dimensions of the Oslo Accords and its various components, refer to Watson 2000, part II.

2 For more on the PLO's quasi-governmental institutionalization in Lebanon and thereafter, refer to Khalidi 1986; Sayigh 1997; Peteet 1991, 1–37; and Sahliyeh 1986.

3 UN Resolution 242 proposes the idea of "land for peace." The resolution stipulates: "Withdrawal of Israeli armed forces from territories occupied in the recent conflict; termination of all claims or states of belligerency and respect for and acknowledgement of the sovereignty; territorial integrity and political independence of every State in the area and its right to live in peace within secure and recognized boundaries free from threats or acts of force." The resolution also calls for achieving a just settlement to the refugee problem. UN Security Council (SC), SC Resolution 242 (1967) Middle East, S/RES/242 (22 November 1967), available at https://www.un.org (accessed on 3 July 2018).

4 UN Security Council Resolution 338 "Calls upon all parties to the present fighting to cease all firing and terminate all military activity immediately, no later than 12 hours after the moment of the adoption of this decision, in the positions they now occupy; calls upon the parties concerned to start immediately after cease-fire the implementation of Security Council resolution 242 (1967) in all its parts; and decides that, immediately and concurrently with cease-fire, negotiations shall start between the parties the parties concerned under appropriate auspices aimed at establishing a just and durable peace in the Middle East." UN Security Council

(SC), SC Resolution 338 (1973) Mideast Peace Conference, S/RES/338 (23 October 1973), available at https://undocs.org (accessed on 3 July 2018).

5 For more on the United States involvement in the Middle East, refer to Peretz 1998; Shlaim 1994; Lesch 2008, 317–325; and Lesch 2006, 99–116.

6 Peretz 1998, 349.

7 For more on this, see Shlaim 1994, especially 104–133; Smith 2013, 419–425; and, for a more critical assessment, Khalidi 2013, 29–65.

8 For more on the PLO's losses after the Gulf War, see Bennis and Moushabek 1991 and Smith 2013, 420–421.

9 For the text of the agreement, see PLO Negotiation Affairs Department, *Agreements* (Declaration of Principles on Interim Self-Government Arrangements), Negotiation Affairs Department, September 13, 1993, https://www.nad.ps (accessed on 3 July 2018).

10 For a summary of the agreements, see PLO Negotiation Affairs Department, *Agreements*, https://www.nad.ps (accessed on 3 July 2018).

11 Supporters included the Fatah leadership. For Nabil Shaath's justification of the accords, see Smith 2013, 445–446, or Shaath 1993, 5–15; Qurei (Abu Alaa) also provides an explanation in his three-volume memoir, Querei 2005, 2006, 2011.

12 For a summary of the points raised, see Smith 2013, 441–443.

13 See, for example, Sayigh 1997, 659.

14 Al-Hout 1994.

15 Bell 2006, 398.

16 For more on this, refer to Public Opinion Poll 4, Palestinian Elections and the DOP, 12 December 1993.

17 Rubenberg 2003, 57.

18 In 1994, Haider Abdel Shafi led a 1994 petition campaign against the Oslo Accords and then was involved in the establishment of a movement that opposed the direction of the Oslo Accords. For more on this, refer to Robinson 2004, 175.

19 For more on the Paris Protocol, refer to Murphy 1995, 35–38; Husseini and Khalidi 2013; and Elkhafif et al. 2013.

20 For more on these agreements and the sequence of events that followed, see Watson 2000, 42–44.

21 See Watson 2000, 44.

22 For a detailed discussion of associated responsibilities in each area, see Watson 2000, 106–115.

23 Other agreements signed between the two parties included the Wye River Memorandum, Protocol concerning Safe Passage between the West Bank and Gaza Strip, the Sharm el-Sheikh Memorandum, and the Trilateral Statement on the Middle East Peace Summit at Camp David.

24 For more on this, see Zavadjil et al. 1997.

25 After the signing of the Oslo Accords, a closure system was put in place restricting travel between the West Bank and the Gaza Strip and WBGS and Israel. Palestinian

residents of the WBGS were no longer allowed to enter Jerusalem without special travel permits.

26 Sayigh and Shikaki 1999.

27 Ibid., 11.

28 Bell 2006, 378.

29 On the creation of a dual system of governance in the West Bank—one for Palestinian Muslims and Christians and another for Jews—see Shehadeh 1994.

30 For an impassioned critique of the Oslo Accords, see Said 1995 and Said 2000.

31 Elkhafif et al. 2013, 7.

32 There would be a few exceptions; the PA would be allowed to impose a minimum price on petroleum that could be up to 15% less than the price in Israel. Additionally, the Palestinian VAT could be up to 2% less than that in Israel, and both parties would apply the same tax percentages on domestic and imported goods (Elkhafif et al. 2013, 10).

33 For more on this, see Elkhafif et al. 2013, 3, and Husseini and Khalidi 2013.

34 Watson 2000, 49.

35 These are my categories.

36 It is important to note that the Palestinian leftist political organizations, PPP and FIDA, and the radical left organizations, the PFLP and DFLP, had not articulated a clear position in relation to the organization of economic life in Palestine, or on the social welfare system, and place more emphasis on civil rights than upon social and economic rights. In general, these groups had embraced free-market economics, including a two-tiered health care system.

37 For more on the post-Oslo political system, particularly in relation to the Palestinian groups, refer to Hilal 1998, Hilal 2010, and Bishara 1996.

38 In some cases, debates ensued between members of these political groups and their leadership abroad about whether not participating in legislative elections was a sound policy.

39 Riad al-Malki would later become a PA foreign minister.

40 Although some Islamists were ready to run in the 1996 elections, they would not fall under this category since they were not necessarily adopting a wait and see approach, but rather were trying to stay politically relevant.

41 Marwan Barghouti, 24 July 2001.

42 For more on the impact of foreign donor assistance on Palestinian civil society, see Hammami 1995.

43 Shalabi and al-Said 2001.

44 Salem 1999, 258–259.

45 Palestinian Central Bureau of Statistics, Estimated Population in the Palestinian Territory Mid-Year by Governorate, 1997–2016.

46 Among the members of any association or organization, the largest percentage (25.7) were members of athletic clubs and organizations. Based on JMCC Public Opinion Poll No. 32-Part Two, Question 23, August 1999.

47 JMCC Public Opinion Poll No. 32-Part Two, Question 22, 1999.

48 Hanan Ashrawi is a PLC member, and a former cabinet minister. She established MIFTAH, the Palestinian Initiative for the Promotion of Global Dialogue and Democracy, a human rights and democracy promotion organization.

49 Mustafa Barghouti founded and is the director of the Union of Palestinian Medical Relief Committees and the Human Development and Information Project. He also was a member of the General Secretariat of the PPP and represented the PPP in the PNC, the legislative body of the PLO.

50 Ghassan Khatib founded and directed the JMCC and was an Executive Committee member of the PPP. He has held several positions in the PA, including director of the Government Media Center (2009–12), minister of labor in 2002, and minister of planning (2005–06).

51 Ziad Abu Amar founded the Palestinian Council for Foreign Relations. He has held several PA positions including being a member of the Palestinian Legislative Council, minister of culture in 2003, minister of foreign in 2007, and deputy prime minister in 2013 and again in 2014.

52 Interview with a director of a donor agency who asked that his name not be attributed to this quote.

53 Interview with Ghassan Khatib, 5 August 2001.

54 In comments on an earlier publication (Jamal 2012), Nathan Brown pushed me to think about the different phases of the changing dynamics of PA and civil society relations. Although we slightly differ about the time frames of these phases, they are important to understanding these changing dynamics.

55 For more on this the drafting and promulgation of the Palestinian NGO law, see Brown 2003, 148–163.

56 Ibid., 155.

57 Ibid., 145.

58 For more on 1996 elections, see Andoni 1996, and Central Election Commission-Palestine, Election Law No. 13 of 1995 for the actual PA electoral laws.

59 Andoni 1996. Prior to the 2006 legislative elections, President Mahmoud Abbas modified the electoral law so that sixty-six legislative seats were elected by a national proportional list system.

60 Andoni 1996, 11.

61 See Jamal 2013, 284–285.

62 For more on this, see Hroub 2006a, 4.

63 For more on Hamas's electoral campaign, see Milton-Edwards and Farrel 2010.

64 Presidential Decree of 2007.

65 Much of the above section on Hamas's electoral campaign is paraphrased from Jamal 2013, 291–292.

66 Presidential Decree of 2007.

67 Central Elections Commission, Local Election Law No. 10 of 2005.

68 These elections were to be held in sixty cities and villages, including Hebron and Gaza City.

69 Deanna Congileo, "Palestine Electoral Study Mission Urges Political Reconcili-ation," Carter Center, October 20, 2012, accessed 14 December 2014, http://www.cartercenter.org.

70 Local Elections Facts and Figures, 2012.

71 For more on the factors leading to the peace accords in El Salvador, refer to Sullivan 1994; Karl 1992; Holiday and Stanley 1993; Byrne 1996, chapter 6; and Montgomery 1982.

72 For more on this, see Stanley 2006, 105–107.

73 Wood 2000, 5.

74 Álvarez 2010.

75 Uclés 1996, 178.

76 Wood 1996, 79.

77 For more on this discussion, see Stanley 2006, 105.

78 Ibid., 106.

79 For more on this, see Stanley 2006 and Álvarez 2010, 25.

80 Stanley 2006, 109. For more on the consolidation of ARENA as a dominant politi-cal party, see Wood 2000, 70–77.

81 Doyle and Sambanis 2006, 201. For more on factors leading to peace negotiations and the peace negotiations themselves, see Negroponte 2012.

82 For more on the peace accords in El Salvador, see Karl 1992; Fagen 1996; and Holiday and Stanley 1993.

83 This term was popularized by Karl 1992.

84 The term "Salvadoran peace accords" refers to these collective agreements. For discussion of the various peace accords, see Holiday and Stanley 1993.

85 Álvarez 2010, 22.

86 Studemeister 2001, 44.

87 For the text of the final peace accord, see Acuerdos de paz de Chapultepec 1992.

88 Doyle and Sambanis 2006, 202.

89 Ibid., 205.

90 For a thorough discussion of El Salvador's failure to establish accountability for former human rights abuses and the longer term implications related to establish-ing rule of law in the country, see Popkin 2000.

91 Wood and Segovia 1995, 2087.

92 Ibid., 2079.

93 See De Bremond 2007 and del Castillo 1997.

94 Phases II was supposed to apply to holdings between 100 and 500 hectares, nearly a quarter of the nation's landholdings. This phase, however, was never imple-mented. The land ceilings affected by Phase 11 were subsequently raised, with Articles 105 and 106 of the 1983 Constitution, to 245 hectares. For more on this, see McReynolds 2002.

95 De Bremond 2007, 1544.

96 Wood and Segovia 1995.

97 Wood 2000, 91.

98 This view was perhaps most eloquently expounded by De Soto and del Castillo 1994.

99 For more on institutional development in postwar El Salvador, see Call 2003.

100 In 1995, the various factions of the FMLN merged into a unified body and dissolved their individual party structures; technically, therefore, the FMLN factions ceased to exist as factions, but survived as tendencies within a new FMLN.

101 For more on this discussion, see Álvarez 2010, and Almeida 2009.

102 Montgomery 1997, 64.

103 "El Salvador: Civic Freedom Monitor," 2015.

104 For more on the uncertainty and crime in postwar El Salvador, see Moodie 2010.

105 Gonzalez 1992, 54.

106 This list includes 189 development NGOs, called private development organizations in El Salvador. Another list compiled by UCA indicates that thirty-seven NGOs were involved in education and training, twenty-five in rural development, twenty-one in environmental issues, fifteen in health, twelve in organizational development, eleven in gender issues, nine in business development, and eight in policy research. Listed in Biekart 1999a.

107 "El Salvador: Civic Freedom Monitor," 2015.

108 For more on the difficulties of transition, refer to Thompson 1997.

109 Ibid., 53–57.

110 For a discussion of the variation among the sectors, refer to Murray and Barry 1995.

111 Ibid., 155.

112 For more on this wave of protests, see Almeida 2008.

113 For more on elections during El Salvador's civil war, see Munck 1993.

114 For more on the different political parties in El Salvador in the immediate postwar period, refer to Zamora 1998.

115 For more on the 2009 Salvadoran presidential elections, see Azpuru 2010, Colburn 2009, and Almeida 2009.

116 Mills 2012.

117 For more on El Salvador's legislative elections, see Almeida 2009, and specifically on the 2012 legislative elections, refer to Gonzalez 2012, 63–64. For more on the general background of El Salvador's elections, refer to Election Resources on the Internet: Presidential and Legislative Elections in El Salvador, parts I and II.

118 Almeida 2009.

119 For more on El Salvador's electoral system, see El Salvador–Election Passport 2015.

120 For more on the development of local government in El Salvador in the immediate postpeace accord period, refer to Macías and Orellana 2001, Galdámez 1997, and Villacorta 1998.

121 Biekart 1999a, 52.

122 Murray et al. 1994, 22.

123 For more on USAID involvement in decentralization schemes, refer to Hansen, Blair, and Ludwig 2002.

CHAPTER 4. FOREIGN DONOR ASSISTANCE AND THE POLITICAL
ECONOMY OF SETTLEMENT OUTCOMES

1 Donor aid programs are often regarded as a unique and do not easily lend themselves to comparative analysis. A number of notable exceptions are McKinlay 1979; Hook 1995; Nöel and Thérien 1995; Schraeder 2002; and Schraeder, Hook, and Taylor 1998.

2 For political critiques of the donor funding enterprise to the Palestinian territories in the post-Oslo period, see Le More 2008; Keating, Le More, and Lowe 2005; Turner 2014, 2012 and Tartir 2011.

3 Carothers 2015. For more on the linking of foreign aid to political reform, also see Crawford 2001.

4 See, for example, Savun and Tirone 2011; Knack 2004; Challand 2009; and a number of chapters in Resnick and de Walle 2013.

5 For more on the political nature of aid in the respective contexts, refer to Beck 2000 and Foley 1996.

6 Although donors may vary in terms of their embrace of the "post–Cold War liberal order," they are more or less in agreement in relation to socialist or Islamist organizations. See, for example, Youngs 2002 for Europe's challenges in promoting democracy in the Middle East. Carothers points out that the Swedish International Development Agency has been a leader in this regard through its embrace of a "rights perspective" that integrates an emphasis on both political and civil rights as well as economic and social rights into its development work (Carothers 2010, 19); their approach to these types of organizations, however, does not vary significantly from other Western donors.

7 Crawford 2001.

8 Burnell 2000, chapter 2.

9 Carothers 2015. For the different approaches to democracy assistance, see Carothers 2009.

10 According to the United Nations Development Program, *1993 Compendium of External Assistance to the Occupied Territories* (Jerusalem: UNDP, 1993), bilateral and multilateral assistance to the WBGS was US$173.9 million.

11 Palestinians refer to the 1948 Arab-Israeli war as *al-Nakbah*, literally translated as "the catastrophe" to refer to the mass displacement of the Palestinian people during that war.

12 Cobban 1984, 45.

13 Nakhleh 2004 and Challand 2009.

14 Roy 1991, 67.

15 Ibid.

16 Ibid.

17 Ibid., 72.

18 Roy 2001, 151.

19 In Arabic *al-ta'awun* means cooperation.

20 Roy 1991, 69.

21 After the signing of the Camp David agreements between Egypt and Israel in 1978, Arab countries held the Baghdad Summit to protest the agreements. During that meeting, Saudi Arabia, Kuwait, and other oil-producing countries pledged to financially assist Jordan, Syria, and the PLO.

22 These amounts, which Philip Mattar based on PLO records, did not include direct funding to the occupied territories, or the tax on Palestinians that was remitted to the PLO. For more on this discussion, see Mattar 1994, 44.

23 UNDP 1993 and UNDP 1994.

24 For more on USAID's role in creating a new model of development, and its support for right-wing organizations, see Segovia 1996, 41–42, and Foley 1996, 79–83.

25 Based on OECD data: Aid, ODA Disbursements to Countries and Regions [Development Assistance Committee, DAC2a], Total Net to El Salvador (Constant 2013 Prices).

26 Ibid.

27 Ibid.

28 For more on USAID's role in creating a new model of development, including these right-wing organizations, refer to Segovia 1996, 41–42, and Foley 1996, 79–83.

29 Biekart 1999a, 33.

30 Foley 1996a, 71.

31 Biekart 1999a, 34.

32 Foley 1996, 71.

33 Ibid., 72.

34 Ibid., 84.

35 Díaconia should not be confused with DİAKONIA World Federation, or Díakonia, a faith-based Swedish funding agency. For more on Díaconia, see Foley 1996, 74 and 76.

36 Biekart 1999, 60.

37 Foley 1996, 75; and Biekart 1999b.

38 Foley 1996, 96 (footnote 13).

39 Per discussion with Katharine Andrade Eekhoff, 15 May 2002. For a discussion about funding patterns to the FPL and the ERP, also see Wood 2003, 185–86.

40 Interviews with Birgitta Tazelaar, 25 July 2001; Peter Borg, 17 July 2001; Anne Brenzelius and Eva-Lotta Gustafsson, 13 September 2001; and Fritz Frolich, 11 September 2001.

41 Based on OECD data, ODA Disbursements to Countries and Regions (Development Assistance Committee, DAC2a), Total Net to El Salvador (Constant 2006 Prices).

42 Based on OECD data: Development Assistance Committee-DAC2a, ODA Loans: Total Net (Constant 2013 US dollars) as Percentage of ODA Total Net Disbursements (Constant 2012 US dollars), and Boyce 1995b, 2102.

43 Ibid.

44 Interviews with Martha Myers, 14 September 2001, and a representative from one of the German foundations who requested that I not directly cite him or her.

45 Interview with Birgitta Tazelaar, 25 July 2001.

46 See, for example, Grant and Nijman 1998.

47 For example, representatives from the Netherlands Representative Office, the Representative Office of Finland, the Consulate of Sweden, Díakonia, the EC, and the Heinrich Böll Foundation expressed this concern.

48 Interviews with representatives from USAID and Friedrich Naumann Foundation, 14 September 2001.

49 These foreign donor agencies include CIDA, the Swedish Representative Office, the Netherlands Representative Office, the Swiss Agency for Development and Co-operation, the Friedrich Naumann Foundation, and the Friedrich Ebert Foundation.

50 MOPIC 2001.

51 Ibid. Commitments and disbursements made by NGOs are not included in MOPIC's reporting.

52 Ibid.

53 CG is common to many aid-recipient countries as a mechanism for aid mobilization and high-level discussion between the recipient and its multilateral and bilateral aid partners. Often the World Bank administers the CG in partner countries.

54 Interviews with Martha Myers, 14 September 2001; Sylvie Fouet, 1 August 2001; and Khader Muslih, 7 August 2001.

55 MOPIC 2001.

56 Brynen 2000, 210.

57 Based on MOPIC 2001.

58 Ibid.

59 For more on this discussion, refer to Karl 1992.

60 Boyce 1995a.

61 Commitments represent a donor's financial obligations that are allocated to specific programs and projects based on signed agreements between a recipient and a donor country or agency. A pledge, on the other hand, represents an initial indication of a donor's intention to provide financial aid for a specified period. Based on Annex 1, Terms and Definitions, MOPIC 2001.

62 UNDP 1997. According to UNDP, this information is not always complete, but based on the amounts reported by the donors themselves. UNDP estimates were also often higher than disbursements documented by OECD. A number of factors might account for this discrepancy: (1) 1997 UNDP figures reflected commitments, or what UNDP refers to as approved budgets and not actual disbursements; and (2) not all NGOs and multilaterals report their funding to the OECD.

63 Ibid.

64 Funding amounts from the EC and Germany are determined on total project costs, and not from direct data from the donors themselves, Boyce 1995b, 2102.

65 See, for example, Fagen 1996.

66 Concessional loans differ from nonconcessional loans in that the former are considered part of development aid, and are often extended at below market terms.

67 Boyce 1995b, 2105.

68 Rosa and Foley 2000, 152. Between 1991 and 1997, the World Bank lent US$451.1 million to El Salvador, along with the IDB, which lent US$1.4 billion for the period between 1990 and 1997.

69 For more on this discussion, refer to Zagha and Jamal 1997, 15.

70 Wood 2003, 95.

71 For a more detailed discussion on donor coordinating mechanism in the WBGS, refer to Zagha and Jamal 1997, 10–12.

72 The Tripartite Action Plan on Revenues, Expenditures, and Donor Funding for the PA was signed in Paris at the April 1995 Ad Hoc Liaison Committee meeting. The Tripartite Action Plan specifically addressed the balancing of the PA's recurrent budget, the reduction of impediments to free travel, and ways to expedite donor disbursements.

73 The twelve sector working groups were Agriculture, Education, Employment Generation, Environment, Health, Infrastructure, Institution Building, Police, Private Sector, Public Finance, Tourism, and Refugees.

74 Rosa and Foley 2000, 139. According to this publication, however, it is not clear how UNDP is defining the sector of economic development.

75 Boyce 1995b, 2107.

76 Rosa and Foley 2000, 147.

77 By November 1993, the NRP had assigned US$41.15 million to Salvadoran NGOs (36% of its total allocations). Of this total, opposition NGOs received approximately 0.62%. The Salvadoran government and USAID claimed that the opposition NGOs were not excluded on political grounds, but rather that many of these NGOs were not institutionally capable of carrying out certain tasks (Murray et al. 1994, 15–17). For more on this topic, also see Foley 1996.

78 Murray et al. 1994, 18.

79 Discussed in Rosa and Foley 2000, 136. For more on this discussion, refer to original article, de Soto and del Castillo 1994.

80 Among their conditions were that some funds be earmarked for peace accord related programs such as the transfer of land and the building of democratic institutions, the modernization of the public sector, including the creation of an appropriate role for the military in a democratic and peaceful society, and the increasing of tax revenues.

81 According to MOPIC 2001, approximately 73% of total commitments were disbursed to the three categories: public investment (US$1.28 billion), technical assistance (US$702 million), and PA budgetary assistance/ support ($480 million). There have been many criticisms of technical assistance schemes in the WBGS. Often, those providing the technical assistance are foreigners who do not speak Arabic, and have little understanding of the actual context. These technical experts are often paid ten to forty times the salary that a local Palestinian would receive for the same job.

82 Boyce 1995a.

83 OECD's sector "Government and Civil Society" includes projects and programs related to economic and development policy/planning, public sector financial management, legal and judicial development, government administration, strengthening civil society, elections, human rights, free flow of information, and women's equality organization and institutions. Based on the OECD list of CRS purpose codes.

84 Del Castillo 2001, 1975.

85 OECD's subsector "Government Administration" includes projects and programs related to systems of government including parliament, local government, decentralization, civil service, and civil service reform. Based on CRS description of "Government and Civil Society" 2002. For a detailed discussion regarding funding to the "Government and Civil Society" sector, and its subsector "Government Administration" in Palestine and El Salvador for the period between 1992 and 2001, refer to OECD, "Government and Civil Society-General'" CRS/Aid Activities-Commitments-All Details: 1973 and 2004 (in Constant 2005 US dollars).

86 For a detailed discussion regarding funding to the "Government and Civil Society" sector, and its subsector "Strengthening Civil Society," in Palestine and El Salvador for the period 1992 and 2001, refer to OECD, "Government and Civil Society": CRS/Aid Activities-Commitments-All Details: 1973 and 2004 (in Constant 2005 US dollars).

87 OECD's subsector "Human Rights" includes programs and projects related to monitoring of human rights performance, support for national and regional human rights bodies, and the protection of ethnic, religious and cultural minorities [other than in connection with peace-building].

88 Interviews with representatives from USAID and Friedrich Naumann Foundation, on 14 September 2001, and Netherlands Representative Office, on 25 July 2001.

89 Interview with Mathes Buhbe, 18 September 2001.

90 Interviews with directors of USAID, Friedrich Nauman Foundation, and Friedrich Naumann on 14 September 2001, and Diakonia on 16 August 2001.

91 This amount is the average for the period between 1999 and 2001. It is important to note, however, that the average amount of funding to Palestinian NGOs was consistently higher between 1994 and 2000, but declined after the start of the Al-Aqsa Intifada in 2000.

92 Although there has been an overall decrease in funding to NGOs during this period, there was an increase in overall state-sponsored and multilateral funding to Palestinian NGOs. For more on this, refer to Hanafi 1999.

93 MOPIC 2001. As in the Salvadoran case, these estimates are not entirely accurate because many donors, especially solidarity groups, nonstate affiliated or representative foundations, and smaller donor organizations, did not report their funding to either MOPIC or to the OECD, particularly in relation to funding to domestic NGOs.

94 Shalabi and al-Said 2001.

95 Birzeit Development Center estimated that there were 1,141 NGO in the WBGS. Sullivan 1996 cited the Palestinian Center for Microprojects Development, which put the figure at 1,200–1,500. According to BESAN Development Center, by 2001, 575 development NGOs were operating in the WBGS.

96 For a more detailed discussion of this topic, see World Bank 1997.

97 Gonzalez 1992, 54.

98 This list includes 189 development NGOs, or private development organizations as they are called in El Salvador. Another list compiled by UCA indicates that thirty-seven NGOs were involved in education and training, twenty-five in rural development, twenty-one in environmental issues, fifteen in health, twelve in organizational development, eleven, in gender issues, nine in business development, and eight in policy research (Biekart 1999a, 53–54).

99 Biekart 1999a, 54. These estimates are corroborated by OECD data, which estimated that official funding to NGOs remained quite insignificant in El Salvador, with total commitments of US$25.24 million, between 1992 and 2001.

100 Biekart 1999a.

101 Solís and Martin 1992.

102 Biekart 1999a, 82. Similar to other donors, the priorities of the Dutch cofinancing agencies shifted from political survival to income-generating activities, with a new criterion focused on gender and the environment in the postwar period.

103 For more on this, refer to USAID 2005b.

104 In the West Bank, these professionalized NGOs were the WATC, PWWSD, Arab Thought Forum, Civic Forum, PASSIA, and PANORAMA.

105 *Tamkeen* means "empowerment: in Arabic. The program has since been discontinued.

106 Tamkeen provided funding to approximately 106 NGOs. Interview with Martha Myers, 14 September 2001, and Mohammed Almbaid, 16 September 2001.

107 The first three program areas were in effect in 2002, and the latter two were in effect in 2005. Interview with Mauricio Herrera Coella, 22 April 2002, and review of El Salvador: USAID Program Profile, accessed on 24 April 2005.

108 I was not able to obtain information regarding the exact amounts of funding that USAID allocated to each of these program areas either from the official I interviewed or from their website.

109 O'Brien and Catenacci 1996; van der Borgh 2005.

110 Carothers 2010.

111 OECD, "Government and Civil Society-General": CRS/Aid Activities-Commitments-All Details: 1973 and 2004 (in Constant 2005 US dollars).

112 Much of my discussion regarding foreign donor assistance and its impact on civil society is in relation to the larger state-sponsored donors.

113 Based on MOPIC 2001.

114 USAID has also helped establish a nonprofit, microfinance institution, the Palestine Credit and Development organization (FATEN), which as of 2005 had provided US$11 million in loans to women.

115 Canada's portfolio as the gavel holder for Refugee Affairs, in relation to peace negotiations, might also explain Canada's greater willingness to fund community projects in refugee camps.

116 See, for example, Stephen, Cosgrove, and Ready 2000, 13.

117 Interviews with Deysi Chayne, 16 May 2002, and Irma Maya, 27 May 2002.

118 As Carmen Medina explained on 13 May 2002, although the Salvadoran women's movement is now very dependent on foreign donor assistance, the amounts are not large.

119 For example, CREA funded a sexual and reproductive health project in Soyapongo for CEMUJER. According to CREA, this project was for US$6,000. The amount of funding allocated to this project relative to the amount of funding allocated to projects implemented by Palestinian professionalized NGOs is illustrative of the difference in scale.

CHAPTER 5. BEYOND PROFESSIONALIZATION

1 For more on this feminist approach to scholarship, see Youngs 2004.

2 Staudt 2002 highlights a number of problems associated with bilateral assistance to women, and asks the critical question about which NGOs receive support and whose interests they represent.

3 Parts of the following discussion about the transformation of the Palestinian women's sector appeared in Jamal 2015.

4 Abu Nahleh et al. 2003.

5 For more on the gendered dimensions of Palestinian civil society and the associated challenges to women's struggles, see, for example, Hammami and Johnson 1999; Abdulhadi 1998; Jamal 2001; Johnson and Kuttab 2001; Qazzaz 2010; Esther-Younes 2010; and Amireh 2012.

6 For a discussion of changes in the Palestinian women's movement, and emerging relations between the grassroots women's committees and the professionalized NGOs, refer to Jamal 2014.

7 The Islamist organizations, al-Huda and al-Khansa', were invited to the lectures but not to the training sessions and workshops.

8 Refer to Staudt 2002 for a discussion of how empowerment requires understanding and engaging within the specific historical context of power operating at the micro and macro levels, as well as in global, national, and local terms. In the Palestinian context, Kuttab 2008 has highlighted the need for empowerment to address Israel's military occupation, but this by itself is inadequate.

9 Interview with Member 4 (WCSW coordinator), Ramallah, 22 July 2001.

10 Interview with Member 1 (executive committee member of the WCSW), Ramallah, 14 July 2001.

11 Interview with Member 4 (WCSW coordinator), Ramallah, 22 July 2001; Member 2 (executive committee member of the WCSW), Ramallah, 19 July 2001.

12 I conducted these office visits on 19, 22, and 24 July 2001.

13 Member 1 (executive committee member of the WCSW), Ramallah, 14 July 2001.

14 Interviews with Member 1 (executive committee member of the WCSW), Ramallah, 14 July 2001, and Member 3 (WCSW coordinator), Jerusalem, 20 August 2001.

15 Interview with Member 4 (WCSW coordinator), Ramallah, 22 July 2001, Member 2 (executive committee member of the WCSW), Ramallah, 19 July 2001.

16 Ibid.

17 Interview with Member 4 (WCSW coordinator), Ramallah, 22 July 2001.

18 The Welfare Association was one of the main administrators of the World Bank NGO Project, and its members have historically been identified as members or supporters of Fatah.

19 Interview with Reema Tarazi, 14 August 2001.

20 Interview with Nihaya Mohammed, 29 July 2001.

21 Interview with Member 1 (UPWC coordinator), Hebron, 20 August 2001.

22 Interview with Member 1 (FPWAC coordinator), Ramallah, 5 August 2001.

23 For more on the post-Oslo political system, refer to Hilal 1998 and Bishara 1996.

24 Interviews with Siham Barghouti, 12 July 2001; and Maha Nassar, 21 July 2001.

25 Interview with Nuha Barghouti, 12 July 2001.

26 Interview with Siham Barghouti, 12 July 2001.

27 Interview with Maysoun Ahmad al-Ramahi, 16 September 2001.

28 Interviews with Member 3 (executive committee member of the UPWC), Ramallah, 24 July 2001; Member 1 (UPWC coordinator), Hebron, 20 August 2001; and Member 8 (WCSW kindergarten supervisor) and Member 9 (WCSW coordinator), Ramallah, 24 July 2001.

29 This situation was exacerbated by Israel's travel restrictions between different geographic locations, which further complicated the work of the committees.

30 The FPWAC, for example, had to close most of its offices. Interviews with Member 2 (FPWAC coordinator) Ramallah, 6 August 2001, and Member 1 (FPWAC coordinator), Ramallah, 5 August 2001. The UPWC, for example, ran only fifteen nursery schools and kindergartens with a deficit, compared to thirty in 1987. Interview with Member 3 (executive committee member of the UPWC), Ramallah, 24 July 2001. Similarly, the UPWWC has had to close down half of its kindergartens. Interview with Nuha Barghouti, 12 July 2001.

31 Interview with Member 1 (UPWC coordinator), Hebron, 20 August 2001; Ali Jaradat, 18 July 2001; and Omar Assaf, 22 July 2001.

32 Interviews with Omar Assaf, 22 July 2001, and Ali Jaradat 18 July 2001. Other political leaders who were involved in grassroots organizing explained that they have been able to overcome these financial constraints by turning to foreign donors. Interviews with Mustafa Barghouti, 24 July 2001, and Mohammed Aruri, 1 August 2001.

33 Interview with Maysoun al-Ramahi, 16 September 2001.

34 Ibid.

35 Ibid.

36 For more on funding to Islamists, see Hroub 2006b, 136–138.

37 Martha Myers from USAID, for example, discussed this at some length in her interview, Jerusalem, 14 September 2001. Member 2 discussed this from the perspective of the women's committees. She explained, "We are not professional enough to fulfill donor criteria: they ask for three years of previous accounting records, and that the organization has a formal administrator. We cannot always fulfill such criteria," interview with Member 2, (FPWAC coordinator), Ramallah, 6 August 2001.

38 Zahira Kamal, 19 August 2001.

39 Hasso 2005, 90.

40 Professionalized NGOs, in general, serve as an important employment sector for the Palestinian economy.

41 Parts of this section are paraphrased from Jamal 2012 and Jamal 2015.

42 The WCLAC provided women with counseling and legal services.

43 The Center housed a feminist library and commissioned reports on the status of Palestinian women.

44 Nuha Barghouti, 12 July 2001.

45 Founders of the new professionalized NGO rationalized that they would only be able to fully develop a women's program and agenda that espoused a feminist perspective if they severed ties with the PPP and fully institutionalized and professionalized.

46 Interview with an organizer from the UPWWC in Ramallah who requested not to be identified.

47 PARC worked in predominately marginal, rural areas, and focused on economic empowerment through training in agriculture, husbandry, and self-reliance schemes. It too turned to advocacy in the post-Oslo period. Alongside these organizations, there were the microcredit programs. Two such programs based in the Jerusalem-Ramallah area are *Faten*, Palestine for Credit and Development, and *Asala*, the Palestinian Business Women's Association (Abu Nahleh 2002).

48 According to Khreisheh, the PWWSD had approximately 300 registered members, and it provided employment for about fifty-seven of them, and by 2003, PARC had 12,702 members, and fewer women in the gender unit.

49 Interview with Maha Khayat, 9 July 2001.

50 The six women's committees that coordinated through the WATC are affiliated with Fatah, the PFLP, Palestinian Liberation Front (PLF-formerly based in Iraq), FIDA, the DFLP, and the PPP. The coalition also included a number of women's study's centers, human rights organizations, and some independent women activists.

51 Among the women who attested to this were Member 4 (WCSW coordinator), Ramallah, 22 July 2001, and Member 3 (executive committee member of the UPWC), Ramallah, 24 July 2001.

52 The larger organizations often provide more generous donor packages to their recipients, with more detailed accounting and follow-up procedures. In general,

it was the larger, bilateral donors that were at the heart of women's discontent regarding the impact of donors on the women's sector.

53 Interview with Maha Khayat, 9 July 2001.

54 The United States is the main sponsor of the Israeli-Palestinian negotiations. Norway mediated the Oslo peace accords and maintains a vested interest in furthering the peace process, and the EU has also played an important mediating role, and is the largest contributor of foreign donor assistance to the Palestinian territories.

55 Interviews with Martha Myers, 14 September 2001; Birgitta Tazelaar, 25 July 2001; and Sylvie Fouet, 1 August 2001.

56 Interviews with Member 1 (executive committee member of the WCSW), Ramallah, 14 July 2001, and Member 2 (executive committee member of the WCSW), Ramallah, 19 July 2001.

57 Worthy of mention is that unlike other activists of professionalized NGOs, the Al-Khansa' director I spoke to, Maysoun Ahmad al-Ramahi, as well as Nada al-Jayyusi, were not at all versed in the NGO discourse of issues pertaining to civil society and democratization.

58 Interviews with Member 1 (FPWAC coordinator), Ramallah, 6 August 2001; Nihaya Mohammed, 29 July 2001; and Maha Nassar, 21 July 2001.

59 Interview with Nuha Barghouti, 12 July 2001. The UPWWC technically was not part of the Opposition-affiliated tendency, but many of their members were unhappy with how the professionalized NGOs began to speak on behalf of the women's movement.

60 Interview with Member 4 (WCSW coordinator), Ramallah, 22 July 2001.

61 The size of the geographic region under consideration, approximately 64 km² for the East Jerusalem and Ramallah access, was further telling of the redundancy involved.

62 Qazzaz 2007.

63 Interview with Nihaya Mohammed, 29 July 2001.

64 Interview with Member 1 (UPWC coordinator), Hebron, 20 August 2001.

65 Interview with Member 1 (FPWAC coordinator), Ramallah, 5 August 2001.

66 Interview with Nihaya Mohammed, 29 July 2001.

67 Ibid. As of 2001, no women's shelters existed in the Jerusalem-Ramallah area, but since then, at least three shelters have been established.

68 Interview with Member 3 (executive committee member of the UPWC), Ramallah, 24 July 2001.

69 Ibid.

70 Interview with Member 1 (UPWC coordinator), Hebron, 20 August 2001.

71 According to many of my interviewees, the notable exception among the professionalized NGOs was PARC's gender desk, which was focused on the economic empowerment of its grassroots base.

72 Interview with Member 1 (UPWC coordinator), Hebron, 20 August 2001.

73 WCLAC Annual Report, 2000.

74 With the help of international donor assistance, the women's movement also pushed for the establishment of a number of gender units or women's desks in the various Palestinian ministries.

75 General Union of Palestinian Women 1994, 2, quoted from Hammami and Johnson 1999, 326.

76 Hammami and Johnson 1999, 326–327.

77 Member 4 (WCSW coordinator), Ramallah, 22 July 2001.

78 Interview with Ghassan Khatib, 5 August 2001.

79 The project was funded by the Friedrich Ebert Foundation and the Netherlands Representative Office in 1997. Joyce Mertz and Friedrich Ebert also contributed to funding the project in 1998.

80 *Palestinian Women's Network: Women's Affairs Technical Committee* (newsletter) 1998, 15.

81 Ibid.

82 Historically, personal status law in the West Bank and Gaza Strip was based on the Islamic *shari'a*. According to the Ottoman *millet* system, the family status laws of each religious community were regulated according to the religious beliefs of each community (Jamal 2001).

83 Quote taken from Hammami and Johnson 1999, 329.

84 Ibid., 328.

85 Jamal 2001, 272; Hammami and Johnson 1999 also provide a descriptive account of the backlash (32–338).

86 Head of Gender Desk at MIFTAH, 7 August, 2001; Member 2 (FPWAC coordinator), Ramallah, 6 August 2001; former member in the UPWWC, Ramallah, 16 July 2001; Nihaya Mohammed, 29 July 2001.

87 For more on the relationship between secular and Islamist women, see Allabadi 2008 and Ababneh 2014.

88 Hammami and Johnson 1999, 334.

89 Jamal 2001, 275.

90 For more on NGO professionalization, see Biekart 1999b, 199.

91 ISDEMU is not an NGO but a government institution established in 1996 to ensure that the ministries are addressing women's interests. The institution provides technical assistance to the government, and provides training sessions to community leaders in relation to issues of gender and domestic violence.

92 St. Germain 1997.

93 As with my discussion of the Palestinian women's sector, this chapter does not address the gendered dimensions of Salvadoran civil society, and the challenges that women face in that context. An impressive number of works have addressed these issues. See, for example, Luciak 1999, 2001; Murguialday 1997; Shayne 1999; Viterna 2006; Hume 2009; and Silber 2011.

94 Interview with Azucena Quintera, 13 May 2002.

95 Interview with Carmen Medina, 13 May 2002.

96 See, for example, Markowitz and Tice 2002.

97 Similarly, Markowitz and Tice 2002 argue that, in other contexts, these schisms may coincide with ethnic, regional, and class differences.

98 Per correspondence with David Holiday on 19 September 2005, he pointed out that although constituencies of women's organizations did not necessarily feel abandoned by these organizations, many individuals at the grassroots level have gradually felt abandoned by the FMLN leadership, as evidenced by periodic fissures and splits in their ranks.

99 Interview with Carmen Argueta, 26 May 2002.

100 Interviews with Deysi Chayne, 16 May 2002, and Irma Maya, 27 May 2002.

101 The reason MAM did not receive funding from CIDA did not reflect political differences, but MAM received funding from another donor for its citizen participation program.

102 In my interviews in El Salvador, directors from the following donor agencies indicated that economic development was among their main priorities: Agency of International Cooperation of Japan, Canadian Center for International Studies and Cooperation, Italian Cooperation, CREA, USAID, Heinrich Böll Foundation, EC, CIDA, and GTZ.

103 Interview with Isabel Fabean, 13 May 2002.

104 Interview with Isabel de Gevara, 23 May 2002.

105 Interview with Yanera Argueta, 10 May 2002.

106 Interview with Jeanette Urquilla, 30 May 2002.

107 Interviews with Sonia Baires, 23 May 2002, and Carmen Argueta, 26 May 2002.

108 Interview with Sonia Baires, 23 May 2002.

109 Interview with Yanera Argueta, 10 May 2002.

110 Interview with Irma Maya, 27 May 2002.

111 For a brief of discussion regarding the different approaches and strategies related to "autonomy," refer to Luciak 1999, 47–49.

112 Interview with Irma Maya, 27 May 2002.

113 Interview with Isabel de Gevara, 24 May 2002.

114 My research findings are supported by works such as Stephen, Cosgrove, and Ready 2000, 4.

115 Interview with Sophia Delgado, 3 June 2002.

116 As explained in chapter 2, this organization was not affiliated with one of the FMLN political organizations but originated from the Popular Social Christian Movement.

117 Interview with Dina Sales, 21 May 2002.

118 Interview with Alba America, 23 May 2002.

119 Interview with Sophia Delgado, 3 June 2002.

120 Interview with Alba America, 23 May 2002.

121 Interview with Dina Sales, 21 May 2002.

122 Interviews with Sophia Delgado, 3 June 2002, and Isabel Ascenio, 6 June 2002.

123 Interviews with Sophia Delgado, 3 June 2002.

124 Interview with Isabel Ascenio, 6 June 2002.

125 Interview with Yanera Argueta, 10 May 2002.

126 Local development programs tended to vary in their exact content, but always included a level of coordination with local government. This level of coordination could involve regular meetings with local government officials, gender-sensitivity training sessions for individuals who work in the municipality, and work on local economic development issues, as well as other projects.

127 See also note 102 above.

128 Interview with Irma Maya, 27 May 2002.

129 Interview with Isabel de Gevara, 23 May 2002.

130 Interview with Jeanette Urquilla, 30 May 2002.

131 Interview with Yanera Argueta, 10 May 2002.

132 Interview with Nora Hernandez, 14 May 2002.

133 Ibid.

134 Interview with Sophia Delgado, 3 June 2002.

135 Stephen, Cosgrove, and Ready 2000, 9.

136 According to Katharine Andrade Eekhoff, for example, NOVIB and Belgian solidarity organizations have and continue to focus on ERP projects. On the other hand, US solidarity organizations tend to fund FPL projects. Per discussion on 15 May 2002.

137 Foley 1996, 82.

138 Interview with Isabel de Gevara, 23 May 2002.

139 Among the first of these organizations was the Comité Unificado de Mujeres Salvadoreñas (Unified Committee of Salvadoran Women) founded in Costa Rica in 1981 to help in the coordination between women living in El Salvador and those living in other Latin American countries. In 1986, the FMLN ordered that all women affiliated with the FMLN come together and form the Frente Unitario de Mujeres (Women's National Front). The initiative was not successful. In 1987 FMLN proceeded to create another organizing structure, Coordinadora Nacional de Mujeres Salvadoreñas (National Coordinating Committee for Salvadoran Women, CONAMUS) for all women affiliated with the FMLN. CONAMUS represented members of various professional unions and committees. In recent years, the organization has been less active. Coordinación de Organismos de Mujeres (Coordination of Women's Organizations) was founded in 1986, and by 1988 its members included CONAMUS, AMS, MSM, ADEMUSA, and OR-MUSA.

140 Interview with Isabel de Gevara, 23 May 2002.

141 Many of the organizations also have direct access to the Legislative Assembly and local government structures, and do not function through an intermediary body like the WATC.

142 Saint-Germain 1997.

143 Ibid., 86.

144 Ibid.

145 For more on legislation passed by the women's movement, see Blumberg 2001.

146 In 2001, the two legislative deputies who were involved in the initiative were Laura Peña and Violeta Menjivar.

147 For more on MAM's Citizens' Initiative for Women, refer to Stephen, Cosgrove, and Ready 2000, 8–9.

148 These donor agencies were Technical and Scientific Cooperation in the Embassy of France, Italian Cooperation in the Ministry of Foreign Affairs, Technical Cooperation in the Embassy of Britain, the Canadian Center for International Studies and Cooperation, CREA, CIDA, Díakonia, Heinrich Böll Foundation, GTZ, Friedrich Ebert Foundation, and the EC.

149 This is an area where women have made important gains in other Latin American countries as well. See, for example, Cluluw 2007, 86–89.

150 Interview with Deysi Chaine, 16 May 2002.

151 Interview with Sonia Baires, 23 May 2002.

152 Interview with Jeanette Urquilla, 30 May 2002.

153 From a discussion with Hector Dada-Hirezi, 26 May 2002.

154 Ibid.

155 Interview with David Holiday, 2 May 2002.

156 Interview with Isabel de Gevara, 23 May 2002.

157 Interview with Isabel Fabean, 13 May 2002.

158 Interview with Deysi Chaine, 16 May 2002.

159 Interview with Sonia Baires, 23 May 2002.

160 For an interesting discussion of other gender-related achievements, see Cosgrove 2010.

161 See, for example, Walsh 2012.

162 See, for example, Hume 2008 and Silber 2011.

163 For a discussion of challenges women face in postwar El Salvador, see, for example, Kampwirth 2004 and Shayne 2004.

CHAPTER 6. HAMAS AFTER ELECTORAL VICTORY

1 For more on Hamas's election victory, see Jamal 2013.

2 For more on the unfolding events following Hamas's election victory, see Brown 2012, 123–124.

3 The Road Map was put forth by the Quartet, and it was agreed upon in April 2003 as a way to move the peace process forward. Phase I required mutual recognition, renunciation of the use of violence, and political institutional reform on the part of the Palestinians. On the part of Israel, the Road Map required Israel to refrain from deportations and demolitions, ease movement, improve the humanitarian situations of the Palestinians in the West Bank and the Gaza Strip, and commit to a complete settlement freeze.

4 For more on this discussion, see Hroub 2006b, 144–146.

5 King Abdallah of Saudi Arabia intervened and brought the two parties together in February 2007 in hopes of overcoming the impasse. The series of meeting

culminated in the Mecca Agreement of 8 February 2007. The agreement outlined measures to end violence between Hamas and Fatah, steps to incorporate Hamas and Islamic Jihad into the PLO, and the composition of the unity government itself. The agreement was based on Hamas's acceptance that a Palestinian state would be established on the 1967 borders, and that it respected previous agreements reached between Israel and the PLO.

6 Middle East Quartet 2006.

7 For a candid critique of the Quartet's policies, see de Soto's *End of Mission Report*, May 2007, that was supposed to be confidential but was leaked to the press. Alvaro de Soto was the Under-secretary General, UN Special Coordinator for the Middle East Peace Process, and UN envoy to the Quartet. http://image.guardian.co.uk.

8 For more on this, see Hroub 2006b, 163–165.

9 According to Mouin Rabani, this move was to put security personnel on payroll and not necessarily to form a new militia of sorts.

10 Ibid., 163.

11 Tamimi 2007, 229.

12 Hroub 2006b, 164.

13 For a detailed discussion of the security situation which unfolded, refer to Sayigh 2007 and Hroub 2006b.

14 Sayigh 2007, 20.

15 Conflict Forum Chronology 2007, 11.

16 Cooper 2007.

17 Conflict Forum Chronology 2007, 13.

18 Although Russia had signed on to the Quartet statement, it technically did not boycott Hamas and maintained that contact with Hamas should continue and also received Khaled Mashaal in Moscow.

19 For more on this discussion, see Sayigh 2007, 17.

20 For a comprehensive discussion of closure policies imposed on the Gaza Strip after Hamas's takeover, see OCHA-OPT 2009.

21 International Crisis Group 2006b, cited in Sayigh 2007, 23 (footnote 53).

22 Sayigh 2007, 17–18.

23 World Bank 2006, 2.

24 Cooper 2007.

25 For more on this, see EC-TIM, 2007.

26 World Bank 2006, 2.

27 For more on these developments, see Brown 2008, 80.

28 World Bank 2007, 21.

29 World Bank 2006, 3.

30 Ibid., 28.

31 Ibid., 22.

32 World Bank 2007, iii.

33 Ibid., 3.

34 Ibid., 1.
35 World Bank 2007, xii.
36 Ibid., 5.
37 Ibid., 5–6.
38 For more on the impact of the closure, refer to OCHA-OPT 2012.
39 For more on this discussion, refer to World Bank 2007, 4–5. Donors disbursed much of this assistance through channels outside the government.
40 Zanotti 2012.
41 For more on this discussion, refer to World Bank 2007, 4–5.
42 Harel 2006.
43 Zanotti 2010, 5.
44 *Haaretz*, "U.S. Begins $42 Million Program to Bolster *Hamas* Opponents," 13 June 2006. Also see Wilson and Kessler 2006.
45 See Sayigh 2007, 17; and for a discussion on Western donor funding to municipalities with Hamas members, see ICG 2006a, 26.
46 INCLE was State Department funded but staffed by the US military.
47 Zanotti 2010, 14.
48 Norway was one of the only Western countries to normalize relations with the unity government.
49 Statement of the Middle East Quartet, 21 March 2007.
50 Hamas has pointed out that Fatah as a movement also has not recognized Israel.
51 ICG 2007, 22.
52 *Haaretz*, "On Rifles," 10 April 2007. Referenced in Savigh 2007.
53 US Assistance to the Palestinians, Hearing before the Subcommittee on the Middle East and South Asia of the Committee on Foreign Affairs, House of Representatives, 110th Congress, 2007.
54 Ibid.
55 For more on these changing policies, see Office of Foreign Assets Control, "Guidelines on Transactions with the Palestinian Authority," http://www.treas.gov.
56 Cooper 2007.
57 Al Jazeera, "Abbas Challenged over New Cabinet: Lawyers Say New Government "Destroys" Foundation of the Constitution," 6 July 2007. http://www.aljazeera.com/news (last accessed 13 February 2018).
58 Conflict Forum Chronology 2007.
59 Ibid.
60 Personal interview with Laurent Marion, 4 August 2009, and personal interview with official from Coordination Unit, UNSCO, 4 August 2009, who asked not to be named.
61 For a concise summary of the impact on financial management, see Sayigh 2007, 24.
62 Roy 2011, 212.
63 Zanotti 2010.
64 Ibid., 5.

65 Ibid., 13.

66 Zanotti 2012.

67 In the Palestinian territories, mosques are under the supervision of the PA's Ministry of Waqf and Religious Affairs. Imams authorized to preach are paid by the PA.

68 For more on this, see Roy 2011, 235.

69 Ibid., 216.

70 Ibid., 215; Schäublin 2011; and Benthall 2016, chapter 4.

71 Schäublin, 42–45.

72 OCHA-OPT 2010.

73 For more on this discussion, see Roy 2011, 216–220.

74 Ibid., 218.

75 Previously, Hamas had observed a six-month cease-fire. Israel had not fulfilled its commitments under the June 2008 cease-fire and did not extend it. Hamas resumed its firing of rockets and mortars into Israel at the end of 2008; their justification was that they had received nothing in return for the cease-fire.

76 These figures are from B'tselem. For more on the aftermath of Israel's incursion on Gaza, see B'tselem 2012.

77 The source for Israeli civilian casualties during "Cast Lead" is the Magen David Adom (the national society of the International Red Cross Movement in Israel), while figures regarding IDF soldiers are based on the Israeli Ministry of Foreign Affairs' information. Sources are cited from OCHA-OPT 2010.

78 UNDP 2009, 5–6.

79 UNISPAL 2009 and OCHA-OPT, 2010, 19.

80 UNDP 2009, 10.

81 Ibid., 14.

82 OCHA-OPT, 2010, 19–20.

83 UNDP 2009, 12.

84 The information excluded any partner financial details. Interview with Laurent Marion, 4 August 2009.

85 Ibid.

86 Miller 2007.

87 Zanotti 2012, 11.

88 See Miller 2007.

89 Personal interview with OCHA official who asked that name not be cited, Jerusalem, 5 August 2009.

90 Transcript of speech by Lieutenant General Keith Dayton, Washington Institute for Near East Policy Soref Symposium, Washington, DC, 7 May 2008, cited by Zanotti 2010, 24.

91 OCHA and the World Health Organization, 30 March 2009.

92 Personal Interview with OCHA official who asked that name not be cited, 5 August 2009.

93 For more on this discuss, see Sayigh 2010 and Berti 2015.

94 Personal interview with OCHA official who asked that name not be cited, 5 August 2009.

95 Ibid.

96 For an incisive and comprehensive discussion of Hamas's reform of the security sector in Gaza, see Sayigh 2011, 43.

97 For more on this discussion, see Brown 2012.

98 Ibid., 200.

99 For an excellent discussion of the tunnel economy, see Pelham 2012.

100 Ibid., 5.

101 Ibid., 4.

102 Ibid., 10.

103 Ibid., 13.

104 As of 2012, most of these tunnels were blocked by Egyptian authorities.

105 Continued international pressure has strengthened the more radical elements of Hamas. For more on this, see Hovdenak 2009; Kubíková 2009; and Brown 2008.

106 Cited from Zanotti 2013, 7–8.

107 OCHA-OPT 2010, 19.

108 Ibid., 21.

CHAPTER 7. NONINCLUSIVE SETTLEMENTS AND DEMOCRACY'S LONG HAUL

1 Uclés 1996, 148–156.

2 Walsh-Mellet 2017.

3 For more on this, see Almeida 2009.

4 For more on the history of labor organizing in the Palestinian territories, see Hiltermann 1991, chapter 3.

5 Interview with Mohammed Aruri, 1 August 2001; and Sovich 2000.

6 For more on the 2016 Palestinian teacher's strikes, see Abu Moghli and Qato 2018.

7 For more on the uncertainty and crime in postwar El Salvador, see Moodie 2010.

8 Ramos and Loya 2008.

9 For more on this subject, see Programa de las Naciones Unidas para el Desarrollo 2009, 64.

10 Wolf 2012.

11 For more on how state institutions contributed to and were unable to address criminal violence in El Salvador, see Cruz 2011.

12 Peña and Gibb 2013.

13 Arato 2016. Although some scholars have highlighted that a multistage constitution drafting process followed by constitution making and amendment by a democratically elected body guarantees legitimacy, detailed discussion pertaining to the different stages is beyond the scope of my analysis. Worthy of mention, however, is that given the inclusivity of the political settlement in El Salvador, the country managed to amend the 1983 constitution, quite significantly in 1991, and then again in 2003 and 2014. In the Palestinian case, the Basic Law, the proposed

constitution, was last amended in 2003. There have been no subsequent amendments given the political paralysis of the legislature.

14 For an excellent discussion on constitutional development in transition contexts, see Benomar 2004. Although the left-wing Pan Africanist Congress boycotted the peace accords, it did not represent significant constituencies. Moreover, though the leader of the Inkatha Freedom Party did not attend, a representative of the party did attend.

15 Ibid., 88.

16 For more on the drafting of the constitution, see Savage 2001.

17 Ibid., 84.

18 Samuels 2006, 675.

19 For more on negotiations with Inkatha, see Friedman and Atkinson 1994.

20 For more on this, see Herbst 1997–98.

21 Friedman and Atkinson 1994.

22 Sisk and Stefes 2005, 294.

23 Ibid., 308.

24 Bratton and Landsberg 2000.

25 For more on this discuss, see Forman and Patrick 2000, 280–282.

26 For more on this discussion, see Habib and Taylor 1999.

27 Ibid.

28 See, for example, ibid. and Kihato 2001.

29 Kihato 2001.

30 Habib 2005.

31 Ibid., 672.

32 For more on this, see, for example, Heller 2001.

33 See Robinson and Friedman 2007.

34 Samuels 2006, 664.

35 Saghieh 2007, 208.

36 Bremer 2003.

37 Hatch 2005, 104.

38 Sissons and Al-Saiedi 2013.

39 Ibid., 17.

40 Ibid., 34.

41 Coyne 2008, 19.

42 For more on the impact on the health sector, see Senate Democratic Policy Committee Hearing 2006.

43 For more on the impact of de-Ba'athification, see Sissons and Al-Saiedi 2013, especially 22, for the statistics listed.

44 Boettke and Coyne 2007, 57–58.

45 Sissons and Al-Saiedi 2013, 21.

46 Hatch 2005, 106.

47 Saghieh 2007, 220.

48 Brown 2005, 7, and Arato 2006–07, 550.

49 For more on this, see Brown 2005.

50 Chaplin 2006, 274.

51 Arato 2006–07.

52 Ibid.

53 For more on this, see Sissons and Al-Saiedi 2013, 15.

54 For more on this, see Brown 2005, 6–7.

55 Ibid.

56 Arato 2006–07, 550.

57 Ibid., 552.

58 Wood 2013.

59 Tarnoff 2008, 8.

60 Special Inspector General for Iraq Reconstruction 2012.

61 Ibid., 4.

62 Ibid., 25.

63 Tarnoff 2008, 19.

64 The Development Fund for Iraq was held by the Central Bank of Iraq. Oil profits and other Iraqi assets would be deposited into it.

65 Tarnoff 2008, 19.

66 Ibid., 26.

67 Ibid., 19 and 33.

68 Urban Institute 2004.

69 For more on the marginalization of the Sunni-dominated areas in terms of education rehabilitation and development, for example, see Chandrasekaran 2007.

70 For more on this overall discussion, see International Crisis Group 2008, 27.

71 Cordesman 2007, 29.

72 See, for example, Tarnoff 2006.

73 Dawisha 2010, 877.

74 Wicken 2013, 14.

75 Dawisha 2010.

76 Sullivan 2010.

77 Al Jazeera, "Iraqi Sunnis Rally Against Shia-Led Government," 2 February 2013. http://www.aljazeera.com (last accessed 13 February 2018).

78 For a slightly more positive outlook, see O'Leary 2009.

79 For a detailed discussion on ISIS and membership drawn from Iraq's former Ba'ath Party, see Richard Barrett, "TSG-The-Islamic-State-Nov14.pdf," http://sou fangroup.com (accessed 20 January 2015).

APPENDIX II. FOREIGN DONORS

1 The main gaps in the CRS concerned Japan, which did not report technical cooperation activities, and the EC, which reported European Development Fund and European Investment Bank projects, but not activities financed through the Commission budget. Information provided is based on e-mail correspondence

with Sophie Lhéritier on 14 April 2004. Despite these shortcomings in earlier aggregate reporting, DAC/CRS has established qualitative standards for aid transfers and maintained this data, allowing for cross-national statistical analysis and comparison.

2 A faith-based Swedish funding agency.

WORKS CITED

Ababneh, Sara. 2014. "The Palestinian Women's Movement versus Hamas: Attempting to Understand Women's Empowerment outside a Feminist Network." *Journal of International Women's Studies* 15, no. 1 (February): 35–53.

Abdulhadi, Rabab. 1998. "The Palestinian Women's Autonomous Movement: Emergence, Dynamics, and Challenges." *Gender and Society* 12, no. 6 (December): 649–673.

Abu 'amr, Ziyad. 1995. *Al-mujtam'a Al-madani wa Al-tahawul Al-dimuqrati fi Filastin [Civil Society and Democratic Transformation in Palestine].* Ramallah: Muwatin, the Palestinian Institute for the Study of Democracy.

Abu-Lughod, Ibrahim, ed. 1971. *The Transformation of Palestine: Essays on the Origin and Development of the Arab-Israeli Conflict.* Evanston, IL: Northwestern University Press.

Abu Moghli, Mai and Mezna Qato. "A Brief History of a Teacher's Strike." Middle East Report Online, 5 June 2018.

Abu Nahleh, Lamis. 2002. "Mu'asasat wa Baramej al-Iqrad' al-'Amela fi al-Ḍ'afa al-Gharbiyyeh wa Qita' Ghaza" [Micro-lending institutions and programs in the West Bank and Gaza Strip]. *Review of Women's Studies* 2002: 32–43.

Abu Nahleh, Lamis, Eileen Kuttab, and Lisa Taraki. 2003. *Empowerment: Between Theory and Practice at International and Local Levels.* Birzeit: Institute of Women's Studies.

Acuerdos de paz de Chapultepec. 1992. *Revista Conservadora del Pensamiento Centroamericano* 47, no. 214 (March): 32–82.

Al-Hout, Shafiq. 1994. *Itafiqiat Ghaza-Areeha Awlan: Al-Hal al-Marfoud [Gaza-Jericho First Agreements: The Rejected Solution].* Beirut: Dar El-Istiqlal.

Al Jazeera. 2007. "Abbas Challenged over New Cabinet: Lawyers Say New Government 'Destroys' Foundation of the Constitution." 6 July. http://www.aljazeera.com (last accessed 13 February 2018).

———. 2013. "Iraq Sunnis Rally against Shia-led Government." 2 February. http://www.aljazeera.com (last accessed 13 February 2018).

Al-Khalil, Ghazi. 1977. *Palestinian Women and the Revolution.* Acre: Dar al-Aswar.

Allabadi, Fadwa. 2008. "Controversy: Secular and Islamist Women in Palestinian Society." *European Journal of Women's Studies* 15, no. 3 (August 1): 181–201.

Almeida, Paul. 2008. *Waves of Protest: Popular Struggle in El Salvador, 1925–2005.* Minneapolis: University of Minnesota Press.

———. 2009. "Social Movements, Political Parties, and Electoral Triumph in El Salvador." *NACLA Report on the Americas* 42, no. 6 (November-December): 16–21.

Álvarez, Alberto Martin. 2010. "From Revolutionary War to Democratic Revolution: The Farabundo Marti National Liberation Front (FMLN) in El Salvador." In *Berghof Transitions Series: Resistance/Liberation Movement and Transition to Politics*, no. 9, edited by Veronique Dudouet and Hans J. Geirrmann. Berlin: Berghof Conflict Research.

Amireh, Amal. 2012. "Activists, Lobbyists, and Suicide Bombers: Lessons from the Palestinian Women's Movement." *Comparative Studies of South Asia, Africa, and the Middle East* 32, no. 2: 437–446.

Andoni, Lamis. 1996. "The Palestinian Elections: Moving toward Democracy or One-Party Rule?" *Journal of Palestine Studies* 25, no. 3 (April): 5–16.

Andrews, Penelope, and Stephen Ellman, eds. 2001. *The Post-Apartheid Constitutions: Perspectives on South Africa's Basic Law.* Johannesburg, : Wits University Press.

Arato, Andrew. 2006–07. "Post-Sovereign Constitution-Making and Its Pathology in Iraq." *New York Law School Law Review* 51: 536–555.

———. 2016. *Post Sovereign Constitution Making: Learning and Legitimacy.* New York: Oxford University Press.

Azpuru, Dinorah. 2010. "The Salience of Ideology: Fifteen Years of Presidential Elections in El Salvador." *Latin American Politics and Society* 52, no. 2 (Summer): 103–138.

Baloyra, Enrique. 1982. *El Salvador in Transition.* Chapel Hill: University of North Carolina Press.

Barrett, Richard. "TSG-The-Islamic State Nov. 14.pdf," http://soufangroup.com (last accessed 20 January 2015)

Baynes, Kenneth. 2002. "A Critical Theory Perspective on Civil Society and the State." In *Civil Society and Government*, edited by Nancy L. Rosenblum and Robert C. Post, 123–145. Princeton: Princeton University Press.

BBC. 2007. "How Hamas Took Over the Gaza Strip." 15 June.

Bebbington, Anthony, and Roger Riddell. 1995. "The Direct Funding of Southern NGOs by Donors." *Journal of International Development* 7, no. 6 (November): 879–893.

Beck, Martin. 2000. "External Dimension of Authoritarian Rule in Palestine." *Journal of International Relations and Development* 3, no. 1: 47–66.

Béjar, Guido, and Stefan Roggenbuck, eds. 1995. *Sociedad Participativa en El Salvador.* San Salvador: University of Central America and Fundación Konrad Adenauer.

Bell, Christine. 2006. "Peace Agreements: Their Nature and Legal Status." *American Journal of International Law* 100, no. 2 (April): 373–412.

Bell, Christine, and Catherine O'Rourke. 2007. "The People's Peace? Peace Agreements, Civil Society, and Participatory Democracy." *International Political Science Review* 23, no. 3 (June 1): 293–384.

Belloni, Roberto. 2008. "Civil Society in War-to-Democracy Transitions." In *From War to Democracy: Dilemmas of Peacebuilding*, edited by Anna K. Jarstad and Timothy J. Sisk, 182–210. Cambridge: Cambridge University Press.

———. 2011. "Civil Society and Peacebuilding in Bosnia and Herzegovina." *Journal of Peace Research* 38, no. 2 (March): 163–180.

Bennis, Phyllis, and Michel Moushabek. 1991. *Beyond the Storm: A Gulf War Crisis Reader*. New York: Olive Branch Press.

Benomar, Jamal. 2004. "Constitution-Making after Conflict: Lessons from Iraq." *Journal of Democracy* 15, no. 4 (April): 81–95.

Benthall, Jonathan. 2016. *Islamic Charities and Islamic Humanism in Troubled Times*. Manchester, UK: Manchester University Press.

Berman, Sheri. 1997. "Civil Society and Political Institutionalization." *American Behavioral Scientist* 40, no. 5 (March/April): 562–574.

Berti, Benedetta. 2015. "Non-State Actors as Providers of Governance: The Hamas Government in Gaza between Effective Sovereignty, Centralized Authority, and Resistance." *Middle East Journal* 69, no. 1 (Winter): 9–31.

Biekart, Kees. 1999a. *El Salvador: NGO Country Profile*. Oegstgeest, NL: Gemeenschappelijk Overleg Medefinanciering.

———. 1999b. *The Politics of Civil Society Building: European Private Aid Agencies and Democratic Transitions in Central America*. Utrecht, NL: International Books and the Transnational Institute.

Bishara, Azmi. 1996. *Musahamah fi Naqd al Mujtam'a al-Madanī* [A contribution to the critique of civil society]. Ramallah: Muwatin, the Palestinian Institute for the Study of Democracy.

Blumberg, Rae Lesser. 2001. "Risky Business: What Happens to Gender Equality and Women's Rights in Post-Conflict Societies? Insights from NGOs in El Salvador." *International Journal of Politics, Culture and Society* 15, no. 1 (September): 161–173.

Boettke, Peter J., and Christopher J. Coyne. 2007. "The Political Economy of Forgiveness." *Society* 44, no. 2 (January/February): 53–59.

Boutros-Ghali, Boutros. 1992. *An Agenda for Peace: Preventive Diplomacy, Peacemaking and Peace-keeping*. 17 June. Document A/47/277 S/24111. New York: United Nations Department of Public Information.

Boyce, James. 1995a. "Adjustment towards Peace: An Introduction." *World Development* 23, no. 12 (December): 2067–2077.

———. 1995b. "External Assistance and the Peace Process in El Salvador." *World Development* 23, no. 12 (December): 2101–2116.

Bratton, Michael, and Chris Landsberg. 2000. "South Africa." In *Good Intentions: Pledges of Aid for Postconflict Recovery*, edited by Shepard Forman and Stewart Patrick, 259–314. Boulder: Lynne Rienner.

Bremer, Paul. 2003. "Coalition Provisional Authority Order Number One: De-Baathification of Iraqi Society." *CPA/ORD/16* (1 May).

Brockett, Charles D. 2005. *Political Movements and Violence in Central America*. Cambridge: Cambridge University Press.

Brouwer, Imco. 2000. "Weak Democracy and Civil Society Promotion: The Cases of Egypt and Palestine." In *Funding Virtue: Civil Society Aid and Democracy Promotion*, edited by Marina Ottaway and Thomas Carothers, 21–48. Washington, DC: Carnegie Endowment for International Peace.

Brown, Nathan J. 2003. *Palestinian Politics after the Oslo Accords: Resuming Arab Palestine*. Berkeley: University of California Press.

———. 2005. *Policy Outlook, Democracy Rule and Law: Iraq's Constitutional Process Plunges Ahead*. Washington, DC: Carnegie Endowment for International Peace.

———. 2008. "Principled or Stubborn? Western Policy towards Hamas." *International Spectator: Italian Journal of International Affairs* 43, no. 4 (December): 73–87.

———. 2012. *When Victory Is Not an Option: Islamist Movements in Arab Politics*. Ithaca: Cornell University Press.

Brownley, Jason. 2012. *Democracy Prevention: The Politics of the US-Egyptian Alliance*. New York: Cambridge University Press.

Brynen, Rex. 2000. *A Very Political Economy: Peacebuilding and Foreign Aid in the West Bank and Gaza Strip*. Washington, DC: United States Institute of Peace Press.

B'tselem. 2012. *Three Years since Operation Cast Lead: Israeli Military Utterly Failed to Investigate Itself*. 18 January. http://www.btselem.org (last accessed 20 February 2018).

Burnell, Peter. 2002. "Democracy Assistance: Origins and Organizations." In *Democracy Assistance: International Co-operation for Democratization*, edited by Peter Burnell, 34–65. London: Frank Cass.

Bush, Sarah. 2015. *The Taming of Democracy Assistance: Why Democracy Promotion Does Not Confront Dictators*. New York: Cambridge University Press.

Byrne, Hugh. 1996. *El Salvador's Civil War: A Study of Revolution*. Boulder: Lynne Rienner.

Caldeira, Teresa. 1998. "Justice and Individual Rights: Challenges for Women's Movements and Democratization in Brazil." In *Women and Democracy: Latin America and Central and Eastern Europe*, edited by Jane S. Jacquette and Sharon W. Wolchik, 75–101. Baltimore: Johns Hopkins University Press.

Call, Charles T. 2003. "Democratization, War and State-Building: Constructing the Rule of Law in El Salvador." *Journal of Latin American Studies* 35, no. 4 (November): 827–862.

———. 2012. *Why Peace Fails: The Causes and Prevention of Civil War*. Washington, DC: Georgetown University Press.

Callaghy, Thomas M. 1992. "Civil Society, Democracy, and Economic Change in Africa: A Dissenting Opinion about Resurgent Societies." In *Civil Society and the State in Africa*, edited by John W. Harbeson, Donald Rothchild, and Naomi Chazan, 244–245. Boulder: Lynne Rienner.

Carothers, Thomas. 1999. *Aiding Democracy Abroad: The Learning Curve*. Washington, DC: Carnegie Endowment for International Peace.

———. 2009. "Democracy Assistance: Political vs. Developmental?" *Journal of Democracy* 20, no. 1 (January): 5–19.

———. 2010. "Democracy Support and Development Aid: The Elusive Synthesis." *Journal of Democracy* 21, no. 4 (October): 12–26.

———. 2015. *Democracy Aid at 25: Time to Choose*. Washington, DC: Carnegie Endowment for International Peace.

Carothers, Thomas, and Marina Ottoway, eds. 2005. *Unchartered Journey: Promoting Democracy in the Middle East*. Washington, DC: Carnegie Endowment for International Peace.

Carter Center. 2012. *Palestine Electoral Study Mission Urges Political Reconciliation*. https://www.cartercenter.org (accessed 14 December 2014).

Center for Policy Research. 1993. *Public Opinion Poll 4, Palestinian Elections and the Declaration of Principles*. 12 December.

Central Election Commission—Palestine. 1995. "Palestine, Election Law No. 13 of 1995." https://www.elections.ps (accessed 17 October 2012).

———. 1996. "The 1996 Palestinian and Legislative Elections." http://www.elections.ps.

———. 2005. "Local Election Law No. 10." https://www.elections.ps (accessed 27 October 2012).

———. 2012. "Local Elections Facts and Figures" https://www.elections.ps (accessed 27 October 2012).Challand, Benoit. 2009. *Palestinian Civil Society: Foreign Donors and the Power to Promote and Exclude*. New York: Routledge.

Chandrasekaran, Rajiv. 2007. *Imperial Life in the Emerald City: Inside Iraq's Green Zone*. New York: Vintage Books.

Chaplin, Edward. 2006. "Iraq's New Constitution: Recipe for Stability or Chaos." *Cambridge Review of International Affairs* 19, no. 2 (June): 217–84.

Ching, Erik, and Virginia Tilley. 1998. "Indians, the Military, and the Rebellion of 1932." *Journal of Latin American Studies* 30, no. 1 (February): 121–156.

Clark, John, and Barbara Balaj. 1994. *The West Bank and Gaza in Transition: The Role of NGOs in the Peace Process*. Washington, DC: World Bank.

Clulow, Michael. 2007. "Women's Organizations and Local Democracy: Promoting Effective Participation of Women in Central America." *Development* 50, no. 1 (March): 86–89.

Cobban, Helena. 1984. *The Palestinian Liberation Organization: People, Power and Politics*. Cambridge: Cambridge University Press.

Cohen, Jean L., and Andrew Arato. 1992. *Civil Society and Political Theory*. Cambridge, MA: MIT Press.

Colburn, Forrest D. 1993. "Post-Cold War Feminism in El Salvador." *Dissent* 46, no. 1 (Winter): 43–46.

———. 2009. "The Turnover in El Salvador." *Journal of Democracy* 20, no. 3 (July): 143–152.

Conflict Forum. 2007. *A Conflict Forum Chronology: The Failure of the Palestinian Unity Government and the Gaza Take Over, December 2005-July 2007*. Beirut: Conflict Forum.

Cooper, Helene. 2007. "U.S. Unfreezes Millions in Aid to Palestinians." *New York Times*, 19 June.

Cordesman, Anthony H. 2007. "Iraqi Force Development and the Challenge of Civil War: The Critical Problems and Failures the US Must Address if Iraqi Forces Are to Do the Job." Washington, DC: Center for Strategic and International Studies (March 28).

Cosgrove, Serena. 2010. *Leadership from the Margins: Women and Civil Society Organizations in Argentina, Chile, and El Salvador*. New Brunswick: Rutgers University Press.

Council on Hemispheric Affairs. 2012. *The 2014 Presidential Elections in El Salvador: The Debate on the Salvadoran Left* 32, no. 3 (April 12). http://www.coha.org (last accessed 20 February 2018).

Coyne, Christopher. 2008. "The Politics of Bureaucracy and the Failure of Post-War Reconstruction." *Public Choice* 135, nos. 1–2 (April): 11–22.

Crawford, Gordon. 2001. *Foreign Aid and Political Reform: A Comparative Analysis of Democracy Assistance and Political Conditionality*. New York: Palgrave.

Cruz, Jose Miguel. 2011. "Criminal Violence and Democratization in Central America: The Survival of the Violent State." *Latin American Politics & Society* 53, no. 4 (Winter): 1–33.

Dahl, Robert A. 1971. *Polyarchy: Participation and Opposition*. New Haven: Yale University Press.

———. 1989. *Democracy and Its Critics*. New Haven: Yale University Press.

Dawisha, Adeed. 2010. "The Long and Winding Road to Iraqi Democracy." *Perspectives on Politics* 8, no. 3 (September): 877–885.

Dayton, Lieutenant General Keith. 2008. "Keynote Address at Soref Symposium.". 7 May. Washington, DC: Washington Institute for Near East Policy. http://www.washingtoninstitute.org (last accessed 20 February 2018).

De Bremond, Ariane. 2007. "The Politics of Peace and Resettlement through El Salvador's Land Transfer Program: Caught between the State and the Market." *Third World Quarterly* 28, no. 8 (November): 1537–1556.

Declaration of Principles on Interim Self-Government Arrangements ("Oslo Agreement") 1993. 13 September . http://www.refworld.org (accessed 8 August 2018).

del Castillo, Graciana. 1997. "The Arms for Land Deal in El Salvador." In *Keeping the Peace: Multi-dimensional UN Operations in Cambodia and El Salvador*, edited by Michael W. Doyle, Ian Johnstone, and Robert C. Orr, 342–365. Cambridge: Cambridge University Press.

———. 2001. "Post-Conflict Resolution and the Challenge of International Organizations: The Case of El Salvador." *World Development* 29, no. 1 (December): 1967–1985.

de Soto, Alvaro. 2007. "End of Mission Report." May. http://image.guardian.co.uk (last accessed 13 February 2018).

de Soto, Alvaro, and Graciana del Castillo. 1994. "Obstacles to Peacebuilding." *Foreign Policy*, no. 94 (Spring): 69–83.

Dietrich, Simone, and Joseph Wright. 2013. "Foreign Aid and Democratic Development in Africa." In *Democratic Trajectories in Africa: Unravelling the Impact of Foreign Aid*, edited by Danielle Resnick and Nicolas van de Walle, 56–86. Oxford: Oxford University Press.

Di Palma, Giuseppe. 1990. *To Craft Democracies: An Essay on Democratic Transitions*. Berkeley: University of California Press.

Doyle, Michael W., and Nicholas Sambanis. 2006. *Making War and Building Peace: United Nations Peace Operations.* Princeton: Princeton University Press.

Dunning, Thad. 2004. "Conditioning the Effects of Aid: Cold War Politics, Donor Credibility, and Democracy in Africa." *International Organization* 58, no. 2 (April): 409–423.

EC Temporary International Mechanism (TIM). 2007. "EC: Key Facts: TIM." 29 June. https://ec.europa.eu (last accessed 17 December 2017).

Edwards, Bob, Michael W. Foley, and Mario Diani, eds. 2000. *Beyond Tocqueville: Civil Society and the Social Capital Debate in Comparative Perspective.* Hanover, NH: University Press of New England.

Edwards, Michael, and David Hulme, eds. 1996. *Beyond the Magic Bullet: NGO Performance and Accountability in the Post-Cold War World.* West Hartford, CT: Kumarian Press.

———. 1997. *NGOs, States, and Donors: Too Close for Comfort?* London: Macmillan.

Election Resources on the Internet: Presidential and Legislative Elections in El Salvador, Parts I and II. 2015. http://www.electionresources.org (accessed 13 January 2015).

Elkhafif, Mahmoud, Misyef Misyef, and Mutasim Elagraa. 2013. *Palestinian Fiscal Revenue Leakage to Israel under the Paris Protocol on Economic Relations.* Geneva: United Nations Commission for Trade and Development.

El Salvador–Election Passport. 2015. http://www.electionpassport.com (last accessed 10 January 2015).

El Salvador: Civic Freedom Monitor. International Center for Not-for-Profit Law NGO Law Monitor. 2015. http://www.icnl.org (last accessed 22 January 2015).

El Salvador: Parliamentary Chamber/Asamblea legislativa)-Elections Held in 1994. 2015. http://archive.ipu.org (last accessed 13 January 2015).

Esther-Younes, Anna. 2010. "A Gendered Movement for Liberation: Hamas' Women's Movement and Nation Building in Contemporary Palestine." *Contemporary Arab Affairs* 3, no. 1 (January): 21–37.

Equizábal, Cristina. 1992. "Parties, Programs, and Politics in El Salvador." In *Political Parties and Democracy in Central America*, edited by Louis G. Goodman, William H. LeoGrande, and Johanna Mendelsohn Forman, 135–160. Boulder, CO: Westview Press.

Fagen, Patricia Weiss. 1996. "El Salvador: Lessons in Peace Consolidation." In *Beyond Sovereignty: Collectively Defending Democracy in the Americas*, edited by Tom Farer, 213–237. Baltimore: Johns Hopkins University Press.

Farsoun, Samih K., and Christina E. Zacharia. 1997. *Palestine and the Palestinians.* Boulder: Westview Press.

Finkel, Stephen E., Anibal S. Perez-Linan, and Mitchell A. Seligson. 2007. "The Effects of US Foreign Assistance on Democracy Building, 1990–2003." *World Politics* 59, no. 3 (April): 404–440.

Fleischmann, Ellen, 2003. *The Nation and Its "New" Women: The Palestinian Women's Movement-1920-1948.* Berkeley: University of California Press.

Foley, Michael W. 1996. "Laying the Groundwork: The Struggle for Civil Society in El Salvador." *Journal of Interamerican Studies and World Affairs* 31, no. 1 (Spring): 67–104.

Foley, Michael, and Bob Edwards. 1996. "The Paradox of Civil Society." *Journal of Democracy* 7, no. 3 (July): 38–52.

Forman, Shepard, and Stewart Patrick. 2000. *Good Intentions: Pledges of Aid for Post-Conflict Recovery.* Boulder: Lynne Rienner.

Friedman, Steven and Doreen Atkinson. 1994. *The Small Miracle: South Africa's Negotiated Settlement.* Randburg, South Africa: Ravan Press.

Galdámez, Ernesto. 1997. *Perfilando el Municipio Como Promotor de Desarrollo Económico y Social [Profiling the Municipality as a Promoter of Economic and Social Development].* San Salvador: Fundación Nacional para el Desarrollo (Foundation for National Development).

Gonzalez, Cinzia Mirella Innocenti. 1997. "Evolución Historica del Movimiento de Mujeres y del Movimiento Feminista en el Salvador Desde 1900 Hasta 1995" [Historical evolution of the women's movement and the feminist movement in El Salvador from 1900 to 1995." MA thesis in Sociology. San Salvador: Universidad Centroamericana Jose Simeon Cañas-UCA.

Gonzalez, Esther Portillo. 2012. "El Salvador's 2012 Legislative Election: Implications and Opportunities." *NACLA Report on the Americas* 45, no. 4 (Winter): 63–64.

Gonzalez, Victor. 1992. *Las Organizaciones No Gubernamentales (ONGs): Una Nueva Expresion de la Sociedad Civil Salvadoreña [Non-Governmental Organizations: A New Expression of Salvadoran Civil Society].* San Salvador: Programa Regional de Investigación sobre El Salvador (Regional Program on Research in El Salvador).

Gordon, Sara. 1989. *La Guerra Politica en El Salvador.* Mexico City: Siglo Veintiuno Editores.

Grant, Richard, and Jan Nijman, eds. 1998. *The Global Crisis in Foreign Aid.* Syracuse : Syracuse University Press.

Gurr, Tedd. 2000. *Peoples versus States: Minorities at Risk in the New Century.* Washington, DC: United States Institute of Peace Press.

Gyimah-Boadi, E., and Theo Yakah. 2013. "Ghana: The Limits of External Democracy Assistance." In *Democratic Trajectories in Africa: Unravelling the Impact of Foreign Aid,* edited by Danielle Resnick and Nicolas van de Walle. Oxford: Oxford University Press.

Haaretz. 2006. "U.S. Begins $42 Million Program to Bolster *Hamas* Opponents." 13 June.
———. 2007. "On Rifles." 10 April.

Habib, Adam. 2005. "State-Civil Society Relations in Post-Apartheid South Africa." *Social Research* 72, no. 3 (Fall): 671–692.

Habib, Adam, and Rupert Taylor. 1999. "South Africa: Anti-Apartheid NGOs in Transition." *Voluntas: International Journal of Voluntary and Nonprofit Organization* 10, no. 1 (March): 73–82.

Haggard, Stephan, and Robert R. Kaufman. 1997. "The Political Economy of Democratic Transitions." *Comparative Politics* 29, no. 3 (April): 263–283.

Hagopian, Frances. 1990. "Democracy by Undemocratic Means: Elites, Political Parties and Regime Transition in Brazil." *Comparative Political Studies* 23, no. 2 (July): 147–170.

———. 1992. "The Compromised Consolidation: The Political Class in the Brazilian Transition." In *Issues in Democratic Consolidation: The New South American Democracies in Comparative Perspective,* edited by Scott Mainwaring, Guillermo O'Donnell, and J. Samuel Valenzuela, 243–293. Notre Dame: University of Notre Dame Press.

Hammami, Rema. 2002. "Palestinian NGOs since Oslo: From NGO Politics to Social Movements?" *Middle East Report,* no. 214 (Spring): 188–202.

———. 2004. "Attitudes towards Legal Reform of Personal Status Laws in Palestine." In *Women's Rights and Islamic Law,* edited by Lynn Welchman. London: Zed Books.

———. 1995. "NGOs: The Professionalization of Politics." *Race and Class* 37, no. 2: 51–63.

Hammami, Rema, and Penny Johnson. 1999. "Equality with a Difference: Gender and Citizenship in Transitional Palestine." *Social Politics* 6, no. 3 (Fall): 314–343.

Hanafi, Sari. 1999. *Profile of Donor Assistance to Palestinian NGOs: Survey and Database.* Report submitted to the Welfare Association. Jerusalem: Welfare Association.

Hanafi, Sari, and Linda Tabar. 2005. *Donors, International Organizations, and Local NGOs: The Emergence of the Globalized Elite.* Jerusalem: Institute for Jerusalem Studies.

Hansen, Gary, Harry Blair, and Kimberly Ludwig. 2002. *Building Democratic Constituencies: USAID and Civil Society Programming after the First Decade. April.* Washington, DC: United States Agency for International Development, Office of Democracy and Governance, Bureau for Democracy, Conflict and Humanitarian Assistance.

Harel, Amos. 2006. "Israeli Defense Official: Fatah Arms Transfer Bolsters Forces of Peace." *Haaretz,* 28 December.

Hartzell, Caroline, Matthew Hoddie, and Donald Rothchild. 2001. "Stabilizing the Peace after Civil War: An Investigation of Some Key Variables." *International Organization* 55, no. 1 (Winter): 183–208.

Hasso, Frances. 2001. "Feminist Generations? The Long-Term Impact of Social Movement Involvement on Palestinian Women's Lives." *American Journal of Sociology* 107, no. 3 (November): 586–611.

———. 2005. *Resistance, Repression, and Gender Politics in Occupied Palestine and Jordan.* Syracuse: Syracuse University Press.

Hatch, Richard. 2005. "A Year of De-Ba'athification in Post-Conflict Iraq: Time for Mid-Course Corrections and a Long-Term Strategy." *Journal of Human Rights* 4, no. 1: 103–112.

Heller, Patrick. 2001. "Moving the State: The Politics of Democratic Decentralization in Kerala, South Africa, and Porte Alegre." *Politics & Society* 29, no. 1 (March): 131–163.

Henderson, Sarah L. 2003. *Building Democracy in Contemporary Russia: Western Support for Grassroots Organization.* Ithaca: Cornell University Press.

Herbst, Jeffrey. 1997–98. "Prospects for Elite-Driven Democracy in South Africa." *Political Science Quarterly* 112, no. 4 (Winter): 595–615.

Hilal, Jamil. 1998. "The Effect of the Oslo Agreements on the Palestinian Political System." In *After Oslo: New Realities and New Problems*, edited by George Giacaman and Dag Jorund, 121–145. London: Pluto Press.

———. 2003. "Problematizing Democracy in Palestine." *Comparative Studies of South Asia, Africa and the Middle East* 23, nos. 1–2: 163–172.

———. 2010. "The Polarization of the Palestinian Political Field." *Journal of Palestine Studies* 39, no. 3 (Spring): 24–39.

Hiltermann, Joost. 1991. *Behind the Intifada: Labor and Women's Movements in the Occupied Territories*. Princeton: Princeton University Press.

Hodgkinson, Virginia A., and Michael Foley, eds. 2003. *The Civil Society Reader*. Hanover, NH: University Press of New England.

Höglund, Kristine. 2008. "Violence in War-to-Democracy Transitions." In *From War to Democracy: Dilemmas of Peacebuilding*, edited by Anna K. Jarstad and Timothy J. Sisk, 80–101. Cambridge: Cambridge University Press.

Holiday, David, and William Stanley. 1993. "Building the Peace: Preliminary Lessons from El Salvador." *Journal of International Affairs* 46, no. 2 (Winter): 415–438.

Hook, Steven W. 1995. *National Interest and Foreign Aid*. Boulder: Lynne Rienner.

Horowitz, Donald L. 2003. "Electoral Systems: A Primer for Decision-Makers." *Journal of Democracy* 14, no. 4 (October): 115–127.

Hovdenak, Are. 2009. "Hamas in Transition: The Failure of Sanctions." *Democratization* 16, no. 1 (February): 59–80.

Howell, Jude, and Jenny Pearce. 2002. *Civil Society and Development: A Critical Exploration*. Boulder: Lynne Rienner.

Hroub, Khaled. 2006a. "A 'New Hamas' through Its New Documents." *Journal of Palestine Studies* 35, no. 4 (Summer): 6–27.

———. 2006b. *Hamas: A Beginner's Guide*. London: Pluto Press.

Hume, Mo. 2008. "The Myths of Violence: Gender, Conflict, and Community in El Salvador." *Latin American Perspectives* 35, no. 5 (September 1): 59–76.

———. 2009. *The Politics of Violence: Gender, Conflict, and Community in El Salvador*. Chichester, UK: Wiley-Blackwell.

Husseini, Hiba I., and Raja Khalidi. 2013. "Fixing the Paris Protocol Twenty Years Later: Frequently Asked Questions for Diehard Reformers." *Jadaliyya*, 6 February.

International Crisis Group. 2006a. "Enter Hamas: The Challenges of Political Integration." *Middle East Report*, no. 49 (18 January). Brussels: ICG.

———. 2006b. "Palestinians, Israel, and the Quartet: Pulling Back from the Brink." *Middle East Report*, no. 54 (13 June). Brussels: ICG.

———. 2007. "After Mecca: Engaging Hamas." *Middle East Report*, no. 62 (28 February). Brussels: ICG.

———. 2008. "Iraq after the Surge: The New Sunni Landscape." *Middle East Report*, no. 74 (30 April). Brussels: ICG.

Jacquette, Jane S. 1994. *The Women's Movement in Latin America: Participation and Democracy*. Boulder, CO: Westview Press.

Jad, Islah. 2004. "The NGO-ization of Arab Women's Movements." *IDS Bulletin* 35, no. 4 (January): 34–42.

Jamal, Amal. 2001. "Engendering State-Building: The Women's Movement and Gender Regime in Palestine." *Middle East Journal* 55, no. 2 (Spring): 256–276.

Jamal, Manal A. 2012. "Democracy Promotion, Civil Society Building, and the Primacy of Politics." *Comparative Political Studies* 45, no. 1 (1 January): 3–31.

———. 2013. "Beyond *Fatah* Corruption and Mass Discontent: Hamas, the Palestinian Left and the 2006 Legislative Elections." *British Journal of Middle Eastern Studies* 40, no. 3 (3 June): 284–285.

———. 2014. "The Palestinian Women's Sector and the Promotion of Human Security." In *The Search for Lasting Peace*, edited by Rosalind Boyd. New York: Ashgate.

———. 2015. "Western Donor Assistance and Gender Empowerment in the Palestinian Territories and Beyond." *International Feminist Journal of Politics* 17, no. 2 (December): 232–252.

Jarstad, Anna K., and Timothy J. Sisk, eds. 2008. *From War to Democracy: Dilemmas of Peacebuilding*. Cambridge: Cambridge University Press.

Jerusalem Media and Communication Center (JMCC). 1999. *Palestinian Attitudes towards Politics, Public Opinion Poll No. 32-Part Two* (August).

Johnson, Penny, and Eileen Kuttab. 2001. "Where Have All the Women (and Men) Gone? Reflections on Gender and the Second Intifada." *Feminist Review* 69 (Winter): 21–43.

Kalyvitis, Sarantis, and Irene Vlachaki. 2010. "Democratic Aid and the Democratization of Recipients." *Contemporary Economic Policy* 28, no. 2 (April): 188–218.

Kampwirth, Karen. 2004. *Feminism and the Legacy of Revolution: Nicaragua, El Salvador, Chiapas*. Athens: Ohio University Press.

Karl, Terry L. 1992. "El Salvador's Negotiated Revolution." *Foreign Affairs* 71, no. 2 (Spring): 147–164.

Karl, Terry L., and Philippe Schmitter. 1991. "Modes of Transition in Latin America, Southern and Eastern Europe." *International Social Science Journal* 128 (May): 269–284.

Keane, John, ed. 1988. *Civil Society and the State: New European Perspectives*. London,: Verso Press.

Keating, Michael, Anne Le More, and Robert Lowe, eds. 2005. *Aid Diplomacy and Facts on the Ground: The Case of Palestine*. London: Royal Institute for International Affairs, Chatham House.

Khalidi, Rashid. 1986. *Under Siege: PLO Decision-Making during the 1982 War*. New York: Columbia University Press.

———. 2004. *Resurrecting Empire: Western Footprints and America's Perilous Path in the Middle East*. Boston: Beacon Press.

———. 2013. *Brokers of Deceit: How the US Has Undermined Peace in the Middle East*. Boston: Beacon Press.

Kihato, Caroline. 2001. *Shifting Sands: The Relationship between Foreign Donors and South African Civil Society during and after Apartheid*. Johannesburg: Centre for Policy Studies.

Kimmerling, Baruch, and Joel S. Migdal. 2003. *The Palestinian People: A History*. Cambridge, MA: Harvard University Press.

Kovacs, Mimmi Söderberg. 2008. "When Rebels Change Their Stripes: Armed Insurgents in Post War Politics." In *From War to Democracy: Dilemmas of Peacebuilding*, edited by Anna K. Jarstad and Timothy J. Sisk, 134–156. Cambridge: Cambridge University Press.

Knack, Stephen. 2004. "Does Foreign Aid Promote Democracy?" *International Studies Quarterly* 48, no. 1 (March): 251–266.

Kubíková, Nataša. 2009. "Political Inclusion as a Key Factor to Moderate Islamists: The International Community's Choice of Policy Impacts on Hamas's Pragmatic or Radical Tendencies." *New Perspectives: Interdisciplinary Journal of Central & East European Politics and International Relations* 17, no. 2 (Winter): 139–162.

Kuttab, Eileen. 2008. "Palestinian Women's NGOs: Global Co-optation and Local Contradictions." *Cultural Dynamics* 20, no. 2 (July): 99–117.

Langohr, Vickie. 2004. "Too Much Civil Society, Too Little Politics: Egypt and Liberalizing Arab Regimes." *Comparative Politics* 36, no. 2 (January): 181–205.

Le More, Anne. 2008. *International Assistance to the Palestinians after Oslo: Political Guilt, Wasted Money*. London: Routledge.

Lesch, Ann Mosley. 2006. *Origins and Development of the Arab-Israeli Conflict*. Rev. ed. Westport, CT: Greenwood Press.

Lesch, David W. 2008. *The Arab-Israeli Conflict: A History*. New York: Oxford University Press.

Lijphart, Arend. 1990. "The Political Consequences of Electoral Laws, 1945–85." *American Political Science Review* 84, no. 2 (June): 481–496.

Linz, Juan J., and Alfred Stepan. 1996. *Problems of Democratic Transition and Consolidation: Southern Europe, South America, and Post-Communist Europe*. Baltimore: Johns Hopkins University Press.

Lockman, Zachary. 1996. *Comrades and Enemies: Arab and Jewish Workers in Palestine, 1906–1948*. Berkeley: University of California Press.

Luciak, Ilja A. 1999. "Gender Equality in the Salvadoran Transition." *Latin American Perspectives* 26, no. 2 (March): 43–67.

———. 2001. *After the Revolution: Gender and Democracy in El Salvador, Nicaragua, and Guatemala*. Baltimore: Johns Hopkins University Press.

Macías, Ricardo Cordova, and Victor Orellana. 2001. *Cultura Política, Gobierno Local y Descentralización: El Salvador [Political Culture, Local Government and Decentralization: El Salvador]*. San Salvador: Facultad Latinoamericana de Ciencias Sociales (Latin American Faculty for the Social Sciences FLACSO).

Manning, Carrie, and Monica Malbrough. 2013. "The Changing Dynamics of Foreign Aid and Democracy in Mozambique." In *Democratic Trajectories in Africa: Unravelling the Impact of Foreign Aid*, edited by Danielle Resnick and Nicolas van de Walle. Oxford: Oxford University Press.

Markowitz, Lisa, and Karen W. Tice. 2002. "Paradoxes of Professionalization: Parallel Dilemmas in Women's Organizations in the Americas." *Gender & Society* 16, no. 6 (December 1): 941–958.

Mattar, Philip. 1994. "The PLO and the Gulf Crisis." *Middle East Journal* 48, no. 1 (Winter): 31–46.

Mayer, Tamar. 1994. *Women and the Israeli Occupation: The Politics of Change.* London: Routledge University Press.

McKinlay, R. D. 1979. "The Aid Relationship: A Foreign Policy Model and Interpretation of the Distribution of Official Bilateral Economic Aid of the United States, the United Kingdom, France, and Germany, 1960–1970." *Comparative Political Studies* 11, no. 4 (January): 411–453.

McReynolds, Samuel A. 2002. "Land Reform in El Salvador and the Chapultepec Peace Accord." *Journal of Peasant Studies* 30, no. 1: 135–169.

Mendelson, Sarah. 2001. "Democracy Assistance and Political Transition in Russia: Between Success and Failure." *International Security* 25, no. 4 (Spring): 68–106.

Meyer, Carrie A. 1999. *The Economics and Politics of NGOs in Latin America.* London: Praeger.

Middle East Quartet. 2006. *Statement by the Middle East Quartet.* 30 March. SG/2010-PAL/2043. https://unispal.un.org (last accessed 20 February 2018).

———. 2007. *Statement by the Middle East Quartet.* 21 March. SG/2125-PAL/2071. http://www.un.org (last accessed 20 February 2018).

Miller, Lloyd J. 2007. *Audit of USAID/West Bank and Gaza's Implementation of Executive Order 13224—Blocking Property and Prohibiting Transactions with Persons Who Commit, Threaten to Commit, or Support Terrorism (Report No. 6-294-08-001-P).* 10 December. Cairo: USAID.

Mills, Frederick B. 2012. "Debate on the Left: The 2014 Presidential Elections in El Salvador (Analysis)." *Eurasia Review*, 12 April. http://www.eurasiareview.com (accessed 23 February 2018).

Milton-Edwards, Beverly. 2008. "Order without Law? An Anatomy of Hamas Security: the Executive Force (Tanfithya)." *International Peacekeeping* 15, no. 5 (November): 663–676.

Milton-Edwards, Beverly, and Stephen Farrel. 2010. *Hamas: The Islamic Resistance Movement.* Cambridge, MA: Polity Press.

Ministry of Planning and International Cooperation (MOPIC). 2001. "First and Second Quarterly Monitoring Report of Donor Assistance." 30 June. Ramallah: MOPIC.

Molyneux, Maxine. 1985. "Mobilization without Emancipation: Women's Interests, the State, and Revolution in Nicaragua." *Feminist Studies* 11, no. 2 (Summer): 227–254.

Montgomery, Tommie Sue. 1982. *Revolution in El Salvador: Origins and Evolution.* Boulder: Westview Press.

———. 1997. "Constructing Democracy in El Salvador." *Current History* 96, no. 61 (February): 61–67.

Moodie, Ellen. 2010. *El Salvador in the Aftermath of Peace: Crime, Uncertainty, and the Transition to Democracy.* Philadelphia: University of Pennsylvania Press.

Munck, Geraldo. 1993. "Beyond Electoralism in El Salvador: Conflict Resolution through Negotiated Compromise." *Third World Quarterly* 14, no. 1, 75–93.

Murguialday, Clara. 1997. "Mujeres, Ciudadanía y Transición Democrática en El Salvador de Postguerra" [Women, citizenship, and democratic transition in postwar El Salvador]. *Estudios Centroamericanos* 52, nos. 581–582: 282–296.

Murphy, Emma. 1995. "Stacking the Deck: Economics of the Israeli-PLO Accords." *Middle East Report* 25, nos. 3 and 4 (May-June/July-August): 35–38.

Murray, Kevin, and Tom Barry. 1995. *Inside El Salvador.* Albuquerque: Resource Center Press.

Murray, Kevin, with Ellen Colleti, Jack Spence, Cynthia Curtis, Garth David Check, René Ramos, José Chacón, and Mary Thompson. 1994. *Rescuing Reconstruction: The Debate on Post-War Economic Recovery in El Salvador.* Cambridge, MA: Hemispheric Initiatives.

Muslih, Muhammed. 1993. "Palestinian Civil Society." *Middle East Journal* 47, no. 2 (Spring): 258–274.

Nakhleh, Khalil. 2004. *The Myth of Palestinian Development: Political Aid and Sustainable Deceit.* Beirut: Institute of Palestine Studies; Ramallah: Muwatin, the Palestinian Institute for the Study of Democracy.

Negroponte, Diana Villiers. 2012. *Seeking Peace in El Salvador: The Struggle to Reconstruct a Nation at the End of the Cold War.* New York: Palgrave Macmillan.

Nöel, Alain, and Jean-Philippe Thérien. 1995. "From Domestic to International Justice: The Welfare State and Foreign Aid." *International Organization* 49, no. 3 (Summer): 523–553.

North, Lisa. 1981. *Bitter Grounds: Roots of Revolt in El Salvador.* Toronto: Between the Lines.

O'Brien, David, and Luciano Catenacci. 1996. "Towards a Framework for Local Democracy in a War-Torn Society: The Lessons of Selected Foreign Assistance Program in El Salvador." *Democratization* 3, no. 4 (September): 435–458.

O'Donnell, Guillermo, and Philippe Schmitter. 1986. *Transitions from Authoritarian Rule: Tentative Conclusions about Uncertain Democracies.* Baltimore: Johns Hopkins University Press.

Office of the United Nations Special Coordinator for the Middle East Peace Process. 2001. *Closure Update Summary: The Impact on the Palestinian Economy of Confrontation, Border Closures and Mobility Restrictions.* Jerusalem: UNSCO.

O'Leary, Brendan. 2009. *How to Get Out of Iraq with Integrity.* Philadelphia: University of Pennsylvania Press.

Orjuela, Camilla. 2003. "Building Peace in Sri Lanka: A Role for Civil Society?" *Journal of Peace Research* 40, no. 2 (March): 195–212.

Ottoway, Marina, and Thomas Carothers, eds. 2000. *Funding Virtue: Civil Society Aid and Democracy Promotion.* Washington, DC: Carnegie Endowment for International Peace.

Ottaway, Marina, and Theresa Chung. 1999. "Toward a New Paradigm: Debating Democracy Assistance." *Journal of Democracy* 10, no. 4 (October): 99–113.

Paige, Jeffrey. 1997. *Coffee and Power: Revolution and the Rise of Democracy in Central America.* Cambridge, MA: Harvard University Press.

Palestinian Central Bureau of Statistics. n.d. "Estimated Population in the Palestinian Territory Mid-Year by Governorate, 1997–2016." http://www.pcbs.gov.ps (last accessed 23 February 2018).

Palestine Liberation Organization Negotiation Affairs Department. n.d. "Agreements." https://www.nad.ps (accessed 10 February 2018).

Palestinian Ministry of Planning and International Cooperation. 2001. *First and Second Quarterly Monitoring Report of Donor Assistance.* 30 June. Ramallah: Ministry of Planning.

Palestinian Women's Network: Women's Affairs Technical Committee. 1998. Newsletter 3, no. 1 (Autumn).

Pappe, Ilan. 2006. *A History of Modern Palestine: One Land, Two Peoples.* 2nd ed. Cambridge: Cambridge University Press.

Paris, Roland. 2004. *At War's End: Building Peace after Civil Conflict.* New York: Cambridge University Press.

Pelham, Nicolas. 2012. "Gaza's Tunnel Phenomenon: The Unintended Dynamics of Israel's Siege." *Journal of Palestine Studies* 41, no. 4 (Summer): 6–31.

Peña, Uzziel, and Tom Gibb. 2013. "El Salvador's Gang Truce: A Historic Opportunity." *NACLA Report on the Americas* 46, no. 2 (Summer): 12–15.

Peretz, Don. 1998. "US Middle East Policy in the 1990s." In *The Middle East and the Peace Process: The Impact of the Oslo Accords*, edited by Robert Freedman. Gainesville: University Press of Florida.

Peteet, Julie M. 1991. *Gender in Crisis: Women and the Palestinian Resistance Movement.* New York: Columbia University Press.

Petrova, Tsveta. 2014. *From Solidarity to Geopolitics: Support for Democracy among Postcommunist States.* New York: Cambridge University Press.

Popkin, Margaret. 2000. *Peace without Justice: Obstacles to Building the Rule of Law in El Salvador.* University Park: Pennsylvania State University Press.

Presidential Decree. 2007. https://www.palestinianbasiclaw.org (last accessed 23 February 2018).

Programa de las Naciones Unidas para el Desarrollo. 2009. *Informe sobre Desarrollo Humano para América Central 2009–2010.* San José: PNUD.

Putnam, Robert D. 1993. *Making Democracy Work: Civic Traditions in Modern Italy.* Princeton: Princeton University Press.

Qazzaz, Hadeel. 2007. "The Role of Non-Governmental Organizations in Supporting Women's Role in Elections." *Review of Women's Studies* 4: 79–91.

———. 2010. "Ya Nīsa' Ghaza: 'Alimūna b'aḍ ma 'Indakun (Women of Gaza: Teach Us Some of What You Have)." *Review of Women's Studies* 6: 30–52.

Quandt, William B., Paul Jabber, and Ann M. Lesch. 1973. *The Politics of Palestinian Nationalism.* Berkeley: University of California Press.

Quiroz, Román Mayorga. 1982. Introduction to *Revolution in El Salvador*, edited by Tommie Sue Montgomery. Boulder: Westview Press.

Qurei, Ahmad (Abu Alaa). 2005, 2006, 2011. *Al-Riwaya al-filistiniyya al-kamila lil mufawadat: min Oslo ila Kharitat al-Tariq [The Complete Palestinian Story of the Negotiations: From Oslo to the Roadmap]*. Beirut: Institute for Palestine Studies.

Radu, Michael. 1985. "The Structure of the Salvadoran Left." *Orbis* 28, no. 4 (Winter): 682–684.

Ramos, Carlos, and Nayelly Loya. 2008. "El Salvador: Quince Años de la Firma de los Acuerdos de Paz." *Revista de Ciencia Política* 28, no. 1: 367–383.

Reilly, Benjamin. 2008. "Post-war Elections: Uncertain Turning Points of Transition." In *From War to Democracy: Dilemmas of Peacebuilding*, edited by Anna K. Jarstad and Timothy J. Sisk, 157–181. Cambridge: Cambridge University Press.

Resnick, Danielle, and Nicolas van de Walle, eds. 2013. *Democratic Trajectories in Africa: Unravelling the Impact of Foreign Aid*. Oxford: Oxford University Press.

Robinson, Glenn. 1997. *Building a Palestinian State: The Incomplete Revolution*. Bloomington: Indiana University Press.

———. 2004. "Hamas as Social Movement." In *Islamic Activism: A Social Theory Approach*, edited by Quintan Wiktorowicz. Bloomington: Indiana University Press.

Robinson, Mark, and Steven Friedman. 2007. "Civil Society, Democratization, and Foreign Aid: Civic Engagement and Public Policy in South Africa and Uganda." *Democratization* 14, no. 4 (August): 643–668.

Roeder, Philip G., and Donald Rothchild. 2005. *Sustainable Peace: Power and Democracy after Civil Wars*. Ithaca: Cornell University Press.

Rosa, Herman, and Michael Foley. 2000. "El Salvador." In *Good Intentions: Pledges of Aid for Post-Conflict Recovery*, edited by Shepard Forman and Stewart Patrick, 113–158 . Boulder, CO: Lynne Rienner.

Rothchild, Donald. 1970. "Ethnicity and Conflict Resolution." *World Politics* 22, no. 4 (July): 597–616.

———. 2002. "Settlement Terms and Postagreement Stability." In *Ending Civil Wars: The Implementation of Peace Agreements*, edited by Stephen John Stedman, Donald Rothchild, and Elizabeth M. Cousens, 117–140. Boulder: Lynne Rienner Publishers.

Roy, Sara. 1991. "Development under Occupation? The Political Economy of USAID to the West Bank and Gaza Strip." *Arab Studies Quarterly* 13, nos. 3 and 4 (Summer/Fall): 56–88.

———. 2001. *The Gaza Strip: The Political Economy of De-Development*. 2nd ed. Washington, DC: Institute of Palestine Studies.

———. 2000. "The Transformation of Islamic NGOs in Palestine." *Middle East Report*, no. 214 (Spring): 24–26.

———. 2011. *Hamas and Civil Society in Gaza: Engaging the Islamist Social Sector*. Princeton: Princeton University Press.

Rubenberg, Cheryl A. 2003. *The Palestinians: In Search of a Just Peace*. Boulder: Lynne Rienner.

Saghieh, Hazem. 2007. "The Life and Death of De-Baathification." *Revue des Monde Musulmans et de la Méditerranée* nos. 117–118 (July): 203–223.

Sahliyeh, Emile F. 1986. *The PLO after the Lebanon War*. Boulder: Westview Press.

Said, Edward W. 1995. *Peace and Its Discontents: Essays on Palestine in the Middle East Peace Process*. New York: Vintage Books.

———. 2000. *The End of the Peace Process*. New York: Pantheon Books.

Saint-Germain, Michelle A. 1997. "Mujeres '94: Democratic Transition and the Women's Movement in El Salvador." *Women and Politics* 18, no. 2: 75–99.

Salem, Walid. 1999. *Al-munazamat Al-mujtamaiyya Al-tatwwu'yyeh wa Al-sulta Al-wataniyya Al-filastiniyya: Nahwa 'alaqa Takamuliyya [Voluntary Social Organizations and the Palestinian National Authority: Towards a Complementary Relationship]*. June. Ramallah: Palestine Economic Policy Research Institute-MAS.

Samuels, Kristi. 2006. "Post Conflict Peacebuilding and Constitution Making." *Chicago Journal of International Law* 6, no. 2 (January): 663–682.

Savage, Katharine. 2001. "Negotiating South Africa's New Constitution: An Overview of the Key Players and the Negotiation Process." In *The Post-Apartheid Constitutions: Perspectives on South Africa's Basic Law*, edited by Penelope Andrews and Stephen Ellman. Johannesburg: Witwatersrand University Press.

Savun, Burcu, and Daniel C. Tirone. 2011. "Foreign Aid, Democratization, and Civil Conflict: How Does Democracy Aid Affect Civil Conflict?" *American Journal of Political Science* 55, no. 2 (April): 233–246.

Sayigh, Yezid. 1997. *Armed Struggle and the Search for a State: The Palestinian National Movement 1949–1993*. Oxford: Oxford University Press.

———. 2007. "Inducing a Failed State in Palestine." *Survival* 49, no. 3 (Autumn): 7–40.

———. 2010. *Hamas Rule in Gaza: Three Years On*. Crown Paper 41, March. Boston, MA: Brandeis University, Crown Center for Middle Eastern Studies.

———. 2011. *We Serve the People: Hamas Policing in Gaza*. Crown Paper 5, April. Boston: Brandeis University, Crown Center for Middle East Studies.

Sayigh, Yezid, and Khalil Shikaki. 1999. *Strengthening Palestinian Public Institutions*. June 28. New York: Council on Foreign Relations Sponsored Independent Task Force.

Schäublin, Emanuel. 2011. *Role and Governance of Islamic Charitable Institutions: The West Bank Zakat Committees (1977–2009) in the Local Context*. Geneva: Center on Conflict, Development, and Peacebuilding, the Graduate Institute.

Schönwälder, Gerd. 2002. *Linking Civil Society and the State: Urban Popular Movements, the Left, and Local Government in Peru*. University Park: Pennsylvania State University Press.

Schraeder, Peter J., ed. 2002. *Exporting Democracy: Rhetoric vs. Reality*. Boulder: Lynne Rienner.

Schraeder, Peter J., Steven W. Hook, and Bruce Taylor. 1998. "Clarifying the Foreign Aid Puzzle: A Comparison of American, Japanese, French, and Swedish Aid Flows." *World Politics* 50, no. 2 (January): 294–323.

Scott, James M. 2002. "Political Foundations and Think Tanks." In *Exporting Democracy: Rhetoric vs. Reality*, edited by Peter J. Schraeder, 193–213. Boulder: Lynne Rienner.

Scott, James M., and Carrie A. Steele. 2011. "Sponsoring Democracy: The United States and Democracy Aid to the Developing World, 1988–2001." *International Studies Quarterly* 55, no. 1 (March): 47–69.

Segovia, Alexander. 1996. "The War Economy of the 1980s." In *Economic Policy for Building Peace: The Lessons of El Salvador*, edited by James Boyce. Boulder: Lynne Rienner.

Senate Democratic Policy Committee. 2006. "An Oversight Hearing on the Bush Administration's Plan to Rebuild Iraq's Hospitals, Clinics and Health Care System: What Went Wrong?" Hearing, 28 July.

Shaath, Nabil. 1993. "The Oslo Agreement: An Interview with Nabil Shaath." *Journal of Palestine Studies* 23, no. 1 (Autumn): 5–15.

Shalabi, Yasser, and Na'eem Al-Said. 2001. *Al-Ta'adad: al-Munẓamat Ghayr al-Hukumiyyah al-Filastiniyyah fi al-Ḍafah wa Qita' Gaza [Survey: Non-Governmental Organizations in the West Bank and the Gaza Strip]*. Ramallah: Palestine Economic Policy Research Institute-MAS (September).

Shayne, Julia Denise. 1999. "Gendered Revolutionary Bridges: Women in the Salvadoran Resistance Movement (1979–1992)." *Latin American Perspectives* 26, no. 3 (May 1): 85–102.

———. 2004. *The Revolution Question: Feminisms in El Salvador, Chile, and Cuba*. New Brunswick, NJ: Rutgers University Press.

Shehadeh, Raja. 1994. *The Declaration of Principles and the Legal System in the West Bank*. Jerusalem: Palestinian Academic Society for the Study of International Affairs.

Shin, Doh C. 1994. "On the Third Wave of Democratization: A Synthesis and Evaluation of Recent Theory and Research." *World Politics* 47, no. 1 (October): 135–170.

Shlaim, Avi. 1994. *War and Peace in the Middle East: A Critique of American Policy*. New York: Viking.

Silber, Irina Carlotta. 2011. *Everyday Revolutionaries: Gender, Violence, and Disillusionment in Postwar El Salvador*. New Brunswick: Rutgers University Press.

Sisk, Timothy D. 1995. *Democratization in South Africa: The Elusive Social Contract*. Princeton.: Princeton University Press.

———. 1996. *Power Sharing and International Mediation in Ethnic Conflict*. Washington, DC: Carnegie Corporation of New York.

———. 2009. "Pathways of the Political: Electoral Processes after Civil War." In *The Dilemmas of Statebuilding: Confronting the Contradictions of Postwar Peace Operations*, edited by Roland Paris and Timothy Sisk, 196–224. London: Routledge.

Sisk, Timothy D., and Christoph Stefes. 2005. "Power Sharing as an Interim Step in Peace Building: Lessons from South Africa." In *Sustainable Peace: Power and Democracy after Civil Wars*, edited by Philip Roeder and Donald Rothchild. Ithaca: Cornell University Press.

Sissons, Miranda, and Abdulrazzaq Al-Saiedi. 2013. *A Bitter Legacy: Lessons of De-Baathification in Iraq*. New York: International Center for Transitional Justice.

Smith, Charles D. 1996. *Palestine and the Arab-Israeli Conflict*. 3rd ed. New York: Bedford/St. Martin's Press.

———. 2013. *Palestine and the Arab-Israeli Conflict: A History with Documents.* 8th ed. New York: Bedford/St. Martin's Press.

Smith, Craig S. 2006. "Europeans Agree on Plan to Send Money to Palestine." *New York Times,* 20 July.

Snyder, Erin A., and David M. Faris. 2011. "The Arab Spring: US Democracy Promotion in Egypt." *Middle East Policy* 23, no. 3 (Fall): 49–62.

Sogge, David. 2002. *Give and Take: What's the Matter with Foreign Aid?* Global Issues Series. London: Zed Books.

Solís, Francisco Alvarez, and Pauline Martin. 1992. "The Role of Salvadoran NGOs in Post-War Reconstruction." *Development in Practice* 2, no. 2: 51–60.

Sovich, Nina. 2000. "Palestinian Trade Unions." *Journal of Palestine Studies* 29, no. 4 (Autumn): 66–79.

Special Inspector General for Iraq Reconstruction. 2012. *Quarterly Report for the United States Congress.* 30 October. Arlington, VA: SIGIR.

Sperling, Valerie. 1999. *Organizing Women in Contemporary Russia: Engendering Transition.* Cambridge: Cambridge University Press.

Stanley, William. 1996. *The Protection Racket State: Elite Politics, Military Extortion, and Civil War in El Salvador.* Philadelphia: Temple University Press.

———. 2006. "El Salvador: State-Building before and after Democratization, 1980–1995." *Third World Quarterly* 27, no. 1 (August): 105–107.

Staudt, Kathleen. 2002. "Engaging Politics: Beyond Official Empowerment Discourse." In *Rethinking Gender and Development in a Global/Local World,* edited by Jane L. Parpart, Shirin M. Rai, and Kathleen Staudt. London: Routledge.

Stedman, Stephen John. 1997. "Spoiler Problems in Peace Processes." *International Security* 22, no. 2 (Autumn): 5–53.

Stephen, Lynn, Serena Cosgrove, and Kelley Ready. 2000. *Aftermath: Women's Organizations in Postconflict El Salvador.* Working Paper No. 309, October. Washington, DC: Center for Development Information and Evaluation, United States Agency for International Development.

Studemeister, Margarita S., ed. 2001. *El Salvador: Implementation of the Peace Accords.* Peacemaker 38. Washington, DC: United States Institute of Peace Press.

Sullivan, Denis J. 1996. "NGOs in Palestine: Agents of Development and Foundation of Civil Society." *Journal of Palestine Studies* 25, no. 3 (Spring): 93–100.

Sullivan, Joseph G. 1994. "How Peace Came to El Salvador." *Orbis* 38, no. 1 (Winter): 83–98.

Sullivan, Marissa Chochrane. 2010. *Backgrounder: Sunni Politicians Barred from Candidacy.* January 14. Washington, DC: Institute for the Study of War.

Sundstrom, Lisa M. 2006. *Funding Civil Society: Foreign Assistance and NGO Development in Russia.* Stanford: Stanford University Press.

Tamimi, Azzam. 2007. *Hamas: A History from Within.* Northampton, MA: Olive Branch Press.

Taraki, Lisa. 1989. "Mass Organizations in the West Bank." In *Occupation: Israel over Palestine,* edited by Naseer Aruri. Belmont, MA: AAUG Press.

Tarnoff, Curt. 2006. "Iraq: Recent Developments in Reconstruction Assistance." *Congressional Research Service: Foreign Affairs, Defense, and Trade Division*, June 15. Washington, DC: Congressional Research Service.

———. 2008. "Iraq: Reconstruction Assistance." *Congressional Research Service: Foreign Affairs, Defense, and Trade Division*, November 14. Washington, DC: Congressional Research Service.

Tarrow, Sidney. 1996. "Making Social Science Work across Space and Time: A Critical Reflection on Robert Putnam's *Making Democracy Work.*" *American Political Science Review* 90, no. 2 (June): 389–397.

Tartir, Alaa. 2011. *The Role of International Aid in Development: The Case of Palestine 1994–2008.* Saarbrücken, Germany: Lambert Academic Publishing.

Tessler, Mark. 1994. *A History of the Israeli-Palestinian Conflict.* Bloomington: Indiana University Press.

Thomson, Marilyn. 1986. *Women of El Salvador: The Price of Freedom.* London: Zed Books.

Thompson, Martha. 1997. "Transition in El Salvador: A Multi-Layered Process." *Development in Practice* 7, no. 4 (November): 456–463.

Tripp, Aili Mari. 2013. "Donor Assistance and Political Reform in Tanzania." In *Democratic Trajectories in Africa: Unravelling the Impact of Foreign Aid*, edited by Danielle Resnick and Nicolas van de Walle. Oxford: Oxford University Press.

Tucker, Robert, ed. 1978. *The Marx-Engels Render.* New York: Norton.

Turner, Mandy. 2012. "Completing the Circle: Peacebuilding as Colonial Practice in the Occupied Palestinian Territory." *International Peacekeeping* 19, no. 5 (September): 492–507.

———. 2014. "Peacebuilding as Counterinsurgency in the Occupied Palestinian Territory." *Review of International Studies* 41, no. 1 (January): 73–98.

Uclés, Mario Lungo. 1994. "Redefining Democracy in El Salvador: New Spaces and New Practices for the 1990s." In *Latin America Faces the Twenty-First Century: Reconstructing a Social Justice Agenda*, edited by Susanne Jonas and Edward Mc-Caughan, 142–157. Boulder: Westview Press.

———. 1995. "Building an Alternative: The Formation of a Popular Project." In *The New Politics of Survival: Grassroots Movements in Central America*, edited by Minor Sinclair, 153–179. New York: Monthly Review Press.

———. 1996. *El Salvador in the Eighties: Counterinsurgency and Revolution.* Philadelphia: Temple University Press.

United Nations. 2014. *UN Gender Statistics.* https://genderstats.un.org (accessed June 2015).

United Nations Development Program (UNDP). 1993. *1993 Compendium of External Assistance to the Occupied Territories.* July. Jerusalem: UNDP.

———. 1994. *1994 Compendium of External Assistance to the Occupied Palestinian Territories.* July. Jerusalem: UNDP.

———. 1997. *Cooperación Técnica y Financiera para El Salvador, Según Información Proporcionada por los Cooperantes 1992–1997* [*Technical and Financial Co-operation with El Salvador, as Reported by Donors 1992–1997*]. July. San Salvador: UNDP.

———. 2009. *Report from the Early Recovery Mapping Workshop.* 30 April. Gaza City: UNDP.

———. 2016. "Human Development Report: Human Development for Everyone." New York: UNDP. http://hdr.undp.org (last accessed 12 March 2017).

United Nations Information System on the Question of Palestine (UNISPAL). 2009. *Minimum Framework for the Provision of Humanitarian Assistance in Gaza.* 30 April. Jerusalem: UNISPAL.

United Nations Office for the Coordination of Humanitarian Affairs–Occupied Palestinian Territories (OCHA-OPT). 2009. *Locked-In: The Humanitarian Impact of Two Years of Blockade on the Gaza Strip.* August. Jerusalem: OCHA-OPT.

———. 2010. *Special Focus-Impeding Assistance: Challenges to Meeting the Humanitarian Assistance of Palestinians.* May. Jerusalem: OCHA-OPT.

———. 2012. *Five Years of Blockade: The Humanitarian Situation in the Gaza Strip.* June. Jerusalem: OCHA-OPT.

United Nations Office for the Coordination of Humanitarian Affairs (OCHA) and the World Health Organization (WHO). 2009. *Joint Statement of Concern of Halting of Gaza Medical Patient Referral.* 30 March. Jerusalem: OCHA and WHO.

Urban Institute, Center on International Development and Governance. 2004. *Iraq: Community Action Program.* (May 2003-May 2004). http://idgprojects.urban.org (last accessed 20 February 2018).

"US Assistance to the Palestinians." 2007. Hearing before the Subcommittee on the Middle East and South Asia of the Committee on Foreign Affairs, House of Representatives, 110th Congress, First Session, 23 May, Serial No. 110-170.

United States Agency for International Development (USAID). 2005a. "El Salvador: USAID Program Profile, Democracy and Governance" (last accessed 26 September 2005).

———. 2005b. "Palestinian Territories: USAID Program Profile, Democracy and Governance" (last accessed 26 September 2005).

Valenzuela, J. Samuel. 1992. "Democratic Consolidation in Post-Transitional Settings." In *Issues in Democratic Consolidation: The New South American Democracies in Comparative Perspective*, edited by Scott Mainwaring, Guillermo O'Donnell, and J. Samuel Valenzuela, 57–104. Notre Dame, IN: University of Notre Dame Press.

van der Borgh. 2005. "Donors in War-Torn Societies: El Salvador." In *Post-Conflict Development: Meeting New Challenges*, edited by Gerd Junne and Willemjin Verkoren, 249–272. Boulder: Lynne Rienner.

van Rooy, Alison, ed. 1998. *Civil Society and the Aid Industry.* London: Earthscan.

Varas, Augusto. 1998. "Democratization in Latin America: A Citizenship Responsibility." In *Fault Lines of Democracy in Post-Transition Latin America*, edited by Jeffrey Stark, 145–174. Miami: North-South Center Press.

Villacorta, Alberto Enríquez. 1998. *Propuesta para el Impulso de un Proceso de Descentralización en El Salvador [Proposal for Boosting the Decentralization Process in El Salvador].* San Salvador: Fundación Nacional para el Desarrollo (Foundation for National Development).

Viterna, Jocelyn. 2006. "Pulled, Pushed, and Persuaded: Explaining Women's Mobilization into the Salvadoran Guerrilla Army." *American Journal of Sociology* 112, no. 1 (July): 1–45.

———. 2013. *Women in War: The Micro-Processes of Mobilization in El Salvador.* Oxford: Oxford University Press.

Walsh, Denise M. 2012. "Does the Quality of Democracy Matter for Women's Rights? Just Debate and Democratic Transition in Chile and South Africa." *Comparative Political Studies* 45, no. 11 (November 1): 1323–1350.

Walsh-Mellet, Luke. 2017. "More Repression, More Fightback! El Salvador's Labor Movement Defends the Minimum Wage" (last accessed 15 March 2017).

Walter, Barbara F. 1997. "The Critical Barrier to Civil War Settlement." *International Organization* 51, no. 3 (Summer): 335–364.

———. 2009. "Designing Transitions from Civil War: Demobilization, Democratization, and Commitments to Peace." *International Security* 24, no. 1 (Summer): 127–155.

Watson, Geoffrey R. 2000. *The Oslo Accords: International Law and the Israel Agreements.* Oxford: Oxford University Press.

Weigle, Marcia A. 2000. *Russia's Liberal Project: State-Society Relations in the Transition from Communism.* University Park: Pennsylvania State University Press.

Wicken, Stephen. 2013. "Middle East Security Report II: Iraq's Sunnis in Crisis." *Institute for the Study of War* (May).

Wilson, Scott and Glenn Kessler. 2006. "US Funds Enter Fray in Palestinian Elections." *Washington Post Foreign Service*, 22 January.

Windsor, Jennifer. 2006. "Advancing the Freedom Agenda: Time for a Recalibration?" The Washington Quarterly, 29, no. 3, 21–34.

Wolf, Sonja. 2012. "Policing Crime in El Salvador." *NACLA Report on the Americas* 54, no. 1 (Spring): 37–42.

Women's Centre for Legal Aid and Counselling (WCLAC). 2000. *Annual Report 2000.* Jerusalem: WCLAC.

WomenWarPeace.org. 2000. http://www.womenwarpeace.org (last accessed 25 July 2005).

Wood, David. 2013. "Iraq Reconstruction Cost U.S. $60 Billion, Left behind Corruption and Waste." *Huffington Post*, 6 March .

Wood, Elisabeth Jean. 1996. "The Peace Accord and Postwar Reconstruction." In *Economic Policy for Building Peace: The Lessons of El Salvador*, edited by James Boyce. Boulder: Lynne Rienner.

———. 2000. *Forging Democracy from Below: Insurgent Transitions in South Africa and El Salvador.* New York: Cambridge University Press.

———. 2001. "An Insurgent Path to Democracy: Popular Mobilization, Economic Interests, and Regime Transition in South Africa and El Salvador." *Comparative Political Studies* 34, no. 8 (October): 862–888.

———. 2003. *Insurgent Collective Action and Civil War in El Salvador.* New York: Cambridge University Press.

Wood, Elizabeth Jean, and Alexander Segovia. 1995. "Macroeconomic Policy and the Salvadoran Peace Accords." *World Development* 23, no. 12: 2079–2099.

World Bank. 1997. *The NGO Trust Fund for the West Bank and Gaza Strip.* Washington, DC: World Bank.

———. 2006. *The Impending Palestinian Fiscal Crisis, Potential Remedies.* 7 May. Washington, DC: World Bank.

———. 2007. *West Bank and Gaza Strip Expenditure Review.* March. Washington, DC: World Bank.

Wright, Joseph. 2009. "How Foreign Aid Can Foster Democratization in Authoritarian Regimes." *American Journal of Political Science* 53, no. 3 (June): 552–571.

Youngs, Gillian. 2004. "Feminist International Relations: A Contradiction in Terms? Or: Why Women and Gender Are Essential to Understanding the World 'We' Live In." *International Affairs* 80, no. 1 (January): 75–87.

Youngs, Richard. 2002. *The European Union and the Promotion of Democracy: Europe's Mediterranean and Asian Policies.* Oxford: Oxford University Press.

Zagha, Adel, and Manal A. Jamal. 1997. *Mortgaging Self-Reliance: Foreign Aid and Development in Palestine, Phase II Report.* November. Jerusalem: Jerusalem Media and Communication Center.

Zamora, Ruben. 1998. *El Salvador: Heridas que no Cierran, Los Partidos Políticos en la Post-Guerra (Wounds that Will Not Close: The Political Parties in the Post-War Period).* San Salvador, SV: Facultad Latinoamericana de Ciencias Sociales (Latin American Faculty for the Social Sciences (FLACSO).

Zanotti, Jim. 2010. "US Security Assistance to the Palestinian Authority." 8 January. Washington, DC: Congressional Research Service.

———. 2012. "US Foreign Aid to the Palestinians." 4 April. Washington, DC: Congressional Research Service.

———. 2103. "US Foreign Aid to the Palestinians." 18 January. Washington, DC: Congressional Research Service.

Zaucker, Joachim, Andrew Griffel, and Peter Gubser. 1995. "Toward Middle East Peace and Development: International Assistance to Palestinians and the Role of NGOs during the Transition to Civil Society." Interaction Occasional Paper, December. Washington, DC .

Zavadjil, Milan, Nur Calika, Oussama Kanaan, and Dale Chua. 1997. *Recent Economic Developments, Prospects, and Progress in Institution Building in the West Bank and Gaza Strip.* Washington, DC: International Monetary Fund, Middle East Department.

Zhang, Bao. 1994. "Corporatism, Totalitarianism, and Transition to Democracy." *Comparative Political Studies* 27, no. 1 (April): 108–136.

ABOUT THE AUTHOR

Manal A. Jamal is Associate Professor of Political Science at James Madison University. She holds a PhD in political science from McGill University and a BA and MA in international relations from UC Davis and San Francisco State, respectively. She has held research fellowship positions at the Middle East Initiative and the Dubai Initiative at Harvard University's Kennedy School of Government, at UC Berkeley's Center for Middle Eastern Studies, and at the Dubai School of Government. During the late 1990s, she worked as journalist and researcher in the Palestinian Territories. Her most recent publications have appeared in journals including *Comparative Political Studies, British Journal of Middle Eastern Studies, International Feminist Journal of Politics*, and *International Migration Review.*

CPSIA information can be obtained
at www.ICGtesting.com
Printed in the USA
FSHW022018280220
67661FS